LOUD AND CLEAR

THE MEMOIR OF AN ISRAELI FIGHTER PILOT

BRIGADIER GENERAL
IFTACH SPECTOR

ZENITH PRESS

Originally published in Hebrew in 2008 as Ram u-varur by Yedioth Ahronoth Books. English edition, translated by Samuel Gorvine, first published in 2009 by Zenith Press, an imprint of MBI Publishing Company, 400 First Avenue North, Suite 300, Minneapolis, MN 55401 USA

Copyright © 2009 by Iftach Spector, translation by Samuel Gorvine

All rights reserved. With the exception of quoting brief passages for the purposes of review, no part of this publication may be reproduced without prior written permission from the Publisher. The information in this book is true and complete to the best of our knowledge.

Zenith Press titles are also available at discounts in bulk quantity for industrial or sales-promotional use. For details write to Special Sales Manager at MBI Publishing Company, 400 First Avenue North, Suite 300, Minneapolis, MN 55401 USA.

To find out more about our books, join us online at www.zenithpress.com.

Printed in the United States of America

LIBRARY OF CONGRESS CATALOGING-IN-PUBLICATION DATA

Spector, Iftach, 1940-
[Ram u-varur. English]
Loud and clear : the memoir of an Israeli fighter pilot / by Iftach Spector ; translated by Samuel Gorvine.
p. cm.
ISBN 978-0-7603-3630-4 (hb w/ jkt)
1. Spector, Iftach, 1940- 2. Fighter pilots—Israel—Biography. 3. Air pilots, Military—Israel—Biography. 4. Israel. Hel ha-avir—Biography. 5. Israel. Hel ha-avir—History. I. Title.
UG626.2.S67A313 2009
358.40092—dc22
[B] 2008054532

Designer: Diana Boger
Maps by Phil Schwartzberg, Meridian Mapping

On the cover: *Israeli Air Force*

On the back cover: The site of the fall, 1964. My poor Ouragan No. 22.
Author's collection

Contents

Chapter

1

The Letter

We, veteran and active-duty pilots alike, who served and still serve Israel every day, are opposed to carrying out attack orders that are illegal and immoral of the type the State of Israel has been conducting in the Occupied Territories . . .

We, for whom the IDF and the Air Force are an inalienable part of ourselves, refuse to continue to harm innocent civilians . . .

These actions are illegal and immoral, and are a direct result of the ongoing occupation which is corrupting all of Israeli society . . .

We hereby declare that we shall continue to serve in the IDF and the Air Force on every mission, for the defense of Israel.

—The Pilots' Letter to the Israeli Air Force,
December 24, 2003

THE FIRST ISRAELI FIGHTER PILOT I ever met was Ladya. He peered at me through the grass and looked a little like cat food, reddish and granular. I collected him carefully in a cardboard box. Around us were low barbed-wire fences, and above stretched the open blue sky from which he had descended a few minutes before—passing over us with a roar, his jet rolling like a big black cross and at last slamming into the ground.

Now, all around the ground was sticky and the air was saturated with the sweet smell of jet fuel.

One of my friends raised his head above the weeds and I saw his pale stare. Then I saw his back bend and heard gagging sounds. When I crawled toward him, my hand sank into a small, steaming pile. I looked at my palm—the dripping porridge of tomato pieces and white slime was not much different from the fiber and broken bone scattered around.

I vomited.

My gorge rose again forty-four years later, when the journalist in front of me combed his hair, checked his makeup in the monitor screen of the TV camera, and turned to interview me for this evening's sound bite for Channel One. A pimple on his cheek drew my attention. Then I saw his expectant look.

"Sorry, what did you ask?"

"Brigadier General Iftach Spector, one of Israel's greatest fighter pilots—are you a refusenik?"

"What?"

What is going on here? My country is under attack. Terrorists with knives attack our citizens on the streets. At night, cars are hosed down with automatic weapons fire. Suicide bombers enter hotels, restaurants, and buses to subject women, children, old people, and babies to fire, shock, and a hail of shrapnel nails. Hundreds are killed, thousands injured. The country is covered with a grid of fences around public buildings, schools, and kindergartens. Armed security stands in the entrance of every mall, cinema, restaurant, and bus station. Security people and soldiers carrying weapons patrol everywhere, stand in doors and road crossings, checking hand luggage. But in spite of all this, the terror continues. And, of course, passive defense is not enough. The enemy must be attacked in his base, and so the Israeli Defense Force (IDF) and the security services are activated.

The IDF moves its center of gravity to the occupied territories. Our soldiers focus on "dealing with the civilian population," breaking into houses, making arrests. Our soldiers smash walls and tear up floors, searching for weapons. Sometimes they catch terrorists and their handlers. When a home has been used in this manner, the family is evacuated and the house demolished. The IDF surprises the enemy time and again in the cities and in the villages, day and night. Sometime the operation ends quietly, and sometimes clashes occur in streets and on rooftops, with dead and wounded on both sides. Many terrorists and suspects are caught. The prisons are packed with thousands of Palestinians, and new prisons are being opened.

The Palestinians react with escalating savagery. Terrorists are caught—but new ones are born all the time, some of them mere children. The mullahs seduce them, promising heavenly virgins, and terrorists continue coming like zombies with their bomb belts. They launch homemade rockets that they manufacture in secret factories at night. In the mosques, on Fridays, they get their religion with an anti-Semitic flavor, justifying their abominable terror as "holy war." It develops into a zero-sum game—either us or them.

I am over sixty and am not an active participant in this war. For the past fifteen years I have done my reserve duty as a volunteer, teaching pilots. From the sidelines, I watched my country forced to defend itself against terror.

This is not a simple battle; the terrorists who face us wear civilian clothes. They emerge, strike, and go to ground among the civilian population. Our forces must hit the terrorists without harming the innocent population in which they immerse themselves, and this is a very complicated surgical mission. Still, it is clear that this distinction is very important—indiscriminate attacks on populations, besides being immoral, are forbidden by Israeli law, and turn the whole world against us. Attacks that cause collateral damage endanger our chances to resolve the conflict we are engaged in, and they tarnish our self-image and our way of life.

It is a tough war. I cross my fingers for the IDF every day.

The air force is the main tool to do that important "surgery," and for good reason. An airplane, soaring high over the conquered areas, sees without being seen. From on high it detects figures who can be identified as "bad guys" by somebody else, locks onto them, and fires on or bombs buildings reported by somebody as containing enemies.

And terrorists do get taken out, but the process is not perfect. Many noncombatants are hit as well. The ratio of combatants to noncombatants is 1:1—meaning for every terrorist we kill an innocent, and other noncombatants are wounded. This ratio is very bad. The terrorists are the ones who profit from the collateral damage. They, who target our children intentionally—exploit our misses to win the hearts and minds of the Palestinian population and world support. Sometimes, after a botched operation like this, it seems that the loss from the operation is greater than the gain. But this is the nature of war. And throughout this book you will hear about war.

On the night of July 22, 2002, the "surgeon's scalpel," while excising a cancerous tumor, slipped deep into living flesh. A fighter jet was sent at midnight to take out a notorious terrorist named Salekh Shkhade. The fighter dropped a one-ton bomb on a house in a heavily populated suburb of Gaza. The bomb hit, and the house collapsed on all its inhabitants. When the dust cleared, it was found that fifteen women and children were blown to pieces together with the terrorist.

When that outcome was known, the world cried out. In Israel hard questions began to be asked. People wondered whether this was intentional, and began inquiring about the limits set upon the military. Officials began making excuses, explaining that they hadn't imagined that so many people were living in that house. Knowing Gaza better than that, journalists dismissed this explanation. On the other side, the shrill voices of self-proclaimed patriots thundered in the streets and markets, "What the hell is all the soul-searching for? Woe to the villain and woe to his neighbor!" And if one listened hard, one could hear the thrill of satisfaction and the joy of revenge.

This bombing woke me from my long lethargy.

I have to confess that in the beginning it was not the moral question that troubled me. I saw in all this something different: What was happening to the operational standards of the IDF? "A terrorist was eliminated—great," I thought and cheered, "Hooray for the Israeli Air Force. But why did you have to get such results in such a miserable way?"

The results of this operation—one terrorist for fifteen children—seemed to me like a pound of gain for a ton of loss. I saw it as a reproach to military competence. To put one bullet in the target you had to tear the whole neighborhood down? This looks like a complete screwup, done by a soldier who doesn't even know how to fire his weapon. Is that what you learned in the occupied territories, to put fire on the target in erratic bursts? What kind of standard is that, my dear Israeli Air Force (IAF)?

Even having uttered this criticism, I was still not that angry. I was aware that the mission was complex and that there might be many factors that could have affected it. Perhaps, I thought, the pilots and their commanders really did not imagine that there might be so many people in the target house (although simple common sense mocked the idea that in Gaza, packed with a million people, the terrorist Shkhade would be sleeping alone in a large house). So I kept saying that "had the IAF commanders known in advance that the house was full of innocent civilians, they definitely would have halted this bombing, and caught Shkhade in another location, eliminating him in a surgical, precise way, the way it should be done." This was what I kept saying time and again, to myself and to everybody who asked me.

Today I realize that in the past few years I had been repressing bits and pieces of information. Occurrences of this nature, on a smaller scale, had been taking place in the territories daily. After the Shkhade incident, I realized that this is the way things had been managed there for some time. It was upsetting, but I still argued, "Surely there was some mistake."

Everyone knows that wars are an arena of mistakes where innocents die. In the three years of the War of Attrition, 1968–1970, against Egypt and Syria, for example, we in the IAF hit an Egyptian school full of children, shot down a Libyan airliner, and more—all by mistake. I myself was involved in a very serious operational mistake in 1967 where non-combatants lost their lives (more about this later). Tragic indeed. But a mistake can have some positive value—provided you internalize it and learn from it. This way, new and better ways to fight can be discovered, and new and improved weapons created. "Recognition of mistakes is the way to turn a failure into success."

That is what I was taught and what I taught others. “There is no shame in acknowledging mistakes. On the contrary—credit and dignity derive from it, benefiting all of us.”

In short, I had no doubt that collateral damage—as happened in the elimination of Shkhade—was taken seriously in the IDF as a grave mistake. I took it for granted that the IAF works constantly to develop new methods to hit its targets—and the targets only.

But then, to my complete surprise, the IAF published a press release that showed me I had misunderstood the whole thing. The air force commander, Maj. Gen. Dan Khalutz, made a public appearance. The commander is a charismatic and very likable person. He is especially known for a glib tongue and plain speaking.

“How do you feel, sir,” the interviewer asked him, “when you drop a one-ton bomb on a populated neighborhood?”

“How do I feel?” the commander replied with a smile. “Nothing. Just a light buffet on the wing, that’s all.”

His black eyes flashing with good humor, the commander completed his answer: “I sleep well at night.”

Well, we know about schlock journalists, the kind who specialize in “How do you feel?” questions. Many times the answers come out foolish, too. I don’t know this officer very well personally and have no clue whether he misunderstood the impact of his words. But the reality was there for everybody to see: immoral and unlawful actions were happening every day in the occupied territories. And when some of the soldiers protested, the IDF and the IAF used their power to punish in order to silence them. This officer’s callous words, on the contrary, were said loud and clear for everybody in Israel and in the whole world to hear. All this shed a new, bright, and ugly light on the IDF’s ways of making war—both operationally and morally.

I began paying attention, and the more I saw and heard, the sadder and more surprised I became regarding the lack of discipline, the defects in personal example, and the short-sightedness of our commanders in this complicated war. I began to see the problem not as just a tactical military mistake but also as a much deeper failure our military commanders were part of. The protruding component in this case was the separation between the principles (and the law of the state) and the deeds done in the area.

This was not the first time, nor the last, when I saw friends and comrades, air force people, pilots of my own level, who were raised on the same values, separating their actions in the field from accepted moral values. In other words, compromising their principles.

Of course, "compromising your principles" is the easy way, isn't it? Why dig, why rake up the muck? It's just a wing buffet. Why deal with it at all? Just let it go. Why rock the boat? Hadn't Ezer Weizmann, the great, the glorious IAF commander of the 1960s, taught us all, "Don't explain and don't apologize"? So what do you expect from the IAF? Don't be dumb. Sit down and shut up.

But I could never follow this principle. Time and again I found myself twisting, investing effort, explaining, and giving excuses. And later, in my forty years of flying, I had had some friends who explored those easy ways and found where they led. The first stage in compromising principles was always easy. But after you began, there was the second stage, and suddenly the path twisted and soon was shrouded in fog. And my mother, too. She used to say, "Now listen well, Iftach Spector" (this is how she would begin when she wanted to make a point), "we are not rich enough to buy cheap things."

I perused the letter I had signed three weeks ago. This time it was not the rough copy put on my desk by a young pilot with a flushed face. Now the text was in bold type, black and red, spread over the entire first page. The headline shouted, "Refusenik Pilots!"

The journalist glared at me with his beady eyes.

"Well?"

He didn't say it directly, but I, like the entire crowd watching us at home, understood exactly the reason for the ugly devolution of the word, from "refusal" to "refusenik." This change is intended to suppress the simple fact that I declare that I shall refuse to take part in war crimes—and to connect me with words whose meaning is repulsive and ugly: "evasion," "cowardice," "treachery."

Or to put it bluntly, treason. Betraying the State of Israel.

"Well?" the interviewer persisted, "What do you say?"

What could I say? It is correct, I do refuse. Here it is written in black and red on yellow. And then I recalled Ladya again. The smell of the mound of vomit of forty-four years ago rose in my nostrils, warm and sour.

So I answered the journalist somehow, and the media did their thing. As expected, the tumult broke even before the interview ended. The IAF reaction was strong: the twenty-eight pilots who signed the protest, including myself, were discharged from the air force. Since there had been no crime and no military offense, they argued that we had violated *esprit de corps*. It was a clever tactic; could I say that in our senior winged ranks, some were not worthy to be called fighter pilots in my corps? I couldn't make my mouth utter those clear, hard words. I hadn't had the fortitude to accuse my air force of incompetence, and the IDF high command of war crimes. Even today, three years later, I find it very difficult to write these words.

So I was struck dumb, and right away some of my friends publicly cut me dead. I noticed that every one of them used the opportunity to show off his medals. I stood empty-handed—I never received nor asked for a medal; I just gave a few to some of them. A friend who had flown with me on perilous missions wrote me a note: "Our ways part," and for a moment I was scared for him; perhaps he had a terminal illness. Another fighter ace suggested I should be executed; another asked me to commit suicide. Public figures, philosophers, and pundits used my name to further their own causes. Important people declared they would not speak with me nor agree to meet me (though I never asked any of them to do any such thing). Economical brains looked for ways to halt my military pension payments.

Reporters who feed on the IDF led a public campaign focused on personal attacks against us. We were presented as deserters and traitors. One reporter was especially nasty—he invented a nickname for the signatories of the pilots' letter—"the Air Force 28," and used the loss of my father, Zvi Spector, at sea with twenty-three commandos who sailed to fight the Nazis, to humiliate me. The public followed through, and all kinds of people I never knew called me and sent faxes. My mailbox at home as well as my e-mail boxes began filling with trash. After some time I gave up and began separating out my utility bills and throwing everything else away.

But all the trouble of that time was nothing in comparison to the moment when my daughter Noah asked me, wide-eyed like the small girl she was, "Daddy, are you a refusenik? Is that what you have taught us?" My face fell.

"There's no better way to wake up than a good slap in the face," my father would have taught me, had I a father and not a shadow drowning nightly in my dreams. So I had to learn this lesson by myself.

So I stood in front of her, shocked, and tried to find something to say. And some noise probably came out of me, since my wife, Ali, raised her head from her book.

"What's the matter?" And when she saw the look on my face, she noted, "Sour? Never mind, sour is piquant." With all her exquisite delicacy, Ali can be pretty tough.

Noah rose angrily to my defense. "Mom, stop it! Don't you see how bitter it is for Dad?"

"Bitter?" said Ali with a smile. At that time she was translating the cookbook *Cordon Bleu* into Hebrew. She was swimming in the spices of haute cuisine. "Even better, then. Bitterness adds finesse to the dish."

It took me time to realize how right she was.

So I had to answer her. My thoughts over Noah's question were so painful that I even had moments from visions in the night, fear and trembling came upon me—when I wondered whether my refusal to take part in immoral and unlawful deeds was not in itself an immoral and unlawful deed. And so, wandering among the rooms in the small hours of the night, confused, washing my face with cold water, I even played out a little drama of reformation. It was so easy. I just had to enter the air force command post. Then I would say wide-eyed, with a disarming smile, "Forgive me, gentlemen. I was wrong. Just a passing whimsy. So sorry!"

And in this context, would you believe, I fully understood the meaning of faith and repentance. Uh, the security within the system. All the difficult aspects of my life—responsibility, authority, guilt—evaporated into space like purple clouds of hashish. Hear, hear, they are accepting me back into the angels' choir. They are going to let me start the engines of the Fouga trainer. My name is going to be cleared, my family relieved of their agony, the aching knot in my gut loosened, and peaceful sleep will visit every night.

A moment later, when I saw my face in the mirror, I burst out with such a laugh that Ali rushed to the bathroom to see what had happened to me.

ABOUT THIRTY-FIVE YEARS before those difficult days related above, I was a fighter pilot in the Fighting First and found myself in a situation that seemed hopeless. I was caught alone in the heart of Egypt, between two enemy jet fighters, and my Mirage was flying on empty. The MiGs kept diving on me, trying over and over to shoot me down as I struggled to stay alive. This unequal contest continued with no end in sight. The moment came when I lost all hope of getting out alive and free.

And at that moment, exactly when I began sinking into despair and was about to lose my fighting spirit, there arose from nowhere a short sentence, only three words, that I have been cherishing since then like a mantra.

The words were "All from inside."

Which means, "Listen well, Iftach Spector. It all depends on you. The question is only what is inside you, how worthy you are."

And this is the whole story.

Chapter

2

December 1960

Super Mystere: A single-seat fighter-attack jet built by Marcel Dassault, France. It was a first-line interceptor in the late 1950s and early 1960s. Armament: two 30mm cannons, four hard points under the wings carry fuel tanks or bombs.

The first eighteen Super Mysteres arrived in December 1958, and the Scorpions squadron formed at the IAF Base Hatzor, under Maj. Yaacov Nevo (Yak), the aerial combat star of the air force.

The initial engagements between Super Mysteres and Egyptian MiG-17s ended with no results. In late 1959, during a dogfight with a MiG-17, a Super Mystere pilot went into a spin and had to eject from his aircraft. In two more engagements, in May and October 1960, two MiGs were hit but made it back to base.

Things changed on April 28, 1961. Two Egyptian MiG-17s penetrated Israeli air space near Nizzana, and this time it was the turn of the Egyptian pilot to abandon his spinning aircraft. The Scorpions had gotten their first kill.

ON A BRIGHT BLUE DAY flooded with sun and the freezing wind of mid-December 1960, five newly minted second lieutenants arrived at the Scorpions fighter squadron, Air Base Hatzor, in the south of Israel.

We climbed the four stairs up to the balcony of our new home, carrying on our backs rucksacks full of flight gear, and halted on the wide and empty balcony. Five doors, painted yellow, were shut. Nobody was there to welcome us.

The Israeli Air Force at that time had six fighter squadrons plus several transports and a few helicopters. That was it, and it was still a hell of an air force. Only five months before, every last one of its pilots—all in all, a few dozen—had crowded into the officers' mess at Tel Nof Air Base for a party to celebrate our wings, get us drunk on disgusting medicinal cognac, and hoist us from the pool table to the ceiling. Fifteen graduates we were, a large bunch in those days, and we punched fifteen holes in the rotten planks of the ceiling. The officers' mess, an old barracks left over from the RAF during the time of the British Mandate in Palestine, was spacious enough to hold the whole Israeli Air Force and even Yalo, a robust fighter pilot with blue eyes and a clownish bent, who made us bunny hop with all the girls at the party till our starched khaki shirts with the new wings above the left chest pocket were drenched with sweat and were taken off and thrown aside. The cement tiles buckled under our feet as we danced the Horah. Before morning, we had overturned the tables and broken the chairs, so our training as Israeli fighter pilots was complete.

Among those six fighter squadrons, the Scorpions were the top of the heap. Two years earlier, the Scorpions had dethroned the senior squadron, the glorious Fighting First Fighter Squadron, with her aging Mystere aircraft. Only the Scorpions were lucky enough to receive the new jet, the crowning achievement of the French aviation industry, the Super Mystere. Even as air cadets we had dreamed of the Super Mystere. Unlike its elder brothers, the Ouragan and the Mystere, which looked like Dutch uncles, the Super Mystere had a menacing presence. It had the face of predator. Under its nose was a giant elliptical mouth, and inside the aircraft's guts roared a huge jet engine full of power, with an afterburner. The Super Mystere was a large and beautiful aircraft, with elongated lines like a viper. It also flew well, breaking the sound barrier in level flight. In addition, it could achieve fifty thousand feet—seventeen vertical kilometers from Earth. We were told that the sky at that height—above most of the atmosphere—is almost black, and that if one trains his eyes well enough one could see the stars in broad daylight.

This was the ultimate aircraft, and this was the Scorpions, the new spear point of the Israeli Air Force.

Everybody knew that the Scorpions accepted only the *crème de la crème.* Who hadn't dreamed of getting here? And there we were on that balcony, a bunch of rookies who had just finished operational training. It was electrifying. It was scary.

So we trembled there in the cold wind, proud and glad, and looked around.

On the tarmac in front of us sat five large, beautiful Super Mysteres. Their crystal canopies hung over their open cockpits, as if hovering in the air. The shining Plexiglas sparkled in the morning sun. Each of the aircraft sported two round, plump fuel tanks that peered at us from beneath the wings, their tips bulging like aroused nipples. With their long, sleek body lines, the Super Mysteres looked to me like a group of women lying on a rug, chatting and waiting.

I lowered my eyes. My friend Zur, called ZBB, smiled at me in wordless complicity.

I looked again at the Super Mysteres and felt a wave of excitement. Within a week or two I would make my first flight in this advanced, powerful machine. Could I handle it? And immediately the momentum would begin building—within two months we would try the aerial firing range, and whoever hit the towed flag—the drogue—would be inducted into the small, elite group of fighter pilots, those few who defend the skies of Israel daily.

I knew which of us would hit the drogue. I knew it would not be me.

Suddenly the whole process seemed too fast—way too fast. Only yesterday I was a kid, the shepherd of Kibbutz Givat-Brenner, a boy humming pop tunes in the fields and admiring Col. Ariel Sharon's paratroopers. Then the Sinai War of 1956 came from nowhere, blackouts were in force, and our teachers carried guns. My sixteen-year-old classmates dug trenches in the lawns. And after that came my flight craze. At night in the underground shelter of the kibbutz, I built model planes and tried to figure out the laws of aerodynamics. When the girls put on black skirts and white blouses and went dancing in the evenings, I stayed in my room, immersed in books about war that smelled of long use, most of them translated from Russian. For some time I read randomly, immersed in things such as Hannibal's tragic fate. Then I discovered World War II. I became entranced by Alexei Merseyev, a Soviet fighter pilot who fought the Nazis (like my own father), lost both his legs, but returned to aerial combat to shoot down Messerschmitts. Merseyev became a hero of the USSR, and I walked the fields, waving a stick and cutting wild flowers the way he did, and swearing aloud.

Finally my induction notice came, then the smell of the high-octane fuel of the Harvard trainer and the propeller's noisy, dissonant whine. Then the heart-stopping takeoff—as if I were being sucked right up into the sky between two screaming Meteor jet engines—and before I knew it I had my wings, and I stood looking at the Super Mysteres from the balcony of the Scorpions squadron.

It was so fast.

A door opened and a head with thick, short, red hair peered out. Nissim noticed us standing there and rushed back in, roaring in a loud voice in his Bulgarian accent, "They're here!"

A long sh . . . sh was heard from the inside of the room. Nissim slammed the door. We looked at each other, wondering. A thin black dog crawled out from beneath the building, stretched herself, yawned, and finally rose to smell us and lick Uri Sheani's hands. We all crowded around to touch her fur for luck. Lira was the famous mascot of the Super Mystere pilots.

Dogs and all kinds of animals loved Sheani. He was a nature boy who used to raise swamp cats in his parents' room at his kibbutz, Ein-Harod, in the Izreel Valley. His little tigers tore the curtains to strips and frightened the neighbors. When we went AWOL from base, the vicious watchdogs guarding the fences stopped growling and cowered before Sheani, begging to be petted.

He was a short, muscular young man with straw-colored hair and a square face. His eyes were pale blue above a charming smile flashing lots of white teeth. His broad jaws and the dimple in his chin hinted at the tremendous willpower hidden behind the smile. Two years earlier, when we air cadets were tested for strength of character in the thirty-five-kilometer field run with full equipment, Sheani made it first to the end, limping badly. But when he took his shoes off, the faces of the instructors went pale. The soles of his feet were bloody minced meat. I was always an admirer of good sportsmanship, but this was something more than athletic prowess.

Uri Sheani was superb at orienteering. In one of our few breaks in the flight course, we decided to drive around the whole Negev—Israel's southern desert—to survey the benchmarks and take pictures. It was a ten-day trip. We were five boys on a rented jeep, and only one of us had a driver's license, but we all abused the small vehicle over hundreds of kilometers of sand and rock. The jeep rewarded us in kind when we had to carry it on our backs through the wadis and down the steep slopes of the Yehuda Desert, down to Ein-Gedi on the coast of the Dead Sea, three hundred meters below sea level.

Uri sniffed the air like an animal and found water for us. When we fell asleep, dead tired, near the bonfire, he would listen to the night sounds and in the morning would show us fine footprints and wild animals hopping in the distance. When we arrived at the operational training and became acquainted with the gun sight and gunpowder, Sheani's powerful hands could manage the Ouragan aircraft with gentle and economical nudges. He proved to be a first-class gunner. In aerial target shooting he set a record, doubling the old one.

And still we stood there, before the closed doors of the Scorpions, waiting. Nothing happened. Finally Umsh sneered and said, "Guys, what a Zikago." We grinned at each other.

We had been together for more than two years since the five of us were in Tel Nof with a hundred other rookies brought for flight school, dressed with baggy clothes, and given over to a sergeant to the torture of the obstacle course. Then, in the middle of it all, we all were ordered to go under the rusty barbed-wire fences and thorns to collect pieces of aluminum and human flesh—all that was left of an Ouragan jet that passed over us, did a roll in the air, and augured in with a boom and a big splash of kerosene. A small fire was soon put out that left a black, fatty layer over everything and a cloying, sweet smell that stuck to skin and clothes. "What a Zikago" was the phrase Umsh coined then for any snafu.

At the end of "Ladya's day," our first day in the air force, many of us decided they had had enough. They smelled the stench and had second thoughts. We—the fifty boys who stayed—were sent to casual company on the base, cleaning, whitewashing, shoveling, painting—in short, waiting for the real stuff to begin. That's how I came to know the air force, and my friends at the thirty-first pilot course.

The door opened again. A short, solid man came out on the balcony and faced us. The back of his thick neck was shaven and the flight suit was tight on his barrel chest. He wore no rank insignia on his worn flight suit that was almost white from many launderings.

Uncertainly, we saluted him.

"You must be the trainees!" he announced.

We nodded.

"Welcome to the Scorpions!"

And suddenly he gave us a warm, beautiful, contagious smile, which lit up his big, heavy face. We all smiled back at him. This was our introduction to Capt. Zorik Lev, the legendary vice commander of the legendary commander of the best fighter squadron in the Israeli Air Force. Zorik never wore rank insignia on his shoulders or wings on his chest. This was a kind of coquettish modesty; just looking at him told you who and what he was.

"Put your rucksacks here. Here! And go into that room! Hurry, move it!"

It seemed that every sentence here had to end with an exclamation point.

We were pushed inside, one after another, and on entering, scanned the room. This was the squadron briefing room, the heart of its existence. The room had a large central table, covered with maps of the Middle East. Around the table, leaning against the walls, sat twenty or so pilots of the elite jet fighter community. We realized that they had all come here to welcome us and to get to know the trainees.

I looked at the men cautiously, surreptitiously. The first impression was one of—a festival of mustaches! Almost everyone here sported one: Yalo's clipped mustache was next to David Ivry's Cossack-style flowing yellow one. A black enormous mustache on Beit-on's upper lip contrasted with the two red brushes sported by Nissim and Yozef Salant. And the cat's whiskers mustaches that belonged to Aki and Avihu were better than the blurry shadow on Khetz's beak. Mustaches and more mustaches. They surrounded us challengingly. Oh, my God, I thought, awestruck. We trainees hadn't much to add to the glory of the Scorpions in this respect, even if you considered the yellow thread under Goldie's nose. And what's more, though ZBB's and Umsh's cheeks were shadowed, Sheani and I had no hope: the shrubbery hadn't even begun to grow.

I scanned the unknown faces, searching. Who among them was Yak?

However, Zorik was the dominant figure. His sharp eyes searched the room; he decided, enough, and banged the table with a heavy fist. Silence. Then he addressed the new arrivals. The introduction ritual had begun. Each of the trainees was invited to stand up in turn and introduce himself to the group.

After much pushing and shoving, Umsh got to his feet. He was two or three years older than the rest of us. Black-haired, virile, tall, and athletic, Zvi Umshweiff was the handsomest guy in our group. He towered over the rest of us.

When Umsh began talking, I looked again to try to spot Yak. A character, Yak was the one whom air cadets discussed admiringly as "the best fighter pilot in the history of the IAF." Recently, while in the operational training stage, we were given the manual on aerial combat theory. Yak had written this manual. I spent nights on the crude but clear sketches he drafted there—an aircraft gets on his adversary's tail, and suddenly, as in a sophisticated jujitsu exercise, is catapulted forward, instantly transformed from predator to prey. And, of course, Yak was one of the very few in the world who had shot down MiG-17s, the most modern jet fighters built in the USSR. Yakir Laufer, the ex-mechanic who knew everything, said that nobody in the world could sit on Yak's tail. And then he would add humbly, "for now." This naive arrogance—which, as we advanced in our training, was gradually proving itself true—annoyed the rest of us.

Yak was already nearing the end of his command of the Scorpions. His successor, Maj. Shimon Ash, joined us in the conversion course on the Super Mystere, and he also was watching us, but Zorik, the vice commander, was the boss. Still, I knew that Yak was hidden among the men, and he was the player who would separate the sheep from the goats. Whoever he didn't like would wash out and go back to the old planes, the Mysteres or the Ouragans.

So, I wondered, who was Yak?

There was something odd about Zvi Umshweiff, some internal conflict that endowed him with an enigmatic, mysterious aura.

His strange family name—Umshweiff—reeked of terrible and evil places. But in spite of this, there was no trace of the Diaspora in him. On the contrary, Umsh was the perfect Sabra, a kibbutz product, full of smiles, a good dancer, and a superb athlete. There was no hint of a Polish accent in his speech, but we all could sense ghosts shadowing him. Slowly and gradually we learned some details. He had come from Umshweiff—a village near Auschwitz—and he had spent two years in the extermination camp as a child, lost both parents, and somehow, by a miracle, made it out alive. When World War II ended, the nine-year-old boy wandered the roads of Europe and eventually arrived in Palestine and Kibbutz Ein-Hamifratz near Haifa. There he grew up an orphan.

In those years, the 1950s, such a story was not very unusual. The classrooms were filled with children who came from God knows where, speaking foreign languages. Gradually a perfect, throaty Hebrew replaced Zvi's native Polish. The Holocaust seedling grew, acquired a tan, and became a superb sportsman and an excellent student. That is what Zvi Umshweiff let us know about him, that and nothing more. But when they ordered us to change our family names to Hebrew ones, Zvi stubbornly refused to part with his strange name.

In our cadet barracks and on some hard marches he proved a good friend. One evening on the "hunger hike," when the night had enveloped our small group on top of a hill in the Negev desert, and we lay on the ground shivering, weak from three days of marching with no food, suddenly Umsh spoke up.

He proposed a prize of ten pounds from his own pocket to whoever could fart the smell of fried chicken. The contest aroused new spirit and got a good laugh from all of us. Zvi was a good sport, but he still jealously guarded his privacy. He always played his cards close to the chest. He was not unsocial, but kept to himself, meticulously squared away, ironed and shined. He lived the moment, every moment, as if it were his last. When we started flying he was immediately successful, but was satisfied with whatever he did and didn't strive to do better. He studiously avoided any extra effort.

On one occasion when he did go out of his way, he took me with him.

We were learning the basics flying Harvard trainers. Suddenly Zvi took me aside and challenged me to a one-on-one aerial combat—a dogfight. We stood away from the others, whispering together worriedly, because this idea was mad and criminal. At that time we were just at the initial stage of our solo flights, and were only beginning to get a preliminary understanding of how to manipulate the controls of our chubby propeller trainer. Naturally, none of us had any clue whatsoever as to the real meaning of those two words "aerial combat" and what happens in one. And above all, it was clear to us that what was cooking between us was a very serious offense against army regulations. We knew that if anybody even heard us talking we would instantly be washed out of the course, and the school's commander would definitely lock us both up.

We were just looking for big trouble.

The next morning we met over the eastern edge of the deserted British runway at Faluja, where nowadays stands the town of Kiryat Gat. At that time there was only the open expanse of the northern Negev Desert. I held a left-turn holding pattern and waited for Zvi's arrival.

The Harvard trainer that came toward me rocked his wings and blinked twice with his landing lights. I extended my landing gear and then retracted them, as a signal. The area around us was clear and no other plane was in sight, so I went to full throttle and flew right at him, not knowing what exactly to do next. His barrel-round nose turned toward me, and within a minute we found ourselves chasing each other with roaring propellers. The more I tightened my turn, the more he tightened his, and the circle shrank and shrank. I could see his face as a white mark in the frame of his glass canopy.

We continued this way until I lost my temper and pulled back hard on the stick. My airplane began to stall, shuddering and skittering from side to side, like a car on a wet road. For some reason, Umsh's plane had stopped turning and was flying straight ahead. Had he given up? Had I won? With pounding heart I hurried to complete the rest of the turn and came in on his tail, disregarding the shuddering of my Harvard, which was threatening to stall again under the pressure of the pulled-back stick, chattering victoriously "Rat-tat! Rat-tat!" And then I sensed something else, big and gray, moving ominously at the fringe of my vision. A second later I passed a rocky hillside within a whisker of my right wing.

When I came to my senses again, I was skimming over a white dirt road, still in the air and trying to regain speed and escape from the low hills around me. Umsh had disappeared somewhere. I saw his plane again only later, when I got behind him in line for a landing at Tel Nof. When we shut our engines and dismounted our aircraft, we ignored each other.

In the evening, in our room, when the two of us were safe from any eavesdropping, Umsh shot me a mocking smile. Hurt, I said to him, "Come on, Umsh, what's that smile on your face, huh? I beat you, didn't I?"

He didn't respond, so I continued, "So what if I didn't see the fucking hill? I was concentrating, I was locked on you!" And when again he didn't reply I said angrily, "Well, are we fighter pilots, or not?" I was insulted, because I felt I deserved praise. In this mock engagement I had succeeded, finally, in flying the way my instructor, Lieutenant Rosenberg, had tried to teach me. "You're absent-minded, Spike!" he used to thunder at me during every flight, in a hoarse and thick voice that came from the rear cockpit as from a deep barrel. "Concentrate, ya-Allah! Focus! Fo-cooos!" stressing the last syllable to get to the Arabic word for "cunt."

And here I did concentrate all right, didn't I? And I sure got results—I shot down Umsh the Great!

Umsh shushed me. "Don't shout. Somebody will hear us—"

I lowered my voice but didn't calm down. After all, the teacher in the children's house at the kibbutz used to call me "scatterbrain." And our schoolteacher, Yos'l, used to ask, "Where was His Majesty hovering lately? Would His Highness be kind enough to descend?" So absent-mindedness had always been my curse, but not this time.

"So what if I took some risk, Umshweiff, eh?" I demanded. "So what the fuck?" I had adapted that from Harry Barak, our Australian commander with the long mustache.

Umsh just chuckled at me. He was two years older than I, going on a hundred, and felt no need to phrase survivability skill in words. So while I was fuming, I found myself alone. Zvi Umshweiff turned to the wall and covered his head with a blanket, retiring for his regular evening interview with Kim Novak.

And now Umsh concluded, introducing himself to the squadron and sitting back in his chair. Zorik handed him a present, a cardboardbound file full of his study materials—Super Mystere manuals, flight rules, etc.—with his name on it. They shook hands, and the group applauded.

It was evident that a splendid pilot such as Zvi Umshweiff would be a very fine addition to the Scorpions, and most of all to Giora Furman, who needed a world-class striker on the squadron's volleyball team. And Yozef Salant also vetted plots. He coached the basketball team.

Uri Sheani then presented himself in a few quiet sentences. Uri never liked to talk much. But it was obvious from the looks on the faces of the people present that the Scorpions had checked this shrimp out before. The best shooter received his file with a handshake from Zorik and sat down. Zorik, with his pointy nose, had already sensed with whom he was dealing, and within a couple of days Sheani would be selected leader of the "fast turnaround" team of pilots, who must put an end to the irritating ascendancy of the wild mechanics of Lt. Gad Sandek, the technical officer of the squadron.

Fast turnaround contests were common competitive events back then. The rival teams, ten players each, would careen crazily out of the ammunition dumps, dragging and pushing trolleys loaded with external fuel tanks, heavy bombs, fuses, and strips of cannon rounds. The competitors then would jump and climb all over the aircraft, crawling under it, all at full speed—all you could hear was wham, bam. Arm it, fuel it, and prepare it to go out again. As in a festival, the whole squadron would be around cheering and shouting encouragement, smearing the name of the opposing team. When all was done—this would be in minutes and seconds—Sandek would arrive to check that all was done right. Then the winning team would collect its prize—an evening pass in town, or something like that.

Everybody in the air force was involved in the fast turnaround contests. We all knew that this was the "force multiplier" of the IAF, the trick that could produce the equivalent of two hundred aircraft from the mere hundred we actually had. These contests required intelligence, a lot of physical power, and strong leadership. Uri Sheani was definitely the right man.

In the last weeks Uri began dating Shula, a petite parachute-folder, who also brought a friend for me. Madlene was a very good-looking girl who sat with long legs crossed, holding her cigarette between slim fingers, but when they went out to the rustling eucalyptus leaves and the perfumed darkness, I didn't go. I preferred to stay sitting on a stool in front of the bar in the officers' mess. I was in love with a girl from the kibbutz—a supple, flat-chested primrose—and preferred to listen to "Tammy" and "For Alize," sucking slowly the Coke bottle and dreaming of those virgin lips.

The room warmed up.

The flight jackets came off, and finally I was able to discern—thanks to the major's insignia on one of them—which of the men was our commander, Yak. I stared at the slender, modest, pensive figure who sat in the corner, totally silent, as if he were only a guest, and let Zorik flood the room with his bubbling energy. Yak had a fine, delicate face with a straight nose and small brown eyes with long lashes. On his upper lip was a thin pencil mustache. He looked soft, almost feminine.

I nudged Umsh. What, is this Yak, the pride of the Israeli fighter pilots? I was expecting somebody very different—a bull of a guy like Aki or Daniel Vardon. At that time I didn't perceive the intense intelligence radiating from this slender person. Neither I nor anybody else imagined how distant from the Scorpions Yak already was, cooking inside his brain the historic victory that was going to save the Jewish state within seven years. And no one at the time could interpret correctly the early signs of alienation and aloofness that were already showing in Yak's behavior and that would eventually lead to his own destruction.

But now he searched in his pocket, produced a pipe, filled it slowly, and lit it. The sweet scent of tobacco filled the room. I was thrilled, for this finally was a real sign. Douglas Bader, an amputee hero of the Battle of Britain, used to smoke a pipe all the time, even in the cockpit of his Spitfire.

I vowed to get me a pipe as soon as I could.

It was Goldie's turn. Immediately, the room was filled with smiles.

Ami Goldstein, Goldie, the most distinguished member of our class, was a small, fair man with blue eyes and a yellow mustache. His unflappable good humor and quick wit inspired everyone. When his fast thinking and meticulous implementation, and the way he cut directly to the heart of things became evident, we understood he was a serious guy. Goldie became the golden boy of our class.

He had a sense of humor and a skill with language that could define a person or an issue in a few words. He coined phrases with staying power. All the time he introduced or invented new, funny ideas. Soon we all were speaking his idiom, which became our secret language. I myself received from Goldie for free the nickname "Spike." Having been raised on a kibbutz, I hadn't been exposed to American films and didn't know the cartoon dumb bulldog who always reacts too late and too much. The nickname Spike, since it came from Goldie, did not offend me. After a time I thought that maybe there was something to it.

Besides his humor, Goldie had clear goals in life.

"Life is divided into two stages," he would say. In the beginning, according to his theory, you are in the stage of "BSA" (being shouted at), because everybody reprimands you. Later you develop and become an "SAEE" (shouts at everyone else). "I have no time or patience for the first stage," he told me. "My aim in life is to shorten it, and get up to the level of the 'shouters' as soon as possible."

Later, when we got to night flying, Goldie had a tough time. For some reason his Harvard went wild time and again in the darkness. Sometimes he would run out of runway while landing, go off into the fields, and flip over. By dumb luck, Ami was not injured on such occasions. In one of those accidents, when he crawled out from under the upended airplane among the smoking gooseneck kerosene lamps that served for runway lights, the boss was waiting for him with a long face.

"What was it this time, Goldstein?"

The small man, covered with mud, giggled. "Suddenly the Harvard growled at me, like a wolf."

"So what did you do?" asked Maj. Harry Barak, our commander, in his heavy Australian accent. This was the moment of truth—Harry was going to determine Goldstein's fate, whether he would continue with us or go back to the ground troops.

"I growled back at him, like a bigger wolf."

The flight instructors around Harry howled with laughter, like wolves, and he was fascinated. He decided to give Goldie a few more lessons. Finally Goldie got night landings figured out, too.

Goldie was purposeful and charming. We all knew that before any of us would be toddling, Goldie would already be running. And as Goldie finished his presentation to the Scorpions and returned to his seat, one almost could hear the "click." Goldie was already one of the gang.

ZBB, ZUR BEN-BARAK, was no doubt the smartest of us, and a heavyweight by any measure. In spite of his cumbersome body and his flat-footed goose gait, he was quick in biting. From the dark, wrinkled, almost old face shone amazing eyes, gray-green and alive, that saw everything. And there was a brain behind the bright eyes that recorded and cataloged to the minutest detail, and retrieved at the appropriate moment for use, though not without adding a little extra something wicked. Zur's brain was a rare calculating tool, sharp and acute. It lost no item of information. He was in love with details, remembered them, knew how to caress them into a whole picture and to produce witty, surprising inferences. He had mastered numbers and was fond of demonstrating his exceptional ability. Even though he was the best pupil in the class—an able painter with notebooks full of elaborate drawings in dimensions and colors—he was slow to grasp the mechanics of flight. But he improved his performance daily, not repeating any mistake. The flight instructors appreciated this and were competing to teach him.

His body was another problem.

In the evenings he was torn by intense desires. Restless, he would drag me along to the soldiers' mess to watch him undressing the girls with his eyes. He would weigh breasts, legs, and buttocks, evaluate and analyze them. He would approach the girls, court them and flatter them, distribute cigarettes and chocolate—a rare item that was given to us air cadets as a nutrition additive—then corner two or three girls with his body against a wall. I was an innocent; I hated this approach and was ashamed of such behavior. All I wanted was to go back to my room to study or sleep. But Zur needed a squire and was trying to teach me.

"Why did you volunteer for pilot training? Huh?"

I was both scared of and attracted to him.

There was something mysterious in ZBB, something similar to my mother, Shoshana. Like her, he had a frightening quality that enabled him to know things he had no way of knowing. Those bright eyes could, at times, be like an X-ray machine. This capability to assemble banal details and produce unexpected generalizations—to infer the missing piece of the puzzle—sometimes seemed magical. On occasions he caught a glimpse into the future.

Once I invited him to join me in an Independence Day event at my kibbutz, Givat-Brenner. We arrived a little late, and the festival had already begun. It was a golden spring afternoon in mid-May. The sun was a great orange ball lowering behind the Sereni building, the community hall of the kibbutz. Hundreds of the kibbutz members and their children, all in white shirts and blue trousers, were crowded on the vast lawn in the golden light.

Above us fluttered our national white-and-azure flags together with the red flags of the workers' movement.

A trumpet sounded and everyone became quiet. The kibbutz choir began singing, and many members joined in. Then, from the second-floor veranda, a boy and a girl recited "The Silver Tray," a poem about the youth who were the tray upon which independence was given to the Jewish nation. The words poured from their lips like silver. The trumpet sounded again, and we all stood at attention. The kibbutz's spokesman read aloud the name of each of the fallen in the struggle for statehood. He read the name of my father, Zvi, and at that moment I saw my mother sitting by herself, smoking a cigarette. The choir went on in four-part harmony, and we all followed and sang together, in one mighty voice, the anthems: "Hatikva" (The Hope), the anthem of the State of Israel, and then the "Internationale." The air was full of positive energy.

When the event was over, families began gathering to continue the festivities. I was about to approach my mother, and suddenly ZBB elbowed me. I turned toward him. He indicated with his eyes, and when I followed his look, I saw the girl I was falling in love with. She stood apart from us, slender and slight, part of a covey of girls her own age. Zur grinned at me. I felt a heavy blush heat up my face. How in the world could ZBB have known that this was the one I wanted? There were a lot of girls around, some of them very good-looking. But Zur saw something, and somehow he knew.

After the grand feast with the entire kibbutz in the public dining room we had to leave and return to base. We parted from my mother and the lit, flower-filled hall and walked in the dark to our Willis. Zur drove the pickup; he never gave the wheel to anybody else. And I sat looking at him from the corner of my eye, confused, as if he had somehow found a way to control me.

It took me years to be able to explain in logical terms how he had done it. Life taught me also, gradually, how to fill in the missing pieces in the puzzles put before me. First it happened in aerial combat and then in commanding men. Time and again I was faced with situations where the facts available to me were only part of a larger whole, and some of them were questionable, too. Still, these were the premises upon which I had to decide and act. Under pressure, I learned to see—that is, to infer and create a complete picture. It was necessary to do it that way, though it was a delicate and even dangerous act. In combat flight, which is—like playing jazz—a fast performing art form based on deep culture and improvisation in varying situations—the necessary base for creativity and invention is the ability to collect diverse pieces of information and fill the missing parts with imagination and association, to create a multidimensional mental picture. This is the meaning of seeing. Finally I came to realize that seeing does not come just from the outside. A major part of it wells up from the inside. Zur knew how to see.

Only after this event did I get up enough courage to propose friendship to this girl. Ali, in her direct way, answered with a short note that ended, "Yes, I accept."

YES, ZBB WAS BOTH SCARY and attractive.

What made it easier for me in his company was this clumsy and anxious body of his that caused him so much suffering. He trembled when we were about to train at being taken prisoner by the enemy. This is the toughest part of the training in the flying school. We knew we were going for a hike in the mountains, that we were to try to hide and escape, but there was no chance. Somewhere along the way, we would be caught and taken to an unknown location, where interrogators would exert physical and mental pressure to extract information from us. Zur was pitiably frightened of this. He felt he would be unable to stand the physical pressures and the abuse, and believed he was going to bring shame on himself and on his father, Itamar, who was a high-ranking and respected officer in the reserves. So he began to try to toughen up. He wanted me to box with him and to punch him in the face. I didn't want to do it, so he pushed me by banging his head into a light pole.

After we finished wrestling, he dragged me to the base swimming pool and demanded that I teach him to dive from the highest board. He shook with terror. Again and again he walked to the edge with trembling legs, stopped, and sat down to think it over, unable to take the plunge. Eventually he climbed down, in despair. Those sweet guys in our class, mainly the veterans such as Umsh, Goldie, and Yakir, scorned him. They changed his nickname from ZBB, Zur Ben-Barak, to RBB—Run, Bloody Bastard.

But he passed the prisoner survival training with flying colors, and after that I saw him break the fear barrier.

It began with an accident. We already were flying Stearman biplane trainers, and one day ZBB taxied his plane a little too fast. He saw the other plane a little too late and was a little too slow to brake and crashed into it. The airplanes crunched together, their propellers flailing and sending cloth and pieces of wood flying. This was an unforgivable screwup, and nobody doubted that this was the end of ZBB's career in the air force.

Saturday passed with fraying nerves. Zur hid in a corner under his blanket for the whole weekend, refusing to taste the food I brought him from the dining room. Suddenly he got up, pulled me to the swimming pool, climbed to the top springboard, closed his eyes, rolled in the air, and did a belly flop on the water. I understood; he wanted to die.

Next morning he was summoned to see the commander. He was judged and punished but not washed out. Later, because of his talents and strong character, he stood out more and more, and when we got our wings, Zur Ben-Barak was already known as a winner.

My turn came. I rose to my feet and faced them all, blushing.

I was of medium height, very thin, and suffered a lot because of my round and childish face. I didn't like myself. My hair especially irritated me: it was black and curly. Elderly ladies loved to pat it, so in protest I shaved my head. I most hated my eyes, inherited from my mother, Shosh, who got them from her father, Nathaniel. My younger daughter, Ella, looks at me with these same eyes. When I saw these eyes in the mirror, light-colored and vulnerable, they made me feel restless.

And now, exposed before Yak and all the Scorpions, I had difficulty saying anything. I was never the kind who found speaking easy. I always found the right words, but later, after time had passed.

At least I had a hero to remember: the amputee Soviet fighter pilot Alexei Merseyev. Many times I have dreamed of the moment when they all were waiting for his return from the fight for the motherland, against the Nazi Messerschmitts. I imagined the squadron commander spitting, "Enough. Merseyev is out of fuel. He is not coming back. Let's go." And right then, in total silence like a shadow, Merseyev's aircraft arrived, gliding down, down, his propeller stopped. His airplane clipped the birch treetops and touched down on the first meter of the runway. But this was neither the place nor the audience to blab my dreams to. And I had no way to tell that like Merseyev within just a few short years, I would come back from air combat, my fuel tanks dry, dead-stick landing like a leaf on the first meter of a far-off runway. When I took my helmet off, two cuts would drip blood from where I had bitten through my lower lip.

Here I was, a mere second lieutenant, the new kid in school. My mother had taught me that things should be kept inside. One does not hang one's laundry out in public. I chose to limit myself to absolute basics: name, rank, and serial number.

Zorik watched me, waiting. I added something in a low voice.

"What did you say? Give us something on you, Spector! And speak up!"

I repeated, "I came here to defend our country."

They thought this was really funny. In the healthy roar of the laughter the investigation was all but forgotten. I flushed as I stooped to collect my file and hurried back to dive in among my friends. I dug into the box and found in it a notebook, a pencil, and two books: *Aerial Combat* by Yak Nevo, and *Air Gunnery* by David Ivry. This was the top wisdom of the air force, and for me—two worlds of knowledge, heroism and battle experience I had to make my own.

When I looked up again, I found those two figures themselves, bent over the table, watching me intently. Yak's eyes were brown and pensive; Ivry's pale blue, large and stern. Opposite them, Sam Khetz made a face and winked.

Then I relaxed. I passed the examination, and all would be well. And most important, everything had been kept inside.

Chapter

3

Palmach

Palmach (assault platoons): The strike force of the Hagana (Defense) organization.

Established in 1941, under threat of Nazi conquest of the Middle East. In the beginning Palmach was supported by the British Mandate government of Palestine, but later on it fought against it. During the covert years, Palmach boys and girls trained for half a month and worked in kibbutzim in the other half. Palmach emerged from the clandestine struggle as a commando force with clear battle doctrines and set values like love of the fatherland, comradeship, and purity of arms.

After the UN partition resolution of November 29, 1947, when the War of Independence broke out, the Palmach was the first force ready to fight the enemy. In the war, Palmach operated three brigades—Iftach, Harel, and Negev. Of the five thousand who served in Palmach, more than a thousand men and women fell. In November 1948 Ben-Gurion decided to dismantle Palmach, a controversial decision. Some of IDF's chiefs of staff were former Palmach members, including Yitzhak Rabin, Haim Barlev, David Elazar, Mordechai (Mota) Gur, and Raphael (Raful) Eitan. The first commander of Palmach was Yitzhak Sade. When he was nominated chief of the Hagana, his deputy, Yigal Allon, replaced him. His vice was Uri Brenner. The adjutant officer of Palmach was Shoshana Spector.

The eyes: the first things you would have noticed when looking at Shoshana Spector. They were terrific eyes, bright and extremely intelligent. The wide pupils were surrounded with bright green, almost yellow irises, and the colored area all plowed with miniature labyrinths like tree-root systems, and speckled with tiny marks.

She lost me at Kibbutz Givat-Brenner.

She arrived at that big kibbutz in the autumn of 1951, three years after the War of Independence had ended. The struggle for the revival of the Jewish state was over—at least so they thought at the time—and the time was right to settle old scores. My mother, the number one woman in the Palmach, was sent for a year of study in America (she had hoped to establish a rehabilitation plan for handicapped veterans), and when she returned, she was fired. Apparently the newly organized Israel Defense Force didn't need her and all the knowledge she'd accumulated. Like some of her comrades, she decided to try a new life in a kibbutz. This is how she showed up at Givat-Brenner, dragging behind her an eleven-year-old boy she didn't really know.

Later she used to blame me, half seriously, for this decision. "The boy wanted to live on kibbutz," she would complain, spreading her arms sideways, grinning as if hiding something. Perhaps she knew that the truth was that I did want to live on a kibbutz, but on a different one, Hulatta, which was on the other side of the country, where I had other parents.

Her memories from her childhood in Jaffa were sharp and colorful.

She liked to remember herself as a barefoot urchin running around the Arab market, cheeky and dirty, with two wild braids, which, when not washed with kerosene, were crawling with lice. In the winter, hot sahlab (a Middle Eastern pudding) was sold from a container carried on the back of the seller and poured out over his shoulder into a cup. In summertime there were cold, sour drinks such as suss and tamar hindi. All her life she longed for that Jaffa market that disappeared after the 1948 War of Independence, and she sought it in other markets. Sometimes she pulled me after her to the Carmel Market in South Tel Aviv, where she would pry and bargain and snoop into all the stalls, an olive here and a piece of salt fish there, and I shrank with shame hearing the vulgar language that suddenly came from this smart, sophisticated woman and the replies of the vendors. For her, this was romantic, although she herself was not romantic. Her Arabic, anyway, was always strong and convincing.

In her childhood in the twenties, there were not many Jewish families living in Jaffa. Her father, Nathaniel Tatar, wrote in his diary, "I was almost the only Jew who lived among the Arabs." Shoshana was sent to school at the Christian mission. There she was taught in Arabic and English. To show me her mastery of the languages and to amuse me, she used to recite all sorts of poetry she had been required to memorize in both languages, and would preach to me in forceful Arabic, "Rach A Shitta, Jaa Seif" (the winter has gone, spring has come). Sometimes she would sing off-key, "Di Yea Ken John Peel" or "Elsie Marley, the wife that sells the barley honey" and Shakespeare's "the hei and the ho and the hei." I especially enjoyed when she taught me a song she called a ditty, and to this day I remember part of it:

Master Bullfrog, grave and stern,
Called the classes each in turn;
Sitting there upon a log,
Taught them how to say "Ker-chog."

Actually, she disconnected herself from her family, and saw her parents—in comparison with her friends from the Palmach—as "provincial." Even when she took me to the north, she didn't stop to see them, and they didn't visit us and never called or wrote.

Her connection with her past existed only in her stories, not in the reality I saw as a child. Even her weird family name, Tatar, didn't connect to anything I knew. Shosh seemed to me some force of nature, existing by itself and with no origin.

Only once did I spend the night at her parents' house, and then I realized that they really existed. I was about five years old then.

It was close to the end of World War II, perhaps in mid-1945. I don't know what caused their daughter, Shosh, to visit them on that day and leave me there for the night, but the memory remains sharp and clear.

A heavy summer heat hung over the Izreel Valley. My grandparents—they were about sixty—had a small house and a small farm on the outskirts of the provincial township of Afula in the valley. The house had two rooms. Both doors opened to a veranda in front. The veranda was closed in, and served as foyer and guest room. Bracha's kitchen was a cubicle at the right side of the veranda, and inside were two kerosene stoves coated with gray enamel. Blue flames shone behind two little glass doors, and two large aluminum pots stood on them, boiling, full of laundry and food. The floor's cement tiles had sunk, and Grandpa used the cool dents under the bed to store watermelons. I squeezed in there and lay down on the clean floor. My grandfather pulled me out, stuck a book in my hand, and ordered me to leaf through it.

Nathaniel Tatar was a sinewy man in his undershirt, and his eyes were bright and hard like my mother's. His face was dark and furrowed. When he found out that I knew how to read, he tested what I could understand, his stiff finger moving along the lines of the book. Grandma Bracha, in cotton dress and apron, hurried to save me from him. She brought hot tea in glasses, and dry biscuits. She looked small and shriveled near her husband, and her Hebrew—in contrast to his—was poor and distorted, and suffered from a heavy Russian accent. I once heard Shosh, my mother, calling her "the hen."

"Ess, ess, Yingale," the hen told me by the table, and when I didn't understand she explained, "Eat, eat. No horror."

My mother left and went about her business, and I was left with the old folks.

The smell of kerosene filled the entire house from Grandma's tiny kitchen. At noontime another smell joined it, the DDT she sprayed from a pump, to keep the flies and gnats away. I liked the smell, which hovered like a cloud of tiny, cool particles. After lunch, which was chicken guts (she taught as she fed me: "belly button," in Russian, is "pupik"), she closed the windows against the hot wind, lowered the curtains, and sent me to their bed for a forced noontime nap. When I opened my eyes she was sitting at the corner of my bed, sailing into a long and vague story about the city of Bukhara, and then she passed somehow to anecdotes from the life of the Bedouins. Most of what she said I couldn't understand. Grandfather was out at work, and my mother hadn't returned yet. Grandma dressed me and sent me to shred fresh clover with a bladed wheel ("You kerfooyl, kerfooyl!"). I scattered the cut clover around for the chickens and they came running over to me, croaking and pecking. I tried to touch them, but the colored rooster drove me away. The excrement stuck between my toes. At last Grandma washed my feet, fed me a soft-boiled egg, and lay me down again, this time on the sofa in the second room.

There was still light in the window, and I couldn't fall asleep. Grandfather came in, dug in the glassed-in bookshelf above me, found what he was looking for, and put a notebook before me.

"Read it," he pleaded. His face was different this time, soft and supplicatory. When he left, I opened the notebook and found handwritten script, in blue ink. At my age handwriting was still not easy to read, and only the many strange names attracted me. Kusseima, Suez, they sounded like magic words as I muttered them. Most of all I was fascinated by a name that sounded as if out of the Arabian *One Thousand and One Nights*, and I rehearsed it time and again, whispering, "Darb El Hajj." Finally Grandma came and put out the lamp. Across from my couch a big radio hissed and muttered. It was made of wood, and had a round window coated with cloth like straw. The radio sported a lit frequency dial, and had a green indicator and a green eye that flickered all the time, opening and closing. It hypnotized me.

When I woke, mosquitoes sang. Yellow, vibrating electric light and jets of cigarette smoke entered through the slit of the door, mixed with the jingling of glasses and the screeching of chairs. Spoons rang on saucers. There were guests in the entrance room. They argued about something, my mother's voice rising above all of them with a strident tone. From time to time there were long periods of silence and then I heard the old man grunt, and the sounds of sipping of tea. Sometimes Grandma Bracha squeaked, her voice cajoling. I understood that she was trying to find a compromise among the hard people of her life.

Suddenly the radio near me began the tones indicating a news broadcast. The chairs in the next room scraped the floor. The door opened carefully, and they all came in on tiptoe. My mother sat on the couch, near me. The narrator spoke in a low, deliberate voice. She spoke words I knew already: Allies. Nazis. Jews. Russia.

That evening, when everybody had gone and my mother arranged to sleep near me, I learned that I was a Jew too. I listened with a lot of interest to the Nazi plan to kill all the Jews. Before I fell asleep I thought about it a long time, a little surprised and proud of the fact that the Nazis—creatures I knew nothing about—knew about me and were interested in me. When my mother pulled up the blanket and turned over, before dozing took me over, I asked her silently what "Darb El Hajj" was. The Road of the Celebrators, she told me, and suddenly asked, "What, he already stuck you with his notebook? Oh, that bookkeeper, what does he hope to accomplish with that?"

Nathaniel Tatar, a bitter, hard person, left behind him thirteen pages written with a scratchy pen in blue ink, in basic, sometimes archaic Hebrew. In this notebook I found buried a vanished world.

My mother's parents began their journey to the land of Israel (there was no country then, just the land) in the township of Rezina, near Kishinev, in Moldova. Nathaniel was a veteran of the tsar of Russia's army. His odd name, Tatar, had an alien sound, and he was formally registered as a Christian. One can assume that he came from one of the Mongol-Tatarian communities of Eastern Europe. On the other hand, his twenty-three-year-old bride, Bracha (blessing), had a good Jewish name. They married through a matchmaker and settled down in Rezina. Nathaniel managed an agricultural farm for its owners.

One evening, when he was thirty-two years old, he went to the movies.

"The film was called *The Land of Israel*," he wrote in his simple hand. "I saw how they picked oranges, the field crops, and more interesting things, and liked it all. I decided to go there."

He tried to get the passport that was necessary to allow him to leave Russia. "But because I had been a soldier, and there were rumors of war, it was difficult. So I tried something else. Since I had a daughter sick with bronchitis, the doctors advised taking her to a tropical country. This way I received permission from the government to go to the land of Israel for three months. I was delayed, for my wife gave birth. She bore another daughter, Shoshana. This was in February 1914," he wrote.

Three weeks after his wife left the hospital, the family took a ship in Odessa and sailed to Israel.

"After a week at sea we arrived at Jaffa and stayed in a hotel. When we left the ship I managed not to give anyone my name, so they couldn't find me later." That didn't help poor Tatar much.

That was Passover 1914. Within five months World War I would break out.

To this country, Palestine in 1914, Tatar came without a cent. Soon he found that manual labor was his only hope. Even that was not easy to find. His young family first lived in Jaffa, then moved ten kilometers east to a cheaper place, the Jewish settlement of Petach Tikva, established in 1878. There they lived on Tatar's work in the orchards "for a tiny salary, the same as the Arabs," tells Nathaniel, the former farm manager. "Even this kind of work was given me reluctantly, for the orchards' owners contended that the work was too hard for us new immigrants and the salary too low for us to live on. There was only one kind of work where I could make some money, and it was mowing hay with a scythe. I had done this work."

With visible pride he went on to tell how he became a subcontractor and employed others as workers, including men who became important later, such as Shkolnik (Levy Eshkol, fifty years later Israel's prime minister), and Harzfeld (a future important political figure). He even employed the manager of the local labor exchange!

On August 14, 1914, World War I broke out.

The Turks, who governed the country, began checking the citizenship of every one of the inhabitants of Palestine, and either drafting them into the army or expelling them from the country. Tatar was captured.

"I took seven pairs of horses for deep plowing in Mikveh Israel (an agricultural school a few kilometers southeast of what was then the village of Tel Aviv). We had just gotten organized and begun working when some Turkish cops showed up. They ordered me to untie the horses from the plow and tie them to the carts. We were taken to Jaffa and put in front of the Sakkai (a Turkish military building). There we stayed till the evening. We sent a message to the horses' owners in Petach Tikva and informed them what had happened."

Tatar was always very careful with any property loaned to him, and his descendants inherited this from him. "But the owners were too afraid to come and defend their property, and told me to do my best. In the evening I entered the Sakkai and asked one of the officers why we were being kept there. He answered that come morning we would haul a load of cement to Beer- Sheva."

The Moldovan estate manager turned teamster in Palestine was going to learn about the Ottoman Empire.

"We watched what happened in the Sakkai. In one of the rooms a commander sat, twenty large candles lit around him. From time to time he called in someone who had resisted confiscation of his property. The commander ordered punishment: fifty falaki (blows on the soles of the feet). This was the way it went all night—verdicts, the punishments executed on the spot, and the people around watching." After this demonstration, there was no more resistance. The next day Tatar's journey began.

"We loaded the cement barrels, and a week's food for the horses, a barrel of water on each cart, and off we went without knowing where we were going, as all I knew about Beer- Sheva came from the Bible. We asked Arab passersby. One said 'go north,' the other pointed south. We decided to go to Rehovot, and see what to do from there."

Rehovot was an agricultural settlement some thirty kilometers south of Jaffa. There, civilization ended and gave way to the wild, wild South.

"From Rehovot there was no road fit for carts going south, only camel trails. Thanks to the light loads on the carts we made it somehow, and after a day and a night we came to Kastina, a Jewish settlement."

So they stopped at Beer-Tuvia, a small settlement among some Arab villages.

"We found there a warehouse, rested for four hours, and continued on our way. From there, there was really no more road, only a narrow trail crossing the wadis (dry streambeds). The barrels were rolling around in the carts and the cement spilled out of the cracks. Another day and night and we reached Kibbutz Ruchama."

The name Ruchama came from the Bible. "Say ye unto your brethren, Ammi (my people), And to your sisters Ruchama," said the prophet Hosea. "Ruchama" means mercy. "I will have mercy upon her that has not obtained mercy." But Tatar didn't know all that, and found no reason to stop there. The place was just a few acres with some shacks. There were fifteen workers planting almond and eucalyptus trees. They couldn't help him with anything—they had brought their own bread from Beer-Tuvia with difficulty, and sometimes personal danger; the Bedouins would sometimes rob them on the way.

So he went on, "There in Ruchama, we found a big wadi with a narrow trail. One of our carts rolled over, and fell to the wadi together with the horses. We worked for half a day until we got it out."

They were crossing the wadi system of Ruchama—a magnificent area, nowadays a national park with many beautiful bicycle trails. Then they came to a plain.

"We found ourselves in a desert of sand. The carts sank to their axles, and the horses couldn't pull them anymore."

Hold it.

There, in this vast plain, I crossed the footsteps of my grandfather Nathaniel for the first time. This happened after I parachuted from my burning Ouragan after an aerial collision. I landed in a desert full of shallow hills, south of Ruchama. I hit the ground, rolled in the floury dirt, and got to my feet. Not far away, I saw a bunch of black, low tents, pitched in what my grandfather had called sand. In fact it was thin, reddish dust.

Bedouins came and gathered around me, interested in my gear. The hot November wind of 1964 stung my burned cheeks awfully, but certainly less than the hamsin (the east wind from the desert) of August 1914, when Tatar and his drivers had struggled to pull their carts through. Finally they had found a solution.

"We tied two pairs of horses to one cart, then drove five kilometers ahead and came back to take the next cart. In this way we advanced fifteen kilometers a day."

Finally they arrived in Beer-Sheva tired, hungry, dirty, and covered with dust.

"I found a military office. A senior Turkish officer sat there. Luckily he could speak Arabic. From the initial load of 2.8 tons, only about one ton was left, but I told the cart drivers to move the barrels in a way that they seemed heavy." Tatar was cunning, but he didn't know the Ottomans yet. "The soldier didn't even approach to see if there was anything inside the barrels."

If he thought his mission ended, he was wrong. His story had just begun.

"The commander called me and asked if I had a bag. I told him I hadn't. He opened his desk drawer and counted eighty-four Turkish pounds in gold. He produced a cloth bag and put it together with a letter, and said we had to deliver pipes from Ramleh—an Arab town near Rehovot—to Kusseima, in the heart of the Sinai desert. That meant two weeks in each direction."

This way Nathaniel Tatar, formerly a soldier in the tsar's army, was conscripted to the service of the Young Turks' post–Ottoman Empire.

For an additional year and a half Tatar continued to work as a cart driver in the service of the Turkish army. "We drove our carts from Beer-Sheva to the Suez Canal, transporting supplies and rations for the soldiers one way, and coming back loaded with the wounded.

"But," continued Nathaniel, "at that time we were not paid anymore for the work, and we no longer even got food for the horses, so they began to die one after the other."

All this time his wife, Bracha, raised her two baby daughters alone in a hut made of eucalyptus branches, its walls covered with towels and sheets, near Petach Tikva. They survived on pita from sorghum flour they baked themselves on an open fire.

At last Tatar decided to desert.

"I ran home on foot, half naked. On the way I got food and shelter from Bedouin and farmers till I reached Petach Tikva. I didn't enter the settlement, but stayed hidden in the orchards. I was a deserter, and the penalty was death."

After some time he managed to buy a nefus (Turkish identity card) under a different name, and resumed work as a teamster on the line between Petach Tikva and Jerusalem, hiding all the time from the police.

In 1918, when the British offensive struck from Egypt and pushed the Turks across the Sinai and out of Gaza, the Turks began to expel the Jews from Jaffa and Petach Tikva. They moved them to concentration camps in the North. Their cruelty reached new heights, but Turkish control of Palestine was over. The roads were filled with deserters who offered their rifles for a slice of bread. Eventually, when the army of British field marshal Edmund Allenby took Jerusalem, my Grandfather Nathaniel came out of the cellar he had been hiding in with his cart and horse.

The Turks were driven out, and British rule was established over Palestine. Foreign Secretary Arthur James Balfour, Lord Balfour, made promises of "a homeland for the Jews in Palestine," and at the same time contradicting promises were given to any Arab who happened to be around. Anyway, a temporary peace prevailed in the country. Nathaniel and his family returned to the mixed city of Jaffa, and he looked for a way to make a living. Initially he continued to drive his cart. He transported rice from Jaffa Harbor up to Nablus in Samaria, and returned with homemade soap. Gradually his cart took him farther away, to Tiberias, and even to Damascus.

For a while he tried to become a businessman. There was a shortage of onions, so he hurried to organize a caravan of camels that returned from the South loaded with onions. But during his journey, a ship arrived from Egypt full of onions, and the price plummeted. His second daughter, Shoshana, five years old, was old enough to remember what happened. During my own childhood she used to regale me before bedtime with her stories about those onions, which rolled around in all the rooms and all about the yard. She acted out for me how the whole family ate onions in the morning, onions for lunch, and onions for supper, and how at the end her sister and she were sliding down from the top of their father's heap of crumbling hopes, which had begun sprouting and rotting.

‡

After World War I ended, the economic situation of the family improved for a while. I found proof of that in a photograph from that time; from a yellowing panel, cracked and framed in green, the family Tatar stares. Mr. Tatar sits on a chair, as befits the master of the house, and all the other members of the family stand around him. My grandmother, Bracha, wears a long cotton dress. She stands near him like a soldier at parade rest, her hands joined behind her back. The two girls, in two identical dark dresses with bright white collars, peep over his shoulders. The two small boys are pressed against his knees. The master himself is mummified in a suit, his face serious, mustache well clipped, and his white tie matches his white shoes. By then he was no longer a newcomer from Russia or a cart driver whipped down the roads of Sinai by Turkish soldiers. Before the camera sits a Levantine aristocrat. He runs, in partnership with a "good Arab," a Jaffa khan (hotel) and a fleet of dilijances (horse carts). The family waits for the flash of the camera. From the center of the picture shine Shosh's unbelievable, bright, disquieting eyes.

In the bedtime stories she told me I heard about the pogrom of the first of May 1921, when an Arab crowd assisted by policemen began attacking and killing Jews in Jaffa and the outskirts of Tel Aviv and looting stores and shops. The family Tatar was smuggled to Tel Aviv. Her father, Nathaniel, wrote, "I stayed alone in the khan, since many Jews who had stabled their horses and stored their merchandise fled and left everything. I was responsible for all of it. I closed the gate and sat alone inside. There was a high wall, but hundreds of Arabs began to force the gate. I climbed the wall and ran to the saraj—the British police station. I stayed there till night, and then they sent me to Tel Aviv in an armored car."

Shosh also remembered something from the 1921 "troubles." "I was six or seven," she told a reporter on one of the rare occasions she was interviewed. "I went to the school for girls in Nve Zedek (a neighborhood on the border between Jaffa and Tel Aviv) and on my way I was swept up by a violent demonstration of Arabs on Bostros Street. A hand reached in and pulled me out of the vortex, otherwise I would have been trampled. Our house at Suk El Dar became a field hospital for the wounded." And she summed up in her dry, curt manner, "These events were burned into my memory, and no doubt they affected my later life."

The events put an end to Tatar's economic success, and he gave up on Jaffa. He heard that in Balfuria, in the Izreel Valley, a new Jewish settlement had been established. One of the settlers, an American, sold his farm and left the country, and Nathaniel bought nine hectares and a shed from him, with a pair of mules and six cows.

"I moved to Balfuria at corn planting time, so I managed to sow about five hectares. I began to work in the fields. The children were still in school—the oldest of them twelve—and my wife and I worked almost day and night to get it all done. And still, after picking large crops and selling milk and eggs, we couldn't make a living since prices were so low."

They sank into deep poverty.

The children were also put to work and given adult responsibilities. Once Shosh, age fourteen, was sent by her father to Haifa to buy a plow. He hadn't given her enough money. She didn't return but stayed for several days in the Arab city, who knows where or how, till she found a workshop to repair an old plow for her to take home.

"No excuses," she explained to me when she told me that story. "Just results."

LIFE WAS HARD, AND EVERYONE in the family did his part. The boys stayed in school up to ninth grade and then left home to work as apprentices.

"The girls," tells Nathaniel apologetically, "saw that the situation in the house was not good, so they left, too. Sara, the older sister, found work in Jerusalem, and the younger Shoshana moved to the youth village in Ben Shemen." Nathaniel sold the farm and moved to the near town of Afula, where he tried his luck at dairy farming.

Since leaving her parents' home, Shosh hadn't had contact with them. On the few occasions when she spoke of them to me, she called their town mockingly "Afulevke." The youth village of Ben Shemen lies in the hills on the way to Jerusalem. There, instead of a farmer's poor and narrow vision, the new world of a renascent Israel was opened to her—a "state in the making."

The founder and manager of the youth village was Dr. Zigfried Lehmann, an educator who believed in tilling the soil, Zionism, and the value of people. Shosh admired him. More than once she told me Lehmann was the best person she ever met. She would compare him with Yanush Korchak, a great writer and educator who went to his death in a Nazi extermination camp with his orphan students.

According to Lehmann's vision, the youngsters ran the life of the village without adult help. The students of Ben Shemen lived in dormitories, studied and worked in all the branches of the farm, and sold its products. They created a vibrant social and cultural environment, celebrated holidays, and did scouting activities on Saturdays. They lived in groups, each group in its own house, so that family units were formed that functioned at work and while studying.

At Ben Shemen the ideal was personal accomplishment. The goal was taming the land, and indeed many of the graduates established new kibbutzim or joined existing ones, and almost all of them joined the Hagana, the Jewish defense force, the forerunner of the IDF. There Shosh found herself in a new and special company, the military avant-garde of the Jewish settlement movement in Palestine in the early 1930s. Since then and to the end of her life, this society was her world, and its values hers. In the fervor of beginning a new society and a state for the Jews, her provincial parents, the poor bookkeeper and his wife, the hen, were pushed out of her life and left behind. They were ghetto folk, bourgeois, leftovers of an old world that no one took pride in.

After finishing her studies in 1932, Shosh—like all her friends—found her way to the Hagana. On March 9, 1940, on a Saturday night, Shosh Tatar married Zvi Spector. I was born on October 20, 1940.

By then, the world was at war. In the beginning it seemed that the British, who controlled the Middle East and Palestine, were going to lose and be driven out. The fear was great. To our north, Syria and Lebanon were controlled by the French Vichy government, a Nazi puppet state. To the east, in Iraq, the pro-Nazi Rashid Ali rebellion broke out. To the west,

Erwin Rommel's Afrika Korps marched toward Egypt and the Suez Canal on its way to close the pincers.

The Jewish settlement in Palestine, which numbered less than half a million, was scattered among more than a million Arabs, who began to smell an opportunity to get rid of the Jews. Many of the Jewish youngsters joined the British army and went to Europe to fight against the Nazis. The Hagana, which had organized for a desperate defensive battle in Palestine, looked for a way to cooperate with the hated British Mandate regime to get arms.

On May 18, 1941, Zvi Spector went to sea in command of a boat with twenty-three men, and a British liaison officer aboard, and never returned. This was a top secret and perilous mission, coordinated between the Hagana and British intelligence, and for that mission the British lent the Hagana a patrol boat, the *Sea Lion*. The boat was lost with all its men on the way to attack the refineries at Tripoli in Lebanon. The men were declared missing in action. The theory nowadays is that the explosives they took with them for their mission (these materials were not British, but taken from the stores of the Hagana, and were nonstandard and extremely unstable) blew up, perhaps when they were being prepped for the mission. Anyway, the rumors and hypotheses about what had happened were ugly.

In 1941 Shosh was left alone with a seven-month-old baby. She was matter-of-fact about it. Among her papers I later found a typed document stating, "Since my husband, Zvi Spector, volunteered for activity connected with the war effort, and since he didn't return and his fate remains unknown, I hereby agree to take the sum of six hundred Palestinian pounds as final indemnity. I hereby free the military authorities, the government of Palestine, and all Jewish foundations in and out of country from any financial responsibility, and undertake to indemnify them for any charge connected to the above." At the end of the page was her signature, in her beautiful script. Since then nobody owed her anything, and she owed nothing to anybody, and kept all inside her.

She made her own decisions, and decided to invest herself totally in the military wing of Israel's national struggle. She was one of the founders of the Palmach, the strike force of the Hagana, headed by Yitzhak Sade.

"If anybody wants to know the actual date of the establishment of the Palmach," she once told the press, "it was on the eighteenth of May 1941. It's over forty years that I have lived this date." It was Shosh Spector together with Zehava, Sade's wife, and a cleaning woman, who were the founding three women in the first group. In the following years the Palmach was Shosh's whole life.

By nature she was meticulous and punctual, obsessively responsible. The missions she took on were fulfilled to the last detail. From the beginning she took on the job of adjutant for manpower and administration. When World War II ended, the struggle against the British Mandate regime was renewed, mainly because of their refusal to allow immigration of the remnant of European Jews to Palestine. The Palmach went underground, and the Brits issued warrants for their arrest. Shosh kept the master list of the names of the Palmach members. She dragged the box of cards with her and hid it first at Kibbutz Mizra, then at Kibbutz Alonim. When she visited me there—I was taken in by her close friends there, the Admons—the box was under her bed.

I found that card box once, when I crawled under her bed to catch a small bird that had flown in the room and vanished.

"Get out of there!" she ordered me sternly. And when I asked her what all those papers under the bed were, she gave me a grown-up lecture. "If the Brits come and ask questions we both die and reveal nothing regarding this black cardboard box."

I was five or six, and I shall never forget the excitement of that moment. I had become partner to a conspiracy, like Emil and the detectives. The body of the bird was finally found pressed between the card box and the wall, her tiny body dried up. For some time I kept a feather that changed beautiful colors in the sunlight and didn't tell the other children what I knew.

The Brits didn't come that night, but on June 29, 1946, remembered as "black Saturday," they surrounded the kibbutzim that hosted Palmach training camps. The leaders of the Jewish settlements were arrested, and thousands were taken prisoner and sent to detention camps in Latroun and Raffah. The Palmach List—that black box—was discovered at Mizra.

But the data were coded, and Shosh had the key. Meticulously, she reconstructed the lost data.

When the War of Independence broke out in 1947 I was with her in Tel Aviv. We lived in a small top-floor apartment at 78 Allenby Street. As long as my secondary school studies continued, I returned home at noon. It was a considerable walk from the "Education home for workers' children" at 13 Bezalel Street. We children would cling to the fences and watch the British officers playing tennis with Jewish ladies. They all were dressed in white. Then, past Allenby Street to King George Street, at the intersection, I used to stop to watch a blind mandolin player. This was an interesting corner, with news bulletins scribbled in large script on a placard above his head. This blind man with his two vacant eye sockets was indeed a sorry sight. Each day a new disaster visited him: on Sundays, he was struck and robbed of his belongings; Mondays were when his house was burned about his head, and so on, each day of the week. We were taught at school about compassion and love of humanity, and all mine concentrated in this thin skeleton of a guy. I also read about little Hanna'le who helped an old woman to carry her sack of coal although she was dressed for Shabbat with her white dress, and the reward she eventually received from the good fairy. Looking at the blind man filled me with a sweet and agonizing pity.

Then I walked up Allenby Street, pressing my nose to the display window at Peel Shoes, then studying the jewelry and the cream cakes in the other windows along the road till I finally reached No. 78. Then I climbed up the four flights of stairs to the top, inhaling the smells of cooking potatoes and jellied meat from behind the doors. Near the topmost door stood a bottle of milk. I opened the door. Inside, after a sip, I could go hurriedly out to the flat roof and into the sun, to squash with my thumbs the softened, warm tar.

On this flat roof, on its peeling whitewashed surface, beneath the sky and among many similar roofs with thickets of electric wires and radio antennae, I built castles from leftover building blocks and planks. The sea could be seen as a blue line few blocks away, and it sent me its fresh breath. There, on the roof, I had my own kingdom. I fortified my castles and ordered my battles and told my stories until evening and the time for homework came.

‡

On one of those mornings I became a man.

My mother entrusted me with the annual school fees, thirty Palestine pounds, a lot of money for her. The bills were to be handed to the school bursar in person. My mother stapled them to my breast pocket with a pin, exactly as in Kestner's *Emil and the Detectives,* and I went out to the street happy and proud. On the way to school I passed by the blind man. I took the money out, together with the pin, and put it inside the beggar's box.

Several days passed with no repercussions, and then my mother was called to school. She returned furious and dragged me out of bed. We searched the streets to find that blind man, but he had vanished without a trace. I was very sad that he had disappeared—it was clear he found his destiny—but I was even sadder to learn that I was just a useless parasite and was no help to our survival as a family.

For this I had a solution: on the next morning I began working and earning my living. In the evening my mother came back and found me near the Izersky Library—not far from the big synagogue and Café Brazil—with her shoeshine brush and polishes. Proudly I gave her half a pound in shillings and pennies. Only I was out of black polish, I told her. She gaped at me. Could she please get some more?

Two healthy slaps straightened me out and sent me back to the school for parasites.

The semester was over and the summer vacation of 1947 arrived, but I lost the use of my flat roof. I was stuck inside now, for the enemy was shooting again from the nearby town of Jaffa. I spent the first week in my room, getting the full milk bottles in and the empties out and listening to the continuous chatter on the radio. Then Uncle Shaike arrived.

Shaike, Yeshayahu (Isaiah) Spector, was my father's youngest brother. He stayed with us for couple of days. Shaike was about twenty, dark-haired and quiet, and to me he looked like a child himself. But he was a Palmach member, of the Negev brigade. He took me for a walk along the seaside, and to the Mughrabi cinema. He didn't have enough money for the movies, but he bought us instead salted corncobs. That was fun.

On the morning after the decision of the United Nations on the partition of the country—that was on the twenty-ninth of November—there was a knock at the door. They explained to me that Shaike was needed in the Negev, where the water pipeline between Mishmar-Hanegev and Hatzerim was subject to sabotage. Shaike hurried to pack his knapsack and was gone. A few days later my mother came and told me that Shaike had been killed. She explained that now only two of the four brothers were left: Israel and Aaron (Aronchik) Spector.

Many years later I learned how Shaike died. The guarding of the water pipe was being done in small foot patrols. Due to the presence of the Brits, the military gear of the scouts was limited and consisted of wooden clubs, and some pistols and hand grenades that were hidden, taken apart in pieces, on their bodies. On December 11 a company commanded by Yeshayahu Spector encountered Arabs on the line. The molested bodies of Shaike and two of his men were returned few days later by the British. They were buried temporarily in the Negev, and later passed to a graveyard. The other two were missing and their fate unknown. Shaike and two of his men were members of Amelim (workers), a youth group preparing to settle in the mountains of Jerusalem and raise a new kibbutz, to be called Tsuba.

THE SUMMER WAS ENDING, as well as with the peaceful days when I was permitted to walk down Geula Street to the sea, barefoot and wearing only my bathing suit. Bullets were whistling over the city. During the day I was kept locked in the apartment, and in the evening the city was under curfew. At night, only the tires of the British armored cars were heard, whining on the asphalt. Their headlights painted passing squares of orange on the ceiling of my room. Sometimes a single shot was heard, or the mad shout of somebody down in the street. Shosh vanished. She worked and slept at Palmach headquarters in Beit Romano house in the south of the city. Suddenly she would appear, sleep like the dead, and vanish again. The radio said all kinds of fearful things. Some nights there were shots fired from nearby Jaffa. I knew, as did everybody else, that the Palmach was aligning itself clandestinely to face the expected great Arab assault. I expected my father to come back, take his place, and change everything.

One morning I was alone at home. Somebody knocked on the door. I opened it, and my Uncle Aronchik entered. He was the third brother, the one between my father and Shaike. Aronchik was the tallest and most good-looking of them, and his smile was charming. He presented me with a sheet of Syrian ledder, an almost forgotten sweet made of pressed apricots. We packed a backpack for me. Down the stairs, a large BSA motorcycle was waiting. Aronchik sat me on the fuel tank in front of him. We chugged noisily northward, crossing hills and passing towns. The wind sent insects flying into my face and chest. The one thing I recall from this trip was the fuel tank—black, shining tin, and on its face a white indicator hand quivering over a green and red arch.

In the evening we came down the mountain past Safed on the twisting, potholed road, and reached Hulatta. Immediately I joined the kibbutz's first class of children.

Aronchik and his girlfriend, Dvorah, lived in a plywood barracks at the lower camp, the initial settlement. This camp stood on a thorny, rocky hill, few dozen meters from the lake shore. I see them both there in a small photo from that time. It is a gray postcard with scalloped edges, as was common at the time. They are very young. They stand erect and serious, close to each other, as if to stress their kinship. Behind them, out of focus, is the barracks. They live behind one of its four doors. Each door has one room behind it. In the background of this photograph, the blurred vista of the Syrian Golan mountain range looms up, like a dark and barren wall, cracked and dotted with stains of remote vegetation. The picture radiates a feeling of disquiet, as if it were underwater or in shadow. Perhaps this feeling ensues from the fact that this was 1947, and it was all about to happen. And perhaps there was another reason. Maybe the anonymous photographer instilled into this photograph his own feeling of confinement, with another mountain ridge towering behind him. Indeed, Hulatta was imprisoned inside a long and narrow valley. Chains of mountains rose above it on both sides, and on each of them sat enemies: the Syrians on the Golan Heights on the east, and the Lebanese on Naphtali Ridge on the west. North of the valley, those two ridges converged at the nine-thousand-foot-high, snowcapped

Mount Hermon. On Dvorah's lips I see, or imagine seeing, a slight smile. Her eyes—the real and the glass one—look directly into the camera, straight and bright and brave as they were all her life, until the night she died.

Shortly before her death, Dvorah told me about that first year I spent with them. "Suddenly you just showed up. Listen, I really had no interest in a seven-year-old boy. I had no idea of how to care for children. And especially one like you, a nonstop talker who couldn't shut his mouth." I disagreed. On the contrary, I told her, I was shy and introverted, a daydreamer immersed in himself and reading books.

"What the hell were you supposed to do?" I asked. She laughed, in that same girlish way that even the pain couldn't take from her.

The heart of Hulatta was the lake. In the heavy summer heat the upper layer of the water cleared, and mirroring the sky above, became almost blue. On Saturdays, under the burning sun, we floated boxes and planks among the water flora and the leaves of the blue water lilies, the nymphaeas. Giant colorful dragonflies hurried about with loud buzzing voices. We fried carp and conchs over fires and ate them, stirring the brown water with our thumbs.

The muddy water was mysterious and scary. When you went deep it darkened fast, as if pulling you down. I would jump in and paddle like mad to the beach, feeling safe only when I felt firm ground under my feet. Dvorah laughed at me and my fantasies. She loved the water and was a good swimmer. I still can see her, swimming far away on a wide expanse of clear water, her black head floating like the head of an otter. She was narrow-waisted, light and sleek, and did not disturb the surface of the water when she dove deep, searching for the cool, secret places. She would disappear for a long, scary time and then return laughing to the surface.

Across the lake lay the big swamp.

Early in the morning all of us children got out of bed and were led to the jetty. A fishing boat took us across the lake and into the forest of phragmite reeds. The canal divided into secondary narrow channels that expanded in places to make pools. It was like wandering in a maze. The brown water passed the boat slowly and silently. Hulla buffaloes, the jamusses, raised heavy, horned heads. The crowns of the cyperus, the papyrus rushes, closed over our heads like a roof, and the pink of the morning sky disappeared in the blue shades of the tunnel. Around us sailed huge rafts of yellow nuffar water lilies and white and blue nimphaeas. Their massive floating roots banged the boat's sides like logs.

Pairs of us were unloaded in different places and vanished in the thickets. The boat pushed off with a big paddle and continued deeper into the swamp. The number of kids who remained on board diminished.

Finally our turn came. Sweet Ronnie and I left the boat and entered, on all fours, into a tunnel among typha reeds and tendrils of stinging "holy" raspberry. A narrow path opened before us, dark and secretive and thrilling. Our soles chirped like frogs in the black slime. Wild pigs and swamp cats were listening and knew we were coming. I trembled, for we had lost the golden thread that led out of the black forest, but just when I was getting really frightened, a green light appeared. A bale of hay floated in the clear water of a small pool. This was the bird-watchers' hide allotted to us.

On the raft was a low shelter covered with straw. We entered it and squeezed, shaking and whispering to each other, plucking black and red leeches from our ankles and cooling the burning mosquito stings with water. Our mission was to keep absolutely quiet, watch and remember anything that went on around us, and bring back a detailed report. Anxiety filled me.

"We are hunters," I whispered in sweet Ronnie's ear. "I am Vinetu."

"Minnehaha, the avenging Indian," she introduced herself. The color of her eyes was rich brown, almost red, like her hair.

The morning sun finally peeped over the wall of canes, and all turned gold and azure. The air warmed. The vegetation around us woke up and spread out toward the light, and the birds rose, about their business. A magnificent kingfisher, all shining green and blue, appeared and stood right above us, sharpening his large beak with a harsh zik-zakking sound and inflating his red chest to show the clear white of his belly. He searched the water with his beady eyes. Under the shallow, slow going and diamond-clear water, crabs ran merrily around, leaving strings of fine footprints on the muddy bottom, vying for the tiny, elegant cyprinodon fishes that glided in the underwater thickets like multicolored lightning. Sweet water oysters opened, breathed water, and closed in small dust clouds. A big fin of a catfish emerged and slashed the surface. Black grebes turned over on their heads.

The sun was high already when a gray Nile goose came out of the canes near us and sat herself on the water of the small pool. Soon a convoy of goslings followed her. And suddenly Ronnie pointed with a pounding heart to the other side of the pool. Less than ten meters away a heron fed its nestlings. When we observed her, she straightened up, long and thin, and vanished into the reeds.

Heavy heat descended on the swamp, and all around us fell asleep. We woke when the wind came up and the surface of the water was covered with green-gray waves. The forest of canes around us was agitated, whistled and swished and moved to and fro under the blows of the hot wind. The air above our heads filled with powder and flying pollen, a golden rain falling on our heads. Light arrows penetrated in, combed the space, and lit the ground.

Suddenly we recognized prints in the mud—small split hooves. Wild boar. After they had reconnoitered the area with their snouts, the dreadful beasts hid in their dark dens among the plants and waited with their yellow tusks for the right moment, when the light dims. All the birds took screaming to the air and circled over us. The sun sank and disappeared behind the papyrus tufts, and the first wave of cold wind passed. Exactly at that moment the boat sounded its horn, and Mussa was calling us back.

We collected our notebooks and pencils and ran. Back on the quay a bonfire waited, and we were served slices of bread spread with margarine, olives, tomatoes, and eggs toasted in embers that smelled like burned hair. We yawned, but Mussa didn't give up until he had debriefed us and investigated every detail. He checked the sketches in our notebooks and examined every finding we brought from the marsh: flowers, leaves, insects. Coppery wings suddenly shone, glowing green, and a wave of excitement rose among us: can this be the golden bug?

"No," said Mussa, and a quick smile crossed his face. "Just *Potosia cuprea*—an ordinary pest."

He turned the specimen over and over again, checking plants' leaves and testing names: Hizzanit. Arzaff. Laana. And maybe shkhelet? Or khelbna?

His black eyes glowed over the *Eretz-Israel Plant Guide*, which didn't have an answer. After a while I thought he might be attaching ancient biblical names to species of plants he couldn't recognize.

Then war came to the northern valley. Our kibbutz was shelled. One day an airplane appeared and scored a direct hit on the cowshed. When we emerged from the trench the elders took us away, so that we didn't see the cows. There were rumors. Apparently the Syrians had taken a nearby settlement, Mishmar HaYarden, killing settlers, taking some prisoners, and destroying everything. Faces of men and women we used to see, we saw no more.

One morning we were hurriedly packed up, clothes and toys bundled into blanket covers, and a truck backed up to our door. The children and the caretaker climbed into the truck and for the next year, 1948, we lived in different places. One day somebody came and told me that Aronchik was badly wounded. I thought Aronchik was dead. After all, this was the way they told you, right? I had experience with this. And then again they came and told me that my mother had gone to America.

The war ended, and we returned to Hulatta. The lower camp was deserted. The kibbutz began resettling in a new place in the fields, a little farther away from the lake. The Arab village, Tleil, didn't exist anymore, and the mud building blocks from its houses were taken for secondary use or were left to melt in the winter rain, returning bit by bit to dust and ashes.

It turned out that Aronchik didn't die. I was taken to visit him. He was in a hospital in Haifa, on the slope of Mount Carmel. He sat on his bed with his leg in traction, and smiled at me with an obvious effort. Dvorah was also there, taking care of him. We returned to Hulatta, and another couple adopted me temporarily. After some months Aronchik arrived, limping badly.

School studies resumed. Somebody said that Shosh was the highest-ranking woman in the army and that David Ben-Gurion proposed that she become the staff officer for women in the newly established Israeli Defense Force. I know why she refused. She told me more than once that she opposed different military organizations for men and women. I was very proud of her.

In the final photo of the Palmach, a moment before its dissolution, the staff officers stand in a half circle. Major General Yigal Alon is in the middle, and around him the men I admired: Uri Brenner, Nahum Sarig, Mulla Cohen, young Yitzhak Rabin, and others. Among them all, shorter than the men but an equal among them, stands Shoshana Spector, in a midcalf skirt with a duty belt around her waist. All the men look like serious sourpusses, but she has a wide smile, clearly refusing to give in to the general sad mood.

IN 1951 MY MOTHER RETURNED from America and took me with her to another kibbutz, Givat-Brenner, in the South. There, there was neither lake nor mountains, just orchards and burning sandy trails between acacia fences, and the kibbutz was a huge community, noisy and full of people.

My mother was a special person, very capable and with lots of personality. When she arrived at the kibbutz she was a woman in full bloom, about thirty-five years of age, extremely smart and good-looking. But she didn't know how to compromise and never deferred to men. Once she told me that after she finished school in Ben Shemen she found work in the offices of the Jewish Agency, an organization that advised the British on issues involving the Jewish homeland, and actually functioned as a government of sorts. She was then a nineteen-year-old girl, and was sent with some documents to one of the bosses. When she entered his room her hands trembled and the papers slipped to the floor. The great man watched her, smiling, and said, "My girl, calm down. Perhaps you think I am a big shot, but when I go to the restroom my shit is as brown as anybody else's." She remembered this lesson and took pains to remind me of it every now and then.

A strong, single woman, she was an odd duck at Givat-Brenner. Men saw her as one kind of threat and women saw her as another kind. Like other war widows I knew later in my life, she radiated threat. Life in the kibbutz did not suit her. Indeed, though the kibbutz was a society of high ideals, in fact it was just a suburb full of petty, personal quarrels. Large clans controlled the social life at Givat-Brenner: The warm, vulgar Polish were different from the crafty Litvaks from Lithuania, and the Yekes—immigrants from Germany—were something else again. Shosh Spector, and accordingly I, didn't belong to any of these cultures. We were outsiders—different.

In Givat-Brenner my own situation was rather better than hers. I was thrown into the seven-hundred-strong children's society, to sink or swim among them. But I was young and still flexible. Actually, what happened to me at Kibbutz Givat-Brenner was similar to what happened to Shosh herself twenty years earlier. When she was fourteen, her father—who couldn't support his family—sent her to a youth institution. There, in the children's village of Ben Shemen, she found her way and her friends for life.

This is exactly what happened to me at Givat-Brenner. The beginning was tough, but eventually I made friends. The youth society I became a part of—the "brigade," in the semi-military jargon of the kibbutz—was stormy, zealously Zionist, and naively socialist. So, like all the kids, I vowed to defend Israel, save the Jewish people, and fight for social equality and for peace and fraternity among nations. Like all of us, I was unaware of the contradictions among those conflicting goals. To find favor in the eyes of the girls, and perhaps to compensate for my incompetence on the basketball court, I became a "cultural promoter." I became the editor, publisher, and sometimes the art director of our weekly magazine, which was displayed on walls. This was a wonderful periodical with stories and poems of local talents, such as "Captain John Marley Flies to the Moon" by Daniel Vardon, or political commentaries discussing the problem of who was going to inherit Comrade Stalin's job when the black day would arrive. The editors bet on Georgi Malenkov, since he had no mustache. We were wrong. Khrushchev was clean- shaven, too.

On summer vacations I took every course I could get into: a month of premilitary scouting in which we traveled by foot some six hundred kilometers; a course in building model airplanes; a gliding course, and the next year piloting light aircraft. I led hikes with heavy backpacks to the three craters (unique geologic formations in the Negev Desert), and hitchhiked to Eilat on the Red Sea. Soon I was selected as a scoutmaster, and invested my evenings and weekends in my young pupils, teaching them to tie knots and make fires in the rain.

‡

Shosh yearned to love me, but the situation had become impossible for us. My mother's social problem, and the fact that she was a stranger in this big kibbutz, threatened my standing in the children's society. Sometimes she tried to make me her confidant and poured her toils and troubles on my head. She described her encounters with people (she was a great mimic), but this put me in an awkward situation: I had to choose whether to be on her side, or on the side of my friends. These people were their parents and elder brothers and sisters. So I listened, dissociating myself, and saw how hurt she was, but I couldn't really sympathize enough. Soon I stopped listening to her stories and sealed myself off from her. I rolled up like a hedgehog toward my mother.

The hurt feelings between us became stronger. I began hiding to avoid being seen with her. Instead of going to her room after school, as was normal kibbutz custom, I went out to the fields or to the vacant sports arena, where I worked long hours on the horizontal bar and the parallel rings. I became the kibbutz shepherd. I took the animals out to pasture. Once in the fields, I spent many hours alone composing endless poems while my four hundred sheep ran wild and raided people's gardens. Sometimes I woke up to the cries of furious farmers whose crops had been destroyed, and sometimes I got hit. I walked the fields and prayed for somebody to come and take me away from this place back to my real home, to Hulatta.

In 1953, when I was thirteen, I ran away from Givat-Brenner and my mother. Before the running experiment, a dream was visiting me in the nights: I lay on a vast plain all striped in gray lines. Beyond it, heavy black lumps towered, their heads vanishing up. When I woke up I didn't know whether this was my bed with the mattress and the lumps of blankets, or that I was on the coast of a huge marsh, and the lumps were the black mountains over it. Anyway, I felt I was home.

I decided, and at supper I filled my pockets with bread. At ten o'clock in the evening, while the kibbutz slept, I slipped out of bed and sneaked in the shadows to the entrance of the kibbutz. The road that led down to the highway to Rehovot was dark. I ran through the orchards crazily, dying of fear. I hoped to hitchhike north on the highway, to Dvorah and Aronchik and my sweet Ronnie in Hulatta.

I got to the road. It was silent and dark. Tall cypress treetops swished in the light wind. I sat on the ground beside the road and waited, accustoming my eyes to the night. I thought if the way north proved long, I would find work, and if my foster parents in Hulatta tried to bring me back to my mother in Givat-Brenner, I would run away from them, too, and hide, and no one would find me again.

It began to get cold.

After some time I saw lights in the distance. I jumped to my feet, gripping the signpost at the bus stop. A bus came and stopped, orange light shining dimly through its windows. I climbed in, but the driver demanded money and I had no money. I got off and the bus left, the whining of its tires fading in the distance.

Dogs were barking. I thought perhaps I should begin walking. And then the sound of approaching footsteps was heard in the distance, coming toward me down the road from the kibbutz. I recognized the ticking of those sandals; there was only one person who ran like that. I fled and hid among the orange trees in the dark orchard. From my hideout I saw Daniel Vardon coming, halting and turning around, shouting my name as loud as he could. Daniel got farther away, and his voice diminished. Another car passed. And then Daniel returned down the road. He was a boy from my own class, a year older than I. He was very dark-skinned, tall and strong. He could sing beautifully, and run faster and farther than anybody else. And he didn't give up on me.

At last I came out of my hiding place. I tried to argue, to convince him, but he just caught my hand and dragged me after him all the way back, not letting my hand free, while I sobbed, flooded with a mix of failure and relief. At age fourteen, Vardon radiated charisma and physical power, and he could subordinate anyone to his will. On our way back he promised me with dignity, swore, that he would never tell about this to anybody, ever. Danny kept his word, but throughout the years we grew up together I felt the eye of this special young person watching me, making certain that I did not go astray.

Not a long time was left for him. In 1958 we all were drafted, and Danny began as a soldier in the Golani Division. His first decoration for valor came almost immediately, when he stood out in the attack on the Syrian position at Tel-Dan. A friend of his told me how he skipped across the trenches, fearlessly, almost happily. In 1962 Lieutenant Vardon got his second medal after taking the Syrian outpost Nukeib above the Sea of Galilee; the outpost used to snipe at Israeli fishermen and the kibbutzim below it. Danny excelled in fighting, and more so in his human behavior. He rose up under Syrian fire and stopped the firing of his own men, to let Arab citizens from the nearby village, who were caught in the crossfire, run away. Only then did he lead his soldiers down to the trenches. The commanding officers of that time saw this action of his as a shining example. Daniel Vardon won his third medal postmortem, in the Six-Day War. On June 8, 1967, he consciously risked his life to save wounded soldiers, and fell in a battle in an alley at the Egyptian town of El-Arish.

As a rule, the grown-ups in my family didn't tell stories about their past. Aronchik would dismiss the past with a disdainful wave of his hand, and Dvorah would just grin and change the subject. My mother, on the other hand, had an exception to this rule. While I was a small child, before going to bed, she liked to tell me stories of her youth.

Shosh knew how to tell stories that were alive, detailed, and full of color. Many a time she made me, and herself, laugh to tears. On such occasions there was strong affection between us. But anything that happened after the end of school in the youth institute of Ben Shemen was hidden behind a curtain of silence. She didn't tell and I was afraid to ask, and gradually the conversations between us ended. Her true, thrilling life was hidden from me.

She never talked to me about Zvi, the father I never knew, but his name was always hanging between us, an open wound. Once I took courage to ask, and she dismissed me.

"A true gentleman," she told me, "doesn't intrude in other people's privacy." And when I flinched, she cleared it once and for all, "even when he is left alone in the room."

‡

One day, after one of his rare visits, my Uncle Israel—the eldest of the four brothers—left me a picture of Zvi. It was a copy of a copy, a very grainy photograph. I hid the photograph under the folded clothes in my compartment of the common cupboard, the second one from the top. At nights, when my three roommates in the children's houses of Givat-Brenner were asleep, I would take a light under the blanket and study it for a long time. I saw the head and shoulders of a young man, very good-looking, somewhat similar to his brother Aronchik. The young man's head was tilted to one side. His hair was blowing in the wind and a slight smile, really just a hint of smile, played on his lips. Sometimes I talked to him, but his face was turned away from me. He seemed listening to something else in the distance. I knew he was smiling at the songs of Sirens of unknown seas.

This picture is still on my table.

Chapter

4

By Myself

IMAGINE ODYSSEUS DECIDING to write his story in the first person. Would that be possible?

Not a simple question.

And that's not just because Odysseus was too busy between Scylla and Charybdis to take up pen and paper. After all, he might have taken to writing later in calmer times, say, when he returned to his always-waiting Penelope from his second voyage, the more magical voyage of the two—to remote lands where the inhabitants didn't know what the sea was and couldn't recognize an oar. Well, then?

No, that's still not it. Because there is another difficulty, arising from the limitation of Odysseus's own viewpoint. While blind Homer sat with the gods and saw everything, Odysseus was struggling against the wine-dark sea and saw very little.

And there is another problem, small but irritating, the writing in the first person: me, and again me, me. I know well that behind every word I write are many friends who were there with me, fought, laughed, acted, lived, and died near me, but can I tell all their stories?

AND INDEED IN ANOTHER BOOK that I wrote—its title was *A Dream in Black and Azure*—I wanted to tell about a small odyssey of mine (forgive me, dear reader, for the immodest metaphor), which occurred in 1973, in a very difficult and terrible war. But at the time I wrote it I was still young and afraid to expose myself. And so it came to pass that eventually I wrote the entire book in the third person.

And this is what happened as a result of my reservations about using "me": I invented a person and sent him out to replace me. I gave him a name: Toledano. Just like that, without much thought.

Toledano was the name my father, Zvi, adopted in his youth, the name of his deceased mother. Zvi Toledano is the name written on the few documents he left behind, papers from school and such. Somehow the name Toledano didn't pass to me.

And so I wrote a book, and in page after page about that war in 1973, I kicked this guy, Toledano, around in the same way all of us were kicked around. Toledano kicked back, and he developed his own point of view, and he was stressed, sometimes to the breaking point. And I watched him from above through the microscope, and saw him struggling down there, the same way I waged my own Yom Kippur War. I controlled him and his actions, and he was dependent on me. I could pull the strings and operate him at will.

But then something strange happened: This guy Toledano, whom I invented to serve my needs, developed a will of his own. From the moment he received his name from me, Toledano grew more powerful and drew from me things I had no intention of giving to anybody, ever, and he reacted spontaneously in ways that nobody could have instilled in him, definitely not me. You see, I never knew my father. I invented him.

And so, throughout the year when I wrote that book, I felt as if my clothes and then my skin were gradually peeled away. And in the end I found myself running around naked in the small, empty flat I was working in, looking for clothes to cover myself. This process extracted from me things that people don't talk about, even things I never knew I ever knew. There were days when I fled my writing desk and ran into the street, being driven half crazy by the devil pushing my pencil across the page.

Time and again I decided to retake control of my book and to return it to the path I had chosen for it—just a simple war story—but Toledano wouldn't submit. He was there, he had a forceful personality, and he wanted to speak. So whenever I returned to that small flat and the piles of scribbled pages, I found that my control of the situation was at best partial, and I couldn't do with my hero what I initially planned. There came a moment when I considered killing him off, but I failed. It was Toledano's fault that the entire book charged off in another direction, and other characters began their own revolution, and also tried to rewrite their stories through me.

And I cannot blame anybody, because *A Dream in Black and Azure* came out okay in the end. At least that's what people told me, and to this day occasionally people grab me on the street, call me up, or send letters telling me things about it and about themselves from its pages. That book even won me a literary prize. I was invited to share the stage where none other than the prime minister, Mr. Yitzhak Rabin, was waiting for me. So Yitzhak shook my hand again and again, and then he turned from me to the microphone and said in his deep bass voice, "Iftach Spector surprises us again."

And, all in all, it was really nice, although I couldn't remember any previous surprises I had given Mr. Rabin. And in truth, it should have been Toledano standing there on the podium before that big audience and getting an award, not me. Because it was Toledano who had surprised the prime minister no less than he surprised me.

Days and years later, I have decided that there is still something special in the first person: it is mandatory. And over it, together with it, comes the special flavor of authenticity. Now I realize that it was with good reason that for the hardest of Odysseus's tribulations, Homer gave him the mike, telling him to speak for himself. The dilemma is clear: How does the poet get inside the head of the man who tied himself to the mast and listened to the singing of the Sirens until he went mad? And who, except the one who dared to descend to the underworld, could imagine the emotions and the thoughts that flooded him when he met his dead mother there?

So now, having started another session with blank pages, I recall Toledano and think that though the word "me" irritates, it still has one exclusive quality: this word is at least clear and binding. Surely it's much easier to blur things; obscurity would have made the telling much easier on me, but I fear that compromises may damage the final product. Take *A Dream in Black and Azure*. With all the praise and the award, who remembers it now?

Well, for sure, one man—a high-ranking officer in the IDF does. He swore, after I declared I would refuse to take part in war crimes, that he was going to destroy and annihilate my book. Erase it from under the sun.

When I heard about him and his threat, I was astounded. Initially I thought there might have been some mistake in the last edition that somehow insulted him personally. So I checked in my copy, and the text was okay. On reflection, I decided that the book had nothing to do with him, and the important thing to this person was just the proclamation of its annihilation. I thought that probably his reward would be an invitation by his superiors for a macho pissing with the wind, a hell of a promotion. If this was really the case, I salute him. This officer must be practical, a man of action, and surely he has the "right stuff," a man with a great future. I am glad my book helped him to get there.

So this is my conclusion after all these deliberations: I have decided that my small odyssey will be told by myself, under my own name. I shall not compromise anything intentionally.

Now here we are back in the early 1960s, at the Scorpions.

Two months have passed since our arrival; I haven't yet passed my flight test. Yak himself was invited from headquarters and came down to the Scorpions to check out the trainees on the Super Mystere in aerial combat, one on one, against him.

Now it was my turn.

"Turn out," he ordered. We separated, turning away and preparing for battle. Then he reversed direction and turned back toward me. He came nearer and nearer, the master battle tactician, and—wham!

We passed each other head on, at supersonic speed.

I ignored his wake turbulence rocking my ship and pulled up hard on the stick. My aircraft climbed vertically to altitude. He climbed, too, and we met again, this time at low speed, joining aggressively.

My Super Mystere shook under me, exactly like the Harvard a year ago, but this time I was not a kid anymore and knew what to do. Yozef Salant had already prepared me for this test.

"Don't give him an inch. Yak wants to see that you know how to be aggressive." And he continued his lesson, "Be careful of Yak. He is cunning as a Greek. He'll offer you his tail like a whore, but if you take it, he'll throw you forward all the way to Baghdad."

And so I almost smiled when Yak waggled his tail at me, and instead of jumping on it, I pulled up over his aircraft and caught "a good seat on the veranda" over his head. Yak changed tactics, climbed toward me, and we circled again like two mad dogs till the red fuel lamp came on with a beep. I sighed with relief; it was over, and I hadn't lost.

Yak led me back to land. When we were back on the ground, my feet hovered an inch above the tarmac.

In the squadron briefing room, after a glass of cold water, Yak uttered only five words that I shall never forget: "You impressed me some today." I blushed, and looked around to see if anybody else had heard it. Hell, where was Zorik? Why, on this day of all days, was he not here, eavesdropping, as usual?

On Friday night, when all the kibbutz youth were singing and dancing in the main dining room, I gave Ali the eye to meet me in the corner. Would she come? She was not mine yet.

She came, curious. I told her I had had a dogfight with Yak.

"So?" She didn't get it.

"Yak," I told her excitedly, "the man who broke all the rules, who opened new vistas in aerial combat. It was Yak who taught the IAF how to split and fight independently, in a coordinated way, rather than in tight pairs, like that."

I demonstrated the meaning of coordination with my hands, and knocked over a stack of china cups. And as we crawled together on the floor collecting the broken china I whispered, unable to hide a quiver of pride from my voice, "I was his equal today. We came out even."

In the shade, below the table, I stole a fast sniff of her neck.

For long time after this special flight, I believed I knew the secret of how to win in aerial combat. The lesson I learned from that flight was that it was all about aggressive handling of the aircraft. Just fly it to the limit.

Big mistake. Yak had been testing me that first semester, and I thought it was the whole story.

But not all is flying, and not just Super Mysteres, either. The time was young and rough, and wherever there are men there are women, too. And where there are men and women, things that are better kept secret happen. Even I was finally roused from my long sleep by a woman. When this was over, the shy courting of my delicate flower changed gear. The time was ripe for decisions. It all happened one afternoon on a summery Friday.

A lazy weekend dawned on Base Hatzor. Work was over, the roar of the jets silenced, and everybody scattered every which way to gulp lunch and grab a quick nap. Hush. No cow mooed, no donkey brayed, no bird chirped. The skies emptied, too, and the radar controllers slept before their screens. One Harvard waited silently at Hatzor.

I decided that this was the perfect time to seduce Ali away from the kibbutz to go with me for a trip to the Galilee. An aerial trip, to be sure. After all, this was what I had to offer.

I waited with a pounding heart. School was over. The sun set. Finally she showed up at the base entrance.

Our Harvard mooed like a bull as it grazed the corn and cotton fields in the Izreel Valley, twisting among trees and hopping over power lines. When we arrived at the old Crusader castle Belvoir, the Jordan Valley divided under our nine roaring cylinders, and we pulled up to five thousand feet. The Kinneret, the Sea of Galilee, stretched before us gray-blue, its waters rough and opaque in the strong early evening wind. In the yellow light of the setting sun I lowered the landing gear, and instantly we landed at Mahanaim landing strip, a deserted old British runway made of cracked white asphalt, among gray thorn fields. This was my home, the Upper Galilee.

Down there my family from Hulatta was waiting. Oh, the joy of meeting my foster mother, Dvorah, my Uncle Aronchik. They already had two children.

Dvorah asked with a cunning smile, "Hey, you, so—are you two going to get married?"

Ali and I looked sideways at each other and blushed. I kept quiet—why say that she hadn't said yes yet?

Ali stammered, "What an idea, of course not! I'm still in tenth grade; I have to finish school first, then two years in the army, and besides, who talks about stuff like this?" Her cheeks flamed.

A big laugh.

I took Dvorah for a spin in the Harvard to show her the kibbutz from the air. We toured the whole Hula Valley. The Harvard came close to the dark mountains of Syria. They held their fire.

When we finally landed, the family invited us for a late lunch at Gitt'l's Restaurant in the nearby town of Rosh Pinna. But I had a problem: I couldn't shut off the aircraft engine, since if I did, there would be no way to start it again. I had forgotten to bring the manual crank starter with me. But it was difficult to say no, and in the end we went to town and left the Harvard with the engine running and stones wedged under the wheels, sitting on the tarmac rattling, waiting for us to finish our business and return.

At night we returned, stuffed, and found our loyal Harvard waiting in total darkness, milling the air with its propeller. With faltering feet we climbed the slippery wing in the back draft of the propeller, stumbling and slipping, and finally got in the cockpit. I lit up the cockpit instrumentation and in the faint red light put the parachute on Ali's shoulders and fastened the belts around her waist. Then I entered the front cockpit, and with a wave good-bye, pushed the throttle forward. We took off, swaying through occasional pools of light thrown by the car headlights on the darkened strip, and finally were airborne among the stars.

I thought, "Ali, you are going to be mine."

That affectionate nickname, Ali, was my own invention.

Everybody else called her Aliza or "Lizchen." Adella—her foster mother—called her lovingly "Lisyen."

She was one of a multitude of small, almost invisible girls we bigger boys never paid attention to, but one day Miriam told me, "You don't look where you should. Look down a little, look at the smaller girls." Miriam and I, before we went into the military, used to talk about things while sitting on the stone fence of the dining room, after the evening activities of the Labor youth movement were over. We both were scoutmasters there.

I said to Miriam, "Those little ones? What, they don't have any . . . "

"They'll grow," she said with a laugh. "You should evaluate the potential."

Miriam was a clever girl. She had a good head for math and used to listen to serious music, Bach and such. I took her seriously and began to look where she had suggested. Among them I found one with a gentle face and a light step. She was silent and introverted. Though an athlete and a fast runner, she moved silently, as if keeping a secret.

At the end of 1958, all my classmates were drafted. First, the girls were scattered to IDF bases all over the country. Then Moishele and Zikky went to the paratroopers, Gabi to tanks; Daniel Vardon became the hero of the Golani infantry brigade. We missed each other and kept exchanging letters, which passed from hand to hand. Eventually we decided to distribute our letters among ourselves in the form of a monthly newsletter. So it turned out that in the rare weekend leaves from Tel Nof, I was collecting letters and editing them for publishing.

Then the newsletter had to be typed. This indeed was a chore. Somebody said there was a girl from the ninth grade, Lisyen, who knew how to type. So we sat together monthly on a Saturday night, in the deserted office center of the kibbutz, I reading the letters aloud to her and she typing them.

She was fifteen, a nice girl, and I was a soldier. We were very shy and cautious with each other. We didn't speak much, and our eyes avoided contact. When she was done, late at night, she collected her things and vanished, and her scent went with her, and I was left alone to illustrate and decorate the folios smelling of stencil wax, and to smear the black, creamy ink and turn the handle of the mimeograph machine.

We really talked only once. I told her of the long hours on guard at the base's fences. She offered me an unknown magic: a transistor radio—a plastic box she had gotten from her South African uncles. It was a working radio with a large, transparent broken dial. All the air cadets used her present in turn, until one of us was caught and the thing was confiscated. Listening to the radio was not allowed on guard duty.

She was not one of my own kind.

In the evening she went to Shlomo and Adella Dgani's room. They were Yekes—immigrants from Germany. At first I thought Shlomo and Adella were her parents. Then I learned that they had taken her into their home when she was four, after Otto Samuel, her father, was killed in 1948, and her mother, Jenny, fell seriously ill.

Shlomo and Adella Dgani (Feldblum) were different from us and even from how their own children turned out. In the Middle East, the Yekes were a strange community with different habits and a different language. They had high cultural aspirations and a deep longing to be somewhere else, in another climate, under a different sun. Most German Jews didn't leave their lethal fatherland. They stayed and died. Those who came to Palestine remained chained to the culture and the language of their murderers. Most of them never could adapt to the melting pot that was Palestine, soon to be Israel.

Being aware of this conflict, I took measures. When finally the delicate adoptee of Shlomo and Adella invited me to their place, I was on my best behavior. I even washed my feet before putting my sandals on.

And there, surrounded by Yekes, I first came to know that miraculous powder, instant coffee.With the sure smile of a man of the world, I loaded a full spoon of the powder into the boiling water in my china cup. The powder shrank immediately and consolidated into a black, sticky ball that floated on the surface. I redoubled my stirring, but the damn ball refused to melt. Puzzled, I tried once or twice to push it down to the bottom and crush it with the spoon, but it was agile and evasive and resurfaced. Suddenly I realized that everyone was watching me with raised eyebrows, sipping their coffee seriously. I had to do something, and soon.

I trapped the slippery rubber lump between the spoon and the side of the cup, and gulped it. It leaped up, and fastened to my upper palate like bitter toffee, but red hot. In agony, I pointed to the white china pot in the middle of the table.

Adella hurried to hand it over to me. *"Schlack zane, bitte?"* Some cream?

"Mein Gott, yes!"

I turned the pot over into my mouth, but the cursed milk stayed up there and never came out. It was the whipped cream they prepared for our five-o'clock meeting. Through a curtain of pain I saw the polite Yekes nodding at me gloomily. I replied with a stern nod of my own, my mouth tightly shut. Had I opened it even a crack, I would have breathed fire.

Sweet Ali and her brother Yair—he was the elder son of Shlomo and Adella—watched it all, bursting with cruel laughter. Those two enjoyed mostly slapstick humor, as when someone slipped on a banana peel and fell. I swallowed and ran out the door. Behind the house, among Shlomo's well-groomed flowers, I found a hose and hurriedly put it in my mouth.

Yair Dgani was three years older than I. He was the best brother Ali could wish for, always looking after her, from the time she came to them from Tel Aviv. Yair was a hell of a guy. He played the clarinet, coached the girls' basketball team, and later became a battalion commander in an armored division. Back in the kibbutz, he managed the carpentry shop. When we were children I used to give him a wide berth, for I feared his cynical humor.

Summer came. I arrived for a weekend, and Givat-Brenner was empty. It turned out she was sent for a summer program in another kibbutz. I heard a rumor she already had a boyfriend.

I took courage and wrote to her from the air base and asked if she would consider being my friend. After several long days a blue envelope came through the military mail. For two days I carried the envelope in my pocket unopened, and finally I tore its side bit by bit, like a girl plucking the leaves of a chrysanthemum. Somebody grinned above my shoulder. I turned around and saw ZBB; he knew beforehand.

The first engagement with enemy MiGs of our class's graduates came very early, exactly four months after our first flight on the Super Mystere.

On April 28, 1961, I was put on alert. Suddenly the first pair scrambled, and right afterward my section went aloft, too.

"South, full power! This is for real! No drill!"

We raced south at full speed, Shimon Ash, the new commander who had replaced Yak, leading, and me bringing up the rear with my sixty flight hours on the aircraft.

Flying supersonic and with guns switched on, we arrived in the arena on the Egyptian border, but the dogfight had just ended. In the distance I saw a tiny white MiG-17 spinning in the air down toward the dunes. Suddenly a parachute sprouted and the aircraft hit the ground.

And then I saw a Super Mystere spinning, too, not far from the MiG. This was also the first real mission for my friend and comrade ZBB. But Zur kept his cool and pulled out of the spin. So the four of us got together and circled the defeated Egyptian pilot, swinging beneath his parachute.

Finally Ron, the leader of the first pair, said on the radio, "I'm going in to take out the pilot."

Zorik's angry voice broke into the communication channel, coming from the transceiver of the squadron in Hatzor, "No way! Leave the parachutist alone. All of you back home, on the double!"

The radar controller—he was the voice of the air force commander—didn't utter a word. Shimon Ash apparently chose to obey his vice commander's order. We left the Egyptian parachutist twisting in the air and came back to base. On the ground, an argument started.

Major Ash said, "I am not sure we did the right thing when we left that pilot. Tomorrow we will have to face him again."

Captain Zorik was certain of his position. His green eyes flared in his round, speckled face, and he stood firm against his new commander with a restrained, polite voice. "Shimon, there are laws in the world. And there are things that one simply doesn't do. One doesn't shoot at people in parachutes."

This was the first time I had heard a real, practical discussion of law and morality in war, and I didn't know which of the two positions to adopt. Was I in favor of killing the fallen pilot? Or against it? At the end I chose to agree with Giora Furman's response—he had a dry sense of humor, which ended the argument.

"Since we all will have to engage MiGs in the future, I, for one, prefer to fight this guy again. We all saw his performance."

"True, especially since now he received one good lesson," added Goldie.

And ZBB, who was in a funk for having put his plane into a spin, consoled himself by saying, "Let him share his experience with his friends."

So the Scorpions registered her first downed MiG.

Some nonoperational flights become the most serious of them all.

Saturday afternoon. The end of a spring day, and everyone was taking naps. That was life before 1967. But in the Super Mysteres' hangar, hammers were banging away. The Scorpions had demanded that one more aircraft be serviceable for the next day's training. Yawning, the technicians worked on. Finally, when the last screw was fastened and the sun was low in the west, the phone rang. I was called to test-fly aircraft number 35.

I took off into an empty sky. The Mediterranean spread endlessly before me, the red path in its center led to an orange sun. I turned north. The coast of Israel passed along my right-hand side. Gradually the land began to blur as a white layer of early summer clouds blew in. The sea on my left shone yellow and red. Here we were, just the three of us—the sun, me, and number 35—and we had the sky to ourselves.

What joy!

I got to forty thousand feet over the sea, north of Israel. Now I saw no sea anymore beneath me—just a white desert of clouds. This was the time to begin testing the engine, and I had to stop fantasizing about wonderful lands beyond the horizon.

First, check the afterburner. I moved the throttle forward, over the detent. A pause, then a choking sound—a sharp deceleration. I heard two loud bangs under me. I recoiled and throttled back. Then a whining sound, which slowly faded. Then the engine died.

At this altitude, forty thousand feet, it is impossible to restart a jet engine. One has to be at lower altitude, where there is more oxygen.

So I headed east, toward the coast. My Super Mystere glided slowly, the blanket of clouds streaming under me like a layer of foam seeded with large and small bubbles. Cold air caressed my shoulders as cockpit pressurization failed and the outside cold air penetrated. Still, I was not afraid. Soon I would initiate a restart, but I began to feel uneasy when my repeated emergency calls on the radio brought no answer.

Okay, down to restart altitude, twenty-five thousand feet. By now, the clouds were closer, a landscape of individual lumps and crevices, with no ground visible. The Earth hid from me beneath the clouds. Now I was in a hurry to restart. First one attempt, then a second one, but no sound whatsoever from the engine and no response from the instruments. Looking back, I noticed a long white trail behind me. That meant that fuel was spilling into the exhaust behind my plane. This was really bad, and restarting attempts had to stop. I had to find a place to land, and fast.

There was only one airport in the vicinity, Ramat-David, Israel's northern fighter base. I searched my documentation and found the frequency of Ramat-David's control tower. Thank God, somebody over there was alert. The controller updated me on the situation there. "Low clouds, low visibility in the whole valley," he said. "Scattered showers in the whole area around Ramat-David." Winter had returned to the north of Israel.

It all began to look pretty grim. My dead Super Mystere and I were already shaving the pink off the cloud tops. Among the peaks there were gray depressions, and I peered into them. The color inside them was the color of evening, gray-blue. One after the other, I could see no hole through which I could catch a glimpse of the ground. I flew the vectors I received, but all beneath me was obscured. I had no way of telling where I was.

Where the hell was Ramat-David down there?

Now I thought, maybe I should enter the clouds and descend through them? Not a good idea. I remembered that Ramat-David is in the Izreel Valley, but this valley was surrounded by hills. And there was also one pretty high ridge—Mount Carmel. It might be touching the clouds. If I happened to come out right there . . .

What now?

I tried again to restart the engine; perhaps this time it would work. Once and twice, and now I had to force my fingers to be steady. But no luck: the engine wouldn't start. And all the time my Super Mystere continued dropping like an elevator. No doubt, in such conditions the right thing to do was just to bail out.

I began moving in my seat, pulling here and there, tightening seat belts.

And then, suddenly, magically, I saw a hole ahead of me among the clouds, perhaps the one and only hole in the entire cloud cover. I glided there, passed over it, and lowering a wing, stared down it as into a deep well. Way down—between the vertical gray-blue walls—I could see the slope of a mountain, black and wooded. And this sighting would have been of no use had there not been glaring, from the side of the picture, lit by a red ray of the setting sun magically shining through the fog, the one and only building that cannot be mistaken, because there is none like it: the monastery on the Mukhraka, on top of the Horn of Carmel.

Now I knew where I was in relation to Ramat-David. The airport and indeed the entire valley were very near, at eleven o'clock, just left of my aircraft's nose. The hole was passed and gone. Should I descend into the clouds?

My body acted for me.

It was my body that left the seat straps alone and decided on its own to land, and my Super Mystere followed, veering a little to the right, to open distance from the base, and then lowered its nose into the clouds, accelerated, and turned left in the direction of the valley. And when this had been done, here I was, driving the aircraft in the clouds, flying on instruments.

In the dense fog I made one important decision: if at two thousand feet on the altimeter we were not out of the clouds, I will pull up and bail out. Again I tightened my belts, and mumbled words of farewell to my Super Mystere. I hoped that if I ejected it wouldn't hit a populated area.

At 2,500 feet the clouds around me thinned, and instantly the air cleared. Close on my left side, I saw beyond a screen of drizzle, a runway, glinting like polished silver. Ho, Ramat-David.

And immediately a tight turn toward it. My speed slowed in the turn, and I lowered the landing gear. Clunk, and another clunk, in maddening slowness, the three wheels lowered one after another and locked. Three green lamps on, and the runway was already very near. Eucalyptus trees passed on both sides.

And so, still in the turn, my number 35 hit the runway heavily, wheel after wheel after wheel, and rolled to a stop.

When I opened my canopy and the cold drizzle caressed my face, a small Citroën Deux Chevaux car beeped at me from below. A heavyset man in pilot's jacket came out and waved both hands at me.

I slid down the aircraft's side, and he caught me like a bear and stood me firmly on the tarmac. Major Kvody, the base maintenance officer, a warm-hearted guy, enveloped me in a hug.

"You are not leaving before you have a drink at my place!" I didn't know yet that he wasn't talking about a cup of tea. "Then we'll find a car and send you home to Hatzor."

"Where is everybody?" I wondered, searching around for firefighters, ambulances, tow trucks, people, anything.

"Where is everybody? Sleeping," the nice man said, dismissing me. "Come on. Your aircraft will be taken care of tomorrow. All in good time." And suddenly he added a sentence from Ecclesiastes, totally unexpected from the muzhik he was: "To every thing there is a season, and a time to every purpose under the heaven."

Chapter

5

Doubletalk

As all five of us were good enough, we soon found our niches in the Scorpions. This squadron had something unique and special. ZBB defined it as "another world," and we, the five trainees, had fallen in love with the Scorpions, and together we wrote a song of praise that we sang loudly at the next air force's Independence Day party: "Every Country Has a National Squadron, but the Scorpions Is International!"

Naturally, that song became the anthem of the squadron.

The most prominent difference was that in the Scorpions they flew speaking Hebrew.

Before, in flight school, the language was a pidgin aviation English built on terms and figures of speech left by foreign volunteers. Those volunteers came to Israel in 1948 to help in our fight for independence. They came from all over the world, mostly America, England, Australia, and South Africa, and at that time no one could fly speaking Hebrew. After the war most of them returned to their homelands, but some remained for a few years. And some of them—all World War II veterans and very respected—were still training cadets at Tel Nof. So it turned out that the actual language in use was aviation English. As a consequence, we were split in two; at ground school we were taught in Hebrew, but once we climbed into the cockpit, all the terms changed into foreign ones. This mixture of languages and terms caused many misunderstandings and a lot of confusion.

In one of the flights on the Harvard, my compass stopped functioning. My flight instructor in the backseat, Tsutsik, wanted to know what was going on. He roared at me, "Hey, is your compass US?"

"You—what? . . . I didn't understand what you said, sir," I mumbled.

The name "Tsutsik" was an affectionate nickname, one with an ironic twist. Not small *(tsutsik)* at all, Lt. Moshe Rosenberg weighed at least a hundred kilos. He was a big man with two mighty, black, hairy arms. He had heavy eyebrows over a big nose, enormous shoulders, and his voice was very deep and smoky. At that time I still didn't realize that this frightening giant was really a big pussycat. I simply feared him.

"Look at your compass," he said hoarsely, "and see whether it is US or not!"

I looked carefully on the compass and didn't see anything. I felt like a complete idiot.

"Well?" the booming voice in my earphones made it clear that his patience was nearing an end.

Then I had an idea.

I loosened my seat straps and bent down forward, twisted around the stick, and stretched my neck forward ahead between my knees. Turning, I squeezed my head into the dark niche under the instrument panel and looked, squinting, at the underside of the instrument panel. The backs of the instruments were all there, looking like small black barrels. Fumbling with my hand, I found the compass box. An electric cable emerged from it like a pig's tail. Around it stuck several inscriptions in English. I read them.

"Well, what's up with you, Spector?" brayed my earphones. "Is your compass US or is it not US? Huh?"

Sweating, I corkscrewed myself back to daylight, yelling, "No, sir, it says 'Made in England'!"

The aircraft and the whole world froze in the air. A hoarse whisper bellowed, "Ohhhhhh, what an asshole!"

We landed. Before I brought the Harvard to a full stop, the flight instructor jumped out of it and went contemptuously to the file room. I knew what he was going to write. I shut the engine and dragged, beaten and dejected, to ask my comrades. They shrugged. Finally Yakir appeared. As usual, he knew everything. "US? What's the problem? The meaning of 'US' is 'Unserviceable,' out of order." And then he rubbed salt in the wound, asking, "How could you not know that, Spike? Everybody knows that."

Soon we cadets were showing off with this jargon. It smelled like hundred-octane gas to us, and we practiced pronouncing its words with harsh facial expressions, spitting them from the side of the mouth, like Humphrey Bogart. You croaked "contact," and for a moment you were Jack Robinson scrambling in his Spitfire against the "Boshes" together with Tom, Dick, and Harry Barak.

After we got our wings our pidgin language was enriched with the perfume of Chanel No. 5. *Disjoncteur*, for example, were a bunch of tiny plugs or circuit breakers scattered in the depths of the cockpit. *Base de niveau* was the name of a certain yellow lamp. And the air conditioning system of the cockpit was operated by a handle with two positions, the names certainly invented by the paperback author Georges Simenon: Miserable *Chauffage* knelt, chafing the floor, and over her, from behind, the impassionate Monsieur *De Zambouage* bent, lifting her skirt.

"*Monsieur, ques-ce que tu fait?*"

"*Rien, mademoiselle,* just a quick '*zambouaging.*' "

In the Scorpions they didn't admire this colorfulness. They demanded we fly speaking only our national language.

There was another exceptional characteristic of the Scorpions: everybody worked hard, trying to establish order and discipline. At noon after the day's flights had ended, Capt. Giora Furman would assume command, and ground-school studies begin. We learned and relearned and then were tested on the minutest details of the body and engine of the

Super Mystere, its gunsight and electronic range finder. We were loaded with tactics, navigation, meteorology, and more. Industriousness and discipline reigned in the Scorpions.

The best personal example was set by Lt. Rami Harpaz. He was a kibbutz kid who demanded of himself that he knew everything. Another self-taught genius was Ephraim Ashkenazi. He had taught himself engineering and sciences. For some time I was received as Ephraim's guest in his room, with the condition that I turn my face to the wall when Lilly, an energetic, slender girl soldier, came to visit.

At night I woke and saw him through a split in my blanket. He sat, sunk in books and notebooks, filling them with drawings and graphs. At that time computers didn't exist, but Ephraim's natural talent for mathematics was such that in a few years he revealed a serious error in the calculations of the French engineers in the gunsight of the Mirage fighter aircraft. Ephraim fixed their mistake using only paper and a pencil.

This accomplishment was historical: until then the Mirages—which had replaced the Super Mysteres as interceptors—couldn't hit anything. Their cannon rounds always missed the MiGs, and the MiGs always got away. Only after Ephraim's solution did the Mirages become lethal.

So if Yak taught us how to get into firing position, it was Ephraim who enabled us to hit our targets. One cannot overemphasize the contributions of these two exceptional men to the fact that the IAF shot down hundreds of MiGs in the next twenty years.

Surrounded by supportive people, I opened up, stopped being so closed, so defensive. Slowly a new rule of life ripened in me. Initially I just felt it building up, but in time it phased itself into two words that stayed with me: "always positive."

There was much to be admired in the Scorpions. In 1960 this squadron was a very serious outfit. It was the most professional of all the squadrons, working hard on the science of battle.

Such an approach was the exception in the early days of the Israeli Air Force. At that time, flying fighter planes was considered by many as an adventure rather than a profession. Flight instructors and formation leaders took their students down for mock attacks on trains, and buzzed vehicles on the roads. So when they were on their own, the students did the same thing. On one occasion I was taking a senior pilot back home. On the way he asked for the controls of the Stearman biplane, and taught me the way a father teaches his son how to fly under power lines, as "any pilot worthy of the name" should do. On the way back to Hatzor, I flew low in the Izreel Valley and brought home strips of corn straw wound around my propeller and wheels, smelling of the perfume of the fields.

Only in cases where things got too crazy—for example, when somebody once dove his Stearman on a helicopter carrying the air force commander—was some punishment meted out, but nothing too harsh. A pilot who broke all the rules with an outrageous air show right over the base was fined ten Israeli pounds, but at the same time was patted on the shoulder by his commander as a sign of manly appreciation. A few days later, in a second show, this pilot hit the ground.

We were working in an environment characterized by many so-called accidents-in-training. When somebody spoke about rules and regulations, he would get a flippant response: "Well, are we pilots or college professors?" The more sophisticated among us had more elaborate rationalizations, such as, "The security of the state demands it!" Or, in other words, to prepare ourselves properly to defend our country, we pilots had to train in outrageous ways.

We bought into this bullshit readily. Knowing the law, we violated it all the time. We loved to fly, and no one protested against the confusion of high-performance flying with hooliganism in the air.

This is how the night acrobatics scandal happened. While in the flying school, in the ground class before night flying, we were introduced to a pilot's worst enemy: the loss of spatial orientation, the lethal "vertigo."

Vertigo lurks in the darkness to drive pilots into the ground. Without proper references outside the cockpit—at night, or in bad weather—it is a constant danger for pilots of any experience. Aerobatics or extreme maneuvers make a perfect recipe for such confusion.

The flight instructor concluded his lecture. He bent forward over his table and said with a hiss, “No radical maneuvers at night! You can get disoriented and crash. Get it?”

We, all the flight cadets, nodded.

“Write this down: ‘No night acrobatics under any circumstances!’ ”

We had already been flying for six months, and felt this order was pretty insulting, but he spoke so forcefully that we felt obliged to do as he said. He scrutinized us all.

“Did everybody write down what I said?”

Again we nodded. He seemed satisfied.

“Dismissed.”

We stood up. The instructor grinned a little, and suddenly said in low voice, “Only pussies don’t do night acrobatics.”

Night with a full moon. My first night flight.

Tsutsik, my instructor, took the controls, and off we went. We flew around the training areas. The air about us was full of light and shining; moonlight spilled over all like milk and lit the world white. I could see fields below us, brooks, canals, and trees. The roofs of the houses in the villages shone under the starred, almost pale blue skies. “What a night!” said my instructor with a growl like a bear.

“Bright as day,” I said.

“Let me show you something!”

He jammed the throttle forward, and the Harvard roared with all nine cylinders of its radial engine. Six hundred horsepower accelerated us to maximum dive speed; then Tsutsik pulled up hard. G-force crushed our asses into the creaking seats. The fat, round nose rose up and up into the yellowish sky, and stopped with the propeller pointing right at the Milky Way. As we lost momentum the engine coughed, and sparks from the exhaust pipe spattered near my right leg. The smell of gas filled the cockpit. Then at zero airspeed the Harvard stopped in the air and stood still vertically, its tail pointed at the ground. After a moment of hesitation, the chubby trainer shook and fell back on its tail and then rolled sideways in a perfect stall turn. The airspeed indicator vibrated, revived. The nose now pointed at the ground. The engine coughed and backfired. A blinding stream of fire wound around and slid in through the canopy's slots, licking and burning my face.

"What a beautiful night, huh?" Tsutsik gleefully said with a howl. I happily agreed. The skin on my face burned a little, but I loved it.

Back from the first night flight, in our rooms, we all had difficulty falling asleep. We gathered in Goldie's room. A jabber of voices, impressions, chattering, laughing. Oh, what a night!

"Is there anybody here who didn't get an acrobatics lesson?" inquired ZBB. Nobody answered. If someone wasn't lucky enough, he didn't say. We were men enough to guard our instructors' dignity and our own.

Two weeks passed. We went out for a second night, this time dark, with no moon. We were to practice takeoffs and landings. The rear seat was manned by Assaf, a famous fighter pilot, superior flight instructor, and the leader of the IAF's aerobatic team. We started up, and made our way cautiously onto the darkened taxiing strip. Finally we got permission to line up on the runway, a path of black void between two rows of kerosene lamps along it. The Harvard raced forward, became airborne, and the two rows of lights disappeared behind us. We closed the canopies over our heads, and the aircraft sank into the darkness like a sea of black ink. Only the constellations of the settlements' lights glowed in the empty darkness streaming under our aircraft's belly, punctuating points on the dark background not unlike the heavenly constellations that shone from space. It was hard to discern the horizon and difficult to stay oriented. A frightening experience for a rookie.

Assaf was "sitting on my controls" and guiding me. He taught me patiently how to combine outside vision with the instrument readings. He handled the ship with a gentle affection that for many years after I strove to imitate.

Finally we finished circling and got ready for the first landing, but then, "A Harvard has landed badly, and is upside down on the runway," the radio informed. "Enter a holding pattern," Assaf instructed me, then explained, "Just circle the field."

I did as he said. The backseat went silent. Once around, twice around. Boring.

"Hey, tower, how long is this going to take?"

"Stand by, checking."

On the third go-round Assaf took an interest in my performance in the course. "How are you doing?"

"So-so," I answered, concentrating on the turn-and-bank indicator.

"Good," the team leader volunteered. "Come on, show me a barrel roll."

And from here to there I got one of the best lessons ever in acrobatic series performance, together with all the exercises. Assaf was flying the aircraft smoothly and precisely. He worked on my handling, and taught me to change the pressure on the pedals gently from one foot to the other, together with changes in airspeed and engine power. "Close your eyes," he told me in the vertical climbs, and I learned how to avoid the blinding bursts of fire from the exhaust pipe. On the third practice run I could already keep the aircraft looping in a straight line parallel to the row of the kerosene torches along the runway. On the fourth, I succeeded in rolling it in a vertical dive, with the nose pointed directly at the cluster of fire trucks blinking in the darkness around the turned-over aircraft.

After midnight, when we were leaving after a meal of cold, oily sunny-side-up eggs, Assaf turned at the dining room door to tell me conscientiously, "Listen, Spector. Whatever you saw tonight, well, it's not regulation. Don't do that stuff in the future."

"Of course not, sir," I said with my best innocent, blue-eyed gaze. "Night acrobatics just aren't done."

Night navigation class. In the beginning we circled the country under the supervision of our instructors, but we were waiting impatiently for the next stage, solo navigation. We already had a secret plan involving what we would do when we could work unsupervised. The program was exciting. We developed it in complete secrecy. Finally the plan was ready down to the last detail, and written down. We approved it in a secret meeting in the barracks.

This was the program: We would take off from Tel Nof one after another, five minutes apart, and go north. The first "practice station" would be half an hour later, over Mount Tabor in the Galilee. There, everyone would do acrobatics for five minutes. That done, each one would clear out and navigate west. The next station would be over the small beach town of Atlit, on the Mediterranean coast. There we would form pairs, each odd number waiting, circling, for the next one behind him. When they met, take another five minutes for a mock dogfight. When that was over, they should separate and return home the same way they came, and say nothing to anybody.

And as in every well-planned operational scheme, we put in our plan all the necessary topics, such as "communications," "concealment," and "deception." Regarding communications, the whole operation was to be done under strict radio silence, except for the mandatory reports each aircraft had to make to traffic control on the way. All the acrobatics, dogfights, and departures would be executed without uttering a word on the radio.

We still had no idea what a dogfight really was, least of all how to do it at night, and so everybody began to imagine tricks to surprise and beat his opponent. This night flight was going to outdo anything our commanders and instructors ever dreamed of.

Goldie, our leader, summarized it. "This operation must be top secret, before its execution and after it. Is that clear to everybody?" It was clear to all of us. But Goldie didn't settle for that. "Let's see some hands!" We all raised our hands and took an oath not to reveal anything to anybody outside the room. We were already ripe soldiers; we created our liars' club.

A cold, dark night, February 11, 1960. Our canopies were covered with dew. Twenty Harvard trainers started up at five-minute intervals. Each took off at the same interval and headed north. In every aircraft an air cadet sat alone with his map in his left hand under the dim red cockpit light, passing alone over the dark land. Only one instructor was on duty in the squadron ready room, just in case. Terribly bored, he sat close to the kerosene stove, warming his hands and joking with the clerk, yawning and looking at his watch, waiting for the last aircraft to land so he could close up shop and get to bed.

I don't remember much about Mount Tabor. I was one of the later arrivals, and when I got there it was pretty late. I recall there was some mist down there, and the mountain's round top protruded from its white veils. The night was so dark that I probably passed on doing acrobatics. But I am not sure; maybe my memory is fooling me. Was I really brave? Did I lift my propeller and aim it right at the cold diamonds of Orion's belt, shining like torches over the mountain? Who knows? Perhaps I didn't do that and only rocked my wings a little, if only to keep my self-respect. I'm not sure.

In any case, if I didn't accomplish great feats over Tabor that night, others did. Yakir no doubt did much more. Yakir was brave as a wildcat and flew like a devil. Yakir the innocent, who in the first week of flight school wrote a song and even composed its music: "To the sky we yearn, there to soar among the clouds," he would sing in a high-pitched, sentimental voice. "There we shall defend our country from all its enemies!" The same Yakir who suddenly demanded that we erect a memorial stone for the fallen in our class (tonight we were going to lose the second one), and was silenced only when ZBB said maliciously, "Yakir, you turkey. Tomorrow you yourself will be history." We looked at each other and shivered.

I remember Atlit perfectly.

As planned, I circled, holding a left turn over the beach at two thousand feet, waiting for Brutus, the next guy after me. The town under me was dark except for a few streetlamps, and I was looking into the darkness around me. Suddenly something emerged, flying right at me, felt rather than seen. Startled, I broke right. A stream of sparks poured into the air nearby as from a grindstone, issuing from a point in the middle of nothing and spilling out to space. It immediately vanished. I heard two clicks on the radio. I answered with a click of my own. The burnished sea beneath me glistened dimly in the pale starlight. A great fear came over me and I turned and fled Atlit, racing south along the beach toward home.

When I finally shut down my engine and ran back to the ready room in the freezing night air, the search had already begun. The officer on duty counted us once and twice, talking nervously on the phone. Somebody was overdue. Who?

Our commander, Maj. Harry Barak, arrived from home, his big mustache wispy and the pleasant smile gone. Then other men arrived, and the ready room of the basic training squadron filled with noisy people. It was late when the last of us landed, the last engine coughed and choked in the line, and silence enveloped all. We cadets wandered about on the outside balcony, freezing, waiting. Finally somebody noticed us, and sent us to our rooms to get some sleep.

As we marched on the wet asphalt, Brutus nudged me with his elbow. "I fucked you over, eh?"

"What are you talking about, Brutus?" I asked. "Where the hell have you been?"

"For by wise deceit shall thou make thy war," he answered me with his brutal sense of humor. "When you grow up, you will learn to switch your lights off at night, and you will not be seen. Why are you opening your baby blues at me?"

In the morning, we were called to the ready room.

We already knew that Khativa was missing. Outside, it was raining. All of us, all the Harvard squadron's instructors and students, were pressed into the small briefing room, whispering.

"Attention!"

The air force commander, Gen. Ezer Weizman, strode in, followed by our base commander, the school commander, and many others we didn't know. The number of big brass squeezed inside the room that morning was greater than our number. The floorboards creaked.

Only Weizman spoke. It was evident that when he talked, others shut up.

"Cadets, has anyone here done night acrobatics?"

Our instructors squinted at us. Our commander, Major Harry, looked at us, his mustache twitching. Colonel Shieh, the flight school commander, kept shifting from leg to leg. We knew that death and life lay in the power of the tongue. We kept silent.

"Sheani Junior, on your feet!" Weizman already knew our names.

Uri got up, stretching his short, stout figure.

"Did you do acrobatics?"

"No, sir!"

"Spector?"

"Not me, sir!"

The general turned to the instructors, to our commanders. They all shook their heads no. Some kept their eyes on the floor.

"Is there anybody here who wants to say something?" For the first time, a tone of hesitation was heard in that energetic voice. Nobody answered.

Weizman waved his hand: "All right. Officers, all of you, out of the room. Leave me alone with the cadets."

After Weizman gave us his word of honor that what we said would stay in the room forever, and that no action would be taken, we broke our silence. And the general kept his word.

That day and in that room, we buried Air Cadet Khativa. Nothing was ever found of his body or his aircraft. Seemingly they joined the silent flotilla in which my father's boat sails. But his parents, whom we were sent to visit all ironed and polished, were never really told why their son died.

Chapter 6

Bastille Day

Mirage 3: a supersonic jet fighter by Marcel Dassault, France. Began development in the 1950s. Can fly twice the speed of sound. Designed to serve as all-weather interceptor, in day and night, and for this end was equipped with Cyrano radar that can detect aircraft. Its armament included a pair of 30mm Defa cannons, a French air-to-air, radar-directed Matra 530 heavy missile, and two heat-seeking Shafrir missiles produced in Israel. The Mirage had three hard points to carry bombs or external fuel tanks that could be jettisoned in flight.

The main prototype 3C flew first in October 1960; the Israeli Air Force gave it the name "Sky," and ordered seventy-two single-seaters and four two-seater aircraft. During the 1960s the Mirage was Israel's main fighter, operated by three squadrons: the Fighting First at Hatzor, the Bats at Tel Nof, and a third squadron at Ramat-David. After 1970, Israel developed the basic design and produced homemade versions of the Mirage—the Nesher (Eagle) and the Kfir (Young Lion).

THE AIR FORCE WAS A GREAT PLACE, but it was not heaven. True, the majority of us could be called good guys, but there were exceptions. One of these was a classmate at flight school. Let's call him Hal.

Hal was a very good-looking young man, and girls were crazy about his fair hair, his oily-brown eyes, and the polite, smooth sound of his voice. In our own eyes—his fellow cadets in the class—Hal seemed simply a sycophant. The trouble was that soon other qualities, much more repulsive, were apparent in him.

It began with his habit of disappearing in the evenings on his own business instead of working on his studies. There were many exams in flight school, and so on the morning of the test Hal would appear and suck up to people, looking for someone he could copy from. In flight school of that day, a code of honor was expected from the students. True, that code was not always observed; in one of the previous classes, students were caught stealing advance copies of tests. And there was even a case of one student who tried to cheat on a flight examination. But as a rule, people could tell right from wrong.

Hal, on the other side, had no moral compass. He didn't hesitate to get us all in trouble. You could try to evade him, but nothing helped. He would rub himself against you and finally take a seat next to you and begin winking. The moment the examiner left the classroom, you felt a hand on your knee or a paper ball landing between your shoulders, and Hal's voice whispering in your ear. If you turned away from him, he might even raise his voice and demand the answers from you, calling you a coward and guilty of "betrayal of comradeship."

Besides being a nuisance, Hal was selfish and a liar. His word was worth exactly nothing. In short time, we all hoped that this guy would wash out of our class. Unfortunately for us, it seemed he was not going away. He flew well, as far as we knew. At least that is what he told us, bragging how he "gave lessons" to his instructor. Among the base personnel he had many, ever-changing girlfriends, and they passed around bizarre stories of how he, with his courage and wit, saved his aircraft and landed safely with a fainting flight instructor. At the end we gave him a ridiculous nickname: the Perfect Pilot. Those girls, who had many times defended him, began to tell about nasty things he had done, some financial and others uglier still.

In short, if in the beginning we were just chuckling about "Hal's pranks," the more we came to know him, the more he annoyed, repelled, and shamed us. When we were still many in number, and four or five boys crowded in each room in the barracks, a volunteer was needed to share a room with Hal. His personality became such a social distraction, that evenings before going to sleep, you could hear in each of the rooms, discussions not of the eternal subjects among our kind of young men—girls and flying—but about "the Hal question."

One of the evenings we all got together to discuss this issue seriously. Hal was not there; as usual, he had disappeared after dusk.

First there were the usual discussions, and somebody asked, "Can this guy be the image of the Israeli pilot?" This question put the argument on a higher level. Others said, "Can we trust a guy like this? Can we go to war with him?"

Some criticized our instructors and commanders. Why couldn't they sense what type of person they were dealing with here? And then one of us stood and said, "Enough complaining. The responsibility rests with all of us here. If class thirty-one resents Hal that much, it's our duty to act and bring about his dismissal from the air force."

This idea made sense. Immediately someone volunteered to prepare a letter for all of us to sign, which would demand Hal's removal. This letter was to be handed to the school commander the next morning. But then Zimmer got up and spoke to the other side, and his words were forceful and well argued.

"Israel is in danger," he said, "and pilots are needed. Fighter pilots are a rare commodity in particular, and the nation pays a high price for them." Then he came to the point. "Hal is a pig, no question about that, but what has that to do with the defense of our country? Perhaps Hal may turn out to be the best combat pilot of us all." Silence fell.

"Who are you to decide to wash out a potential pilot," Zimmer went on, "and waste a national investment?" We were stunned.

"You've overstepped yourselves," Zimmer summed up his impressive speech. "What's happening here is like mutiny. There are flight instructors and officers here, and all of them are able and authorized people. They are the ones who determine whom to dismiss and whom to keep. Certainly not you"—he stabbed the audience with his pointed finger—"you spoiled brats!"

Zimmer was a clever and powerful person. He later became a lawyer. None of us could answer his argument. The anti-Hal organization was dismantled. We channeled our frustration in a vicious ditty we performed in one of the school's parties, called "The Ballad of the Perfect Pilot."

"My baby shall be the best of pilots," chants Hal's mother merrily from the window, hanging his diapers to dry.

"By God, how can you tell that in advance?" the next-door housewife asks, clasping her hands in awe.

"That's easy," the proud mother sings, her voice embellishing. "He floated to me through the air."

"Flew in the air? From where?"

"From Mr. Smith, the neighbor."

This was the first time I had to face the question of whether our national situation was so bad that it demanded employment of undesirable elements.

In the coming years, this was a dilemma that kept recrudescing, and sometimes it was my call to determine whether state security justified compromise with pigs. There were always people around who argued that there was no other alternative, that one must use what's available, and that the security of Israel justifies all means. Some even forwarded the theory that since war is a dirty business, dirty types are better fit for it. In a certain kind of American film you find this theory, too.

I want to testify to something I learned from experience. There is no functional connection between swinishness and effectiveness in war. The myth is false. I have never seen good things coming out of the trash can.

Hal got his wings with the rest of us and became a pilot and an officer, if not a gentleman. But he never justified the expectations or the investment in him. Shortly after a stupid accident, he vanished. I heard he left the country, and there were rumors that he became involved in illegal businesses. Many years later, when his name came up by chance, one of our instructors from back then said, "We were all waiting for you, the cadets, to get rid of him."

This taught me something about where the buck stops.

The early 1960s passed slowly, and without me noticing, time began accelerating downhill toward the earthquake of June 1967. The dominance of the Super Mystere dwindled, and a new magic fighter landed in Israel. This was the Mirage III, whom we called in our language "Sky." If the Super Mystere was a plump, black-haired beauty, the Mirage was a blond courtesan, slender and cheeky. My Super Mystere suddenly looked to me a little cumbersome and round, like an overripe woman. She was not fat yet, still attractive, but . . .

The Mirage brought on delta wings a new epoch in the history of the air force and eventually in my own life, too, but I didn't know it yet.

In the beginning, just a few chosen pilots were sent to France for training on the new fighter. This was such an honor, and a marvelous opportunity to leave our claustrophobic little country and see the greater world outside, that pilots who were not chosen for Mirage training got really mad. They even wrote a blues ballad, and soon angry and disappointed people sang it all around the air force.

"How is it?" asked the poet who wrote that song. "How, by all that's holy, does it happen that among all of us so fine, Lieutenant Liss will go to France? Huh? For fuck's sake, why is he the only one to eat croissants?" And Lieutenant Liss was further immortalized like this:

To the Mirage he proudly strides, to fly Mach 2 high in the sky,
Have fun in France, but not until he passes the whorehouse
drill . . .
He walks down Paris streets, and suddenly happens on Brigitte,
To Place Pigalle they go, of course, and she suggests some
intercourse.

The crowd roared the chorus "How did it happen?" to an old tune from a Tel Aviv nightclub.

The solo continued to abuse Liss, who apparently crumpled under the sexy star's lust for the pilots of the IAF. "Says Lieutenant Liss, 'Oh, yes, indeed, but I am just a Boy Scout kid, and keep your distance, let's not kiss, I am afraid of syphilis.' "

But then our Mirage boy was gentleman enough not to leave the star in an empty bed for the night. "I have a friend, his name is Nick, he comes along and shows his stick. If you don't mind, then I shall keep behind the door to take a peep."

"How did it happen?" roared the crowd, enjoying immensely this abuse of the brown-nosing pilot and his mother.

In admiration, I asked the poet about the wonders of his art. "Writing songs? That's no big deal," answered Lieutenant Arnon. "Just put a prick in every other line and you will always have good lyrics."

The year was 1963. Peace in Israel.

The end of our first five-year enlistment was nearing, and our small group scattered to the winds. Umsh left active service and went to fly transports at El Al. Soon he was mostly abroad, and lost to us. Uri Sheani, the gunnery champ, married Shula and fathered two girls. The young family was sent to Uganda, where Uri taught military flight training. Our mutual affection kept us in contact in spite of the distance, and from time to time I received letters and magnificent black-and-white photographs of exotic African women with exposed breasts.

Yakir, the rooster, went an inch too low. His aircraft hit the surface of the Sea of Galilee when he was demonstrating low flight to a student. I saw the splash and the gray water close over them. Their remains were never recovered. After I got back, I had a long, dreary drive to take Yakir's just-widowed bride back to her parents in the north.

Zimmer was already a law student at Hebrew University in Jerusalem. His protégé Hal disappeared into thin air, and nobody missed him. Brutus, my opponent that horrible night over Atlit, went back to his kibbutz and turned into an inventor of agricultural machines.

ZBB got promoted and was selected to fly Mirages at Ramat-David. Soon his special talents stood out there. We didn't see each other as much.

I almost missed his piercing, clever look. And Goldie—he was upward bound, as foreseen by all. While we all toiled to learn to lead formations in the air, he had already finished a term as squadron deputy, and the IAF sent him to college.

All my original friends were gone now, and I found new ones. I got closer to Nissim, the redhead Bulgarian who saw us first on the veranda of the Scorpions. His home in base family housing was always open to me and to the shy soldier-girl who sometimes came to visit me. Nissim's clever wife, Etty, knew how to listen to us and give advice when needed. Zorik, a commander who became a friend, also used to invite confused youngsters to his home, and his wife, Tali, saw to it that they did not get out hungry. Another close friend was Mossik, a happy-going and crazy flier who loved to wrestle on the lawn and break bones. He brought to the squadron's parties a stunning brown-eyed girl with honey-colored hair, also named Etty. Soon the likable young couple Ilan and Judy Gonen joined our small fraternity.

As for me, I was on my way out.

I was already twenty-three years old, and after three years in the Scorpions, flying fighter planes had nothing more to show me. I gave up any desire to fly Mirages, since it required another enlistment. I preferred to return to my friends in Kibbutz Givat-Brenner and to join them in the grand, righteous partnership of building a socialist-Zionist society in Israel.

On Saturdays I was in the kibbutz, picking oranges and cotton, loading hay and raising my hand in the general assembly on behalf of equality and similar principles. I hoped to marry the girl who loved me, and study medicine in Jerusalem. In my imagination I saw myself as Dr. Spector, distinguished physician and kibbutz member, who once a week puts aside his scalpel and does his reserve duty flying Super Mysteres at Hatzor.

This was a beautiful dream. I even obtained a pipe and began practicing with it in front of the mirror.

I shared these thoughts with my friends and commanders, and it never crossed my mind that I had hurt somebody's feelings, especially not the special and stormy commander of the air force, Gen. Ezer Weizman.

Weizman had never said two words to me before, but when he appeared one day at Hatzor and gathered all the pilots for a pep talk, he suddenly pointed a long finger from the podium at me.

"You! You decided to become a doctor!" Weizman knew every pilot by name, and knew all about us.

Embarrassed, I rose to my feet.

"Yes, sir."

"You want to be released from the service? What, flying isn't good enough for you?"

I didn't answer. What could I say?

"You want to be a dentist!"

Laughter. I blushed.

I heard in Weizman's offended tone a feeling of insult and began to heat up myself, but suddenly I grasped that from his point of view as air force commander I was doing something against him. At the time Weizman was leading a campaign to mobilize the best youth for aviation. It was clear and public knowledge that he wanted the air force to become the leader of the Israel Defense Force, and perhaps all this involved his career as well.

And another thing: Only shortly before, Weizman himself had sent me for a two-month leave to appear in a feature film full of propaganda for the air force. This movie was showing at that time all over the country, and for a time I was a media item—the handsome, curly-headed Israeli pilot. I was interviewed in ladies' magazines, and my name and picture were on walls everywhere. I was flooded with letters from ambitious boys and romantically inclined girls. And lo, this symbol was going to betray him. Weizman raged, and he wouldn't let me off the hook.

"A dentist, eh? Answer me!"

"I was thinking psychiatry could be helpful." I told the truth, and instantly bit my tongue. I believe he never forgave me for this reckless answer.

DURING THE FOLLOWING MONTHS I took the bus to Jerusalem to visit the school of medicine. I audited classes, and even bought *Human Anatomy and Physiology* in a used bookstore, and began memorizing the volume.

Then another surprise. The kibbutz also viewed my intention to become a physician with an unsympathetic eye.

One evening Jos'l, who had been my class's teacher and later became the kibbutz's treasurer, called me for a talk. He sat me in the office of the kibbutz and treated me to a jeremiad on those degenerates who frequent bars and nightclubs and drink alcohol. The members of the steering committee sat around, nodding like Chinese sages. I didn't understand what any of it had to do with me, and suspected it was a prank. At last they got to the point: Hooligans and drunks from Weizman's flight school must first get cleaned before they approach the kibbutz with applications of any kind.

This was perfectly fine with me. I said I would happily invest a year or two in the fields and the dairy, to go to medical school. They smiled, but the committee was just the first step. Within a month I was invited to present my case to the general assembly of the kibbutz.

As usual, the assembly took place after Saturday night dinner. The long tables were cleared of white cheese and jam cans, and aluminum teapots were scattered about. Hundreds of members took seats or roved around, talking. The secretary rapped with his fork on his cup time and again, and finally it was quiet enough. He had put my case first on the agenda.

"Iftach Spector applies to go to medical school—"

Before he could finish, the storm of noise resumed. The ladies crocheting in the first row put their needles aside and began discussing my personality and what my mother was doing.

"He is Shosh's son, isn't he?"

"She won't stay on the kibbutz."

"I hear she has someone in Tel Aviv."

"Really?" Ringing of a needle falling on the floor. "Do you know who this one is?" And they stopped, looking at me.

Then the men said to each other, "It's mandatory that he sign a letter of obligation. Otherwise he'll just get an education and never come back here to do anything."

I stood there in the crowded dining room, waiting to be called to the table to stand before them and present my case. I couldn't avoid hearing comments behind my back. Among the kibbutz's older members, especially the women, some saw me as a "jobnik," not a real kibbutznik but one who just wants a cushy job. They said I intended to go "white collar" at the expense of the kibbutz and evade hard physical work. I looked left and right at the hundreds of faces I considered friends and family. I heard them speak. The children from my class with whom I had grown up, hid in corners. I was on my own.

I raised my hand and asked the secretary to end the discussion.

"I'm withdrawing my application."

A tumult broke out; I felt stares on my back as I went to the door and left the hall. From behind, I heard the fork ringing against the cup.

"Silence! Next item."

I went to the scales room, the small house at the entrance of the kibbutz where trucks stopped for weighing. It also housed the telephone switchboard. Suzy, the operator, let me place a call to my base. I found my friend Mossik there, and he came from Hatzor with a military truck. We threw my bed, mattress, and clothes in it and drove away. At Hatzor we unloaded my few belongings in the bachelor officers' quarters and went to sleep. So I was homeless and broke until next payday. My dream blew away like fog in the wind. This is how I remained "temporarily" in the military, where I made my living.

And while this intermediate period continued, Ali finished her military service. A chaplain married us in a ratty office with dusty windows, on the second floor of the military rabbinate in Jaffa. A minyan was required—a quorum of ten men, mandatory for any religious ritual—and some guys were pulled in off the street. Ali looked very beautiful, thin and slender and fragile in a white dress prepared for her by the seamstress who lived near her mother (a small belly had to be hidden under the dress). On her head Ali wore a garland of tiny white flowers. The dress and the flowers looked out of place in that dreary room.

In the beginning there was no housing available for us, and we had to stay apart during the week and meet at her mother's on weekends. Then a flat was freed up at Hatzor family housing, and eventually we had a floor on which to unroll our first joint acquisition—a rug. We got a table from the base quartermaster. We slept on my narrow iron single bed from the kibbutz at night, and during the day it metamorphosed into a sofa for visitors to sit on. The jewel in the crown was a brand-new Amcor refrigerator, donated by Ali's South African uncles.

Mossik—my closest friend at the time, until he was killed a year later—also got married, and the young couple moved in next door to us. A warm friendship bloomed among the four of us, on the common lawn. The summer days were beautiful, and the pain and disappointment after the loss of our home dulled slowly.

News of my son's birth reached me exactly according to the pilots' wives' myth, over the radio. In early November 1964, Ali had been taken to the hospital, and just as I was in the middle of a mock dogfight, the news broke in my earphones. I landed hurriedly, grabbed a vehicle, and sped to Kaplan Hospital, near Rehovot. My beauty was exhausted, her face pale and her lips dry and cracked. I looked around; there was nothing else.

"Is there a baby?" I asked suspiciously. At last they let me watch my newborn son through the glass. He looked like a tent peg, with his big head and the pointed small cylinder that was his body wrapped in cloth. We called him Etay, after the name of one of King David's heroes. This also was the name of one of the children of the Admons, who adopted me for three years in Kibbutz Alonim.

After two days in the hospital, Ali returned home. There was much washing of cotton diapers, and nights with no sleep from his crying, and one fine morning I collided with another aircraft. We both crashed, but survived. Again I had thoughts whether this is not the place for me, but life had to go on, and the air force was the one place that wanted to pay me a salary. The studies had to be postponed for another year, and meanwhile we became a family and began to build a home. Our baby looked like an angel, fair-haired and round-faced. Zorik came to visit us. He marveled and praised the baby, and we were filled with pride and affection. Zorik was an expert on kids, as he himself told us.

On December 30, 1965, on the turn to my landing approach, the control tower asked me to go around again. I opened the throttle, and my small world exploded with a bang. My plane was engulfed in flames, and before I knew what happened, I found myself rolling in the air in my ejection seat, waiting for the parachute to open. I remember with absolute clarity that very brief moment, with my eyes closed and my mind coolly asking what had happened.

My parachute opened. I opened my eyes and there it was, my Super Mystere, still not far from me in a flat turn and trailing a long plume of fire. I saw it sinking toward a house in the near village—a great fear enveloped me—and then it missed the house, hit the field beyond, and burst into flames. Another swing in the air and I smashed into the mud like a sack of potatoes.

I lay on the wet ground, struggling to breathe through this pain in my chest, and thought, "Motherfucker, that Super Mystere went up like a torch!" And then, "What luck it didn't fall on that house." And suddenly I got the point: this fire . . . there was no way I could have caused it. "Well then, this time it is the aircraft's fault, not mine. This time I was not guilty." I groaned. That was not the case in my former bailout, after the aerial collision. Then I was guilty. And how.

And again I thought, "Ah, this time it was marginal! The parachute opened right at the minimum height, perhaps twenty meters above the ground. And if that's true, then I ejected from the burning aircraft in the last split second. How did it happen so fast?"

I didn't remember any thinking or any conscious decision when the fire boomed around me. I simply found myself outside. And while I was trying to get up, pushing the mud with my boots and exerting a lot of effort just to get to my knees, a strange idea came to my mind. Was it possible that my hands were "preset" to pull the seat's handles?

Could it be that some "actions at threshold" are hidden in my limbs and muscles, waiting to be activated by danger even without any command from the brain?

And then I remembered something I had seen once on a bus. An elderly man stood in the aisle, carrying two baskets of groceries. Then the driver braked, and the old man fell on his face and lay full length on the floor. The amazing thing was that his hands kept hold of his baskets. Did this senior citizen forget to prepare the "action on threshold," cocking the mechanism letting the baskets go and grabbing the post?

And then I wondered whether there might be other kinds of automatic mechanisms hidden in our subconscious, waiting to activate themselves in moments of need. And if so, what are these actions, and how do they know when to deploy? How had this reaction, which had just saved my life, been programmed and set to execute from somewhere deep in my body? Those thoughts amazed me. I thought, "Here is a serious matter to be learned."

While I was still moaning with pain and amazement, I heard a loud whup-whup above. A helicopter came to take me for a medical examination.

Benny Peled, the commander of Hatzor Base, was waiting for me. "Are you okay?"

"Yes," I said, and immediately went on, "Listen to what came to my mind, sir . . . "

Benny listened attentively. When I was done, he patted my shoulder. "I understand. You are going to Mirages. Report tomorrow to the Fighting First; they'll give you a private conversion course."

"But Benny, I'm planning to be released." All that time we lived on borrowed time, saving money for the release. I still hoped to study medicine.

"Good. First do what you are told."

And so I also got to fly the wonderful triangle, and the anatomy book went into the trash.

What was it like to fly the Mirage for the first time? Namely, the primordial experience of encountering a new world . . .

Forget it; it's no use. This is a cliché that turns up in every aviation book ad nauseam, beginning with George Berling's *Spitfire* and ending with the astronauts in their space chariots. The description is always similar: the climbing into the "strange" and "complicated" cockpit (and then the inventory list of all the instruments and knobs), and the doubts. Am I good enough for this machine? Can I control it?

Then the standard continuation: a stanza of poetry follows, complete with the sounds of engine startup, and so on till the fake climax—fake because the real thing can't get on the page. Initially the aircraft feels like a bucking bronco, but soon enough the writer wrests control over it and they fall in mutual love, the machine becoming "a part of him." And if you are the romantic type like Pierre Closterman, you surely won't stop there. You will tell about your last flight, how you looped and rolled your aircraft for the last time, and the tears filled your eyes in spite of all you could do when you were listening to the growl of the engine that carried you through the blah blah blah, et cetera, et cetera.

Well, this is exactly how it was between me and Mirage No. 82. She accelerated and climbed so fast and at such a steep angle that I indeed had to fight vertigo. This aircraft's performance was really amazing—in acceleration, rate of climb, and top speed it still could rival today's modern fighters, and it had some interesting innovations. And as in all the stories, after a few more flights I fell in love with the Mirage, and also in love with the Fighting First, which had renewed itself with this outstanding aircraft. And the Fighting First became my new home, my true home.

The Super Mystere had been my first love, but I never flew one again. The Scorpions were already a second line unit, and the archenemy wasn't the MiG-17 anymore, but the fast and modern MiG-21, capable of twice the speed of sound, and the pinnacle of Soviet technology. The Super Mystere had changed from a racehorse to a plow mule. I knew I owed much to the Scorpions, but from that moment on I became a man of Mirages.

The year was 1966, and the air was charged with energy and uncertainty.

While we were looking inward, polishing our capabilities in aerial combat and ground attacks, the world around us hissed and bubbled. Revolutions took place everywhere. Every other week a new military coup in Africa. Charles De Gaulle withdrew France from NATO, and white Rhodesia was crumbling. Indira Gandhi was chosen prime minister of India. Nobel Prizes were awarded to the Israeli author S. Agnon and the poet Nelly Zakash. Martin Luther King Jr. marched in Chicago, and there were race riots in Michigan. Mao began the Cultural Revolution, and China spiraled into chaos. The Beatles—more popular than Jesus, as John Lennon proclaimed—gave "definitely the last concert" in San Francisco. Soviet Lunas landed on the Moon and Venus, while the Americans fought back with Gemini flights around Earth and space walks. A quarter million American soldiers were fighting in Vietnam, heavy American bombardments hit Hanoi and Haiphong Harbor, and the North Vietnamese declared full national mobilization. The first artificial heart was implanted in Houston, Texas. Turkey and Greece threatened one another over Cyprus. In Yemen, where an endless war dragged on, Egyptian bombers dropped poison gas. Every other week a plot against Egyptian president Gamal Abdel Nasser was unearthed. Executions took place in Al Mazza Prison, Cairo. A military coup in Syria, and the Baath Party, led by Jedid and Hafez Assad, took over the government. Syrian strongholds overlooking the Sea of Galilee shot down at Israeli fishermen. The Israeli-Syrian border heated up—and the days were still so fair.

I loved to get up very early in the morning, before sunrise. I washed and shaved quietly and quickly, and left our small housing apartment in silence, tiptoeing carefully in my flight boots so as not to wake up Ali and the baby. Outside, I stopped momentarily on the stairs, breathing the cool morning air laden with the scent of eucalyptus trees, feeling the clean cloth of my flight suit on my skin, and seeing the pearls of dew glittering on the lawns.

One by one we gathered near Hatzor's old cinema and waited for the truck to take us down to the Fighting First. Then came a morning full of action and light, working with young men and fast aircraft that smelled of burned gasoline. This smell was sweet in our nostrils. In the afternoon, after debriefing two or three training flights, the workday was over. Only the men on duty remained in the squadron building, preparing to sleep in full gear with their boots on, and everybody else searched for a lift back home to base housing. We usually got home before sunset.

The world was an orderly place, and step by step we settled in. We skimped and saved on my military salary and Ali's work as a typist. Her mother, Jenny, helped us buy our first car, a blue Citroën Deux Chevaux, well used, and soon I found myself lying under it on Saturdays, greasing, changing oil, installing lamps. In the nearby town of Gedera we got seeds and planted a large garden behind the house: tomatoes, cucumbers, radishes, green onions, lines of dill and parsley for our own salads. I built a hut from planks of wood

I found in base salvage, and creepers with bottle gourds, good for drying out and making into artifacts, soon covered it. I began flirting with painting. I painted aerial landscapes that soon became abstracts. I couldn't get rich colors, so I used hued white toothpaste. With it, I dotted carpets of shining points over a black velvety surface, and created a vista of the breathtaking coast, hovering in oblivion, as seen coming home from a training flight on a dark night far away over the sea. But after a while the toothpaste absorbed moisture and disintegrated, and the pictures were lost.

On one summer Saturday we succeeded in getting a military pickup truck—a great coup—and the three of us drove north to Kibbutz Afikim, on the Sea of Galilee. There, in the salvage of the kibbutz's plywood factory, we loaded the car with a huge slice of a tree trunk prepared for us by Aki. After lunch with Aki's family in the kibbutz's public dining room, and a swim in the Kinneret, we drove back to Hatzor, the pickup swaying under the enormous weight. It was two hundred kilometers of bad road to Hatzor.

We placed the wooden slice on our lawn, among the blue eucalyptus trees, and used it as a large outside table. We hung over it a lamp I made out of a burning jar taken from a jet engine I found in the dump. On this round table we feasted occasionally on Friday nights with our friends Nissim and Etty, Sam and Rana Khetz, Judy and Ilan. Mossik was dead by then. He was killed in an accident.

These were wonderful evenings, with every couple bringing a dish from their small kitchen, and the kids romping on the grass. When the children fell asleep, we put them to bed and continued the evening in one of the apartments, cracking sunflower seeds and chatting into the night, the men with the men and the women with their own interests. By today's standards we were miserably poor, but that's how it was for everybody. Our lives were on a small island detached from the world, where jet engines roared day and night until we no longer noticed them. Sometimes we went off base to the short main street of Gedera, to dine at Auntie Leah's, a shabby roadside inn run by a grumbling old woman, to chew shreds of burned rubber with onion that she insisted was steak.

The greater world around us became French, and Paris was its center. The lingo changed, and the accent. The American hits that had melted our hearts in the fifties on Radio Ramallah from Jordan ("Caroline Husseini sends her wishes to Diana Nashashibi, on her birthday, with Paul Anka in 'Diana' ") were replaced by the hoarse, smoked humor of Charles Aznavour, the sophistication of Montaigne and Edith Piaf, the lyrical choir Compagnon de la Chanson.

Ali was ready to invest a full month's salary to see Zizi Jeanmaire and Roland Petite performing in the Hall of Culture in Tel Aviv. When we managed to get places for Maurice Béjart with "The Rite of Spring" and "Bolero," we both felt on top of the world and couldn't sleep the whole night after. Money was scarce, and we stood with empty pockets eyeing mouth-watering miracles such as the newly introduced pizzas, hamburgers, or whipped Italian ice cream dispensed from a machine.

At that time there was still no television in Israel, and on Saturday evenings we all gathered and danced with romantic lighting around the record player, necking in the dark to the sounds of the Platters and the Golden Guitar, coming with "My Prayer."

Not that there were no security issues. The Syrians kept shooting at us, and even tried to divert the source of the Jordan River to dry us out. There was a lot of rapid arming of our aircraft, many ready alerts, and a lot of scrambling aloft. One time I was scrambled with a four-ship formation of Ouragans, loaded with bombs to hurry north to attack the Syrians. On the way I heard Goldie's voice on the radio—he had led four Mysteres and hit the Syrian post Khamra at the source of the Dan, a major tributary of the Jordan River. Before we could get there, too, we were called back, to our great frustration. On another occasion some Super Mysteres—Nissim and Umsh were in the bunch—had an inconclusive scuffle with some MiGs. All such events excited us. We young pilots all hoped to get a piece of the action.

We Mirage pilots had our special dream: MiGs. Every one of us was praying to his God that his MiG would appear, the one designated just for him. But at the end, one day of training followed another, and the important fight was that of the next morning, against the one comrade who shall be set against you. The wars of the mid-1960s were still in the future. The days were fair, nice days of the end of autumn, before the storms came.

Only at headquarters in Tel Aviv serious men sat, watching with somber eyes the Arab military buildup. They felt the sky darkening; they planned and worried. And somewhere in Tel Aviv, in his apartment, Yak was turning over restlessly in bed, sleep elusive. He drew from his stormy brain various ideas—some of them a bit crazy—and proposed them to his superiors, endangering his reputation and status.

At the end he stood before the commander, Ezer Weizman, and presented him with the answer.

And just like the showers of an early autumn, a small series of air battles and victories began. Each case was single, as if it were the last one. When the first ever shooting down of a MiG-21 occurred, an Israeli Mirage of the Fighting First, my squadron, did it. It happened on July 14, 1966, Bastille Day.

I was in Paris then. I met there with Peel, nicknamed Elephant, a friend from the squadron. We both were in Paris on our way back to Israel, after short courses abroad, and luckily we happened to be there on the French national holiday.

We wandered, happy and excited, on the sidewalks of Boulevard Houseman, among a large and colorful crowd streaming toward the Champs-Élysées to watch the grand military parade. Loudspeakers on the chestnut trees trumpeted military marches. We were dizzy. Paris was colorful, noisy, and tempting.

In front of the supermarket Prisunic, a small gathering crowded around a couple of hippies, a young man and a woman, who painted flowers on the ground and collected donations. Passersby threw centimes for them. In Israel you didn't see things like that. After watching, I told Peel, "I can paint better than those two."

Exactly at that time the music stopped, and a loud voice broke out over the loudspeakers, speaking with great excitement. The entire crowd froze and listened. The speaker got enthusiastic and shouted in a high-pitched, breaking voice, and suddenly everybody around began to yell and whistle. They all jumped up and down, cheered, waved their hands, hugged, and yelled. We looked around, amazed. We could identify a familiar word—

"Mirage"—over and over, but it made no sense. We looked at each other. What did all this mean? Was it a joke? What was the big deal? And all the time the hoarse voice kept shouting,"Mirage! Mirage!"

"Qu'est-ce que il dit?" We pulled the sleeve of this one and that with our basic French, and finally we understood that an Israeli Mirage fighter had just shot down a Syrian MiG-21 over the Golan Heights.

"Le Mirage is a French-made fighter," they informed us, "and the MiG-21 is the best of the Soviet industry."

"It's ours! A French fighter did it!" yelled a man in a fancy suit.

"Not an American!" cried his wife, and he spun her in a dance. Everybody around jumped and applauded. "On Bastille Day!"

Peel and I looked at each other in amazement. Who made the kill, the French? Bullshit, it was us!

"Paint it!" roared the Elephant, and so our demonstration began.

I grabbed the box of chalk from the surprised hippies and began stretching fat yellow lines along the walkway. The crowd backed under the physical pressure of the Elephant, whose name reflects his bodily measurements, and left us an elliptical space of ten or fifteen meters.

Soon the lines of the long bodies of the fighters were drawn on the pavement; the MiG in front with the Mirage sitting on his tail. I didn't bother much with scenery and clouds; general outlines were enough. On the other hand, the aircraft were painted in great detail. I spotted the Syrian MiG with brown and black and green, but the Mirage's skin glowed white and silver.

Big drops began falling from the clouds above us, but the gathering around us grew and grew. I drew from the Mirage's nose a line of yellow chalk stars hitting the MiG's fuselage. Yellow and red fire broke out with a black trail of smoke. After some thought, I drew an ejection seat from the burning cockpit, with a small pilot sitting in it.

"Mustache, mustache!" somebody in the crowd cried, and immediately a whole bunch of people joined in. The Elephant, ever responsive to the demands of the people, snatched a piece of chalk and drew on the Syrian's helmet a large black mustache, bristling in the wind. The mob cheered and applauded, women shrieked for joy, and when I added blue and white

David stars on the tail and wings of the Mirage, the money began flying and covered the picture. Our hippies hopped around us and collected notes and silver in their hats and squeezed them into their backpack.

“We could have asked for a commission, at least,” Peel scolded me when we pushed in to watch the multicolored French parade. Our work of art was already washed from the pavement by the rain, lost to humanity forever. “At least we could squeeze them for a good dinner, don’t you think? And not couscous again. Did you ever hear of Maxim’s?”

I shrugged. All I wanted was to return to the squadron and get my own MiG.

Chapter

7

Savage

One more impressive person squeezed into my life in the last months before June 1967. This was the extraordinary pilot and commander Ran Pecker.

On January 1, 1967, I was posted to the Bats—a sister Mirage squadron—together with eight other pilots of my age group who had been gathered from the rest of the fighter squadrons. We were sent there for two months to take an advanced aviation course called the senior leadership program (BBN for short). This squadron's exceptional commander, Ran, impressed me greatly, as he did the whole air force in the coming years.

The Bats was the newest among our three Mirage squadrons. It was stationed at the large base of Tel Nof, and was tasked—besides all the normal missions—with intelligence-gathering over enemy countries. The reconnaissance flights were secret, of course, but everybody knew that the Bats were crossing borders. It was the only squadron in which pilots endangered their lives almost daily. They flew deep over Egypt and Syria and brought back pictures of airfields, army units, bridges, and all kinds of installations. Their photos were making the rounds to us in the other squadrons, with the notation "taken on the date of . . ." When we filed those photographs in our target packages we could only guess which of our friends in the Bats had taken it because they would never tell.

Ran was already a legend. As a fighter pilot, and especially as a leader, he was the best of the best. He wasn't an ivory tower intellect developing theories, like Yak, nor did he have an analytical mind, like Ephraim. But he was energetic and daring, a charismatic, open man who had learned the Mirage well and who knew how to wring out of it all it had for speed, maneuvering, and range. The frequent reconnaissance operations connected him, a young lieutenant colonel, directly and daily with the gods: the air force commander, the chief of intelligence, the IDF's chief of staff, the minister of defense, and the prime minister. They all saw him frequently, and soon his name was known all over the country. He knew everyone personally, and everyone knew him. His close friends, his houseguests, were the top military men who commanded brigades and armor and paratroop corps, the leaders of special units, politicians, and spooks.

Shortly before the opening of our course, Ran had shot down a Jordanian British-made Hawker Hunter in a dogfight that, befittingly, had to have been the hardest and most dangerous in the whole history of the air force. Under his command, the Bats shone. His subordinates admired him. Other squadron commanders couldn't hide a bit of jealousy.

This was the man on whose office door we knocked.

A MAN SAT BEHIND A TABLE leafing through papers. His hair was dark blond, and on the white wall behind him hung a piece of art: a rusty triangular piece of iron, a broken blade of an Arab plow made into a Mirage silhouette.

Ran looked at us. His sharp, piercing stare was immediately replaced by a big smile, and he jumped from his seat and rounded the table to shake our eight hands. He overpowered us with captivating, physical warmth. He was not a particularly tall or large man, but on every occasion all eyes swung to him, and every ear listened to his hoarse, ringing voice. For me, this was the second time I met this rare human phenomenon of vibrant leadership, and at such volume. The first time was with my classmate at Givat-Brenner Daniel Vardon, the boy who could animate hundreds of schoolchildren and their teachers. Vardon owned this magic until, on June 8, 1967, he lost his life in the Six-Day War.

Ran also had plenty of this charisma. And right away, as we followed him to the briefing room to start the course, I noticed that all of us were imitating his sturdy, rocking gait, pushing our chests out like him. Even our voices sounded flattened, and we languished in his rolling, choking laughter.

HE PRESENTED US WITH an astounding agenda. We were going to visit all the important, secret installations and meet the key figures and leaders. We would visit and explore in detail the country and its borders. Divided into small teams, we would research and devise new combat techniques, and then fly and test them in the air. Our flights in the context of the course would not be confined to the regular air force limits. Suddenly we felt special, important.

And so it turned out. For the next couple of months Ran devoted himself and all his time and resources to our course. He opened his squadron to us as a guinea pig and research subject. In fact, he put the Bats at our disposal. And he kept his word—in the following weeks we lived in the eye of the storm, one event following another.

We were fascinated. When we went back to our homes on weekends, I went down to my own squadron, the Fighting First, and compared it to its younger sister, the Bats. True, my Fighting First also lacked nothing, but for some reason it looked faded and dusty. Sadly, I had to admit that though every category was okay—command, aircraft, technical support—and though one-on-one our pilots were no worse than the Bats', the final product was somehow less convincing. Ran's personality extracted from everybody living in his halo something extra, so that the whole was made greater than the sum of its parts. He set people in motion, he guided them, he criticized, he sometimes frightened them—he was always there. Even when he was not around, the Bats were his personification, vibrant and full of energy.

The studies were great, too. There I was exposed, for the first time, to serious discussions—led by excellent teachers—of how to run a military unit, command in battle, and lead warplanes to their targets. Colonel Motta Gur, a distinguished paratrooper who later became the IDF's chief of staff, astonished us, urging us to stand behind our opinions and not give in, even within the chain of command, even when those ideas were rejected by our leaders.

Professors of psychology engaged us on the phenomenon of fear and discussed ways to deal with it. Senior civilian managers came to talk to us about their experience in personnel management.

Ran went nonstop. He strove to put us through every possible experience in the short time he had. Some days we flew or went traveling along the borders on foot and in jeeps. In the evenings we didn't go home: he dragged us out ("You can sleep on Saturday," he would say with a snarl) to join police patrols in the underworld of Jaffa, for a bowling lesson in Haifa, to take a sauna in Beer-Sheva, or for a fancy dinner on a ship in Haifa Harbor. Or he would send us to drag our wives out of the house and head together to the Singing Bamboo nightclub for an evening of dancing. Everything, everywhere, was free of charge. Everybody knew Ran and was glad to serve him, and we just blossomed in his shade. Only after midnight did we arrive home with ringing ears to read the stuff for tomorrow, prepare a project, write, or rehearse. Ran cast a spell on us all, and we all loved it.

In addition, there was the flying. Here also, promises were kept to the letter. We took off in twos and fours and went out to check the ideas and methods we invented. All the shooting ranges and training facilities were at our disposal, all the flight areas evacuated for our course. Scarce munitions were given freely to us. And in any formation where Ran flew, usually manning the rear aircraft, you could expect surprises.

"Idle your engine!" he would suddenly order, and the designated pilot had to pull up and look for a place for a forced landing, and always find one far away that could be reached only by planning and finesse. When Ran was around, the air hummed with energy. He was a dangerous and surprising guy, and we were constantly on guard. He kept teaching us his motto that the only proof of a fighter is his results. In his words, "The courage and integrity of a warrior are measured by the number of holes in the target."

On January 31, 1967, we went down to the squadron for some night flying. This was to be one of the special flights of the BBN course. The plan was to take off from Tel Nof in pairs and navigate south to the southernmost city of Eilat, and from there at low level over the Red Sea to the limit of the Mirage's range. The mission was to do a sea search in the dark, locate and record all ships.

This mission had immediate relevance: just two weeks before, Ran and I—we were together in the ready room of the Bats—were scrambled down to the Red Sea to attack a Saudi vessel that had opened fire on a Israeli ship some fifty kilometers south of Eilat. We reached the place at dusk and found a small black boat chugging after a fat, white whale of a ship. The plump lady was by far faster, and fled leaving a long white wake behind her in the dark sea. Our flight ended when we buzzed the black leech a few times and finally convinced it to give up the chase and point its bow back toward the Saudi coast.

Then an operational question was asked: how to defend Israeli shipping in our southern port at night? How do you find vessels in the dark? The BBN course was certainly the right laboratory, and this was going to be the first test. The night that was selected for it was during a full moon. But the choice of this night was not lucky. Deep winter lay over the country; strong winds blew, rain fell, and all the roads were awash, and all the time lightning flared and thunder boomed.

During the preflight briefing we looked at each other skeptically. The IAF of the 1960s didn't fly in such conditions, especially not at night. We thought, when the briefing was over, that we would get a night off.

Then Ran took the floor. "What if it were wartime?" he asked us.

I LED THE FIRST PAIR. We took off in close formation, and after wheels up Yoeli, my wingman, stuck close by, our aircraft just a few meters apart. Together we burrowed into the clouds. Inside, the air was dark, turbulent, and unstable, and my Mirage pitched and yawed. In the mirror above my head I could see the dim lights of Yoeli's ship dancing close on my left wing, blurring and brightening at times together with the thickness of the black fog. We passed through spurts of rain and hail, and I increased the intensity of my running lights to the maximum, to help Yoeli see me. Then I focused on my flight instruments.

I knew that Yoeli could not take his eyes off me for a split second, lest he lose me in the dark. He had put his trust in me. I had to get him through this soup. I was his compass, his artificial horizon, and his aerial speedometer. Wherever I went, he went, too. As we climbed, conditions worsened. Our two Mirages bumped along and made noise. We were going through a storm, and my hands on the controls were aching from excessive pressure. Yet I felt a mix of anxiety and pride in myself and in Yoeli, who held on and kept tight with me all the way up. I knew well that he also—just like me—was pushing out of his mind any thought of Khativa. In the group picture at the flying school, air cadet Khativa stood between Yoeli and myself.

At last, at thirty thousand feet the world cleared and we broke out into a clear, bright night. A lonely, cold moon bathed us in white light. We breathed deeply, postponing for now the question of the return to base. Yoeli slipped away from my wing into a looser formation, and we both gazed across the expanse that spread beneath us to the horizon. The cloud tops were like white and fantastic mountain ranges washed by moonlight. From time to time bubbles of yellow electric light inflated inside their huge masses in crazy spasms, vibrated for some moments, and were gone.

I checked my chronometer, got out a map, and set up to continue the mission. First I had to find the Red Sea. Just as I was getting ready I heard nervous, rapid chatter on the radio. I froze to listen.

Somebody asked, “What’s that?”

Another voice broke in, “Horizon! Watch your artificial horizon!”

The first voice returned—now I recognized it as ZBB—and in complete tranquillity he said, “It’s all right now.”

We waited in silence, and I do not know whether the short flash we both saw to the north was a flash of lightning that lit the clouds from inside, or ZBB’s Mirage as it hit the ground under them. The lights of Eilat flickered beneath us through a hole in the clouds. The second voice was now on the air, shocked. It couldn’t stop talking.

I pulled Yoeli back on my wing, and we turned for home.

For us from the thirty-first class, ZBB was the fourth casualty from the fifteen young men who had stood at attention to get their wings (two more were devoured earlier by the Harvard trainer), and the wars hadn't even begun yet. This was a high price to pay, but by no means unusual.

Training accidents and losses were viewed at the time as a necessary evil, just a part of becoming a fighter pilot, and not as a plague that must be eradicated. And though accidents might occur—friends auger in, collide in the air, spin out from vertigo—this was their contribution to the defense of Israel. This way I accepted, like all my friends, the disappearance of Khativa in the Mediterranean, Yakir's crash in the Sea of Galilee right under my nose, and today, the loss of Zur Ben Barak in the clouds behind me. That's life. What can be done about it? Hope for the best.

Believing this, I was stunned to meet somebody who thought otherwise and who was not scared of saying it loud and clear to his commander's face and the whole world. This happened early on, while we were still juniors in the Scorpions, flying Super Mysteres. Umsh passed through a flock of birds, and his engine choked. He punched out and parachuted to earth. As he was brought safe and sound back to the squadron, we all crowded around him to hear what happened. Then we were happy to see our squadron commander write in the accident report as expected: "Accident caused by force of nature."

Captain Yozef Salant raised his hand and remarked, "It's the pilot's fault."

We all were stunned. Birds—what can you do about that?

"What, my fault?" asked Umsh. "How's that? We flew in high speed, in formation, and how on Earth could I see those goddamn small chicks?" All looked at Yozef in dismay. He wasn't a guy who entered a quarrel lightly.

Salant asked, "Umshweiff, is the aircraft guilty?"

"No."

"Are the birds?"

"Of course not, but—"

"So who's left?"

Umsh spat out angrily, "Some people here are assholes. What should I do when the exercise requires high-speed flying where there are birds?"

"Who told you to fly at high speed with birds around?"

"The commander said—"

"Then the commander is guilty," said Salant in the voice of a teacher who had just written the solution on the blackboard. We looked at him, but it took all of us a long time to get the message.

Zur Ben Barak was buried with us standing at attention among the cypress trees at the cemetery of Hanita, his kibbutz. We listened to the singing of the shovels and spades and the lumps of dirt falling upon his coffin, each of us thinking thoughts like well, now we've buried ZBB, too. Yael, his young wife, wept, holding their baby girl. Itamar, his father, stood bent over the grave of his first son. The grave was filled, and each of us stole a look at the others: Who's next?

What could we do, anyway? Vertigo had beaten Zur, nobody was guilty but he himself, right? So that night we celebrated on the deck of a ship in Haifa Harbor. The next morning we got up and returned to Tel Nof, to continue our training.

FOR THE END OF THE BBN COURSE—one of the best experiences I ever had as a pilot—Ran saved the best for last. We went through a series of discussions and workshops on battle command and leadership.

The climax came when the old American movie *Twelve O'Clock High* was screened for us. This film tells the story of an American bomber squadron in World War II, stationed in England and flying missions over Germany. The squadron is crumbling from the pressure of long flights over enemy territory, through punishing ack-ack and relentless Messerschmitts. One bomber after another is shot down; in each of them a crew of ten die or become prisoners of war.

The squadron sinks into self-pity and accusations against a high command that continues to order more "suicide missions." The commander finally breaks down, and is unable to continue sending his men into battle. Just then, when the squadron is on the verge of ceasing to be a fighting unit, Gregory Peck appears. The tall, dark, handsome hero takes over and saves the day. His name in the film is appropriately Frank Savage.

Savage volunteers to replace the ailing commander. But first he shakes up his men, putting them through training until under his stinging whip they get back the right order of things, forget the whining and remember the mission, the bombsight, and their profession. As Savage promised them on his arrival, they begin to fear him more than the Messerschmitts. And then Savage goes again into the heart of Germany, leading his men into the lethal ack-ack and Nazi fighters. His personal example and leadership have raised the squadron from the dead and put it back on its feet.

Ran's eyes shone when he taught us this subject. From this film he singled out for us all the components of battle: the situation factor and the team factor. He pointed out for us the signs of fear and disintegration, and showed us the tools in the quiver of the good commander to remedy them. And he underlined the key role of the commander's personality: the leadership factor. Ran Pecker was wonderful and convincing. We gazed starry-eyed into the complicated world he opened for us. Each of us admitted after this lesson that it had been Frank Savage himself talking to us at Tel Nof.

After this lesson I, too, for the first time, wanted to command people and be a leader.

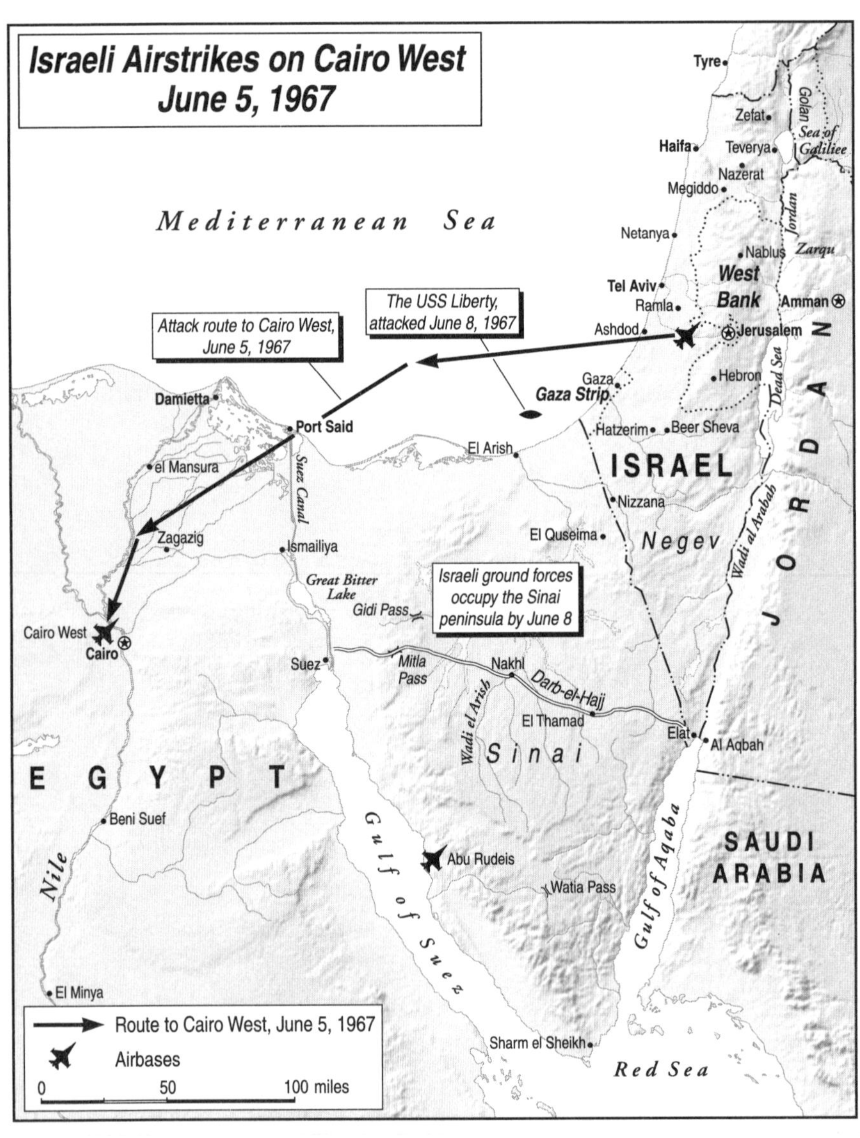

Israeli Airstrikes on Cairo West
June 5, 1967
Mediterranean Sea
Attack route to Cairo West, June 5, 1967
The USS Liberty, attacked June 8, 1967
Israeli ground forces occupy the Sinai peninsula by June 8
Tyre
Zefat
Haifa
Teverya
Sea of Galilee
Golan
Nazerat
Megiddo
Jordan
Netanya
Nablus
Zarqu
Tel Aviv
West Bank
Ramla
Amman
Ashdod
Jerusalem
Gaza
Hebron
Gaza Strip
Dead Sea
Damietta
Port Said
Hatzerim
Beer Sheva
El Arish
ISRAEL
el Mansura
Suez Canal
Nizzana
JORDAN
Zagazig
Ismailiya
El Quseima
Negev
Wadi al Arabah
Great Bitter Lake
Gidi Pass
Cairo West
Cairo
Suez
Mitla Pass
Nakhl
Darb-el-Hajj
El Thamad
Wadi el Arish
Elat
Al Aqbah
Sinai
EGYPT
Beni Suef
Gulf of Suez
Gulf of Aqaba
SAUDI ARABIA
Nile
Abu Rudeis
Watia Pass
El Minya
Route to Cairo West, June 5, 1967
Airbases
Sharm el Sheikh
Red Sea
0
50
100 miles

Chapter

8

Operation Focus

SUNDAY, JUNE 4, 1967. Tomorrow, the six most fateful days of our lives begin.

All through the weeks before, the sword of Damocles hung over us. On the fourth of June, the sword swayed and jangled in the wind and we covered our heads. To the ground and air skirmishes that had occurred along the Syrian border, a Soviet provocation was added: for their own reasons, the Soviets put it about that Israel was preparing to go to war with Syria. The Syrians became frightened, the Egyptians vowed to defend their Arab brothers, and the whole thing started rolling downhill.

On May 17, while I was on a regular training flight, the controller suddenly called for an immediate return to base. The air force's readiness was raised. Back at the squadron we were told that a large Egyptian force had just moved into the Sinai Peninsula—an area that had been demilitarized since we evacuated it in 1956—and was advancing toward our southwestern border. Soon Jordan joined the Syrian and Egyptian military alliance, and the three were preparing their armies for a coordinated attack on us, from three sides.

Jordan posed the most immediate danger. The Jordanian army threatened to descend from Judea and Samaria, which protruded like a wedge into Israel's narrow waist, and by advancing to the sea, cut the country in two. The Jordanian Arab Legion was parked just a few kilometers from the sea. And in the North the Syrians also mobilized in their fortifications. They waited in the mountains overlooking the Sea of Galilee.

But the largest and strongest enemy, the engine of the Arab juggernaut, was Egypt. It was a big country and especially important in the Middle East. Egyptian dictator Gamal Abdel Nasser called back his armed forces from Yemen, where they had been conducting their own colonial war, to take part in the war against Israel. These forces brought back with them their Russian jet bombers. These were not tactical aircraft; they carried heavy bomb loads, and their targets couldn't be anything but cities such as Tel Aviv and Jerusalem. We knew that these bombers had already dropped poison gas on civilian populations. And on the ground, Gen. Saad Shazli's elite Egyptian division entered the Sinai and plunked itself down on our border.

The secretary of the UN, U Thant, acceded to Nasser's demands and timidly withdrew his team of observers, which until that time had supervised the partition lines between Egypt and Israel since the 1956 cease-fire. This action removed the last obstacle to an Egyptian attack on Israel. With success, Nasser got even more belligerent and blocked the Strait of Tiran—an international waterway—to Israeli shipping. When Israel turned to the UN and the United States of America and asked them to open the strait in a lawful, peaceful way, it was fobbed off with promises in spite of explicit treaty obligations made after the 1956 war. Our ambassador, Minister of Exterior Abba Eban, ran around begging, but no country was ready to take any form of action on our behalf. The French declared an embargo on arms to the Middle East that actually was against us.

Egypt had special influence and importance, and now its threats stoked the Arab world into orgasmic enthusiasm. Arab radio stations screamed hysterically for the annihilation of Israel. Newspapers showed pictures of columns of tanks rolling down Cairo streets on their way to battle, and battalions of paratroopers marched by on their way to Tel Aviv. The Arabs were aroused; their time to avenge their defeats in 1948 and 1956 had come! Finish off the Jewish state!

‡

Confronted with all this, the government of Israel sputtered and stammered. We seemed to have no answers to the dramatic developments. We, the Israeli people, listened with growing alarm.

In the first days of June, Israel was terrified, trenches were dug everywhere, and it became clear to us in the air force that war was coming. When and how it would start—those were the questions.

We sat for long hours in our cockpits, and occasionally were scrambled against Egyptian MiGs that crossed our southern border at high altitude. We achieved no results. Evenings, we stayed at the squadron until late and went over mission plans, especially for an operation named Focus. We studied intelligence data and maps over and over. I was just a Mirage pilot, captain, leader of a four-ship division, and third in command of the Fighting First, Lt. Col. Amos Lapidot commanding. I was just a junior actor watching uneasily the rapid unfolding of events around me, and sometimes feeling that my government was botching the defense of my country.

President Nasser of Egypt appeared before the media on a visit to the military airfield Bir Gafgafa in the Sinai. From there, laughing, he threw down the gauntlet. "If Israel wants war, *Ahlen weShalen* [welcome]."

I remember that famous photograph of Nasser's visit to Bir-Gafgafa. In the center Nasser and his chief of staff, General Ammer, were sitting wearing well-decorated military uniforms. Their mouths were open in roaring, exultant laughter. Their pilots surrounded them, squeezing to get close to their leaders. In the center of the picture, close to the generals, a young and very handsome man stood. He was a pilot in a full pressure suit, not just a flight suit. His hands were folded over his rugged chest. His dark face was square and intelligent, his hair short and thick. He smiled slightly at the camera.

When this picture was published in the newspapers, I studied it for long time and tried to imagine the hopes and dreams that hid behind that broad brow. I couldn't avoid seeing in my mind's eye my own home and family, and the kibbutzim I grew up in. I gave this man a name: Hassan.

Many times since then I have imagined Hassan's face in the cockpits of the MiGs that fought against me.

‡

On the night of the fourth of June our squadron commander, Amos Lapidot, called me to his office. Outside on the balcony there was no light. The darkness of the moonless night was total. We checked again all the maps and plans. On Amos's order, I opened a sealed envelope and handed the technical chief the Focus specifications for arming our aircraft. Soon lights lit up in all the underground hangars, and the mechanics, who had lived, eaten, and slept there all the past week, began loading the Mirages with bombs. At midnight, when nothing was left for me to do at the squadron, I returned home. In base housing they already sensed that something was cooking. All the houses shed thin lines of light from the blacked-out windows, doors opened and slammed, women ran across lawns to each other's homes.

I found Ali and our three-year-old packed and ready for evacuation. Ali didn't say anything to me, but I could see in her eyes the certainty of war. I couldn't help her with any added information. I took a shower, scrubbing myself several times with hot water, soaping two or three times. I shaved in both directions and put on aftershave lotion. I changed underwear and prepared a clean flight suit and new socks. I even sat down to shine my flying boots.

We went to bed. Ali didn't sleep, passing the time biting her nails. And inside me, anxiety grew. Something roiled my stomach constantly, like convulsions. Suddenly, like a fool, I scolded Ali to stop fussing and let me sleep. She froze.

I had a few short bouts of dreamless dozing. Finally I got up. I brushed my teeth once and again, anointed my toes with antifungus cream, and scattered talcum on them. When I came out of the bathroom, nobody was moving in the silent house; only my son breathed quietly in his bed. I went out on tiptoes and closed the door silently behind me.

In the fresh air outside I heard the deep sound of truck engines. Vehicles were parking near the movie theater. I was sure that very soon the families would be awakened and evacuated somewhere. This day, June 5, 1967, I didn't think of Ali and Etay anymore.

‡

It was five o'clock in the morning, and the headquarters of the Fighting First was dark. We all gathered in the briefing room, and this time the base commander, Col. Benny Peled, also was in the room. The morning flight program was written in chalk on the blackboard, business as usual, but it had over it a big headline in capital letters: "Operation Focus. Zero hour—0745."

All the targets were airfields in Egypt. The fog of the last weeks lifted. Now everything was clear.

I peered around and saw that some of my friends were still uncertain. Slapak sent an uncertain smile in my direction: Wasn't this just another drill? Would we be stopped before we get on the runway and sent back to the hangars? I shook my head. I had just returned from the hangars for a last check. All our aircraft were armed and fully fueled, and most significantly, the operational fuses had been taken out of their boxes and screwed into the bombs' bodies and noses. There was no going back now. This time there would be a fight. At long last our government had gotten it together and decided. From now on it was all in our hands.

Amos concluded his short briefing with "good luck." Benny Peled also said a few words. We all left. On the walk to the hangars, bellies grumbled. Fighter pilots waited in a long line, safety gear on their shoulders, for a visit to the bathroom.

The sun was up. Dozens of fighter aircraft—arrow-nosed Mirages, chubby Super Mysteres, barrel-bodied Ouragans—were parked around the runway, engines whining. Everybody was waiting for his own time and the green light to climb in and take off. At 0700 the first afterburner was lit: Sever took off first, collected his division of four, and faded into the distance going south. They opened the attack. We would pass over them, striking deeper into Egypt. Now everybody was thinking, "What is waiting for us on the way? How will we break through to the target?"

But most of all, "How will I behave at the moment of truth?"

Desk flight was called. We were a three-ship division—not enough aircraft to make four, but never mind. We lined up on the runway. Fortunately, the pain in my gut had passed. This was an encouraging sign, and now I was sure I would be okay. Throttles forward, racing down the runway, wheels up, and we joined up and crossed the coast, going west, out to sea, flying low and practically parting the waves along the lengthy leg westward. Once "feet wet," each of us flicked on the armament switches in his own time. There were neither orders nor reminders on the communications channel; all was silent. Our radio sets were switched off to prevent any possibility of noise that might warn the enemy of our approach. Now we could not be stopped by anyone.

After some long minutes at sea we turned left and crossed a foreign beach. We flew very fast and low, forming a triangle: Maj. Oded Marom in the front and Yair Neumann and I spread behind at the other two points, guarding our six o'clock, our backs. At first we passed over sand and salt flats, and here and there shallow marshes. Waterfowl fled before us on pink wings. To the right, a white tower stuck up over the dunes. The map said this should be Port Said, the northern entrance of the Suez Canal. We looked forward, and suddenly white cones jumped out from the sands, white sails. A second of wonder, and then the Suez Canal passed under us: a thin line of water, many boats, a big ship trailing smoke, the iron grating of a bridge.

Marom corrected our direction, and we accelerated to even higher speed. Now we were flush over the delta of the Nile. Green and brown fields seeded with people and beasts, groups of palms, water tunnels. Villages, mud huts standing on barren circles of land like ant mounds. Minarets, checkered black or red stone. In the squares, people crowded, their faces turned up: our predecessors had awakened them. In the sky above us remnants of morning clouds shed a mix of light and shade on them and on us. We raced on, now at full throttle.

I looked backward: Neumann was in place. No MiGs; our six was clean. So—here we go. Just a few more minutes to the target.

The last, short leg. The target was very near. Full power, maximum speed now. We streaked among the sand hills of the Western Desert. Beyond the hills in front of us a large black pillar of smoke was rising. This was it, the target! Our predecessors had left their mark. They had just finished, and left the area free for us. Another look backward: nothing. A flutter of disbelief. Where is the enemy?

Top! Target in sight.

We pulled up, and instantly the large military airfield of Cairo West spread under us. The concrete and asphalt runways were flat on the sand, like in a painting. On the field's circumference fiery stakes burned, throwing up dirty flames and enormous pillars of black smoke. The pillars climbed fast and expanded above like huge mushrooms, creating dark shadows over the field. These great fires were enemy planes our predecessors had already lit up. It was clear now. The Egyptian bombers were caught full of fuel, ready to take off.

From altitude we rolled over and dove along the axis of the runway. I was full of cool and pleasant purpose, neither rage nor battle joy. Just a calm, straight dive until the runway filled my gun sight like a long, black strip, broadening as I went lower. Exactly at the right height and on target I gave the bombs button a nice, long press. The aircraft rocked; bang one, bang two, and it was over: two half-ton bombs released and gone to earth. I pulled up and out of the dive. Good. The runway passing under me was blocked; no takeoffs today. And now to more exact work: my cannons.

I expanded the radius of my turn and moved away from Marom, to open some working space for Neumann and myself. We all spread out to get some distance from the airfield, very fast and low, and when we were lost in the distance, hidden among the hills, we toggled switches from "bombs" to "guns" and prepared the gun sight for a strafing run. When all was ready, we turned back and returned to the burning hell.

The place actually looked like hell. The great smoke pillars, and the shadows of the cloudy "treetops" above, showed from far away like a huge, dark jungle. Only a few rays of the sun penetrated from the eastern side among the huge trunks, painting marks of gold here and there. Kerosene fires belched red, sending black and white balloons among the bellows of the blacksmith's fantastic shop.

Marom pulled up in front of me, rolling high over my head, and dove in. I followed him through the smoke, and found a Tupolev 16 bomber, its tail sticking up between the walls of a revetment. There it stood, the size of a Boeing 707, but longer, narrower, and painted dark green. It looked like a lizard. The sun glinted off Marom's Mirage two or three times and then he vanished into the shadows and smoke.

My turn. I pulled up, leading Neumann in. Each of us was looking to get a Tupolev. A tall tail peered through the columns of smoke and I jerked my aircraft sharply once left and right, and the bomber was exposed. Under the black clouds darkening the whole airport, it all felt strange, like winter. I dove toward my prey. Slowly and patiently I walked my gun sight's pipper up and into the large aircraft. There. Hold it. Fasten and lock the pip exactly on the wing root. When the range became short enough and the bomber loomed large in my windshield, I gave the trigger a long, gentle squeeze. Sparks flitted about the nearer wing, crossed the center of the fuselage, and continued onto the other wing. Suddenly, point-blank range. The Tupolev was enormous in my windshield. I stopped firing and pulled out hard. When I passed over the bomber, a big explosion and a belch of oily fire knocked me and my Mirage upward, banging my head twice on my Plexiglas canopy.

I cleared the smoke out to the sunny, clear air. On my way around I could see the bonfire I had started. My tree of black smoke was still young and slim and black, but it was definitely a healthy plant. It grew fast and surely would continue to grow and become a respectable tree for President Nasser to see, no less so than the others in the area. Ignoring streams of ack-ack sent in my direction by a brave antiaircraft gun position, I passed through them untouched and proudly added another smoke tree to the growing garden.

All along the way through the Nile delta, we cruised among tall towers of smoke. From Inshas and Abu-Zweir in the delta, from Kabrit on the Suez Canal, and from other, more distant military airfields. We rejoiced. Israel was no longer under threat by long-range Soviet bombers.

On the way home, from altitude, I could see dust rising on the border between the Sinai and the Negev. That meant that ground battle had begun, too.

On my landing approach to Hatzor, the base looked odd: two Super Mysteres were stuck with their noses in the mud on both sides of the runway, and one Ouragan was lying near the control tower in a pile of dirt, blocking the last section of runway. I understood: not everyone got home untouched.

"Request clearance for the other runway, please."

"The other one is even worse, Desk. You are clear to land."

"What a Zikago," I mumbled to myself, deploying my braking parachute just off the ground, braking hard, and making it to a stop just before the pile of dirt, clearing the runway at the halfway point.

When I shut my engine off in the hangar, the mechanics pulled me out of the cockpit, going nuts: "Where were you? What did you do? Speak up, man!"

"It was all right," I answered them, knowing very little. For the past hour I had been caged in my cockpit, seeing only details without the big picture. The mechanics, on the other hand, were full of confusing information. The radio transmitted news. It seems that things were going well with Egypt, but there were rumors of casualties, especially in the Scorpions. On the squadron balcony I saw Ilan Gonen's face go pale: he already heard names of friends. Someone waved to advise that Yak shot down a MiG. I was amazed: I didn't know the old wolf was back from his year of studies in America.

That was how the noose around our neck was removed. The continuation of the war went like a dream. In the following days our enemies around us crumbled one after another. The radio reporter went nuts when East Jerusalem was taken. I shed real tears, together with all the mechanics around me, when thc hangar loudspeakers trumpeted the voice of the paratroopers' brigade commander, Col. Motta Gur: "the Western Wall is in our hands."

Operation Focus, the demolishing of enemy airfields that had opened the Six-Day War and determined its military outcome, was extraordinary in military history because it was a tactical operation that had strategic significance.

Focus had a tactical goal: to abolish the aerial threat to Israel and secure air superiority for the continuation of the war on the ground. But unintentionally, Focus had achieved a strategic result: victory in the war.

Why did this happen? Because Focus struck directly through the pupil of the eye of the enemy, right at the symbols of his power. The enormous bonfires that flared all over Egypt were seen in Cairo, the Suez Canal, and in the fields of Sinai. They gave each Egyptian soldier and citizen an astounding answer, sharp and merciless, to the bombastic boasting of their leaders. The successful neutralizing of the Arab air forces was much less important to the results of the 1967 war than the theatrical effect the lighting of these fires achieved. Into the arrogant, inflated show President Nasser staged, the Israeli Air Force broke in, kicked ass, flattened the set, and deflated the balloon.

To be sure, one must not fake such a performance. The drama is in danger of becoming a comedy (or a tragedy, depending on the viewer). And the greatness of the genius scriptwriter Yak and the outstanding directors Maj. Gen. Moti Hod and Cols. Rafi Sivron and Rafi Harlev and their assistants, came through here: the lightning flashed at the right place and the thunder roared on cue, and all the lines were recited correctly by us actors. Within three hours the Middle East was on fire, and the audience was left open-mouthed in their chairs.

Yak and his men never imagined that they were producing theater. But it was the theatrical effect that dismantled the Egyptian government and its army, led to Nasser's resignation, and sent General Shazli's division running home without shoes, even before it bumped into Israel's ground forces. True, our armor and infantry had much pounding and crushing left to do, but they fought against an enemy who already lost his spirit, and his command and control systems were disintegrating at all levels. The fall of Egypt led to the crumbling of Syria and Jordan, which were hit less severely.

And this strategic performance—taking an enemy state and army and taking it apart in one aerial strike—wasn't planned at all. The possibility wasn't even in the minds of the planners and commanders. The greatest achievement of Focus came completely by accident.

Like Saul, the first king of Israel, we searched for donkeys and found the throne.

‡

The cost of Focus was not cheap. In the 490 sorties of this operation, we lost twenty aircraft. This was a casualty rate of more than 4 percent per sortie, a price four times higher than what the military world sees as acceptable. And indeed this number was put on the table in full knowledge that there was only one chance. The windlass of fate turned, and when it stopped, the gamble was successful: twenty pilots dead; one country saved.

And it should be clear that in this case it was really a gamble. The success of Operation Focus depended totally on fair weather, absolute surprise, and perfect data. The existence of all three conditions was far from certain. In fact, the launch of Focus was a challenge to fate.

Suppose, for instance, that we had chosen to attack at an earlier hour in the morning. There were officers who argued that we should attack the Egyptians at dawn, a more conventional hour, instead of 0745, as was actually done. Then the plan would have failed totally. When our first attacking formations arrived over their objectives, several airfields in the Nile delta had been partly hidden by low clouds, and the targets were almost completely concealed from above. Some of the first leaders had had difficulty finding their targets, and others in attacking them. But as things happen in the Middle East, the skies cleared fast, and the following waves of attackers had no difficulty getting the job done.

Another bet, no less dangerous, was on absolute surprise. The last week before the war the enemy was at peak readiness. Had he learned of our coming—or just had he raised the alert level—the MiGs would have been in the air in time. In this case, each of us would have had to fight his way in. Had this been the case, the results would have been totally different, and surely the demolition of our opponent's air force wouldn't have ended in three hours, if anytime at all. The war would have proceeded very differently.

And the greatest gamble of all was certainly the reliance on intelligence. Our maps showed us, the attacking pilots, where each enemy aircraft was parked. When we got there, we found them all in place. All was frozen; the intelligence map was static, a "dead" map. If, on the other hand, the Egyptians had kept moving their bombers among distant airfields, and kept a considerable part of their fighter force in the air, patrolling, then we would have found the airfields empty of targets (an ugly experience that awaited me in the next war— more on that later).

None of this actually happened. The Egyptians thought of their deployment as if it were a chess game. They set up their pawns for the big attack and waited. Our knight, in turn, jumped and struck. And as fate would have it, the move we had been planning for years beforehand, Focus, worked out better than all expectations. To the amazement of all, the king himself was on the square where our knight landed.

Our air force couldn't do much more than that. After this amazing solo display, Focus, the enemy had no way to tell that this was the last show in our air force's repertoire. But the fact was we had no other convincing acts up our sleeve.

And on second thought, perhaps every addition Israel made to Focus was superfluous.

Chapter

9

The Black Flag and the USS *Liberty*

Kafr-Kassem: In October 1956, at the opening of the Sinai campaign, a curfew was ordered in the Israeli Arab villages. The beginning of the curfew was at five in the afternoon, and the village heads were notified only half an hour before. The Arab farmers who went out to the fields on that morning naturally didn't know about the curfew.

Battalion commander Major Malinky was called to his brigade commander, Colonel Shadmi, and ordered to "shoot to kill" every violator of the curfew. To the question of what about those returning from the fields without knowing about the curfew, Shadmi answered, "May Allah have mercy on them."

Malinky passed the order to the platoon commanders. The commanders listened, but only one of them, Lieutenant Dehan, followed the order. His company massacred civilians from Kafr-Kassem, on the pretext that they had violated the curfew. According to the company commander's report, returning villagers were stood in line and shot in cold blood. Forty-three people were killed, including old men, women, and children.

The soldiers were court-martialed and argued that they just followed orders. This was the same argument given by Nazi criminals accused in trials at Nuremberg. The court, headed by Judge Benjamin Halevy, determined that the order was manifestly unlawful, an order that must not be obeyed. All involved were found guilty. Colonel Shadmi was fined one cent. Major Malinky got seventeen years in prison, Lieutenat Dehan fifteen, and each of the soldiers seven. They were all released before November 1959.

On the fourth day of the Six-Day War, my two-ship section, code-named Kursa, was sent to patrol over the Suez Canal. My wingman was Lieutenant Y. The Mirage fighter I flew had been armed for aerial combat with one Matra 530 air-to-air, French-made heavy missile, and two 30mm cannons with antiaircraft explosive rounds.

On our way westward I observed again, as in the morning, a big ship cruising off El-Arish, an Egyptian town on the Sinai coast where battles were still taking place. And again, as in the morning, I reported it to central control. This ship stood out like a sore thumb in the empty sea, and every pilot who passed had reported her, so I was not surprised when there was no particular reaction to my report. We continued to the west, looking for some MiG activity.

For a time we circled over the Suez Canal with nothing happening, and then we got a call from air control. The controller ordered us to leave our patrol area and go check the identity of a ship that was sailing off El-Arish. It was instantly clear that the vessel was the same one we had seen before; it was the only ship around. So we turned north and headed out to sea, and after some vectoring I saw her again in the distance. I set my wingman in a swept-back formation and approached her.

A ship's identity can be checked in one of three ways: by identifying her profile, by identification of signs she displays (such as flags), or through radio communication. Control passed us through to the general maritime radio channel, but those who answered us on it were from the Israeli Navy. This ship never answered any radio calls. So we approached her from astern, and began circling to check her out.

Although there was no other object around for reference, the ship seemed pretty large to me. She was gray, and looked to me like a military vessel. The profile of the ship was totally unfamiliar to me. Before the war we had studied all the enemy vessels, like the Soviet Skury destroyers the Egyptian Navy operated, as well as others. But this one was definitely not one of those.

I began transmitting its physical description to air control and the navy. I was hoping that they might have something in their manuals to help with the identification. I described the shape of the hull, the lines of the forward superstructure, stacks, and mast. Most of all, I was looking for the sea-to-air recognition sign of our Israeli Navy. That sign was a large red "X" in a white square. It should have been painted all over the upper deck, to be seen clearly from the air.

I saw no such mark. But other signs weren't found either. Above the ship protruded a chimney, a mast, and some antennae. Both of us—Lieutenant Y. and myself—searched for flags or signals but saw nothing. As pilots, we both had excellent vision, at least twenty-twenty. To get a better look, I reduced my airspeed to 350 knots—a lower than optimal operational speed, and unsafe in wartime. Then I approached the ship even closer, carefully. I was concerned, and kept a safe distance from that ship—several hundred meters—because I had no idea what kind of antiaircraft measures she had.

The conversations between the air controller and me lasted for five to six minutes, in which time we made two full circles of the vessel. At last I finished my description and waited for orders. Finally I heard, "Kursa flight leader, if you are certain that this is a military vessel, you are cleared to attack."

"Roger." But I was still not sure.

I sent my wingman to fly high cover, and I came in low and flew parallel to the right side of the ship. Only then did I see the lettering "CTR-5" on its side. I spelled it to air control. "Charlie Tango Roger five."

To me this meant nothing. This wasn't a name in any language I knew. It seemed just a serial number, like the number 73 on the tail of my Mirage. This convinced me that this was indeed a military vessel. The letters were not in Hebrew, so it was not one of ours.

Later I was to learn that I had made a mistake in reading the letters. Another pilot, who came after I left, read it as "GTR-5." I don't know if misreading the letter G for C had any effect on what followed.

Then air control came back on, and he sounded more confident. "This ship has been in action against our forces in El-Arish. She is disengaging to the west." He went on to give the order, "Attack her and stop her."

From my point of view, there was no problem. We were at war, and for the past days I had been attacking enemy vehicles and installations and setting them on fire. This ship was certainly a military vessel, and she didn't have Israeli markings. And this part of the Mediterranean Sea was in the heart of the battle zone, bordered only by Israel and Egypt. It was clear as daylight that the controller who had commanded me to attack knew who she was, and why she should be stopped in place. And this is exactly what I was going to do.

The only problem was technical: how do you stop a ship that big? I was sorry we weren't carrying bombs. A half-ton bomb would surely have stopped the ship, and perhaps even have sunk her. But we were armed only for aerial combat. For a moment I even considered launching our Matra missiles at her. The French radar-guided missile had a thirty-five-kilogram warhead, in itself a small bomb. But I changed my mind. The Matra was a rare and expensive weapon designed for shooting down aircraft. So all I had left were our guns.

Here I had a problem, too: 30mm cannon rounds are just like fireworks hitting the steel side of a ship. But 30mm rounds are like small hand grenades, and their shrapnel can hit people and installations on the ship's decks. The two Mirages in my flight had four cannons, 125 rounds in each. Five hundred rounds are at least something; they can inflict considerable damage on the surface of the target. I was hoping we could at least harry her—prevent her from getting away. And during this delay, another, properly equipped force might come up and finish the job.

I came in first, my wingman following. Each of us attacked the ship two or three times. I did a good job, and the bursts from my 30mm cannons strafed the deck and superstructure. I saw my rounds exploding, and streams of fragments and splinters flew off the ship and into the water beside her and turned it white, like spray from a fountain. Even before we were out of ammunition, smoke was rising from the ship. It was my impression that we had slowed her down.

That was all I could do. All four cannons were empty, and we left the ship and returned to base, satisfied with our attempt to delay her escape.

This sad story had one small coda, not a thing that would have interested the investigators who questioned me a few weeks later. Just something a person like me keeps deep inside. And today, in retrospect, perhaps that was a mistake.

When we landed back at Hatzor and went down the stairs to the Fighting First's underground operations room to report and receive our next assignment, the officer of the day, Lt. Col. David Ivry, met me with a strange expression on his face. He had been managing the squadron's missions during the past hour.

He said to me, "Spector, you attacked a ship."

"Yes, sir!" I was pretty proud of myself.

"For your information, you made a mistaken identification. The ship was one of ours."

What?

For a moment I thought this was just an ugly joke. But David Ivry—a man who later became commander of the Israeli Air Force—was not the joking kind. I saw from his face that he was not kidding. I was stunned. I needed time to pull myself together.

I let my flight gear slip to the ground and left the room. I climbed up the stairs and found myself on the outside balcony, darkness before my eyes even though it was full daylight. I ended up somehow at the end of the building, across from the restrooms. I entered and locked the door behind me. There, sitting on the bowl, I put my head against the cool tiles and tried to think.

I thought I had brought disaster on everyone. It was certain. I was there, I saw the hits. How could I fuck up like that? I tortured myself, convincing myself that yes, I had seen a red "X" on white background there, and surely there had been an Israeli flag flying from that mast.

What gotten into me? What had I done?

Here, in the restroom of the Fighting First, I lived the last moments of my former life. I knew that in a short time, within minutes, the windlass of fate would begin to turn, crushing me and all I had in the world, my dear Ali and my three-year old son, Etay, my mother, and my foster parents from the Galilee. What would they all say? What would everybody who knew and raised me say? What would my friends who were fighting and shedding their blood just then, think of me? What had I done to my squadron, my Fighting First? I had shot up my friends, fact. There is no way I can live in this country anymore.

Plans began rushing around my head. Perhaps I should commit suicide? But how to do it, and where? Or maybe flee to America, Australia, or Brazil? How to sneak unseen out of this room, change clothes, change my name? All sorts of crazy thoughts, some practical and some fantastic, ran though my mind, and even one important thought, that before anything else, I had to get my wingman out of this mess. After all, he was only following me.

Inside the fog in my head, I heard voices coming from the outside. I heard somebody calling my name again and again. Doors banged open and closed. Then Ivry was there, standing in front of the door to the men's room.

"Spector, are you in there?"

"I'm here," I answered after he shook the door.

"There was a mistake; that ship was not one of ours. Come out of there!"

I got up and went out. "Whose ship was it then?"

"French."

I collected my flight gear. Before dusk I was scrambled again to patrol over the Suez Canal. The ship was still there, farther out to sea.

Only later did I learn that this was not a French ship either, but an American spy vessel, the USS *Liberty*. How did she get there? What was she doing there? All that was none of my business, and the thing was totally suppressed during the flights and fighting that came after. A few weeks after the Six-Day War was over, an investigating committee came from the

United States and I gave a deposition. I told them what I have said here, and answered their questions in my high school English. When I left the interrogation room into the light of day, the issue was closed as far as I was concerned, and I gave it no further thought. Another sad event, neither the first nor the last of its kind. In war, mistakes happen.

A decade later I learned that a conspiracy theory was being advanced about the attack on the USS *Liberty*. One day a friend came in and put before me a copy of *Penthouse* magazine. Enormous tanned tits stared at me as I began leafing through it curiously; one didn't find such pictures in Israel.

"No, not that." He pointed out an article. "Read this."

I read. There was a long and interesting story that claimed Israel had attacked the *Liberty* on purpose. Israel, according to this article, decided to attack the *Liberty* to silence it, and prevent the ship from discovering Israel's plans, such as capturing the Golan Heights. The reasoning seemed odd to me, but the story was well written, and I enjoyed reading it.

"You were there," asked my friend. "Could this be true?"

Initially, I chuckled and dismissed the whole thing as ridiculous. But then I stopped and began thinking again. I recalled the voice that spoke to me on the radio, ordering me to attack. Had he known something he didn't tell me? I sank in a sea of question marks.

I thought, "All in all, I was just the tip of the spear. It's the point that pierces for sure, but it's just a dumb point. I was manipulated by somebody from a distance."

My friend kept looking at me, and I didn't know what to say. As a tool, how could I tell whose hand manipulated me, and what its intentions were? Was I deceived and sent to shoot up a friendly American ship? Did they cheat Ivry, too, telling him the ship was French? For a moment I was really confused.

Then I remembered the simple fact that the *Liberty* had carried no signs or flags clear enough for two sharp-eyed fighter pilots to discern (and after us, several other pilots, and a number of capable sailors who soon arrived on the scene hadn't seen anything either). So if there was a conspiracy, which in my opinion is nonsense, it had to come from the *Liberty* herself.

When I remembered that the *Liberty* did not identify herself, it cleared up the issue, because neither I nor any other Israeli pilot would have attacked a ship—even a military vessel—that flew an American flag, or for that matter British, French, Chinese, Upper Volta, Schleswig-Holstein, or the flag of the kingdom of the Martians.

I have no idea what this ship was doing there, in the middle of a war, and why she couldn't have been tapping into our communications from a little farther out to sea. In any case, if there was no conspiracy, there was certainly a mistake. Somebody on the *Liberty* stuck his ship into a forbidden and dangerous place. And while he was there, he didn't do his job: He didn't fly a visible flag, didn't respond in any way to our calls for identification, and didn't signal to our jets when we circled him for long minutes. If he had gotten on deck and sent up a flare—any color would have done the trick—or just waved a white sheet, I would not have fired on him.

This is the truth, the whole truth, and nothing but the truth in the affair of the USS *Liberty*, as far as I know and remember it. And I pray for the souls of those American sailors who perished or who were injured or maimed through no fault of their own.

Every war in the history of mankind is full of killings of innocents. "The aircraft, the ultimate weapon that can reach everywhere, appeared at the beginning of the twentieth century, when technology upped killing capabilities to levels unseen before," taught Maj. Yehuda Massad, the chief ground instructor in the flying school. He gave me a thin black book and ordered me to summarize it and prepare a lecture for class. Such lectures were the academic summit and the final exam in our education as officers.

The name of the book he gave me was *Command of the Air,* and the writer was Giulio Douhet. Armed with my kibbutz English, I toiled the whole weekend on that book. I found that Douhet was an Italian general and that he had developed a complete theory of war. His idea was that airpower was the most effective of all war measures. "A war can be won," said Douhet, "by airpower alone."

Since I was planning to become a pilot, this was interesting.

Armies and navies, said Douhet, were nothing but a waste of resources. All they could do was crawl around on the surface nose to nose and grind each other down endlessly.

"But nowadays"—the book was from 1927—"we have the capacity to build large bombers." Immediately after the outbreak of war, these bombers should pass over the front lines and attack deep in the enemy's rear what he called "targets of value": cities, population centers, intersections of transportation and railway junctions, water and electricity installations, plants and factories—in short, the entire infrastructure, public and private. These all were civilian targets, manned by noncombatants. For these aerial attacks the "most efficient" means shall be used, prescribed Douhet, and he numbered them: explosive and combustible bombs, poison gas, and every other "effective weapon" for causing damage and death. He even went into calculations of damage and death per pound of weaponry put on the target.

The enemy state would lose its will to fight in direct proportion to the aggressiveness and murderousness of the attacks, maintained Douhet, and surrender. This argument had a moralistic dimension, too: the destruction of a vigorous but short war could be less than the damage of a lengthy struggle.

I concluded my lecture with a flourish. I wrote on the blackboard in large letters QED, the Latin acronym of "proven." This was the way Mr. Kagan, our mathematics teacher in high school, used to complete a proof in geometry. Smiling victoriously, I scanned the faces of the other air cadets. From the corner of my eye I could see Massad scribbling in his notebook, and I even caught a glimpse of the grade he gave my lecture: AB—that is, okay, not too bright, but at least he didn't talk too long.

Massad raised his head. "Any questions for the lecturer?"

ZBB's hand shot up. "Yes. Did Douhet consider the possibility that the two rivals may have air forces?"

"Sure." I knew the answer from the book, and proudly I cited it to him: "The bombers would get through."

As usual, ZBB was smarter than I. "Get through they will, and every side will bomb the other. The question is, what's the end of such a process?"

And Umsh remarked from the back row, "What is going to be left of these two rival countries when it's over?"

I was about to try an answer, but my fifteen minutes were up. Major Massad looked at his watch and stopped the discussion, and Goldie rose to the podium to present his analysis of *Air Power in War* by British air marshal Tedder. Unlike me, Goldie preferred to save time and get right away to his conclusions. And Tedder's conclusions, to the astonishment of us all, referred directly to the question that was left open from my lecture: how Douhet's war would end.

Tedder knew something about this subject, since he was one of the top commanders in the Allied air war against Germany in World War II. That air war went pretty much along Douhet's lines and included intensive bombings of cities and industries.

First, the air marshal was not blinded by the euphoria of victory. His conclusion was that strategic bombing hadn't brought victory. Then the end of the book put the whole idea in doubt: "What shall we gain," asked Tedder in the last sentence, "if while winning the war we shall lose our souls?"

Goldie raised his eyes from the book and let the question sink in.

Somebody remarked, as if in reflection, "Douhet was after military victory, but Tedder was looking at the costs, too."

"My conclusion is," said Goldie, "that anti-Semitic elements aside, Giulio Douhet was Hitler's twin brother. They both saw no problem in hitting civilian populations to achieve a goal. Tedder, on the other hand, thought differently."

"Perhaps the whole difference between Douhet and Tedder is," someone broke in, "that Douhet invented his theory before seeing Hitler in action, and Tedder saw it."

"Shshsh," said Major Massad. "Sit down, Goldstein. Very well done."

"At the end of the nineteenth century," Massad summed up, "a new concept was born in Europe: that there should be rules for war, too. In this way," he explained, "the Geneva Convention was born. According to the convention it is illegal to attack anybody who is not a part of the warring forces. It is the obligation of every soldier to defend civilians if they are caught inside a battle zone. It is forbidden to injure enemy soldiers who had surrendered or were captured as prisoners of war. It is forbidden to use any weapons of an undiscriminating nature, such as chemical weapons." He distributed among us mimeographed abstracts.

"Fortunately for us," Massad continued, "Hitler and his gang lost the war, and Hitler's version of Giulio Douhet—aerial bandits such as Hermann Goering—were put on trial as war criminals. The Allies won, and after the war they reinforced the Geneva Convention. All the states who signed this covenant agreed to honor its rules. Whoever breaks those rules," Massad warned us, "becomes a war criminal."

"Was Douhet a war criminal?" I asked, surprised.

"In fact, probably not. Potentially—certainly he was."

We all sat silent, thinking about future missions. And again it was ZBB who put the hard question: "Sir, how about the Allied bombings of German cities in this context? And what about the Hiroshima A-bomb? Are the people involved in these actions—the same people who tried the Nazi criminals—are they not criminals of war themselves?"

"I admit," answered Massad truthfully, "that I cannot answer this question with any logical and moral certainty."

We all moved in our chairs. "If so, then is it just opportunistic? Does the winner make the rules?" A tone of resentment was heard in the question.

"Perhaps. It may sound cynical," said Massad, "but let us return to the subject of this lecture. The Geneva Convention is finally in force, and nations try to behave in a more lawful way. I remind you"—he rose to his feet—"that the Geneva Convention binds us all. Israel is signatory to it, and accordingly this is the law of the land."

"Indeed? So if someone shoots at—uh—"

"Remember what happened in Kafr-Kassem," Massad said harshly, and got to his feet. "Remember the black flag!" This unforgettable lesson was over.

Many years later, in 2004, I was surprised to run into Giulio Douhet again, in the newspapers. The new Israeli Air Force commander,

Gen. Eliezer Shkedy, gave a magazine interview. After giving some insights into his thoughts and feelings—he was the son of a Holocaust survivor—the new commander was asked who his role models were, and to my surprise they were Giulio Douhet and Billy Mitchell.

At first this selection seemed reasonable: both these men were aviation pioneers and among the first to champion the airplane as a weapon of war. But Douhet is known for his radical theory that advocates the attainment of military victory through the massacre of civil populations and the destruction of enemy infrastructure. Mitchell, who was a hero in World War I, had similar opinions. The strategy they proposed was tried several times and never justified itself. Even the dropping of the atomic bombs on the Japanese cities Hiroshima and Nagasaki—the essence of Douhet's concept—doesn't prove the theory: the bombing shortened the war, reduced American casualties, revenged Pearl Harbor, and frightened the Soviets, but its part in the actual victory was negligible. But even disregarding their inefficiency, the strategies of Douhet and Mitchell are reprehensible and contradict the laws of the State of Israel. I couldn't understand how an Israeli Air Force commander with such a family history hadn't noticed this.

I was disappointed he didn't look into the history of his own air force. There were some good role models there. One of them is Yak, the late Col. Yaacov Milner-Nevo, the planner of operation Focus. Yak, the father of Israeli aerial combat, devised a method of fighting in jet fighters, wrote it down, tested it in the air, and taught it to the air force. His theory and practice were the bases for our complete control of the air for decades and for the shooting down of hundreds of enemy aircraft in a heretofore unknown and unbelievable kill ratio. But his excellence in aerial combat didn't prevent Yak from attaining another outstanding achievement. As the chief of operations he analyzed the problem of achieving air superiority in a methodical, profound way, and when the crunch came for Israel in June 1967, the air force had a sharp and efficient answer: Operation Focus. This three-hour operation was the ultimate example of airpower at top efficiency. It achieved decisive results, and Yak Nevo even took part in the operation as pilot and leader.

Yak, a special and original person, never pursued honors, and when he left the military he was forgotten. His unique personality and outstanding achievements passed into oblivion. The Israeli Air Force had produced a first-rate military genius and could take pride in that.

The Six-Day War was over.

Suddenly, no more scrambling. In the mornings we woke up by ourselves—no reveille. We looked up from our maps, looked left and right, and behold: our families were back. Children in colorful clothes ran around in the squadron briefing rooms and hopped about on the balconies. In military housing, women cleaned their homes and filled their refrigerators with new products from the grocery store.

Everyone was standing in line to use the phones, and the military telephone system crumbled under all the personal stories—who had done what in the war, and how he had done it. Then the voices were lowered for stock-taking—who was still alive and who wasn't. In every gathering, people looked around to see who was there and who was gone. People were afraid that someone they expected would not show up, and then they'd be told about his death. And sometimes the opposite happened and the "dead" showed up, causing embarrassed laughter.

In spite of the pain—everyone in the country had lost either a friend, a relative, or a loved one—at that time, we experienced great joy and relief. From a country surrounded, whose neighbors had threatened it daily with extinction, we suddenly felt a great release. The enemy had melted before us like ice in the rays of the sun. Egypt's president, Gamal Abdel Nasser, resigned his office, and after changing his mind and taking office again, he executed his vice president, General Amer. Syria's president Sallakh Jedid lost his job, and his days were numbered. Hussein, the king of Jordan, admitted in public that it had been a mistake to attack Israel.

Vast spaces were opened to us. In the beginning we called them the Conquered Areas, and then the name was changed to Liberated Areas. In the North, our planes danced in the air over the peaks of Mount Hermon and did aerobatics over the Golan Heights. And in the South lay the widest expanses. We made long navigation flights circling the whole Sinai Peninsula. We rejoiced in front of the black mountains of Santa Katarina and delighted over the long, colorful coral reefs that crowned Sinai's long beaches of white sand dozing in emerald waters. And in the vast spaces of the Sinai I found something else.

On the fourth day of the war, I was attacking a retreating Egyptian convoy on a desert road, between the desert forts of Nakhl and Mittleh. During this flight I was on strict firing discipline. My wingman, Poraz, and I fired our guns meticulously, sending short bursts into tanks, trucks, and mobile cannons, setting them on fire and sending defeated soldiers scattering into the hot and dry hills. Poraz was already out of ammunition, and I was pulling my last bullets off their racks when the formation behind me called me on the radio.

"Armchair"—this was my call sign that day—"where exactly are you now?"

I had to vector him in so he could continue my work. I unfolded the map and began reading it, and finally I found a name over a long line that crossed the Sinai horizontally from the west to the east: "Darb el Hajj" was written above it. When I said these Arab words on the radio, I instantly realized that I knew these words from somewhere in my childhood. Yes, they had been written in longhand, with blue ink, on an old, lined page. But where?

On the long flight back I remembered. I saw this name Darb el Hajj, the road of the celebrators, in my mother's father's notebook. Nathaniel Tatar used this name when he told how he drove his cart on this way some fifty years before.

This was the second time I came down from the sky and walked in his faded footprints in the sand.

The air force celebrated wildly. We were proud of the wings on our chests. It was we who had broken the stranglehold and removed the threat from our nation. We went nuts with festivals of victory, and indulged in massive singing and dancing.

But Ran Pecker's Bats squadron outshone us all; it was the jewel in the crown of the air force. Its battle performance was above and beyond that of all of its sister squadrons. The entire air force, and gradually all the IDF and the whole country, reverberated with the war stories of this wonderful

Mirage squadron and leafed through the photographs of the Pyramids her pilots took passing by. Luck, as usually is the case, also played into the hands of this squadron.

"The Bats is the only squadron that didn't lose a single aircraft or pilot," said the air force's commander, Maj. Gen. Moti Hod, when he visited us at the Fighting First. And we, with our three fallen pilots, bowed our heads and felt almost reprimanded. In the gallery of the gods, one step below Moshe Dayan and among very few others, Ran Pecker reigned supreme with his outstanding command. Perhaps only we BBNs, the graduates of his leadership course, were not surprised. We knew in advance.

And then a small, black worm got inside the golden apple, and its poison did a lot of damage for many years.

For me, it all began when A.—one of my friends and a pilot in the Bats—tugged at my sleeve. We, all the pilots and senior officers of the IAF, were squeezed into the entrance of the Hatzor cinema, waiting for the doors to open and let us in to attend the general debriefing of the war that was about to be held inside. This was a few days after the end of the war, and most of us hadn't seen each other since the fifth of June or even before. And so, until the locked doors opened, we were exulting and slapping each other on the back.

A. had something he wanted to tell me, but quietly. His face was grim. We went off to the side and began to talk. Suddenly we were not alone. More pilots of his squadron came and joined us, among them another A. And what the two A's told me, whispering and looking around like conspirators, was not a story of heroism but of murder. The murder of a prisoner. And they blamed their commander, Ran Pecker, for it.

I couldn't believe my ears. "A., what are you telling me? Did you see this with your own eyes?"

"Not exactly," admitted my friend. "But it did happen. Immediately after the war Ran took us all for a short trip into the conquered areas, to see everything. We stopped somewhere near Jericho. A unit of paratroopers appeared. They had some prisoners of war. According to them, one of their captives had taken part in the murder of a downed Israeli pilot, Ben Aaron. Ran wanted to interrogate this prisoner."

The pilots of the Bats crowded around us. They also were there.

"So what did you do?"

"Nothing. Ran took the prisoner and left. Evening came. Ran returned, alone."

"And on this evidence you say the prisoner was murdered? By Ran? You're nuts!"

"Yes, that's what I'm saying. Ran himself told us. He boasted about it."

I was shocked. Ran was my hero.

"Maybe the prisoner attacked him?" I was trying to find an excuse for him. "Perhaps Ran had to defend himself?"

"The prisoner was handcuffed."

We entered the cinema. The general debriefing of the war began, and lasted for the whole morning. Actually, this was not a real debriefing. It was more like a show, a happy chain of success stories and deeds of valor. It started with Gen. Moti Hod, who told us about some of the tense moments at central control. He had sat in his chair, in complete silence, as the leaders of the State of Israel stood behind him, waiting for the first radio calls from deep in Egypt, to know if Operation Focus had worked or if the population of Israel must be sent into the bomb shelters.

Then each of the squadron commanders followed in turn. They all projected chosen gunsight films with bombings and aerial kills. Each touted his own squadron's achievements. In fact, this was an audition of different actors competing for stardom, everyone rehearsing the same Shakespearean speech. It was good fun, but I can't remember even a single word from that whole show. Until the end of the debriefing came.

When the presentations were over, and before we were all to leave and have a festive lunch, the air force commander stood up and turned to the audience. He asked if anybody had any remarks or additions. I looked toward A., who sat with his friends a few rows in front of me. He noticed my signal and shook his head.

"This is it," I whispered to him, bending forward. "It's now or never. Stand up!"

"I'm no fool."

"Then if not you, let somebody else from the Bats speak up."

"Are you crazy? Shut up and sit down, fool!"

The second A. looked away from me, as if he hadn't heard. People around began looking at us, raising eyebrows. My heart pounded. I raised my hand.

When I received permission to speak, I asked, stammering, if the high command had heard the scuttlebutt. No, I had no details, but I had heard that somebody had done something—I don't know for sure. . . .

I could see that everyone knew what I was talking about. I finished suggesting that the matter be investigated, whatever it was. "Just to know what happened, if anything had really happened." I stopped timidly and sat down.

The hall was dead silent. All eyes left me and looked to the podium. At last General Hod answered. He was also stammering as he began. Moti advised us all not to be taken in by rumors and all kinds of sick stories that some people might be spreading around. The debriefing was over. We all went to lunch.

HERE I WANT TO ADD something special.

In the Sinai War of 1956, eleven years before the Six-Day War, a reserve battalion commander, Lt. Col. Pinhas Weinstein, was commanding one of the battalions that stormed into Gaza. Pini, a member of my kibbutz, Givat-Brenner, was formerly a Palmach officer. He was my father's age, and a close friend of my mother's. I knew Pini well and respected him.

Immediately after breaking through the Egyptian lines, Pini's battalion captured many enemy soldiers. He called his commanders on the radio and asked them to send some men to take the captives so that his battalion could continue its advance.

The answer he received was, "We have no men available. Kill the prisoners."

Without hesitation, Pini answered, "Sir, you can kiss my ass."

Then he left part of his force to guard the prisoners, and continued until his objective was taken. But his blunt words were heard on the open communication channel, and high command had heard them, too.

After the war, Pini was called before a board of inquiry. The board was weighing a charge of disobedience in face of the enemy, or at least insolence to a commanding officer in the presence of soldiers. Pini answered the charges: "There are things," he said, "that must be said loud and clear, so that every soldier understands." The charges against him were dropped immediately.

That evening, after the debriefing in the cinema, the air force celebrated at one more victory ball. Hatzor's enlisted men's dining room was cleared of all furniture, newly decorated, and brilliantly lit. Hatzor's base commander, Col. Benny Peled, stood in the open gate and shook hands with everybody. He looked me up and down with a practiced eye and asked Ali in a harsh voice, "What kind of a wife are you? Where is his belt?"

"It's not her fault," I said. I hated belts in my trousers, and probably didn't have one. After all, when did I ever wear a formal uniform? I was afraid I was going to be sent home to search for the belt.

Benny tapped my flat belly, still being a pedant.

"You don't eat, either! Well," he softened suddenly and said with a smile, "You can afford to go without a belt." He pointed to his own considerable paunch, and only then did I realize that he was kidding.

Ali said, "I'll take over." This was fliers' slang, and they both laughed like idiots. "In the future I'll see to it that the boy is dressed properly."

Somebody touched me on the elbow. I turned around. Ran Pecker stood there, his face grim. He beckoned to me to follow him. Of course, I knew this was coming.

I left Ali and Benny and followed Ran. He was sailing deep into the crowd, and I had to rush not to lose him. The hall was already full, dense, and noisy. The orchestra onstage was already tuning up, and the crowd began milling about like one big body full of humming, talking, and smiles, getting warmed up for the dancing and the singing. Ran parted them like an icebreaker, avoiding faces and hands reaching out to him. He directed himself backstage, knowing I would follow him. At last we stopped behind the stage, and he turned to face me. The decorations separated us from the hall. We were alone, surrounded by noise.

He pinned me with a hard hawk's stare. "What was that supposed to be today, in the debriefing? Huh, Spector?"

"Listen, Ran, some pilots of yours—"

"Don't mention names and don't be an informer," he barked at me. He was right. I shut up. "So you heard something. So people say shit. What makes you run in the street and shout it around? Couldn't you come to me first and ask what really happened?" Again he was right. I began feeling like a puppy that had wet the rug. "Is this the way friends behave? After all I taught you, after all the times you came to my home?

"Now let me tell you what's going to happen." His talk was slow and staccato, like a judge pronouncing sentence. "As far as I'm concerned, you're finished. This is the end of your air force career. And perhaps you shall have to leave Israel sometime soon."

We were eye to eye.

"I'm going to finish you." He turned away and was gone, and a moment later I heard his familiar, hoarse voice above all the others while he joined the singing crowd.

For a while I stood there backstage and thought my thoughts. His threats didn't scare me; even if this was to be the end of my air force career, and it definitely could have been, nobody can expel me from my own country. But I agonized over the feeling that I hadn't behaved correctly and had lost an old friend and a man I had respected. And so, only when I rejoined the crowd to search for Ali, did I realize that I never got an answer to what really happened to that prisoner near Jericho that night. To this very day, I don't know.

The victory in the Six-Day War put us on a historical arc that hasn't ended. Biblical Israel, the Land of Israel, opened before us. On Saturdays we went out in sandals to stroll over her hills and in her valleys. They all carried names we had drunk with our mother's milk. We fell in love with the narrow streets of Old Jerusalem. The Old City bloomed anew out of its ancient history. For us, it was the first time we had seen that rich and mysterious world. The forbidden Wailing Wall stood close to the magnificent Muslim mosques of El-Aqsa and the Dome of the Rock. We walked along the Via Dolorosa, from the Basilica of Agony at Gethsemane to Golgotha, where the Holy Sepulcher stands over Adam's tomb. And then into the Jewish Quarter, deserted and destroyed since 1948, when the Jordanians expelled all the inhabitants and took them prisoner. Then up Mount Zion, to Dormition Abbey, which stands over King David's tomb, and down into the three-thousand-year-old Shiloah Tunnel, which brought water from the Spring of Gihon to the City of David, to walk five hundred meters underground in freezing water and come out to the Pool. Then the bells began to toll from all the churches: St. James Cathedral, St. John the Baptist, Dominus Flevit, Ecce Homo Basilica, Mary's Tomb, Mary Magdalene, the Church of the Flagellation, and then Jaffa Gate, from which one entered an Oriental, noisy, smelly, and colorful maze of ancient alleys.

Bible in hand, we plied the markets of the biblical cities of Nablus and Hebron. We peeled grapefruits under the red blossoms of the Regia trees of Jericho. We breathed the air of the summit on the peak of the mountain Joshua named Beit-El (the House of God), and marveled to see the coast of our country spread before us, beyond the low hills of the Sharon, kissing the great, azure expanse of the sea.

Everywhere around, the remains of war were evident. The roads of Sinai were full of the wrecks of burned-out convoys. In the northern territories—the Golan Heights, Judea, and Samaria—parts of vehicles and smashed cars were everywhere. Houses sported shell holes; farms were crushed and blackened.

My family had a special, private experience. We went to visit our family in Hulatta, to share the new feeling of freedom from the threat of the black mountains. First we climbed the Golan Heights, to look for souvenirs in the deserted Syrian strongholds. Then we drove together to Hamat-Gader, the hot springs of El-Hamma, on the southern corner of the heights. This had been one of the points of dispute, from which we had just driven the Syrians. We stood above the Kenyon, and Aronchik pointed to me the remnants of a steel bridge that rusted over the Yarmuk Valley. These were the ruins of a railway bridge, built at the beginning of the twentieth century, connecting Palestine with Trans-Jordan. The Palmach demolished the bridge on the night of June 16, 1946, "the night of the bridges," together with ten other bridges. This was a protest against the British, who were preventing the few survivors of the Nazi Holocaust from entering what was soon to be Israel.

Aronchik shyly told me that he had commanded the Palmach squad that bombed that bridge. It was news to me, and I was very proud of him. I asked him,"How did you retreat after the explosion without being caught by the British guards?" The only way back was a narrow path on the side of the canyon. It surely had been blocked and guarded.

"We didn't retreat," he snapped. Aronchik was not the type to cling to stories of the past. "We crossed to the other side, walked all night in Jordan, and returned to Israel recrossing the Jordan River downstream."

But of course, I thought admiringly. This was the Palmach, the "indirect approach."

All around the conquered territories hummed with Israelis. We all were full of immense optimism. In the street of an Arab township north of Jerusalem, a tank driver demonstrated to us, all smiles, how a black Mercedes sedan could be flattened and made the thickness of pita bread. When we stopped to pee at the side of a road, a corpse was lying among the weeds, raising clouds of flies. But the waiting Arabs were respectful and polite. They looked nice and were exotic in their "Franji" suits or abayas, kaffiyehs, and tobacco-stained mustaches. They welcomed us and entertained us with miniature cups of cardamomed, extra-sweet coffee. Their women, all wrapped up, peered at us sideways, and already had begun bargaining with our women. Some Hebrew words began to be heard with a heavy Arabic accent. The defeated Arab countries could convene and vow their three insulting noes. So what? We were already seeing with our own eyes the truth—or what we hoped was the truth. We saw a bridge of peace beginning to be built between Jews and Arabs. It was happening before our eyes, materially.

It took us a long time to realize the fateful meaning of the path we had unintentionally chosen. Suddenly we became masters over vast areas where an alien nation lived. Immediately after the war, the government of Israel declared that we would hold the conquered areas just as a guarantee, and that all would be returned to their owners when they had made peace with us. The offended Arab states, on the other hand, reacted with the three noes of the Khartoum Conference: no to recognition of Israel, no to negotiations, no to peace. Just no, no, and no.

So days passed and turned into months and years, and our initial intention to hand the conquered areas back dissolved. Inside us, feelings of ownership began to grow. After all, the freed areas were part of the Land of Israel, the cradle of our nation. At the same time, the Palestinian people in the conquered areas lost their former Arab masters and were left hanging. So while we fantasized about "enlightened occupation" and boasted of improvements we brought to the region, a new nationalism, Palestinian, began to crystallize and be directed against us Israeli Jews, the occupiers. Both nations, unable to compromise in any way on their one land, were struggling more and more with each other like two people trying to sit in the same chair.

But my story has only gotten to July 1967. At this time, only very few, extremely visionary people in the Israeli community could begin seeing the coming disaster. Their warnings and demands that we leave the conquered areas as soon as possible sounded ridiculous. We didn't understand the mortal threat to the Jewish state that was building. We saw such people as eccentrics, fools—or traitors.

Chapter 10

Toledano

The Twenty-three of the Boat. Spring 1941, Nazi forces built up in the West African desert. A Vichy French regime was established in Syria and Lebanon. Most Arabs leaned to Hitler and Mussolini. A German takeover of the Middle East meant Jewish annihilation, and the end of any hope of a revival of the nation.

The British needed troops for special operations. Twenty-three commandos were sent to demolish oil refineries at Tripoli, Lebanon, a vital source of fuel for Vichy and the Luftwaffe there. On May 18, 1941, the boat Sea Lion, *under the command of Zvi Spector, went to sea.*

The boat never arrived. The crew vanished without a trace. Their fate remains unknown.

IN 1945 I WAS TOLD HOW my father had died. The story was told to me in rather a surprising way. At that time I was living in a kibbutz called Alonim, in the Izreel Valley. Samuel and Rebecca Admon were friends of my mother's, and they agreed to take her little boy. One day my Uncle Israel Spector, my father's elder brother, came to visit me. It was spring and everything was green. We walked together in the fields near the kibbutz and took pictures—Israel was a professional photographer and had a Leica camera, with a tripod. Once wound up, we could get in the picture while the timer buzzed.

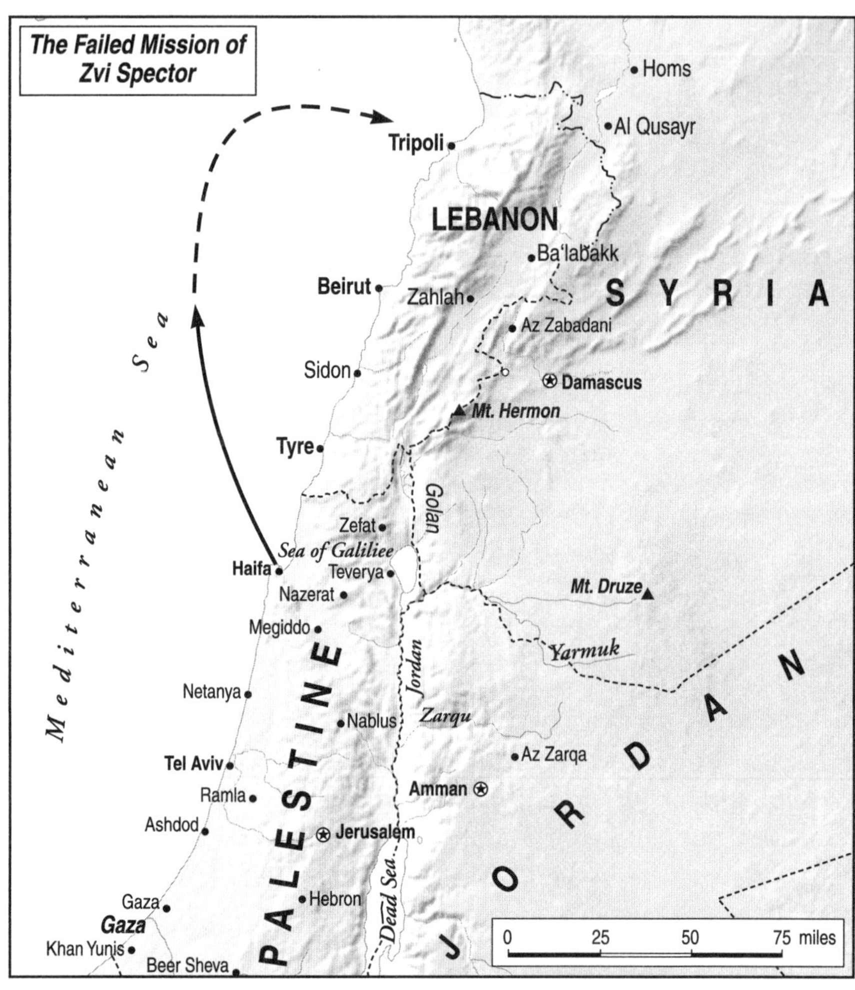

Israel told me that he, too, was a Palmach fighter—in my opinion this was obvious—and then he disclosed a military secret to me. This was the way he located a machine gun nest: the enemy had hidden a Bren gun somewhere in an Arab village near Jerusalem, and fired it only at night. And this is how my Uncle Israel located it: before evening he stood his Leica on its tripod and photographed the village. After night came, he opened the shutter (he demonstrated to me how this was done) and waited.

As usual, the enemy began shooting their Bren gun under the cover of darkness, at the nearby Jewish neighborhood. The muzzle flashes would burn a light dot on Israel's film.

"On the same evening," Israel told me, "after I developed the film, I knew which window they were shooting from!"

I was full of admiration, and we both continued discussing operational matters. And then, perhaps unintentionally, Israel told me that his brother Zvi had been lost at sea. Until that moment all I knew from my mother and my foster parents was that my daddy "was traveling far away."

"So my father is dead?" I asked him excitedly.

He confirmed it.

When I updated my mother, all hell broke loose. Israel immediately was put on the banned list, and I was warned not to believe anything I was told by anybody. "The Twenty-three are missing!" she shouted, "and who says they are dead? They are still looking for them!"

"Yes, yes," I nodded obediently. So I joined the legion of semi-orphans who search for their fathers for the rest of their lives.

I received factual, real information about the man who was lost to me from Dvorah. She gave me a book, *A Hidden Shield*, to read. I read that Zvi was born in Jerusalem on May 18, 1915, finished the Hebrew Secondary School with honors, and was one of the founders of the local Boy Scout community, and its leader for years. "He was outstanding in his diverse talents, his sterling character, and his rich spirit. His was one of the first group of brave youngsters who reconnoitered on foot the whole circumference of the Dead Sea."

Yitzhak Sade had secondhand knowledge of this, or perhaps of another, not less daring trip. "At the time of the Arab Revolt, 1936–1938, when ordinary people thought themselves courageous if they took the bus from Tel Aviv to Jerusalem, Zvi decided with a few friends to go by camel through the Judean Desert all the way to Petra, in the mountains of Trans-Jordan. They wanted to know firsthand what was going on out there in the desert. But when they arrived at Petra, they ran into some agitators. It was clear that two or three Jewish boys in a sea of sand were easy prey for everyone. Then Zvi organized a show of marksmanship, using the Mauser pistol he carried with him. His shooting was so good that it became clear that hunting such boys might end badly for the hunters. So the expedition returned unscathed."

After finishing high school, Zvi went to England, hoping to continue his education. Short of money, he had to cut his studies short and return to Israel. Back home, Zvi devoted himself to security issues. During the Arab Revolt of 1936 (for emotional reasons, the Jews gave it a neutral name: "the Events") he established with his friends Israel Ben Yehuda ("Abdu") and Yossi Harel a small unit of volunteers and called it "the Jerusalem Wanderers." They were the first to go "beyond the fence," mounting offensive operations against the Arab rioters, rather than just passively guarding. Then the older and more experienced Yitzhak Sade came and took command of this squad of wild kids. Sade was a veteran fighter; he had headed armed groups in the Russian Revolution and then led working groups in Palestine. He thought big, and turned the small units he gathered into unified field platoons. This was the first budding of an organized Jewish force, the predecessor of the Palmach.

In the summer of 1939 the "Mossad for the Second Channel of Immigration" (the organizers of illegal immigration to Palestine) decided that an emergency effort was needed to rescue the Jews of northern Europe. The Jews there were already in real danger. Growing numbers were being sent to concentration camps. Agents were sent to Europe and bought a small, old ship named *Dora*. Zvi was sent to Holland to command this immigration operation.

He met the ship and its foreign crew in Amsterdam Harbor. It looked unseaworthy, and the snobby Dutch Jews, after they saw the *Dora*, refused to board. Some even threatened to call the police, to prevent it from sailing. He wasn't deterred; after a lot of discussion and some arm wrestling, the decrepit *Dora* finally sailed from Amsterdam on July 15, with three hundred immigrants on board.

She stopped at Antwerp, where she loaded an additional 180 people who had escaped from Germany. On the night of August 12 she anchored opposite Shefayim Beach, north of Tel Aviv, and disgorged her cargo of immigrants. It was Saturday, a moonless night. The *Dora* immigrants were some of the last to escape from Europe before the outbreak of the war and the Holocaust.

Yitzhak Sade knew an anecdote from this landing. "At night, as the last of the illegal immigrants were being unloaded, a British patrol boat appeared and began searching the area with its spotlight. The *Dora* was totally blacked out, of course," said Sade, "but the captain panicked and decided to give up the ship. He was ready to order the ship's lights on, when Zvi came in. Out of his pocket he took a large key, and stuck it in the captain's belly, ordering him to turn and go to his cabin. The captain surrendered under threat of the 'revolver,' and Zvi locked him in his cabin. Then he told the sailors, 'I arrested your captain, and now I am in charge here. Go on, finish your work!'

"After all the immigrants had been unloaded, Zvi jumped overboard. A kilometer swim got him to the beach. The ship stayed dark and made her escape.

"Surely," Sade concluded with a smile, "the captain must have been grateful to Zvi for locking him up." Zvi was twenty-three then.

When I lifted my eyes from the book I saw Dvorah watching me. Blushing furiously, I read her the last sentences in the story about my father. "Zvi, who was very brave, a daring and talented officer, was selected to command the *Sea Lion* on its mission to Tripoli. His second in command was Yitzhak Hecker, and the captain was Katriel Yaffe." There were an additional twenty-one names, and I learned them all by heart. They are all wandering the seas with the *Flying Dutchman* until they remember to come home.

When the youngest of the four brothers, Shaike, fell in action in the Negev in 1948, I was told that the then-popular song "In the Plains of the Negev" was written about the two Spector brothers. I was proud of the family I came from, and used to hum the second verse to myself, where the mythological mother sums up the situation like this: "I mourned my first in the depths of the sea, and I raised you, the second, to defend the nation."

There was one moment in my life, a crazy, unforgettable moment, when Zvi seemed to have returned.

It happened one morning in 1947. As usual I was playing on the flat roof. My mother was in her room. I heard the noise at the door and ran to open it.

A man was standing on the stairs. He opened his arms and lifted me up in the air and stuck his nose in my chest. I heard Mother ask, "Who's there?" and suddenly she made a strange sound. She flew right past me and fell on this man's neck, laughing and weeping, and if he hadn't caught the railing they would both have rolled down the stairs. I stood beside them, pressed between them and the wall, and watched them hugging, trembling with excitement. A pipe protruded from the man's pocket, and this was the final, absolute sign.

When they noticed me again, Shosh introduced me to Maccabi Mutzeri, a good friend and "Rachel's husband." Rachel was my mother's friend and neighbor. Then I realized he was also the father of my friends Oded and Alona, with whom I played in the sandbox.

Shosh and Maccabi had a long talk over coffee, and I listened. Maccabi talked about Europe. He had just returned after a long time away from home. When World War II broke out he had joined the Jewish brigade and was sent to Europe. There he fought the Nazis, and after the victory remained as an agent for the Haganah, to organize illegal immigration of Jews to Palestine. Now he was back.

In the coming months the connections between our families grew stronger. As he became involved in Palmach operations, Maccabi also began to be away more and more. The War for Independence had begun, and the roads were interdicted by Arab snipers. Word of Maccabi's fall reached my mother in the morning. I was at home, and suddenly I saw her weeping bitterly on the bed. I asked her and asked again and didn't stop until finally she told me: Maccabi had been wounded in the abdomen near Shaar Hagay, in a battle to open the road to Jerusalem. On the way to the hospital he bled to death. We both wept.

Then she got up decisively, dressed us both, and we went to see Rachel, who opened the door and immediately knew. The women sent the three of us children to play downstairs. The kids grilled me, and I told them what had happened in spite of being told not to. Oded ran upstairs. Little Alona and I stayed in the sandbox, and when we got tired of making fierce faces, we began to dramatize some scenes of Maccabi's last battle. As the fatal bullet struck, his hands went up and he cried out, "I'm hit!" and then, at the dramatic moment, "It is good to die for our country."

Years later I learned that in his dying moments Maccabi had really said, "This had to happen sometime. Go ahead, I wish you luck." He died in April 1948, on his thirty-fourth birthday. The operation to open the road to Jerusalem was named Operation Maccabi, for him.

MY MOTHER DIDN'T TALK about my father, but the books were more generous. "Zvi was not a muscular guy," wrote Yitzhak Sade, who himself was a big man and a famous wrestler. "On the contrary, his body was slight and delicate. But when he needed to, he showed unusual physical strength. I once saw him carry a wounded friend on his back over rocky terrain in the mountains for several kilometers. Where did he get this strength?" I internalized this, and went back to it in moments of physical stress.

And Sade concluded, "There was a streak of cruelty in him, a non-Jewish attribute. He had no hesitation about pulling the trigger. Still, justice was his guiding star. He kept this attribute inside himself, like a very dangerous weapon to be taken out of its holster only in time of absolute need—for justice." I kept these things also in my memory.

YITZHAK SADE, "THE OLD MAN," the father of the Palmach, and its first commander, was the one who sent the boat on her way. The Jews of Palestine were torn at the time in two opposite directions: on one hand, the struggle against the British Mandate government, and on the other, the need to cooperate with the British armed forces against the Nazis. The Brits were looking for "natives" to do special operations; at the same time, the Haganah was seeking legitimacy and arms. Their interests coincided. Sade gave the order, and the *Sea Lion* with the Twenty-three was sent on her dangerous mission. Three weeks after her loss, the British army attacked and conquered Syria and Lebanon and caused the loss of the boat to be unnecessary.

The timeline of those events made many people suspicious, and some interpreted the boat operation as a nasty plot of the British to damage the Haganah and remove its next generation of commanders. Some denounced Sade's part in the affair, called him naive, or worse—and never forgave him. But my mother never bore a grudge against him. She saw the operation of the Twenty-three as part of the struggle of the Jewish people, and knew that in such struggles mistakes are inevitable and losses occur. She appreciated Yitzhak Sade, and continued to work under his command in the Palmach, first underground and later in the War of Independence.

After the end of the war, Sade invited us both for several days at his home in Jaffa. This was an old Arab house that stood on top of a limestone cliff overlooking the sea, and Sade's son Yoram lives there to this day. I sensed the affection and the admiration that Shoshana felt for this cumbersome, bearded man, who used to go down to the beach early in the morning to jog on the gray, coarse sand and lift weights.

In those few days we spent with him—this was on our way to settle in Givat-Brenner—Yitzhak was very pleasant to me, too, and talked to me a lot. He took me with him down to the beach to do his gymnastics, and once we went for a long walk in the Muslim cemetery, among the rows of tombstones. There we sat, and he told me stories of his own life. At home he opened interesting books and showed me strange pictures, translating the titles from Russian. One evening he talked to me at length about my father. I was ten by then, and I fell asleep on the sofa near him while he talked. Sade had known Zvi well and loved him, and probably he tried to pass something of him to me so I wouldn't forget. I do not remember much, only his distant, awkward voice. I do not remember if it was he, or perhaps Abdu, who told me about that night in the Jerusalem Wanderers unit, when the Arab sniping at the settlement of Kiriyat Anavim intensified.

Zvi suddenly left his guard post and began crawling among the rocks in the direction of the snipers. When he came close, he began shouting at them (he knew perfect Arabic), "You cowardly sons of bitches, you are afraid to come to us, just hiding in your holes and shooting, not aiming and hitting nothing. All you do is make a lot of noise!" When he came back he was asked why he had endangered himself for nothing. He answered, "What do you mean for nothing? I stopped their shooting, didn't I?"

I wonder why this young man, who didn't need to seek adventure, for adventure sought him, volunteered to command that boat to Lebanon. Was it just for the love of danger, for "nothing?" The original commander of the operation, who had trained the crew for the mission and was slated to go, refused at the last moment, just two days before the departure date. He argued that the operation was too dangerous, with no reasonable chance of success. Perhaps he was right. No doubt Zvi, who was an experienced fighter, understood it, too. And more: "Nobody expected Zvi to take this mission," Yitzhak Sade tried to comfort himself. "Recently Zvi had been injured in a motorcycle accident. His broken leg was still in a cast." But Zvi Spector needed no order to take it on. He always rose with danger, like oil on water. "Even lame," said Sade, "it was hard to imagine a better commander. And the group was worthy of a commander of his caliber." He took command, and they went out and were lost in the sea.

All my life I had followed this man, searched to find more about him, and after many years—this was after the 1973 Yom Kippur War, I was thirty-four already—a stranger told me the end of his story. This happened in the oddest place, on the road, on my way from air force headquarters to my home in Ramat-HaSharon. Suddenly a voice came from the radio, high-pitched and tortured, calling to me in English, "Full fathom five thy father lies. Of his bones are coral made."

I was shocked. I stopped the car on the shoulder and sat frozen. Outside was a dark, rainy evening. A lonely child lies on a faraway, deserted seashore. A clown is bent over him, telling him the news in a choked, hoarse voice. In this way, from Shakespeare's "Sea Dirge," I learned the end of my father and his twenty-three comrades. "Full fathom five thy father lies," said the shrill voice, in an unbelievable lullaby or ancient legend. "Of his bones are coral made; those are pearls that were his eyes; nothing of him that does fade, but doth suffer a sea-change, into something rich and strange."

Children are the loneliest creatures in the world. A child is weak, poor, and ignorant. He is yet to find his only true friend; himself. With no spine of experience, no power, he wanders about in an unknown land like a lost prince, waiting for his father, the king, to come and take him back under his wing, to the light and the warmth. Instead, that horrible joker whispers in his ear, "Sea-nymphs hourly ring his knell: Hark! Now I hear them—Ding-dong, bell." Now I knew he was gone. And when I couldn't hold it in anymore, I wept there in the car, on the side of the road, for the first time in my life.

But when it had all sunk in, Shakespeare's language had lifted the tragedy of my childhood and immersed it in a larger story. I sat there crying for my lost father and for my lost friends.

Zvi Spector, Toledano, grew in my mind until he became a saint. I saw my mother's eyes examine me, criticizing, comparing. Around me, the large kibbutz of Givat-Brenner was full of fair-haired boys who ran faster than I, jumped higher, and knew how to whirl the girls around in the big dining hall at the Friday night parties, and then take them out on the grass. I became a closed young man with a moody streak, and became more serious the more I grew up.

The traumas of adolescence drove me farther from my mother. Perhaps she guessed my problem—that being a living person she could not compete with a saint—but we both were weak and had no tools to find a way out of the thicket. I was an innocent boy, a virgin, and the discovery that she had her own sex life, without any intention of marriage and with no love or future, shocked me.

As an adolescent I was very confused, torn between high ideals and low self-esteem. I clung to one rule of life I had learned from my mother, "All inside," and it protected me. Whenever people approached, I would become silent, turn my back, and hide. Time and again I reminded myself that I was not transparent, that as long as I didn't open a window, nobody could see what I kept inside me. I decided that only I would decide whom to let in, and Shosh was especially not included. Never again did I let her into my life.

I volunteered for military service as early as I could, at age seventeen and a half. She signed my permission for pilot training with her lips tightly clenched. Afterward she snapped, "An orphan is not handicapped."

Chapter 11

From Inside

After the Six-Day War, even as the terrible strain on Israel was lifted, the burden on our shoulders, the soldiers and fighter pilots, increased. The Egyptians and the Syrians started a war of attrition on our new borders, which had suddenly become much longer and farther away. Our country wasn't a small piece of land anymore that a Mirage could cover from one end to the other in a few minutes. We found ourselves scrambled for missions, or patrolling at long distances, burning flight time.

The war over the Suez Canal flared up, and the air force command deployed a forward fighter station in the formerly Egyptian airfield at Bir-Gafgafa, in western Sinai. The name of the airfield had been changed by somebody to Refidim, after some obscure location from the Book of Exodus. In the following years we, the Mirage pilots, were held in constant readiness at Refidim for weeks at a time.

The workload was enormous, but it got my motor going. The more the pressure, the more momentum I developed. Work was abundant, but I asked for more. I didn't notice I was neglecting my family, that Ali and little Etay were leading a life of their own, without my involvement, a life I knew almost nothing about. I left early in the morning and returned late at night. I hung out in Refidim for weeks on end, not understanding why my gentle girl was changing, becoming cool to me, snapping sarcastic remarks, demanding, and getting angry. What was going on? I worked so hard, and whenever I came home I took off my flight boots and tried so hard to be nice. Ali was becoming thinner and thinner, and I didn't know why. I even liked it, and used to call her jokingly "my skeletal friend."

One evening, when I came back from Refidim after a long absence, I found my four-year-old son, Etay, sitting on the outside stairs. I stepped over him, not noticing the bowl full of wet sand with dry canes he tried to show me, and went in. I didn't even imagine that this was a "bouquet of flowers" he had worked hard over for my twenty-eighth birthday. I hadn't even remembered it was my birthday.

In the squadron I had found my own separate world. A great love and a deep trust grew between me and the Mirage, this gray, skinny iron triangle, light of movement and graceful as a coquettish girl, as lethal and loyal to me as Jonathan to David. Through the development of these new, intimate relations, which worked by physical touch, the Mirage taught me to court her every hour of every day. I found myself speaking to the Mirage sometimes in the masculine, but mostly I thought of her in the feminine.

The more I knew about her I realized that the Mirage could not be forced, and it was no use pushing her. All you had to do was ask, but ask in the proper way, politely. Just think first, don't try to hustle her with hurried, hysterical demands. If you prepared her in a nice way and gave her time to warm up, she would go all the way with you, ready and hot, and cut like magic any way you wanted. Thus the Mirage taught me gradually to think things out first, and not just react after the fact.

And it cannot be denied: there always was the other side, the dark side of our profession, the shadow hanging over our lives. This demon was there, too, hiding like a horror inside me, terrifying, since that aerial collision I had four years before.

I screwed up badly. My Ouragan, an old French attack plane, was rolling slowly on its back, listlessly, and I was hanging head down in my straps. Just then another aircraft hit me. There was a loud bang. I was thrown forward in the cockpit, and my head smashed into the instrument panel.

Somehow I didn't lose consciousness. What I remember was the wind that suddenly tore in all over me, my ears deafened from its screams, the skin of my face torn, and the cloth of my flight suit shaving my cheeks and whipping abruptly into my eyes.

The aircraft simply stopped in the air, and strong braking forces hit and then bent me forward like a jackknife. With my head between my knees, I gazed vacantly for a time. Shocked and dumbfounded, I saw a strange spectacle: swarms of clear glass fragments, shining like diamonds, rose from my lap and took off from the floor below my legs, then flew up and were taken away in the rush of the wind to disappear over my shoulders. I didn't think much, but I certainly remember that a feeling of guilt, like sharp fragments, was already there. What had I done? How could this happen to me?

This went on for some undefined time.

Then suddenly something awoke in me, a wild sense of danger. I forced myself to raise my head from my knees, clutched the sides of the cockpit, and with difficulty surveyed the scene with narrowed eyes. My Ouragan was rolling left wildly, and at the same time it was looping forward in the air. The control stick thrashed in my hand uselessly, soft as a dead fish. I looked left and saw that a wing was missing. It just wasn't there, torn away. And still I didn't do anything, till the roar of the wind changed abruptly. Another voice, deeper, joined the whining choir. I saw stains of red light up all the glass. A long tongue of fire slithered from the root of the plucked-out wing below me, wound itself around the body of the aircraft, and came in to lick at me. I smelled kerosene and tar. The fire burned my face. Only then did I act.

Get out of here, punch out, fast! Like an automaton, eyes shut because of the wind and fire, I performed a series of well-rehearsed steps. Sit erect. My left hand pushed a handle, and the metal frame of my broken canopy flew off. Legs back. Throttle all the way forward, to spare my left knee as I went out. Both hands up in the punishing wind, groping to catch the ejection ring handle. A hard pull.

Black canvas covered my face. Well? But nothing else happened. This was not good.

A second pull, harder, with all your strength!

A heavy kick in the ass. Then fast rolling. Heat became cold. The noises changed. Well then, I must be out.

I threw the canvas off my face and opened my eyes. I found myself sitting, tied to my ejection seat, as in an armchair, rolling fast in the air. To my amazement, I was not alone. Around me circled a threatening crowd of broken pieces and torn sheet metal, small and large pieces. I was falling in a cloud of junk. These pieces were all spinning around me and rolling together with me in a vortex, like a swarm of angry bees. I watched and waited for the automatic sequence to come in, open my chute, and stabilize my fall, but nothing happened. The Earth and the sky rolled around me in a nauseating whirl, going blue-yellow-blue, and the heap of trash in a mad dance around me.

A black mass shot into sight, and then there was my poor single-winged Ouragan No. 22, churning in the air not far away. It rolled and whirled, shrouded in flames, a long, corkscrewing tail of fire and black smoke dragging behind it. The empty cockpit disgorged a thin white line of smoke. White clouds of fuel sprayed through holes in its skin, then converted into spiraling sheets of fire. I remembered my burning face, tore off my oxygen mask, and threw my helmet away. The air was cold on my cheeks. The burning Ouragan passed near me, and I suddenly heard it growling, whistling, and whining. Then I noticed the wing, too, above me, fluttering on its own, burning through the blue sky.

And still I fell and fell, spinning in my seat, waiting for the automatic release to open the parachute at the right altitude. It was beginning to annoy me, all that crap coming close and threatening me again and again. Finally I decided to get out of there on my own. I opened the buckle and released the belts, then kicked the seat away from me. When it floated away, I caught the parachute handle under my left armpit and pulled.

Whew! The parachute opened. Far below, the Earth steadied and settled down. All of a sudden the entire swarm of airplane junk shot past and below me like a dark cloud, continuing to revolve around the falling aircraft. Amazed, I watched this small solar system of a large, burning star, surrounded by its many asteroids, all fluttering and sparkling on their way to fall like a cutting rain on the yellow fields of the Negev below.

My face burned. I looked up and saw a torn section in my parachute. I decided that would be all right. Anyway, there was a lot of time; I was still very, very high. Farther above I could still see the whole trail of smoke, beginning up there with the cloud of the collision.

At that instant I recalled the other pilot, my student. Burned and panicky, I searched for him, and was relieved to see him not far away, hanging under his own parachute. For a long time, more than fifteen minutes, I continued to hang in the air, freezing, until finally the ground grew large and all of a sudden came up to meet me. I hit and rolled in the yellow dust of a dry field, near Kibbutz Ruchama.

After this accident I continued flying. But ever since then, a feeling of nausea hit me when in training dogfights metal bodies materialized suddenly from nowhere and passed by my canopy, bumping my aircraft and stopping my heartbeat. Then, after a split second of freezing, ants in my skin would remind me that I was still alive and could continue fighting. The dark shadow was still there, waiting.

And so my friends and I were going out for aerial combat training flights and operational missions once, twice, and three times a day. In each of these we, young men, walked silently together on the asphalt in the sunlight, our helmets dangling, whistling to ourselves. I felt how my feet caressed the ground, stuck to it before I climbed the aluminum ladder and into the cockpit. And I looked around and saw that each of the pilots was visiting his private eucalyptus tree to pee on it, and secretly knock on the warm, sleek trunk so it would wait for him to return and pee on it again.

Sometimes this other side of our world, together with the heavy burden of the war of attrition, intensified, and small cracks opened. Once I stood in the operations room, getting from the clerk the last details before going to my aircraft. A small radio was playing there as usual, whispering, and suddenly several clear strumming notes caught my attention, and I stopped to listen. A honeyed voice came out of the box and said right to me, "Why take it to heart? I have new things in my head . . . "

I thought I was fainting. A dear friend of mine, Asher Snir, also a Mirage pilot, had disappeared from his squadron suddenly and wasn't found for some days. I waited to hear what was coming.

Then a young, happy voice came in and advised me, "Take it easy, walk slowly. After a time you'll be able to run again."

I took a deep breath and smiled at the clerk. The band continued strumming its guitars, and I shouldered my gear and went very slowly to the Mirage, for another sortie. When Asher returned, after five days, it turned out that he hiked to Eilat and lay there on the beach by the Red Sea, out of contact, until he was able to come back and fly again in the war of attrition.

One night the commander of the Fighting First, Lt. Col. Oded Marom, phoned and asked me to come over. He and I took off early in the morning, June 26, 1969. We were a special mission team, and Marom received his orders directly from the commander of the air force, Maj. Gen. Moti Hod. That day's mission was to go deep into Egypt, to find MiGs and shoot them down. At the time, the Egyptians were shelling our soldiers at the canal; there were losses. Our commander chose this way to pay back and deter the enemy.

Accordingly, we didn't sneak into Egypt but flew at high altitude. Anybody with a radar set could see us. We entered Egypt at dawn and cruised directly in at thirty thousand feet. Over the Nile we turned north and then south, waiting for MiGs to show up.

Marom led beautifully, calmly, and I was on his wing in a wide-open formation—a couple of thousand meters away—watching his six while he watched mine. Dawn broke, the sky reddened in the east, and the contours of the land under us acquired a patina of gold.

Suddenly I saw a faraway twinkle—a single MiG-21, some two thousand meters behind us, coming from below and closing fast. We broke together toward him. In the middle of our turn, when Marom was behind me, he warned me, "Another MiG at eleven high!"

I raised my head and saw the MiG, now outside my turning radius, as I had turned inside him. In calm voices we divided the job: Marom would take the first MiG and I the second one, which was still trying to close on me. Within seconds Marom and I lost sight of each other, and each of us was on his own.

And now, time for a kill. Something rumbled in my gut, "Don't blow it."

I began with a disadvantage with the MiG on my six, but I was armed with the cunning I learned from Yak. I eased my turn a bit and reduced power to slow down, in a casual sort of way. Let him come in really fast. Then, when he ardently approached me, I performed abruptly a "pass me" maneuver, and exactly as I anticipated, he shot past me and pulled up. I hurried after him, relighting my afterburner.

This was a mistake.

At that altitude the air is thin, and the Mirage's engine—a variant of the Super Mystere engine—is very sensitive. With a loud bang my compressor stalled, and the engine choked. Here I was, stuck behind and below the MiG, too slow to get to him and with no engine power. The MiG rolled over above my head and turned back toward me.

But high altitude and gravity can be used to give a trained pilot—for a limited time—a good substitute for an engine. I lowered my nose down together with the MiG, and in a dive we rolled down, each opposite the other in a descending vortex. The fall kept me alive and maneuvering, and at lower altitude the air pressure was higher. I caressed my engine carefully, and it sprang back to life. Cautiously I lit the afterburner, and was rewarded by its wonderful kick forward. I was back in the game.

The MiG was still faster and higher than I, pushing itself into me like a dog chasing a bicycle.

"Hassan," I told him, "you're not going to get anywhere this way."

I began to give him what he wanted, leading him on, titillating him. I reduced my rate of turn and widened the radius, accelerating, while he was avidly scrabbling to stuff his nose into me. Now we were at much lower altitude, as in training, but the difference was that instead of the desert of Ruchama, I saw under me strange, red hills. The sun broke out on the eastern horizon, and the MiG's silhouette on the background of the narrow, blinking silver line of the faraway Red Sea looked like a black arrow.

Now my engine was working fine and my Mirage began to do its magic again. My disadvantage was gone, and I started taking command of the battle. I gradually eased my wing bank and lifted my Mirage's nose gently. I began to rise above the MiG's tight circle, moving to its center. I paid with some of my speed, but caught the pivot point high above him. My next move should be to lower my nose at the right moment and nail him from above.

At this point Hassan understood what was happening to him. I watched, and the flight instructor in me nodded approval when in a clear and correct decision he leveled his wings, gave up the fight, and dove straight to the northwest. He fled, using the little altitude he still had to dive to the deck and increase his speed.

I had an answer for this, too. I finished my turn, came in behind him, and launched my two Shafrir heat-seeking missiles after his hot jet exhaust. But this time luck was on Hassan's side—both missiles missed. This was no surprise. The Israeli Shafrir 1 was just a prototype from our research and development laboratories, and usually it didn't work very well.

And still Hassan flew on ahead of me, racing toward Cairo, and it seemed he had made good his escape. All I had left were my guns, and the range was far too long for them. I couldn't continue the chase—Cairo was coming up fast, and I was already at my fuel limit for a safe return. I had to give up. Unhappily, I shut down the afterburner to head for home.

And then things began to happen.

Perhaps Hassan lost sight of me. Perhaps he thought he was home free, where Mommy and Daddy would protect him. I don't know. But exactly when I gave up the chase, Hassan also shut off his afterburner. The flame from his engine diminished. He was a thousand meters in front of me, slowing down and stopping his run from me. This was an invitation that the fighter pilot in me could not refuse.

My left hand pushed the throttle again beyond the detent and lit the afterburner, sucking up my reserves of fuel. My right hand pushed the stick forward, aiming my Mirage into the ground shadows. The distance between us vanished in a flash. In no time I was on him, my gunsight stuck in the center of his black jet pipe and my cannons spitting fire. The houses of a peripheral suburb of Cairo were passing under us when a large piece of aluminum tore off his plane—a part of a wing or a stabilizer—and passed me. Hassan rolled left, turned over, and hit the ground. Shutting down my afterburner, I passed victoriously over him and immediately turned east, to get out of there—fast.

If I flew really carefully, I still had enough fuel to get back. Though I might not make it to Hatzor, certainly I could make it to a safe landing in Refidim, our nearest airfield in the Sinai. But I was not out of the woods yet. I still was alone over Cairo, having to cross a hundred kilometers of enemy country to the Suez Canal, and then another fifty over the Sinai. Fuel was short, so I had to repress the impulse to open full throttle and get out of there. I had no reserves for any hot-dogging. So I began climbing up to the east slowly, flying carefully, not wasting a drop of fuel.

When I reached an altitude of twenty thousand feet, two MiGs caught up with me.

I saw them while they were still far away, two silver specks approaching from the north. They came closer and materialized, long and sharp, right beside me, sniffing at me. I had no fuel to deal with them and continued placidly on my way, so for a while we flew east together, as though we were part of the same formation. It was such an unbelievably peaceful trip together toward the black line of the Suez Canal that I asked myself, "Could it be they don't see me?"

But then they were satisfied with what they saw, and a decision was made. Pulling up, they split into a line in back of me, one of them staying put behind and up to watch from above, while the other turned confidently to attack my six. I could do something, or continue flying forward and wait for the bang.

I decided to do something.

I rolled my Mirage on its back, and for the second time that day, gravity was my engine and accelerated me down to the waiting Earth. The hills were nearing, but the prospect of a safe landing in Refidim was shrinking fast.

When I came out of the dive at low level I was again among flat desert hills, and those two MiGs came after me, one after the other. I watched them pulling out of their dive, and for some reason they seemed soft and easy, like a couple of trained poodles. But even so, I was definitely screwed, and my chances of getting out of this seemed so small that my hands twitched with an abrupt wild desire to go for it and shoot them both down, one after the other, and then see what would happen. But then reason took command over my emotions and forced me to cool off and try to find a way out.

Two MiGs behind me and it played out like this: I couldn't run away from them, and they didn't need to do any tough fighting. All they had to do is run me around in circles here, and here I would remain, forever. All that was left for me was to slip-slide slowly to the east, to try to reach the Suez Canal. I must hug the earth, for only an extremely low flight, following in the ripples of the earth, could save me from their guns and missiles. I had to hope for poor marksmanship from them until I crossed . . .

Crossed what?

Suddenly I realized that I could not continue east to Suez. There was not a chance in the world that I could cross it alive. At low altitude and slow speed, even if those MiGs didn't shoot me down, the canal's dense antiaircraft systems would make mincemeat of me. Without wasting time on any detailed plan I made up my mind and turned south. A wide, yellow valley opened before me, and I glided into it. Certainly all the streams here led to the Red Sea. And beyond the sea was Sinai. I would have to find someplace to land there. I remembered there were some landing strips along the coast, left by the Egyptians: Ras-Sudr, Abu-Rudeis, E-Tur, maybe more. I should be able to find something over there.

And if my fuel should run out before that? It better not, since wherever the fuel ran out would be my last stop.

I cruised slowly at very low level, perhaps two to three meters above the stony bottom of the wadi, hopping over small hills and practically hiding behind bushes. The MiGs followed me. One of them hovered up on my left side, high above the wadi's left wall, and the other came up on my six. In spite of my decision to ignore them and continue flying east, when that MiG disappeared behind my back I got a chill down my spine. I could not restrain myself and broke sideways, up to the rim. Immediately I saw him, eight hundred meters behind me, and nosed out. As I broke, he quit and pulled out.

Then the second one tried his luck. I slipped back into the wadi using the flat slope to regain the speed I lost, and continue toddling along with minimum engine power, preparing myself for the next break. When the second MiG disappeared behind me I broke, and then he quit, too. The first one went in again. We danced around like that for while. They were good-natured kids, educated and well mannered and not scary at all, but meanwhile they turned me around and stopped my progress home. My fuel kept going down and down, while I crawled turn after turn through the endless Wadi El-Khafayer, among the shallow, barren hills, and no Red Sea appeared.

Once I lost airspeed completely and had to open the throttle to stay airborne. There I lost all hope of a landing anywhere. I pulled the gunsight camera from its chassis and hid it in my flight suit, on my chest. Let this proof of victory be some compensation for the Fighting First's Mirage No. 33 that I was about to foolishly destroy.

When I was a child, I learned a dictum from my mother: "all inside." In times of personal distress I whispered this incantation and fortified myself with it. And here in the Eastern Desert of Egypt, when I was sinking into despair and losing my fighting spirit, this mantra returned to me with a slight variation, but a huge change of meaning. I heard it as if somebody were saying it in my cockpit, clearly and calmly. The words were: "from inside."

"From inside." Just a change of one word—in Hebrew it's a change of one letter—but it sounded in my consciousness like a bell and energized my thinking on the spot. From inside, namely listen up, Iftach Spector, it's all in you; all depends on you. The question is only how worthy you are.

This short phrase saved me then and was to support me in difficult times to come. To this day I teach it to my children till they complain, "Come on, Dad, enough with this proverb of yours."

I saw no mysticism in this discovery. Like a great teacher I had, Benny Peled, I never had any inclination to mysticism. All I believe is that in the cacophony of the many voices that thrashed about in my overworked mind during my predicament, the healthy and balanced one won out. This voice was always there. The real miracle, and my luck, lay in the fact that this voice knew not to shout and prate, but narrowed its message down to two simple words that silenced everything else and sent me back to my struggle. And still I wonder why this happened there in Wadi El-Khafayer; how those two words were formed just then, not before and not after, but just at the right moment, and directed me there as they did in hard times that came later.

And so, instead of opening full throttle to accelerate and escape from this trap—and be dead meat in a few kilometers—I recouped my patience and continued to walk a tightrope, watching not the horizon but the next turn of the wadi, shutting off my engine and evading the MiGs' attacks at the rim of the wadi. I used every wrinkle in the ground ahead, and once or twice hills rose up to knock me down but missed. So I slid one kilometer ahead, and then another, and suddenly the horizon lit blue between two hills and a blinding ribbon of sharp blue appeared: the Red Sea.

The wadi descended, and I accelerated. An Egyptian antiaircraft base at the estuary sent long bursts of fire in my direction. I turned south and wafted out to sea. There, over the water, I looked back again, and lo and behold, nobody was there! My pursuers had abandoned the chase and gone home.

Oh, how I gained altitude! I gulped altitude like a man dying of thirst who finds a river and sticks his head in it. A thousand feet and another thousand feet, and Egypt fell farther behind, and the mountains of Sinai appeared in front, still twenty kilometers away beyond the purple-blue surface of the Bay of Suez, the Red Sea. But I kept myself in check; I still had to find a place to land. The fuel indicator was already kissing the empty mark. So again I restrained myself. I didn't bolt, but continued my climb at a low, optimized speed, saving every liter.

‡

When I reached five thousand feet, radio communication, which hadn't worked during the duration of the low-level chase, became available again.

"Control, this is Armchair Two." I tried to keep my voice steady. "Give me data on landing strips on the Sinai coast. Urgent."

"Armchair Two?" I heard the surprise and relief in his voice. "Right away, immediately! Roger!"

But I was not relieved. At an altitude of twenty thousand feet my fuel indicator became rooted to the bottom of the gauge. I stopped climbing, reduced power to a minimum, and began cruising horizontally. I tried to fly as perfectly as possible, not moving any control surface, to minimize drag. I kept counting the passing seconds. Every second meant another 125 meters east.

Zero fuel. The little fuel pressure light began to flicker. I didn't know where the fuel that fed my engine was coming from, but the engine continued to sing its impossible music.

"Armchair Two, come in."

"Armchair Two, go ahead."

"Your only available field is Abu Rudeis. Do you copy?"

"Copy that, control."

I pulled out a map and located Abu Rudeis. Then, scanning the landscape, I decided that it had to be somewhere on that line of sand below that distant high, black mountain to the south, beyond this terrible sea. Then the details came in: Abu Rudeis was a single asphalt strip, 1,500 meters in length. Fit for light aviation, not for jet fighters with a landing speed of 165 knots (300 kilometers) per hour. Oh, shit.

And as if sensing my hesitation, the whining sound of the falling engine revolutions meant that my engine gave up and died. The air pressure in the cockpit fell. I lowered the nose and began to glide down the slope. I had twenty thousand feet to descend, and under me passed the bewitching, frighteningly beautiful surface of the Red Sea, its depths covered with a dark blue curtain. No pilot who ditched there had ever come out alive. Not even their bodies were ever found. This was the sea that had already swallowed up Aki, Dovik, Raz, and Khagay.

And then another call: "On the landing strip at Abu Rudeis," said the controller, "strong northwesterly winds, twenty-five knots."

I was coming in from the northwest, too, and I understood—this strong tailwind was pushing me forward, helping me to reach the strip. But if I did arrive at Abu-Rudeis and came in to land, the tailwind would add to my landing speed. At 190 knots only God would be able to stop me in just 1,500 meters. I knew if I couldn't stop we would go off the end of the runway into the soft sand. My Mirage would flip over. And even if I was not in pieces by then, there was nobody at Abu Rudeis to pull me out of the wreck.

The nose of my Mirage didn't like this plan. It kept trying hard to turn left and take me to the nearest beach. There was no place to land there, but the sand was white, soft, and nice, and I could punch out over there and parachute safely to the ground. And I really wanted to let my Mirage take command and take me there. But somehow something in me was already committed to Abu Rudeis. I already knew that all comes from inside, and that part of me was being tested again. So I forced myself to point the nose at that black mountain in the distance, and we continued gliding toward it, crossing the sea in a long, diagonal line. I knew that if we ran out of altitude halfway, I would have to bail out low into this terrible beautiful water with all the disgusting creatures swarming there, waiting. And so, with chills along my spine, I continued to glide, losing a thousand feet and then another.

My hands were shaking but my Mirage had turned into a glider. We floated silently in a blue space, out of this world, and I felt the plane's body getting cold. Down and down, and to my amazement—not my relief—it gradually became clear that the tailwind was really pushing us. The mountain came closer and closer. Gradually, yellowing sand hills appeared at its foot. And then I saw a comma among the dunes. The comma grew, and a whitish strip materialized, dreadfully short and narrow. But the wind worked in my favor, and the closer I approached, the steeper the glide angle became. At five thousand feet I had to make my final decision, whether to go for this landing, or turn left and bail out safely on the beach nearby. I lowered my landing gear, and this was it.

"We'll make it and land safely," I told my Mirage. "We just have to brake successfully."

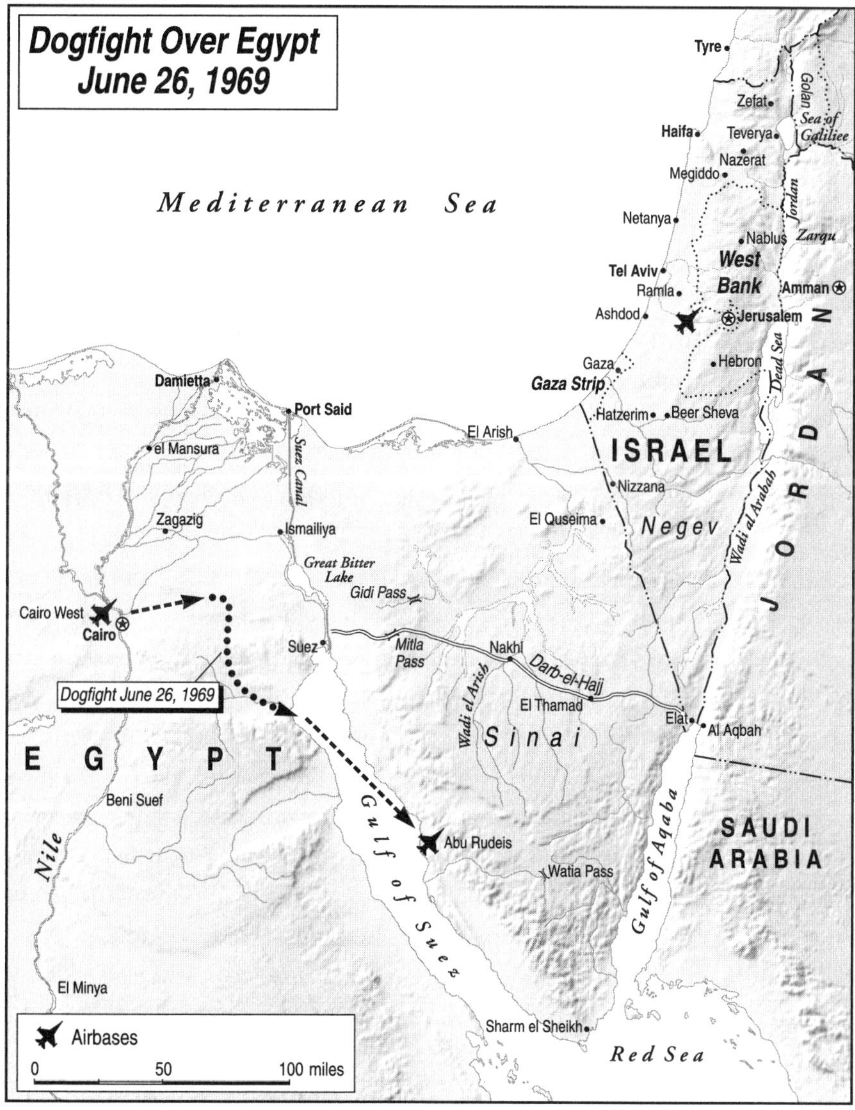

"All from inside," it answered me, and I understood. It was just a Mirage, a speedy metal missile that couldn't possibly stop in 1,500 meters with a strong tailwind. The solution had to come from me, from inside.

And I found it inside, too, the last answer to the last puzzle of this hard, spectacular morning. I told myself to imagine my touchdown point way before the real beginning of the paved runway. I flew my aircraft as if we were to touch down on the coastline, several hundred meters before the actual landing point, and I forced myself to descend between lines of foaming surf. It was weird, and I had to convince us both that that was where we would really touch down.

"And when we get there," I silently told my ship at the last moment, "all we have to do is stay airborne just a bit more, a few hundred meters more, avoiding those white sands." No fighter aircraft flies this way. But this was the only way we could get to the beginning of the tarmac almost "standing on our tail."

Our altitude was gone and we leveled out above the surf and dark blue water. The aircraft felt tired and wanted to sink, but I held it with a firm hand and did not let it go down. I sensed the airflow swishing and growling on our wingtips, threatening to flip us over head down, as Hassan had done before our eyes two hundred kilometers and eons past. Then the coastline slid under us and everything got big real fast. I lifted my aircraft's nose even more to the sky. Nose up, we floated, hurtling, another half kilometer with the wheels caressing sand dunes and rush thorns, totally concentrated on the short runway before us. The stick was already pulled fully back, pressing my belly, and all of a sudden a line of rim stones passed below us.

Airbrakes! We fell like a stone to the tarmac. I deployed the brake chute, and felt with relief its pull take hold. And now the brakes! And again—one more time. Then there was no need for more. My lovely Mirage stopped gracefully a long way before the runway's end, its nose nodding.

I opened the canopy to the oven breath of the morning hamsin. The hot, dry wind hit hard on my wet back. Let me get down and sit on the tarmac near my Mirage. Let me wait for somebody. Somebody will come sooner or later. Let me get down.

I tried to get to my feet but couldn't. My knees trembled and folded under me.

Chapter

12

Nissim

MiG 21: a lightweight, single-engine, single-seat fighter produced in the USSR. First flew in 1956. Top speed, 2.1 Mach. Ceiling, sixty thousand feet above sea level. Armament, one 23mm cannon and four air-to-air missiles.

The MiG 21, lightweight, high-performance, and agile, was simple to operate and reliable, a classic "pilot's plane." It was developed and improved successively and became the most widely flown jet fighter in history. Took part in wars all over the world.

AERIAL COMBAT IN THE WAR OF ATTRITION became more frequent and more difficult. In November 1968 I had an especially tough dogfight that in time influenced my thinking on the matter.

I scrambled with a younger pilot, Gordon, against some enemy aircraft penetrating our area in the northern part of the Suez Canal. The controller sent us to chase them, and we crossed over the Small Bitter Lake and pulled up but saw no MiGs. The interception was so lame that when we looked around, we found MiGs on our tails and launching missiles at us. We broke and separated, each of us carrying on alone.

I closed rapidly on one of the MiGs. He went high and I followed, and we stopped in the air with me close behind him, but before I could finish him off, I received a call for help. I left the MiG immediately and went to help Gordon get a MiG off his tail.

Suddenly the skies around us filled with enemy aircraft. The feeling was like being in a cloud of wasps: I saw targets in every direction, but every time I looked back there was a nose pointed at me with four missiles under its wings, one of them already spitting fire on my six. I broke, and broke again. A missile passed and exploded very close to my cockpit. Another break, and the MiG came in on me. We locked horns. It looked cool: a new, shiny aircraft painted in dark colors. For a moment we came so close I could see that the pilot wore no helmet but only a black leather hood, similar to those we had worn in the Stearman trainer in flight school. As I was lining him up in my sight to take a shot, another MiG came in on my six and spoiled my aim.

This battle was nasty. Throughout the fight, Gordon and I were trying to look out for each other, but we were two against ten. We were forced to fight separately, unable to support each other. The battle was full of action and a strange excitement—many targets passed before my eyes—but the pressure was unrelenting, and I couldn't concentrate on any particular one.

Finally, after I had shot at four MiGs and missed every one of them (my aim was way too hurried), I decided that discretion was the better part of valor. We both turned east and dived to maximum speed. On disengaging we received a parting gift: a Russian Atoll missile hit Gordon's aircraft and luckily caused just minor damage. After landing, I found a long, deep scratch in the Plexiglas of my canopy.

"This is becoming dangerous," I wrote in my report. But it took me some more time till I came to do anything about it.

In April 1969 I was transferred to the flying school to instruct air cadets. The flying school wasn't in Tel Nof anymore, but had moved down south to the Negev, to the new air force base at Hatzerim.

I didn't want to go. The war raged on in the Golan Heights and the Suez Canal. My Mirages fought night and day. My comrades were being worn down with the strain. I felt that the Fighting First needed me, especially since some of our best pilots, especially the deputy commander and my friend Sam Khetz, had been sent to study the new Phantom aircraft in America. Their departures had left a big hole.

But there was something else, too: I was worried about another run-in with Ran Pecker, who was now the commander of the flight school. I tried to avoid it and stay in the Fighting First. But Yak, who was now the commander of Hatzor, refused to listen to my pleas. "We need pilots. You are needed at the flight school. Get over it."

Ran Pecker received me in his office as a friend. Our last conversation seemed to be forgotten. Puzzled, I kept my guard up.

We flew small twin-jet Fouga trainers, the student in the front seat and the instructor behind him. To my total amazement, I found flight instruction interesting and enjoyable. Even more than that, I enjoyed commanding men. I was given a pretty large unit to manage; there were fifty cadets and twenty flight instructors, and a new class came in every four months. Certainly the workload was heavy here, too, but the operational tension was less. We lived in a calmer atmosphere. Hatzerim was at that time just a couple of runways in the desert, with a few concrete buildings nearby, which housed the training squadrons. A little farther on, beyond a dusty Negev hill, three rows of housing were squeezed in, surrounded by yellowing attempts to grow lawns. The wind blew dust and weeds on the roads. The job came with a car, so we could go out on Saturdays for trips in the Negev, or for a dip in the salty, heavy water of the Dead Sea, or to fill bottles with the multicolored layers of sand in the Negev's craters. Sometimes we even drove north to visit family.

MY JOB IN FLIGHT SCHOOL was comprehensive and hard. The air force needed new pilots badly, and we were the production plant. We flew a lot. I was in the air every day, all the day. In my logbook I find months with seventy-five training sorties, plus dozens of operational flights and transport sorties in light aircraft. My subordinates, the young instructors, certainly flew even more; after all, I was a manager. In the evening, when there were no night flights, I had my chance to help Ali feed and wash the children. Ali was also tired after a long day of work and studies in the institute for training for librarians in Beer-Sheva. So after we put the kids to bed—now we had two, when Etay became five we had our second son, Omri—we looked at each other, and instead of going to sleep summoned our last reserves of strength and went out to a show in Tel Aviv, a restaurant with friends at Beer-Sheva, to visit Ilan and Judy in Hatzor, or to sit around Nissim's bed. In the small hours we returned home and hung on to each other with our fingernails.

BEING A FLIGHT INSTRUCTOR captivated me. I became a researcher, breaking new ground. I wanted to explore the secret of military flying and the way to break it down into its component parts, using short, clear, and accurate words and phrases so my students could understand them and later elaborate on their own. I strove to reveal the clean, perfect lines beneath the rococo overlay of operational flying.

I began to sense that behind the rules I had learned hid unplumbed depths. A successful, efficient turn of the aircraft was much more complicated than just manipulating the controls the way they taught me at school. I would input a clear requirement and get back complicated, delicate responses. Sometimes the craft gave just hints; on other occasions it opposed my will by certain side skids, or abruptly tightening its turn, even raging and bucking at me. And if I used force on the stick to compel it, it would take its revenge and put us into a spin. I began to realize that I had partners in the art of fighter flying: the airframe and the engine, together with the air that streamed through and around them, and the force of gravity, were discussing my wishes and processing them. It was like driving a fast car on a slick road in pouring rain: the wheels, the surface, and the wind have something to say, too.

I searched for general rules, for me and for my trainees. I felt that we pilots had no common language to communicate in. I turned to art, trying to draw flight. After landing, while the Fouga was refueled for the next sortie, I sat with my student on the wing and drew on the aluminum surface the maneuvers he had performed, drawing the correct pattern with a full line and what he had done with a dotted one. I tried to draw in three and four dimensions, and all the Fougas were covered with my scribbling.

In my pursuit of the art of flying I followed the footprints of former seekers of perfection. One hint was sent to me by none other than Picasso himself, in Françoise Gillot's book about her life with Picasso. "Try to use colors at a minimum," he once told her. "This way the painting shall acquire stored power." Stored power, energy—that was the thing! Since then I sought that ideal: not to waste energy on futile maneuvers, to use every movement to its maximum.

In this way I discovered that the way to conserve my energy, that stored power, came from foresight: broad vision, understanding the general situation was the key to the next stage. And if you acted early, you won: something you could get from a small move early on, you could not achieve later, even with a radical maneuver.

I defined an order of things to myself: First, you must know what you want to do. Second, you have to achieve it fully; without that there is no meaning to anything. And then comes the art of flying, which is the question of the price. The art of flying, I concluded, is the achievement of the target with the absolute minimum of energy.

But there was more than that to it. One day Ali showed me a magazine interview with a famous Israeli artist, the mime Sammy Molcho. He said, "Every movement must be meaningful, but better yet if it has several meanings." Immediately I recalled General Sherman, who stood the Confederate army on the horns of a dilemma, since his every movement had two possible interpretations and his enemies couldn't decide which way to turn. Now I saw the wisdom behind the route of chase they had taught us in the operational training course: a sharp cut into the opponent's curve combined threat and temptation, and the opponent was confronted with a dilemma. Molcho's words generalized for me that actions are two- and threefold more valuable once they are not simplistic, when they create diversified possibilities. Instantly I envisioned the possibilities hidden in operating several aircraft in varying ways against one target, and I got pale with wonder and joy.

The good artist is neither simplistic nor one-dimensional. He does not do the expected and banal, does not put his nose right on the target, like a dog chasing a bicycle. The sophisticated artist divides his powers into meaningful actions, and enriches his creation with overt and subtle layers, possibilities within possibilities. And all along he builds the moment when he shall put his last brushstroke into place, in one sleek and cruel move, and finish it all with a single speck of color. And at the end of the battle the good artist shall not have all his power spent, shall not have used his entire palette. He has spare energy, fuel, and ammo, and is ready for the next fight. His creation leaves something unsaid; it contains stored power.

"There are many good artisans," I lectured my students, "but the true artist is one who sees the whole, who can tell the geometry of the arc that hides behind the simple stones. Only in this way can he see the next phase, and achieve the result with absolute minimum of waste of effort." Once, when I left time for questions, a young officer rose in the audience. "You were not talking about flight," he said. "You were talking about life in general, weren't you?"

That day I felt I hadn't wasted my efforts.

Hatzerim was remote, but the war found us. Regularly we, the flight instructors, were called to our operational squadrons to help with training or flying operational missions. Every few weeks I spent a busy weekend in the Sinai, on duty in Refidim. There was action all the time. Wild artillery battles raged on the Suez Canal, and every day casualty lists were published in the newspapers. The air force fought also, and all of us pilots—from the colonel to the last first lieutenant instructor—were called on to fly missions with our parent fighter squadrons.

In some strange way, the Mirage pilots among us were given some rest from the hard work in Refidim, in the Sinai. The small, dusty ready room, with its eight beds, was a holy shrine where nobody interrupted sleep. There, once you were in your gear and were ready to scramble if the bell rang, you could loaf around. Only in Refidim we could read books, prepare for our entrance exams, or just play Dominos. We saw plenty of schlocky Westerns—sometimes two, three, and more films a day—and invented gourmet dishes that no man's palate had ever tasted. And best of all, we slept and slept.

Refidim was a crazy oasis in the middle of the desert. It was uncertainty itself, wild and heartbreaking, bursting with men, and overrun with flies. It was in the middle of nowhere—half sublime, half ridiculous. Once, all the pilots pulled emergency duty to help unload casualties from a helicopter that had come in, blackened, from a battle in the salt marshes of northern Suez. None of us will ever forget how the door opened and the doctor fell out with the dead and wounded covering him, all of them blackened and bleeding.

The atmosphere was morbid. Once, I was hanging out with two reservists making a pot of coffee near our aircrafts' hangar. They looked ancient to me, at forty-five or fifty. I was all of twenty-eight. They invited me for a cup with them.

"You get a choice," said one. "A son fucked up at the Suez Canal, or a daughter fucked in Refidim. Which would you choose?" Suddenly I realized that none of them laughed; this was not a joke.

On the other hand, Refidim actually had some nightlife. After dusk just two pilots had to remain on alert while everybody else could take a shower and was free to wander around. There were many attractions: visiting the Sinai Armored Corps headquarters to join the unending discussions; commandeering a jeep to radar station 511 on the hill, five kilometers off base, to peer in the windows at the girls. And there were many parties wherever lights were on; and night rides on the desert's crumbling roads, to roll around in the dunes.

This was a good time, except that the relations between my immediate superior, Ran Pecker, and me were going badly. I knew I had made some mistakes in the running of my unit. Some of those command mistakes were marginal, but a few were really dangerous. Ran reprimanded me, and rightly so, but he chose an annoying venue: he chose to do it in public, sometimes even in the lecture hall in front of my instructors and students. I was in trouble.

I thought I understood what he was after. I had never forgotten that talk behind the stage in Hatzor, and figured there was some plan he was working. I felt he was setting me up. The blowup came one Saturday night in Refidim, the Sinai front-line airfield. We were resting there, six pilots of the Fighting First on ready alert, when the telephone rang. Epstein gave me the receiver, his eyebrows going up.

"It's Ran Pecker, and he wants you," he whispered to me. "Watch it, Spike; he is really steamed."

The voice that came out of the receiver was so loud that everybody around heard every word. "Spector?"

"Yes, Ran."

"What are you doing in Refidim!" The sentence ended without a question mark.

"I'm on duty—" I began, stating the obvious, and then he flared up, cutting me off. He went over all the mistakes that had happened in the unit I commanded since he "unfortunately" accepted me at the school. Ran had an excellent memory for detail, and he connected every mistake with an absence of mine. Once I took leave, in another I was ill, the third time I "disappeared" to fly with the Fighting First.

"Again you're absent from duty? And I have to hunt for you all over the country, and find you in Refidim?"

This was unfair, but I had no way to stop the harangue issuing from the receiver.

"And what about the training of the aerobatic team tomorrow morning! You got out of that, too?" I was the leader of the aerobatic team of the flight school. Every morning, at dawn, we trained for formation maneuvers with six aircraft, preparing for the forthcoming air shows. Aerobatics in formation is a hard and dangerous performance, and only the cream of the flight instructors are selected to take part in it. It also requires much meticulous drilling, over the normal daily routine of flight training.

"I postponed the training to Monday, when I am back from duty."

"You postponed it to Monday?" his voice was hoarse, choking with anger. "And you think you are good enough to cancel a training session ten days before the parade! I have seen how you fly . . ." And so on and so forth. The pilots around watched me with pitying eyes.

I decided to cut this short.

Zvi Spector, my father, who died at sea in World War II when I was seven months old.

With my uncles, Aronchik (left), and Israel Spector, 1947. Shaike, my father's other brother, the youngest, was killed in December 1947.

Air cadets, Course No. 31, 1959. Left to right, front row: Zur Ben Barak (ZBB)*, Yoel Arad (Brutus)*, Zvi Umschweiff (Umsh)*, Yaacov Zik*. Middle row: Giora Yoeli, Yair Khativa*, Nachshon Halperin, Nir Gershoni, Micha Genosar, Ami Goldstein (Goldie)*, Nachshon Gal*. Back row: Uri Sheani*, Dan Zimmerman (Zimmer), Hannan Peled*, Dan Segri*, Iftach Spector, Yakir Laufer*. (* dead)

The French-built Ouragan fighter-bomber jet was flown by the Israeli Air Force (IAF) primarily in the mid-1950s, but it served as a trainer for long after and also saw action in the Six-Day War.

IAF's flight-school Harvard trainers in formation flight, Course No. 31, March 1960.

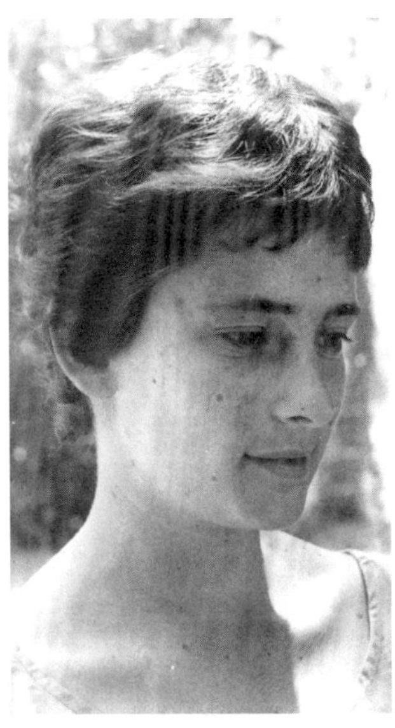

My future wife Ali, in the early 1960s. We would marry in May 1964.

During the filming of *Sinaya*, while on a special two-month leave in 1962. For a time after appearing in this feature film, full of propaganda for the air force, I was a media item.

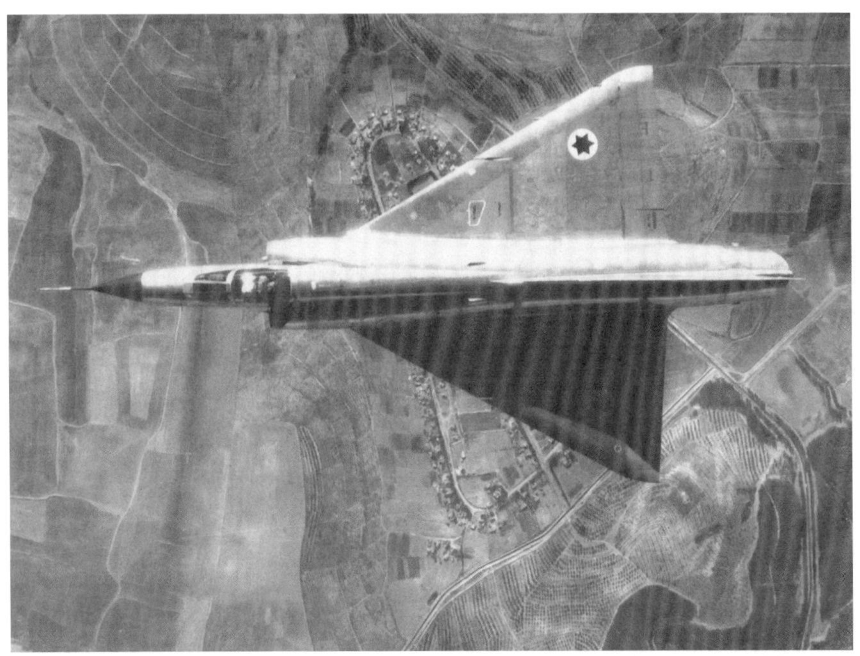

The gray, skinny iron triangle of a Mirage III, a French-built supersonic fighter flown by the IAF in the 1960s.

A Tupolev 16 bomber at Cairo West Air Base finds itself in the gunsight of a Mirage at the beginning of the Six-Day War, June 5, 1967.

Attacking an Egyptian convoy between the desert forts of Nakhl and Mittle in the Sinai, June 8, 1967. We fired short bursts into tanks, trucks, and mobile cannons.

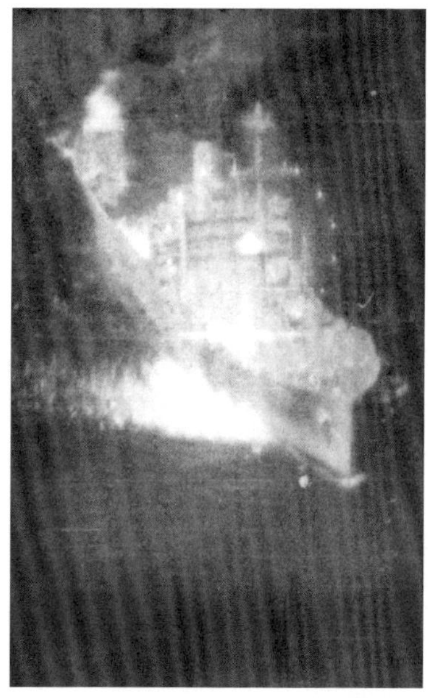

Firing on a ship that carried no signs or flags clear enough for two sharp-eyed fighter pilots to discern; soon identified as the American spy ship USS *Liberty* near El Arish, East Sinai, June 8, 1967.

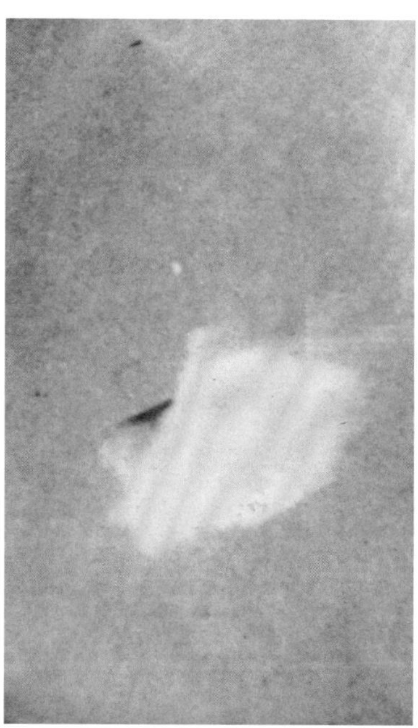

Mirage No. 59 shoots down a MiG-21 over Egypt, March 6, 1970. Gunsight pictures show aiming at the MiG (left) and the successful hit.

My handling of the formal flight procedures wasn't free of problems. An extravagant Phantom takeoff in Hatzerim, in aerial display, July 1973.

Sam Khetz, the first commander of Israeli Phantoms. His wit, and the special grace he radiated, brought him honor and affection all over the IAF.

In the cockpit during the Yom Kippur War, October 1973.

Mechanics under the wing of a Phantom. Every aircraft was loaded with some four tons of bombs.

A thin bridge, very hard to see from the air, and parts of broader one, on the Suez Canal. October 7, 1973.

An F-16 on the tarmac just before takeoff to Iraq, June 7, 1981. Operation Opera seriously damaged Iraq's nuclear reactor, eliminating the threat of Saddam Hussein developing nuclear weapons.

After landing from the attack on the nuclear reactor. From left, sitting: Ofer, Katz, Nahumi, Ramon, Raz, Maimon. Standing: Spector, Mohar, Yoffe, Yadlin, Falk, Sas, Shafir. Ilan Ramon fell as an astronaut in the crash of the *Columbia* space shuttle.

Left to right: Iftach Spector, Chief of Staff Rafael Eitan, and Prime Minister Menachem Begin during the government's visit to Ramat David after the attack on the Iraqi nuclear reactor.

"Ran, excuse me. Just a minute! Yes, I made a mistake. I'll fix it. Tonight I'll return to Hatzerim, and tomorrow morning we'll train—" He slammed down the receiver, and I began looking for a volunteer to leave his home in the North on a weekend and fly to Refidim to replace me. The commander of the Fighting First, Marom, finally arrived after midnight with a Mirage, and I returned in it to Hatzor. At four o'clock in the morning I arrived by car at Hatzerim, shaved, and at six o'clock we performed the aerobatics drill over the base. When, after landing, we entered my office to debrief the flight, yesterday's voice was already booming from the intercom.

"No, this time I have no complaints about the aerobatics, but now I'm going to teach you a lesson about irresponsibility."

The intercom is an irritating machine—there is no way to shut off the loudspeaker and talk privately; everybody in the room hears everything. I signaled to the six pilots that the debriefing was over. When the door closed, I dialed the telephone to Ran's office. The intercom over my head kept rattling on and on.

His secretary picked up.

"Tell Ran I am coming to his office."

A short pause. The intercom went quiet.

"Okay. Ran says he is waiting for you. He said to come in full uniform."

Every soldier understands the meaning of "come in full uniform."

I STOPPED AT MY HOME at base housing to take off my sweaty flight suit and boots and put on a clean uniform. The house was empty and cool. Ali was in Beer-Sheva, at work. Etay and Omri were at kindergarten and nursery. I drank water from the tap, tried to think, and when I went out to the sunny street, I felt my heart beating rapidly. I breathed deeply. Then I decided to go for a moment next door to see Nissim, a close friend since the Scorpions, before I went to the commander's office.

I found Red as usual, lying in bed. His bandaged hand and foot were hooked up in traction. He had multiple injuries after being returned just a short time before from a four-month stint in an Egyptian prison. They showed him a really good time there, and now he was in the middle of a series of operations involving most of his body. He was on pain pills, but every hair in the brush on his head and mustache stood redly erect, his Bulgarian accent cutting, and his black eyes direct and sharp as ever.

In the three years of the War of Attrition, eighteen of our soldiers became POWs in Egypt and Syria. Most of them were pilots who were shot down in battles over enemy territory. A few of them were returned after some months of captivity, but most prisoners—some of them seriously wounded—stayed in an Egyptian or a Syrian prison almost four years and were returned only after the Yom Kippur War of 1973. After interrogation, which included torture, they were put in one room and for some years they established there a "society" of their own, and lived as if out of time. Sitting in prison was hard, but after it another punishment waited for them, even harsher. While they sat there, the outside world went on. Each of them had had his future and plans, and each had a family at home, parents, wife, and children, whose lives changed during his absence. In some cases the cracks that opened could not be mended anymore.

In the Jerusalem Talmud there is the story of Khony, who fell asleep in a cave for seventy years. During that time the holy temple had been destroyed and rebuilt again, and Khony didn't recognize the world. When the prisoners of war emerged from whatever hole or prison cell they were kept in, and returned to the world, each of them was a changed person and met a different reality. For some of them their temples, and their whole lives, were ruined.

Becoming a prisoner of war. This was in the background all the time, like a droning in all of us who continued to fly and fight. The thought of it became the horror of my life.

When World War I broke out, Ali's grandfather Moshe Felzen, of Berlin, was conscripted into the Kaiser's army and became a POW on the Eastern Front. He spent six years in Russia, and definitely didn't imagine that his fatherland, for which he had fought and suffered, was already planning factories to make soap out of him and his family. After the end of the war Felzen returned to a hungry Berlin, where his wife and daughters didn't recognize him.

After time, I saw in Ali's family album a strange photo post card from the time of captivity of her grandfather Moshe Felzen in World War I. A soldier is standing in the snow. He is wrapped in a heavy military jacket, collar up, and with two lines of buttons on the front. The coat is large and calf-length. The sleeves hang down, empty-ended. Behind the soldier there is a massive doorway between walls made of heavy logs. One could only guess what waits inside.

The face of the soldier is square and pale. A black, thick mustache falls from his wide nose down on the contracted jaw, under a helmet that shadows his face. From this shadow gaze two white eyes. The picture was taken in a dirt crevice of a deep trench, and the blanket of snow turns the dirt white, shades and subshades of white, and only around the soldier's feet a large, round stain, like a black puddle, sprawls as a mass of strange shadow in that totally black-and-white world. It seems the soldier was marching in place for long time.

But once you narrowed your eyes, that weird picture would turn, in a magical way, into something else: the dark puddle would turn into some black hole forming its center between the two boots like a thin leg, and over it the dark wall widens and resembles a black wineglass on the snowy background. The soldier stands imprisoned in his black glass, handless, and only his white eyes gaze dumbfounded from it.

I have no idea how Moshe Felzen's picture was taken there, and in what conditions. But this picture, imprisoned in the snow, came to me in my dreams and became my nightmare.

"WHAT'S UP, YEFFET?" Nissim got right to the point. There are no sick visits in the daytime, so something must have happened. I told him everything.

"That's it," I told him. "Tomorrow I'm out of here."

For some time we remained silent together. Then my friend Nissim said, "Look, Yeffet (that is how he nicknamed me a long time ago, when we were flying Super Mysteres), I can't tell you what to do, but I've known you a while. Just stay cool, take it easy. You'll find a way out."

When I left, he sent his voice after me, "And be strong. Tomorrow you'll still be here."

On the stairs up to the commander's office I stopped, and thought that the cellars at the prison in Cairo, with interrogators messing with the open breaks in your limbs and beating the soles of your feet with bamboo canes, were much harder than anything I could expect here. So I took a deep breath and calmed down. Nissim helped me as much as one can help a friend in need.

I knocked on the door. Ran got up to meet me. He was as ready for a fight as a rooster, but this time I was, too. Before he began speaking, I cut him off. "Sir, just so you know. From here, I'm flying directly to Tel Aviv."

He was surprised. "To Tel Aviv? What's in Tel Aviv?"

"I'm going to see General Hod, to remind him about the question I asked him in the Hatzor cinema. He still owes me an answer."

Ran looked at me for a long time in silence and then said, "Go back to work, Spector. Enough of this nonsense."

I rose and stood facing Lieutenant Colonel Pecker, hesitating. Nothing was settled. We looked at each other for long time. At the end I made my decision, saluted, and turned toward the door. At the door he said, "And work more on that responsibility, Spike."

And so it ended. Our relations became friendly again, and since then, I've had no further run-ins with Ran Pecker. But when I left his office I knew well that I had compromised on something very deep. I returned to instructing on the Fougas under Ran and tried not to think of what Toledano would have done instead, or what Shosh would say had she known, and I kept it all inside.

I treasured the only real asset I received from Ran Pecker: his personal example as a fighter and leader in battle. I added to my internal book the rule he taught me, that the courage and integrity of a warrior is measured by the number of holes in the target. This was a very clear lesson, and all the rest I suppressed. I was a soldier, and I was at war.

‡

Ten years later, Ran left the air force, slamming the door behind him. His leaving had no connection to the mysterious alleged murder of the prisoner, or any other moral issue. It was due to a banal struggle for control and ego. The special thing in that struggle was only that not just Michael wrestled against Gabriel, but also a whole bunch of inferior saints and demons were involved. At the end the angels won, and it all ended, in T. S. Eliot's words, not with a bang but a whimper.

When Ran was released from military service I invited him to Ramat-David for a ride in the new F-16 aircraft I was introducing into the air force. He came happily, and we flew together. It was fun and a gift of honor for both of us. After the flight we sat in my office and talked. We both enjoyed comparing the American plane to our common love, that French beauty, the Mirage. Over a cup of coffee I tried to remind him of those two tough talks we'd had.

"What are you talking about?" he replied. "I don't remember anything like that."

I believed him.

Chapter

13

Authority

The Fighting First, the first Israeli Air Force fighter squadron. Established in 1948 with Avia-199 Messerchmitts made in Czechoslovakia. The planes were brought to Israel, dismantled, and assembled at Tel Nof. The squadron's first operation was an attack on an Egyptian column on its way to Tel Aviv, on the bridge named Ad Halom (End of the Way). This aerial attack stopped the Egyptian army.

Soon the squadron was equipped with Spitfires flown directly from Czechoslovakia in a daring flight, and after the War of Independence it added American Mustangs. In the Sinai War of 1956 the squadron flew French Mystere jets, and then it was the first to absorb Mirages.

The first commander of the Fighting First was Mordechai (Moddi) Alon. Moddi died in the War of Independence, when his Messerchmitt crashed.

THERE IS ONLY ONE SQUADRON I'd care to command: the Fighting First, the one and only, the First Fighter Squadron of the IAF. My squadron.

On May 27, 1970, my wish was fulfilled. I stood opposite Marom on the taxi strip at Hatzor. The hundred-odd men of the squadron stood in ranks of three, facing us at attention. The pilots' platoon wore their usual gray, wrinkled flight suits, and the mechanics their well-worn fatigues, black oil staining their elbows and knees. I squinted at the mechanics' platoon, and suddenly I realized I had become their commander, too, responsible for the preparation and maintenance of the Mirages, not just for flying them.

I saluted Maj. Gen. Moti Hod, the air force commander, and he took the squadron's black-and-red flag, with the winged skull, from Marom's hands and gave it to me. Moti and Marom returned my salute, did an about-face, and marched to Yak's car. The three senior officers then drove together to the base commander's office. I was left with my men. My squadron, finally.

Soon I will enter my new office and sit in "Zorik's seat." Above my head will be the picture of the first and for always commander of the Fighting First, the young and handsome Moddi Alon, who crashed his Messerschmitt and died in the 1948 War of Independence. And serious faces will watch from the walls, among them a boyish Ezer Weizman, looking into the far distance, his curly hair waving in the wind. Benny Peled, too, the squadron's commander in the Sinai campaign, who was shot down with his Mystere in enemy territory and rescued in an amazing operation. Many others, too.

And now it's my turn.

I took a deep breath, took a sheet of paper out of my pocket, and cleared my throat to get their attention. This was going to be my first speech as a commander. I was full of plans and intended to read to them the outlines, where I was going to take this squadron. Just then, a blast of compressed air shot out of the readiness hangar. The whole parade froze. A hundred heads turned around to see what was going on. Then a siren screamed, and two jet engines huffed and puffed, accelerating their turbine revolutions. A pair of Mirages emerged from the hangar and sped to the near runway. The pilots lit their afterburners and took off. Another roar of thunder, even louder, rolled in from the other runway, and two F-4 Phantoms from our neighboring squadron—the Falcons under the command of Sam Khetz—scrambled, too. The black trails of the smoking Phantoms stretched behind the little Mirages, diminishing in the western sky.

"Who is in that section?" I said with a questioning look at my new deputy, Capt. Menachem Sharon, who stood in front of the pilots' platoon.

"Reservists," Sharon said, hurrying up to me. "All the active service pilots are here at the ceremony. We put the reserve pilots on alert." And suddenly he asked, "I hope that's all right?"

Hey, I was being asked.

"All right, all right," I answered cautiously. "Let's continue according to plan." But my legs were not steady. I folded my paper, put it back into my pocket, and kept my remarks short. I kept quiet about the ideas I had been working on during the past year, how I would change and improve the Fighting First, put my stamp on it. No time for this now. Let's go.

"Attention! Dismissed!"

The parade scattered in all directions, everybody running to his working place, and only the new commander of the Fighting First walked slowly, restraining himself from running. He has to show everyone that everything here is in order, that he trusts his men, that he is cool. I descended the stairs to the operations room slowly when everybody was already there, crowding around the humming radio.

"Well," I thought, "I haven't been given any hundred-day grace period, not even fifteen minutes, actually. "In the evening," I consoled myself, "there will be some quiet, and then I will find time to sit in my new office, think, organize my thoughts . . . "

I had no idea.

MY FAMILY, ON THE OTHER HAND, had a smooth landing at the new housing.

That same morning, as the truck unloaded Ali with the kids and the furniture near our new apartment in Hatzor, I was still checking out an air cadet on the Fouga trainer. At noon I waved good-bye to Uri Sheani—they were back from Africa and lived next to us in Hatzerim—and took off in a Piper Cub to Hatzor, together with the family cat, Cleo, who hated flying and all along the way glided among the seats, cutting long scratches in the tough seat covers.

Both Ali and I were very happy to get an apartment next to Sam and Rana Khetz. This was good luck indeed; the four of us had been friends for a long time, and our children played well together. Dedi, their firstborn, was about the age of our Etay, and Uri and Omri—the seconds—were both babies. Right away they invited us for dinner.

I had known Sam Khetz since childhood, long before military service. We both grew up on kibbutzim, and met in youth camps in the summers. There was some similarity in our personal backgrounds (what we called mockingly "our stolen childhood"), and there were always things to talk about. Khetz was a year senior to me, and when I arrived at flight school as a new cadet he helped me adapt, and used to lend me his notebooks. In the evening he sometimes came to our room to help us with the more difficult material.

His simple and direct manner couldn't mask his depths. Khetz had a complicated and interesting personality. His wit, and the special grace he radiated, brought him honor and affection all over the air force. At the beginning of the War of Attrition we served together in the Fighting First. Once we drove together to air force headquarters in Tel Aviv for a briefing. When the meeting ended, he told me, "Come, let's visit Moti."

"Visit whom?"

"Moti, the air force commander."

"Is he expecting you?"

"What? Of course not. But if one passes by, one should drop in and say hello."

Moti's secretary, of course, knew Khetz. She cleared the general's agenda, and Captain Sam entered Major General Moti's office, and they sat for an hour. While they discussed matters there, I sat in the entrance and read magazines.

Among his many friends, Khetz had one best friend, Yitzhak Arzi, Aki. Aki was an athletic, handsome guy—very unlike Khetz, who was skinny with a hook nose. These two, from the moment they met each other in the flight school, were always together. When they arrived at the Scorpions, exactly one year before I arrived there, they were given a common nickname, Khezarzi. Everybody thought it was a good name—two for one, as it were. Around this double star we, the newcomers, revolved like satellites.

Then Rana appeared. I met her first in the back of a transport leaving Tel Nof. She was a very slim, black-haired soldier—dark eyes in an exotic face. "Wow, what a beauty," Ali said. Rana had two sisters, both beautiful, and a father, Papa Saul, who had a special sense for finding and picking mushrooms in the fields. We brought the onions and potatoes, and together we made a good dinner and became fast friends.

On December 1, 1967, Aki died. He went down in the Gulf of Suez and vanished, like all the unfortunate pilots who went down there. Zorik and I were in Refidim, and we flew around like mad over the ever-widening petroleum slick in the blue-black water, searching for survivors, annoying ships, and chasing them into the Egyptian harbor at Adabiya to see if they raised anything or anybody, then expelled by ack-ack fire and hanging out again until dusk came and we had to return to Refidim with empty tanks. Nothing was ever found of Aki and his navigator, Raz. From then on, whoever had used the name Khezarzi didn't mention it again. Khetz got another, single nickname, Khetzkel.

He returned to the Fighting First as second in command to Marom, and Khetz and I worked together. He never talked about Aki. I didn't kid myself into thinking I filled the hole in his life. At about this time Rana and Ali became close friends, and remain so to this day. After a short time Sam Khetz was selected to head the Phantom mission—an indication of the regard the IAF had for him—and I took his job in the squadron.

Rana and Khetz went to America to meet the new aircraft, and we in Israel went on fighting. Now the few were even fewer, and the future Phantom jockeys were very much missed. International telephone conversations were out of question back then, so Rana sent us post cards from the American town they were living in—I believe its name was something like Arcadia, a Greek sound that reminded me of green, mythological fields. We missed them both, and particularly Sam's exceptionally bad cooking in Refidim.

When they returned from America, and Khetz began building his new squadron—the Falcons, the Phantoms of Hatzor—Ali and I were already at Hatzerim, in the flight school. Khetz had his work cut out for him building his new squadron, and I was working hard, too, so in the next six months we met very rarely. And so, on our first evening back in Hatzor, when we sat down together for dinner, I was amazed to see how much thinner he was, and that his back was bent more than before. There were shadows under his cheekbones, and the flash of joy in his eyes seemed to have faded. The women were talking about their stuff, so we spoke of ours.

"So, how is the Phantom?" I was curious. This was the new magical aircraft—"a knight in shining armor," some called it. Khetz waved his hand dismissively. He was fed up with talking about the wonders of the Phantom, and he was very tired. The burden he bore was the absorption of magnificent and complicated aircraft and getting them into action in an escalating war. He had begun his squadron from scratch, and was up to his neck in the details, from the developing of fighting doctrine to the integration of a lot of intricate and expensive hardware, with too few trained people to help him. In the Falcons, the competent pilots trained new pilots, navigators trained navigators, and mechanics trained mechanics, while at the same time the Phantoms pushed themselves—and were pushed by the IAF—into battle, with all the power they could muster.

The story of the first two Phantom squadrons in the Israeli Air Force, 1969–1970, is an untold epic. I am not the man to tell it, since I was not there. But the Falcons squadron was my neighbor, and I could see how my friend Khetz was pushed to the wall until he broke.

Meanwhile, I also had a few problems. The two reservists who took off during the ceremony landed safely. But there was a dogfight involving other squadrons, and the radio in my operations room went nuts. The two-ship section from the Fighting First arrived in time but was ordered to patrol the border, and when their fuel was finished they were sent home without doing anything.

Still, I didn't suspect anything. But the next morning fighting broke out again and the whole air force was airborne, but the Mirages of the Fighting First were left sitting in our hangars. Amazed, I called central control.

"What's going on here?" I asked the controller peevishly.

"Just a moment."

Then I heard somebody saying, "Yes, it's him."

"Okay," the controller returned, "talk to the air force commander."

Moti came on the line. He used to run operations personally, and his control of every detail was famous.

"Sir," I began, "I have four sections here in a high state of readiness. Why aren't they in the air?"

"Iftach, they are not going up today."

"Why? What happened?"

"Take a look at your personnel and you'll understand." He hung up.

I was stunned and humiliated. I hadn't yet finished the first day of my new command, and this was a real slap in the face to the pilots of the Fighting First.

I had difficulty even uttering the words to share the bad news. I put the receiver down and left the operations room. I went up to my room and sat there for a while. Then I called Sharon in and told him the story. I was really steamed.

"Take it easy, Iftach," said Menachem. He was a large man with a very centered disposition. "Come on, let's look over the personnel and rethink everything from square one."

When we looked up from the list of the squadron's pilots, we got the commander's message. The menu the Fighting First offered was varied, eclectic, and tasteless. We served a lot of dishes, from experienced aces to rookies, students, desk jockeys, airline captains, and senior officers still putting in flight time. All of them were great guys personally, but many were rusty and others ready for the scrap heap. The Fighting First was not serving a decent lunch, but a dog's dinner. Now I saw the formations I had called ready for battle with new eyes. I also understood that Moti knew us all, and he was watching us closely. Moti was running a war, not a soccer match. And I knew that he didn't have time for any bullshit. He needed super-ready teams—"top guns" and nothing else. I understood I was going to have to give him the real thing, not kids or the over-the-hill gang. It was just my bad luck—or perhaps my good luck—that he decided to deliver his message on my first day there.

I looked closely at the list of pilots and agonized. Some of them were my former instructors, commanders, and leaders. Others were my personal friends who came from my own age group. Still others were my own students. The people of the Fighting First were my best friends and my reference group. Over the past four years we had fought together in the Six-Day War and numerous other battles. These were the men with whom I spent weeks in the bunkers at Refidim on cots, studying for matriculation examinations, soaping each other's back in the field showers, viewing endless films at night, cooking up all kinds of weird shit, telling each other personal secrets, laughing together. Together we ran to the aircraft, took off, flew to the heart of darkness and back. Some of them had protected my tail from MiGs; others I had saved. This was the moment of truth, and I really felt the pressure. I didn't want to do what had to be done now.

Hesitating, I looked at Menachem, waiting to get his opinion. Even he, Captain Sharon, my exec, was not considered a top gun. Sharon got to his feet.

"Iftach, this is your call. This problem you have to face on your own. You are the CO of the squadron." Before he closed the door silently behind him he added, "I'll see you."

That evening I worked late.

During the following weeks I talked to eight of the squadron's pilots. Eight pilots, 30 percent of the force of the Fighting First on the day of my arrival, packed their bags and unceremoniously left the squadron. Some of them got angry, some froze up when I told them of my decision, and their faces hardened. One pilot could not restrain himself and wept openly in my office, another preached at me, a third one seethed with anger and humiliation. But a few understood. Curiously, in this difficult command process I found myself alone. This was like an upside-down situation—I made decisions involving more senior officers than myself, but none of the higher-ups said anything. Yak and Moti kept quiet. No one asked for a report, or gave any advice, or just parted with me in my difficulties. The commanders looked from above and kept their distance. I decided who left and who stayed; the washed-out left offended and their friends who remained watched me with visible uneasiness.

This is how Moti taught me a lesson I never forgot. Since then, the manning of formations for readiness and operations was handled only by me or under my supervision. Within a week from the beginning of the process the ban was lifted, and the Fighting First rejoined the fighting air force.

What happened, moreover, was that once I was burned with hot water, I became careful even about the cold. I began to fly in most of the operational missions. In my logbook I find that in June 1970 I flew thirty-six Mirage flights, a considerable number, but the point is that twenty-three of the total were written in red pencil: operational flights. Clearly I had difficulties trusting my comrades and subordinates.

They felt it, too.

The air war against Egypt, which began to boil over in March 1969, reached its peak in the middle of 1970. The Syrian front was hot, too, and Jordan also made noise, but in relation to Egypt those two were secondary, lukewarm fronts. All our aircraft—Mirages, Skyhawks, old Mysteres—fought day and night. And among us all the special role of the new Phantoms began to appear.

These heavy American fighters that just appeared in the region with their rookie pilots and mechanics who had just learned how to load ordnance on their aircraft went on all the missions. More than that, soon they became exclusive players in two of the hardest missions: attacking strategic targets deep in Egypt, and the dangerous battle against the surface-to-air missile (SAM) batteries the Egyptians stationed beyond the Suez Canal.

The Egyptians could not deal with us in the air, and asked the Soviets for more and more SAM batteries, and they got them. Every day new red circles were added to our maps, indicating danger zones to avoid. These were the killing fields of the missiles; they could get you if you flew there. Initially we attacked the batteries, bombed them, cleaned out some red areas for limited periods of time; but then, like the plague, the batteries returned, modernized and multiplied anew.

At the end of 1969 the Phantoms took this job exclusively. We, with all the inferior aircraft, were sent off the field to watch from the stands the deadly game taking place. The Soviets supplied the Egyptians with more and more replacement batteries, and the missile arrays widened and thickened. Single red circles joined together and overlapped, covering each other until a big, knotty tube was smeared on our maps like a big piece of camel dung going north to south halfway between the Suez Canal and Cairo.

The air war against the missiles heated up, and the few dozen Phantoms began to absorb hits and take losses.

The War of Attrition was strange because the armed forces fought but Israel was not at war. The borders flamed and soldiers killed and were killed there, but inside the country, traffic moved and streetlights shone brightly. Israel's economy bloomed. Restaurants and theaters were full. Every day the newspapers carried casualty notices, but the people of Israel just flipped the newspapers aside and said with a sigh, "That's how it is," and went back to business. Those few who actually fought—in the air, at sea, and on the ground—were not present in the streets, so they were unseen. Only their relatives worried for them but they kept silent, lost in the happy crowd. This was really a war—and what a war—but it was not announced as one, and not perceived as such. Just a nuisance, a fact of life, a thing one cannot change, like the rate of accidents the air force continued to produce, war or no war.

The air force pilots continued to fly combat missions, and in base family housing, the tension, like the mercury in a thermometer, rose and fell and rose again. You could return from the MiGs and the flak, drive to the store to buy bread and milk and stick them in the refrigerator for the wife, and hurry back to the squadron to take off again to battle, or disappear for a week or two to Refidim, as if you alternated between two different worlds. And whenever I returned home I didn't know how I would find my Ali, satisfied and at ease, or withdrawn inside herself, cold and prickly, hard on herself and us for no good reason. When I found her in this mood, we would get into a cleaning mode, shaking out rugs and blankets, sweeping and gardening. She would bend over weeds and uproot them mercilessly, her mouth set hard. Sometimes we had to take a breather, and then we drove to visit the family at Givat-Brenner, or took our two kids to the beach for a few hours of relaxation. Sometimes the air force arranged free hotel stays for us—we had no money for that—and then we would go down to the street and look at the wonderful, vibrant city.

The desire to live bubbled in us until we choked on it. One Saturday night we fell into bed dead tired. Long after midnight we woke up. It was a warm early summer night, and the light from a full moon streamed in through the open window along with the intoxicating smells of flowering orange trees. Noisy dance music came from a party that banged at full power in a nearby apartment, featuring the latest Beatles numbers.

"Should we go?" I asked Ali.

"We were not invited," she answered.

We both got up and stood on the bed, naked. We didn't know any ballroom steps, but we danced in our room till the moon faded, the window filled with pink and rosy light, and the wail of the record player was replaced by the clink of glasses being washed. In our private memories, this magic night became "Lucy in the sky." Not that we had any idea of what LSD was, or who were Hey, Jude and Michelle, Ma Belle.

WE ALSO DIDN'T THINK BIG. We thought just a day ahead. One day the whole government visited Hatzor, to look around and have lunch with the base officers and pilots. When our glasses were raised, the host, Colonel Yak, our base commander, gave a short speech in which he presented a strategic idea of his. "Perhaps we should consider a unilateral retreat from the Suez Canal," he said. "If we let it open for international navigation, a partition might be created, which might lead . . . "

Prime Minister Golda Meir shook her head, annoyed. Moshe Dayan, the minister of defense, rose from his seat and said in a scolding tone, "Military officers should stay out of politics." Yak sat down again on his chair and we lowered our eyes, humiliated, into the hummus on our plates. We didn't notice that the big-shot general Moshe Dayan was ducking a serious question instead of dealing seriously with it. We were ashamed of our commander's question. We didn't grasp the difference between strategy, dealing with vision and thought, and politics, which in essence is the manipulation of people. Some wise guy near me whispered that with such defeatist ideas the air force would lose part of its budget to the artillery. We all thought he probably was right. We thought Yak had lost it, and instead of devising aerial tactics he began dealing with politics.

In truth, Yak was slipping further and further away from us. In discussions, instead of taking an interest in aviation tactics, he sailed into abstract reflections on the best way of war-making, saying it was a mistake to pit aircraft against aircraft, tank versus tank, ship versus ship, like two grindstones that wear each other out. He would pull out his pipe and think aloud on "diagonals," on "getting out of the mental box." This wasn't Yak the MiG-killer anymore. Instead of a fighter commander we had a philosopher. Some sneered behind his back, said he didn't understand what he was talking about. He acquired a nickname, Yak the Clueless. Only Furman, his deputy, said it was worthwhile to listen to what Yak was saying.

Meanwhile, somehow, the Mirages became limited, single-mission fighters. No more were bombs loaded under our wings, and except for a few night scrambles for urgent air-to-ground interventions against artillery shelling on our ground forces in the Suez Canal area, we didn't aim our gunsights at the ground at all. We were just light fighters for daytime air-to-air missions, and that was it.

To this day I don't know how it happened that Mirages—that only three years before had taken out all the military airfields in the Middle East—were totally excluded from the ground warfare in that difficult war. A similar thing happened to the Super Mysteres and Skyhawks. Even though they were aircraft specializing in ground attack, they were limited to second-class missions. We were ordered not to pass the line of the canal, and only Phantoms continued to penetrate deep into Syrian and Egyptian air space and attack the SAM batteries. They began to return with holes in their formations. The Phantom squadrons began to be stressed.

I was not the only one who wondered where all this was going, especially with the stress that began to show in the Phantoms and their crews. Other officers asked this question in a loud and clear voice. The commander of the Mirage squadron at Ramat-David, my buddy Uri Even-Nir, raised his voice once in one of the general briefings and asked, "What is up with those fucking SAM batteries? What in hell requires us to keep our Mirages out of the action?"

But Moti never answered this question. He wanted just one thing from us: MiGs. For Moti, our MiG kills were the only substitute for a real strategy, which he didn't have.

MiGs were not simple, either. I was also having a tough time. I pushed my notebook with all the nice programs I had planned for the Fighting First to the back of my desk drawer. I was left with time and energy only for one thing: dogfights. I found in my squadron two serious problems: leadership in aerial combat, and the launching of our air-to-air missiles.

THE KEY TO VICTORY and survival in aerial combat lies in flight management—keeping the sections together in combat, not letting them scatter. Two aircraft can defend each other, but a lone aircraft is very vulnerable. I, with my narrow escape from deep in Egypt after I separated from Marom, learned that it is mandatory not to leave a lone aircraft in enemy territory. The other pilots understood it, too—we had a daily reminder of it: Avi Kaldes, a pilot from our squadron, was rotting in an Egyptian prison after his section had scattered and left him alone. Clearly, aerial leadership was the key to victory and prevention of losses.

The requirement was to stay together and not separate, but some things are easier said than done. The essence of Yak's breakthrough in the 1950s was in separating the section into two independent fighters who fought individually—each one chasing another target—while coordinating their movements by radio. The separation according to Yak was very aggressive and brought excellent results in small dogfights, but led to the opening of large distances between the partners and eventually loss of eye contact between them. Those separations led time and again to total parting, each fighting on alone.

Our difficulties became more serious when enemy aircraft started appearing in ever-larger numbers. The enemy began to prepare himself in advance and to throw into engagements more and more MiGs, and every dogfight soon turned into mass confusion. Time after time we found ourselves few against many, under pressure, and finally ending up alone in enemy territory, against several MiGs. Instead of attacking, we found ourselves defending, and every now and then one of us was hit by a MiG that appeared out of nowhere.

Hard questions began to be asked: What should we do in a multi-participant dogfight? Did the solution lie in flying in closed formations? This would reduce our aggressiveness and lessen our results. Or was it massing our forces, too? Should we scramble formations of eight and ten fighters? We didn't have enough force for this, and we didn't know how such an armada could be led while in battle. The problem was difficult on all levels.

The idea I brought with me to the Fighting First allowed a pair to separate, but prevented loss of contact between them by introducing a new concept: target specification. The idea was to keep our aircraft together by sending both of them against one target. This idea came to me about a year before, in 1969, thanks to Giora Furman, Yak's deputy at Hatzor. Furman organized an air force discussion of air battles and assigned me to give a lecture on multiparticipant aerial combat. Furman, the intellectual among us, already knew that if one wants to go deep into a matter one should write about it. I resisted, but he forced me to hand him a lecture written in black and white. I had to think.

First, I had to define what a multiparticipant dogfight was. When did a dogfight become multiparticipant? This was not a simple question; the situation was not defined solely by the number of aircraft. I finally concluded that the answer lay in the level of information: the dogfight becomes a melee when the leader loses his orientation and cannot control the situation anymore. This battle was wholly different from the jousts we knew so well—one against one, two against two, and even a few more. In those limited battles a normal leader could see it all, and control what was happening pretty well, keeping himself above the fray. There he can plan and utilize passing instances with no threat, to employ one of his aircraft to attack and kill.

But a melee is a fight loaded with chance encounters, a boiling soup where opportunities appear unexpectedly. And risks, too. Of course, the example in my memory was the mad dogfight with me and Gordon.

Labeling a serious air battle a "red-hot melee of surprises" revealed to me the need to create "cool bubbles"—intervals with no threat. We had to give the pilots in the melee a chance, even for a moment, when they could be relatively safe and could concentrate on a target in relative calm. This could be achieved through planning how the pair would work together.

For a few days all this churned around in my brain. Then I took to the air and did some training experiments, and finally I presented Furman and Yak with a new idea I called one-target specification. It worked like this: The section leader chose one of the adversaries in the area and defined it as the pair's target. They both attacked the same target but from different angles. The adversary, trapped in a pincer, would turn to deal with one of them, leaving his six exposed to the other one. The kill should be quick. All through that process—since we both were after the same target—we would be working together. Eye contact would be maintained continuously, and each could clear a MiG off his buddy's tail and warn him or come to his assistance in time of need. In fact, in this one-target specification method we created a bubble with three objects in it: both of us, and the MiG. Anyone who tried to enter the bubble could be seen, and we would both operate against him in the same way.

"Independent, self-supporting sections in battle," I told Yak and Furman, "override the issue of the size of the opposing force in the area. Each two-ship section is supposed to fight against any opposing force, in any size, and there is no need to send larger formations. In principle," I added, "one can describe the proposed method as 'work in line': the section shoots one MiG down, then the section shoots down another MiG, and so on. Send more pairs to battle only if you want more kills."

Target specification was the one plan I drew from my notebook the moment I came to command the Fighting First. On the first day of my arrival I declared it a mandatory battle tactic. My senior officers, Sharon and Epstein, followed suit, and the method was immediately taught in class and aerial training. This was a not simple, inflexible way of fighting, and it required strong aerial discipline. It was so much easier to pursue targets of opportunity. Some of my pilots didn't like this new method, and called it mockingly "the old bull method." They had some good theoretical reservations, too, but I stood my ground and warned my pilots that if any section leader's pair got separated in a dogfight, there would be hell to pay. They had to do it my way, if they wanted to stay in the First. In this way, in an instant, the First changed its fighting stance.

The problem of launching air-to-air missiles was a totally different issue.

When I dug into Marom's safe I found a top-secret document I hadn't known about, with a report on all the air force's missile launches against enemy aircraft. The results achieved by the Fighting First's pilots were very bad, worse than all its sister squadrons. Most of the missiles launched missed their targets.

I was not upset because our missiles missed. My expectations of the air-to-air guided rockets we were carrying beneath our Mirages' wings were pretty low anyway. The First operated antiquated missiles, even Soviet Atoll rockets we found rusting in the Egyptian munitions dumps at Bir-Gafgafa. The worst thing in my eyes was how my pilots treated them. I found out that most missiles were fired beyond the minimum conditions necessary for a hit. It was as if you shot at a bird without aiming at all. My pilots dumped missiles into the trash. They didn't respect them; sometimes they didn't even hide their shooting them lightly without precise aim. They called them "miss-siles," and some joked about the missile "making like a flare," just light and noise. I suspected that some of the launches were done just to get rid of the extra drag of the missiles, to blow them out on the first opportunity and clean the Mirage to go in for a cannon attack. Our squadron prided itself on gun kills, which are much more glamorous.

Besides being immoral, such behavior seemed to me dangerously anachronistic. As aerial combat became more and more massive, fast, and lethal, the long, tedious closing to gun range endangered my pilots' lives. The future clearly lay in air-to-air missiles, which enabled pilots—at least theoretically—to launch from a distance and finish off the enemy in seconds. I was facing a discipline problem.

I gathered the pilots and reminded them of the situational requirements for a successful missile launch, and then announced that this was mandatory in our squadron. No missile could be launched unless the shot fell within the situational envelope: speed, range, angle off, etc. I warned them that if any of them launched a missile out of that envelope, I would wash him out of the squadron.

AND SO, ONE MONTH AFTER I decided to shelve all my plans to change the First, I found myself shaking it up. To the filtering out of a full third of the pilots, I added target-specification tactics and missile-launching limitations. It all fell on them within a very short period, and came as a tough order given today, to be applied tomorrow. It was clear to me that the pilots were feeling some pressure—and they said it to my face, that the squadron knew how to fight well enough before I took over. That was offensive but didn't surprise me; I knew this squadron well for years. But now it was my call. We were in a war that was accelerating fast toward a peak, and I didn't have time for a PR campaign. I couldn't give them any time to adjust. Their criticism would just have to hang fire for now.

Only Ali remarked once, dryly, that I was gradually becoming like Shosh. My mother lived in Acre, a city on the northern coast, where she managed the national academy for merchant marine officers. She was famous for her high hand there.

HARD MEDICAL OPERATIONS don't always pay off, but on July 10, 1970, I received a small reward for the hard work I had done on my squadron.

We were sent to an integrated battle of two squadrons. The goal was to catch some MiGs. A four-ship division of Super Mysteres from the Scorpions crossed the canal first and began turning for a bombing approach in Egypt. Another four-ship division, of Mirages from the First, followed the Super Mysteres at low level, discreetly.

I had set up a great team for that mission. My wingman was Moshe Hertz, a relatively young Mirage pilot; this was to be his baptism of fire. Menachem Sharon, my deputy, led the second pair, and his number two was Baharav. We went over again the procedures for target specification and the right way to launch missiles. Thirty kilometers inside Egypt, over the Manzala Marshes, we gained altitude and saw the Super Mysteres below us, racing east as planned. The pursuing MiGs came right to us; the battlefield was set.

Right away a four-ship division of MiGs came at us, fast and high. I divided the work between our two sections, and we were ready. I had two MiGs in front of me. Again I divided the work within my own section, and defined one MiG as the target. I sent Hertz up to the "observation position" to gain altitude and be ready to replace me on our joint target while I came in hard under the MiG's belly. And so, while I was still closing on that MiG, grunting under the high g-force, and beginning to pull my gunsight toward his tail, Hertz kept watch on our "bubble."

"Vapor trails approaching fast from the west," he announced.

I looked up and saw them, too, and I saw that Hertz was clean. The vapor trails were still remote, and both our MiGs flew before me. Hertz watched my six, and I had time to do my thing calmly. I fired, one MiG was hit and caught fire, and I passed near it, canopy to canopy. There I had the rare sight of the pilot in his white helmet looking aside, meeting my glance, and then tensing his body, lifting his hands, and pulling on the ejection handles. His ejection seat fired, flew out of his aircraft, and was lost behind me.

We changed target and jobs—I pulled up to the observation post, and Hertz passed in front of me on his way down to get the other MiG. Far lower, under us, Baharav and Sharon were closing their pincers on their pair of MiGs. Just then the radar controller called on the radio,

"Abort battle! Everybody turn east."

"Abort battle," in the IAF's lexicon, required absolute obedience. When you heard those two words, you had to drop everything and return by the shortest route to our area.

I understood what motivated the controller. He had just seen the approaching enemy force on his radar screen. But my view was better than his. I saw those four white trails coming at us at top speed from the west, and I could estimate when they would reach us and in what direction we would meet them. Even though I didn't see Menachem and Baharav with my own eyes, I heard their communication on the radio and knew where they were, and on which heading they were flying down there under me. It was clear they were together on their two MiGs, and defending themselves from any surprise. I had a complete grasp of time and space, and knew everything, including things I didn't see physically. The circle we were drawing in the sky was leading us to a head-on pass with the new MiGs—a classic opening situation. On the other hand, the order to abort combat and turn east would have put the approaching MiGs right on our six. The right thing to do was to continue the same turn another full circle—from the west to the west—and this was exactly the time needed to finish the job on the MiGs we were dealing with.

I pressed my transmit button and commanded, "Belay that order! Everybody continue your turn—and shoot them down!"

When I said that over the radio, it was clearly an offense against air force discipline. And not just an offense; this was real insolence. The voice of the controller is the voice of the air force commander, and usually the air force commander is sitting behind the man with the mike. I had no doubt that they all heard my answer and had recorded it, and I was going to hear about it—not that I had any intention of disowning what I had said. But this was my moment. Not that I wanted to violate orders—definitely not—but I was a commander and leading my men in battle, and I knew what was right and what was wrong. After the last hard month I got it all clear; I was not asking anybody for authority to do my job. The responsibility was mine, no matter what happened. I took over.

Nobody argued, and things lined up like clockwork, tick-tock every ten seconds. First Baharav announced a kill. Then Hertz closed on his MiG and chopped it to pieces while I was guarding him from above and watching the incoming new enemies. I put him on my wing, and we received the four new MiGs in a well-organized formation as they came and streaked between us head-on at ultrahigh speed and passed far to the east, tearing themselves apart and churning the air in an effort to turn back to us. I really felt Hassan sighing under the high g-turn while he tried to keep eye contact with us while maneuvering to avoid colliding with his wingman. I even grinned wickedly to myself.

Then the fourth MiG crashed into the ground with Baharav on his tail, and the circle was completed. Sharon and Baharav were on our right-hand side, climbing to re-form the four-ship division, all facing east at the new MiGs, pressing them to the canal.

"Eye contact?" I asked.

"Eye contact."

"Full power."

Our voices were calm. We were spread aside in a wide formation of two fighting pairs, heading east, and before us the four new MiGs, weary and confused, with no energy. We could start a new dogfight, the conditions were perfect, but there is a limit to arrogance.

"Aborting battle."

We passed among them face-to-face and continued home, leaving Hassan to collect his buddies and hurry to return to his airfield at Inshas, not to miss his friends' funerals. This was the most beautiful dogfight of my life.

On the ground I got a phone call. Colonel Somekh, the likable deputy of the air force commander, had been following the battle. He listened to my explanation and accepted it, even laughed, and I heard he liked telling the story of how I had refused an abort-battle order. I took note of that.

A week later we were ordered to get a formation together for a similar operation. This time I appointed my deputy, Sharon, as division leader. Before he went out, the air force commander called. He asked me to lead the formation myself.

"Sir," I told him, "I am developing Sharon."

"This is not high school," General Hod said. "Remove him and get out there yourself."

"Moti, I trust him."

"For me he is not good enough yet."

I breathed deeply and said, "Okay, I'll do it. But when I get back, I'll wash Sharon out of the First."

After a silence Moti said, "Do what you want, then." Sharon led the division for the mission and brought back good results.

I WAS PRACTICING disobedience.

The rules of my life began to formulate inside me, for now in secrecy and soon loud and clear: You, the operational commander, are responsible to all. An order is just an instruction; its aim is more important than learning its details by heart. You know? So act according to what you know. You already received authority. Don't ask for it again—don't roll the responsibility back to your superiors. You don't need permission to do your job. Blind obedience does not relieve you of responsibility for the results, because a nondecision is a decision in itself. What did they make you an officer for, if not to change the orders when they are inappropriate in your view?

And what about guilt? Who knows? Anyway, it shall be determined only after trial. And who shall try you if not you, and who can punish harder than you, yourself?

WITH A CERTAIN LACK of intellectual integrity, I demanded iron discipline from my subordinates. In the dogfight I described above, Baharav launched his missiles in a way totally contrary to the instructions I had dictated. Both missed. I called him to my room.

"But Spector, both my missiles were Atolls! No Atoll has ever hit a target!"

I admitted he was right, but an offense is an offense. If you were out of the envelope, you were not allowed to launch. And so Baharav, with two additional MiGs to his credit, packed his things with a sour puss and left the squadron. With him went another young pilot who lost eye contact with his leader on the way to battle. Both were exceptionally good pilots, but I demanded discipline.

On the next day in a training dogfight, I scolded Slapak for some flying offense. Immediately an answer came on the radio, "No problem; wash me out, too."

I understood I had passed the limit, and soon I might be flying out here alone.

Chapter

14

Challenge

SAM (surface-to-air missile): weapon in a missile system designed for defense against aircraft. This defense doctrine was prevalent mainly in the Soviet Union and its protégés. In the seventies the most common systems were the Soviet SAM-2 and SAM-3. The West produced the American Hawk and the French Crotale SAM systems.

The basic unit of a SAM system is the battery, which has three main components: the fire-management center with a radar, which should detect and follow the target; the launchers (usually four to six); and the missiles. The missile carries sensors that enable it to home on the target aircraft and detonate close to it.

A SAM battery is a big ground unit, and it defends itself also with antiaircraft guns. A SAM division commands several batteries.

JULY 1970 WAS ONE OF THOSE months when joy and sadness mingled. It went so fast and was so condensed that one thing overlapped the next. That month, my story and the story of Lt. Col. Sam Khetz, the commander of the Falcons, interlocked and separated like wires in a cable till they finally separated forever.

‡

My insistence that my pilots aim their missiles accurately was definitely the way to go. But there also had been merit in Baharav's defense: the missiles he was given to do his job were worthless. We all knew it.

I went with Khetz to see the new air-to-air missiles his Phantoms had just received from America. They were heat-seeking rockets, keying on the opponent aircraft's exhaust pipe. The Americans dubbed them AIM-9D, and their Hebrew code name was Dagger. I loved them. They looked so brand-new and shiny, unlike the scratched and peeling tubes we were carrying. Their noses were pointed, and carried a small, glassy sensor looking for prey like a gray evil eye.

Then, when we sat down to dinner at his home, Khetz opened the technical manual and showed me the specs of that missile, and my eyes widened. The launch envelope was enormous. This missile could be launched at a MiG from unbelievable distances and wide-off angles. It was exactly what we needed. I asked Khetz to lend me a few of those beauties.

Khetz grinned.

"You are as innocent as a child," he told me. "Adaptation of a new weapon to an aircraft is not a simple thing. There are procedures, and if you don't do every step exactly right you will have serious problems. Would you mount a truck wheel on your Sussita car?" he asked me.

"Well, if I were stuck with four flat tires," I tried. Khetz laughed but refused my request. My idea was stupid anyway, and besides, his squadron was short of missiles, too.

But I was already fired up. As I came out of Khetz's house, I turned and went directly to Yak's. The commander of Hatzor listened to me pensively and aloofly. Eventually he took his pipe out of his mouth and assumed a noncommittal position. If I wish to work on it myself, he would not stand in my way. That was all I got. Yak was already in his last days on this duty, and he wouldn't get involved in dubious things. In general, he became a different Yak than the one who ten years ago accepted me into the Super Mysteres. Many years later I recalled that meeting in his house. Only then did it occur to me that perhaps Yak's personal deterioration was already on its way then.

‡

So, I thought, this is about ordnance? Good. Let's see what the ordnance people at headquarters have to say. I called them.

Major Sapir, heavy and perspiring, arrived from Tel Aviv and sat in front of me. I presented him with my idea. Still it seemed to me very simple: let's take a few missiles from the Phantoms—not too many—and put them on our Mirages.

"Can you imagine the tactical revolution?"

"It's not a good idea!" he said immediately. First, the Dagger was too heavy for the thin wing of the Mirage. Second, the impact of jettisoning external fuel tanks—the usual thing we all did before going into battle—would shake and surely break the missile's sensor. When I twisted my mouth he told me that the Phantom didn't have such a problem; it was a much heavier aircraft and didn't shake in the air. And there was a third argument: "Do you have any idea of how expensive this missile is? A hundred thousand U.S. dollars!" Three arguments, indeed!

Although the money didn't mean anything to me, I made out that I was seriously impressed, so that Sapir could see I was a logical person. Then, when coffee was served, I got after him again.

"We both have been familiar with the wing of the Mirage for some time," I told Sapir, "and the Dagger looks to me like a pretty tough piece of pipe, too. I don't see any of them breaking in the air. As to the sensor, if the cow-eyed missiles we currently carry don't, why should the Dagger's eye break?"

I saw his engineer's face sour and hurried to add: "I promise you we'll drop our tanks very carefully."

I was deeply suspicious that all his technical arguments had been prepared on the way from Tel Aviv, and the only reason for refusing my idea was stinginess. Was the Dagger expensive? And what was the cost of a Mirage and its pilot going into battle with improper ordnance?

But Sapir shook his head and got up to leave. I understood that I hadn't passed the first test. But there was a war raging outside, and all we had were shitty missiles that even the sternest discipline couldn't convince to hit anything. And within two weeks we were going to be on alert in Refidim. Gnashing my teeth secretly, I set myself a goal: we would do the Refidim alert with Daggers on our wings. But how?

‡

THE WAY TO CIRCUMVENT the system revealed itself, and amazingly it was that same Sapir, the engineer from headquarters, who in the same meeting presented me unintentionally with the solution. Sapir needed four Mirage sorties to flight-test a new pylon they invented in his department. The other Mirage squadrons, up to their necks in work, already turned him down. This was normal in the air force of the 1970s; headquarters had no aircraft for flight testing and had to use the fighter squadrons for tests. Sapir was a nice person, and he preferred to be considerate; he knew how hard we were working. He didn't want to order us to do it.

"Perhaps the First might agree to do the tests for us?"

"For you, sure," I fawned sweetly, grasping on the spot what a gift I was being given.

I SPENT ALL THAT EVENING at Khetz's home. The next morning, when Sapir's engineers arrived to hang their new pylon under the belly of one of my Mirages, a cart stood near the aircraft with one Dagger missile on it.

"When you are done with the pylon, hang this thing too," my technical officer requested.

They checked their paperwork. "We don't have any orders on this missile."

"That's just a local check we do here. Here are the missile's technical manuals." Engineers love technical manuals.

After some hours of work, the way to hang a Dagger on a Mirage and connect it to the wiring was found. Only then the most senior engineer looked up, and a spark of intelligence shone in his eye. "Is this okay, that's . . . say, what's the hell is going on here?"

"It's okay," he was told hesitantly. While they were arguing about it, over their heads in the cockpit Epstein was already being strapped in.

"I am informing headquarters!"

"Sure, go right ahead."

In the meantime, we acted. We had a test order, four flights to do, and we had no time to waste. The new pylon had to be checked. While the senior engineer was trying to get his phone connection, Mirage No. 15 was already breaking the speed of sound at fifty thousand feet, and checking the robustness of his new pylon in sharp rolls and turns. After twenty minutes he landed. We all gathered around anxiously, waiting for him. The wing was still there, safe and sound, and so was the Dagger—small evil eye and all.

In the evening everybody came to Hatzor. The whole ordnance department left Tel Aviv and came in cars and trucks. Sapir was there, and Dekel, his superior, and even Lt. Col. Joe Aretz himself, the tough head of the department. Fearing what was surely coming for my head I hurried to summon Yak, and as a further defense armed my office with cake from the base kitchen.

A heated exchange broke out. Joe Aretz stabbed me with his spectacles like two white-hot rods of steel. "Where did this chutzpah come from?" he wanted to know, and, "I want to know from whom you stole that missile! Huh?"

But in front of us—I made sure my office's door remained wide opened all the time—Mirage No. 15 stood in silence in the parking lot, carrying the Dagger on its wing, complete and shining. And this is what changed the course of the discussion. After all, we were in a war, and we all were air force men.

After an hour of heated exchanges, things calmed down. Joe gave us permission to continue "the testing of the pylon." Before he got up to go home, I squeezed out of him acknowledgment that the testing included weapons firing. This, of course, was written into the pylon testing order. Nobody mentioned "missile" or "Dagger," but it was all clear. At the door he retorted, "We'll see what will come out of this."

"Joe," I promised him, "this will be a great success!"

"I am really moved," he said ironically. "But let's be clear, Major Spector, this is only a test, nothing more. Is that clear?"

"Yes, sir."

"You will not get Daggers for your squadron!"

"Of course not, sir."

"And no matter what comes out in the tests, don't even think of taking a Dagger operational! You don't have permission!"

"Right, sir."

This was mid-July 1970, and things were coming to a boil.

‡

Both Khetz and I were called to air force headquarters for a special briefing. Some important operation was cooking. Khetz invited me to drive there with him, so as I landed he was waiting to pick me up at the aircraft. He drove his car to Tel Aviv in uniform, and I sat beside him in my sweaty flight suit.

A different crowd was gathered in the barracks that served as a briefing hall. In the first row, near the air force commander sat Minister of Defense Moshe Dayan. This was unusual. In the middle rows sat an odd mix of uniformed personnel I had never seen before, and quite a number in civilian clothes. We, the few invited squadron commanders, sat in the back rows, as usual. It was our habit, from the old days of being the "opposition."

Looking at the strange people, I elbowed Khetz.

"EW," he answered me obscurely, whispering.

"EW what?"

"Electrons," he shut me up, left me, and went to sit in the front, among the VIPs. I didn't know what he was talking about. Colonel Agassi, the chief of operations, finally took the podium. Silence fell; the air was thick. Agassi presented us with the operation, code-named Challenge. The part that involved me and my Mirages was nothing; just a four-ship formation patrolling along the Suez Canal to prevent interference by MiGs.

"First, clear?"

"Clear," I answered. From now on I was free to listen to the crux of the program. It was a large operation to attack the Egyptian SAM array that lay beyond the Suez Canal, on the way up to Cairo. It was a huge array, with many missile batteries, gun points, and radar installations woven into a complete unit. A giant antiaircraft fortress.

Then my mouth fell open. The plan Agassi presented was so weird, and so different from anything I ever imagined, that I couldn't believe my eyes. An armada of Phantoms, flying formation at high level, was to cross the canal and fly directly into the SAM array. I couldn't understand their flight profile. The Phantoms were supposed to fly in large formations directly at the missiles at high altitude in straight and level flight. This was nuts. The enemy batteries would be given optimal conditions, conditions that every Egyptian missile man could only dream about.

I rubbed my eyes. "What is this for, the Independence Day parade?"

"Husshh!" whispers came from all around. If the atmosphere hadn't been so serious, and the people around so tense and somber, and the minister of defense in the audience, I would have thought somebody was pulling our legs. The proposed plan looked to me like a bad joke.

The tactics I was brought up on were that one should penetrate areas of missile danger at low altitude, close to the ground, and at maximum speed. Surprise the enemy like lightning. Approach clandestinely and indirectly, hit the target, and get out of there as fast as possible. The flocks of geese on the blackboard were cruising calmly, directly into the heart of the missile killing zone. This approach contradicted anything I had known.

I stopped laughing, looked around, and was shocked. Then I thought that there must be something here I don't understand. And again my eyes were drawn to the "EW" people who were sitting before me and whispering to each other. Who were these people, and what were they doing? Who invited them here?

There were others in the audience who felt as I did. Stares crossed, people shrugged. I whispered to my neighbor, "Do you understand this *operazia*?" I used that word in the mocking way our East European elders in the kibbutz used to belittle our youth movement activities. "Because I sure don't."

He shrugged. "I don't understand it, either."

And there was something else weird in this briefing. It dragged on, gray and dusty like a sack. I felt there were holes in it, things unsaid. It was strange, and even Agassi was different on the podium this time. He was not energetic, and his voice didn't boom as it used to. He hesitated, and at one point stopped and looked at Moti. The air force commander nodded, and Agassi turned to the room and asked all the pilots, except the few Phantom senior pilots and navigators, to leave the hall and wait outside.

"We'll call you back in ten minutes." I got up to leave, and noticed that most of the audience remained sitting. Only we non-Phantom pilots were sent out. The door closed behind us.

We hung around on the hot, dry lawn, everybody silent and withdrawn. I lay down on the ground in my flight suit and sucked a grass stem. Something mysterious was being discussed inside there, some secret not for us to know. That is the magic, I thought. I was not so curious as hopeful.

When we were invited in again, the briefing was already in its final stage. Moti stood on the podium and summed up. After him the minister of defense got up also and added some formal words. And again a weird sensation passed through me—it all seemed like a ceremony, not like the end of a good briefing before a good military operation.

"All right," Agassi woke me from my musings, "start getting ready. The operation will take place this coming Saturday. Detailed orders will reach your squadrons tonight, through the teleprinter."

When we were released, I walked to the front row to join Khetz. Small groups gathered in the passage, discussing and arguing. When they saw me coming, everybody fell silent. Khetz noticed me coming, hesitated for a moment, and then said, "Listen, perhaps you can find yourself a lift back to base? I have something to do in town."

"What lift?" I wondered. "Nobody here is going to Hatzor. What, you suggest I get out to the road in my flight suit and stick out my thumb?"

"No . . . but perhaps a driver can be found for you in the transportation section here." But when he saw my face, Khetz changed his mind. "Okay, never mind. We'll go back together. But I have a meeting in town. I have to ask you to wait outside. Don't be offended, please."

I had no alternative. On the way to Jaffa I sat by him in silence and asked myself if Khetz was leading a double life.

It was early evening. The small military Citroën stopped in the corner of the road above the small fishermen's harbor in the ancient city of Jaffa. I saw on the stone wall a restaurant sign. Khetz turned off the engine and got out of the car. I began organizing myself for an hour of dozing, but suddenly he returned and opened the door on my side.

"Come on, come with me."

"Forget it," I said. "You go and finish your business. I'll stay here." I hate to be a nuisance. "Go ahead, Khetz, don't worry."

"Forget it. I am not going to leave you here in the car." And suddenly Khetz understood and laughed. "It's not what you think, idiot. I have a friend waiting here, an American. We'll sit, eat something, talk business. Why should you stay in the car?"

"Okay," I finally acceded. "I'll take another table." I was hungry.

I followed him into the restaurant. The entrance was very fancy, all glass and black woodwork. On my own I wouldn't imagine entering such an expensive place. The waiter bowed before the military uniform with the wings but turned his nose up at my unpolished boots and sweaty flight suit. Among the empty tables a man in civilian clothes got up and waved his hands at us.

Suddenly I was terrified, and I caught Khetz's sleeve to stop him. There was something weird here. In those times, air force pilots did not meet with foreign citizens. I suspected that what was going on here might be unlawful. What can a squadron commander in wartime discuss with a foreigner in a restaurant immediately after a super-secret briefing? This was not an affair here; it seemed much worse. It got all mixed together with that awful briefing. Suddenly I was flooded with rage. I felt like a total idiot, was suspicious of Khetz, and amazed at myself. How could I be dragged into this business here? I couldn't believe what he had gotten me into. Why didn't he tell me beforehand so I could come and go on my own? Why had I agreed in the first place to go with him to Tel Aviv?

"Listen, Khetz, I am going back to the car to wait for you there."

"Iftach, what's the matter?"

The rage freed a cocked spring in me. Suddenly I said in anger, "Sam, what are you doing? You are wrong, you are wrong, wrong!" Gasping, I added, surprising myself, "Why did you agree to that operation?"

We stood in the entrance, whispering hoarsely. The man returned politely to his seat.

"Look, Sam, I don't like what you are doing now. I hate this operazia you are about to fly. And I don't understand you. What the hell are you doing in this fancy restaurant? Who is paying for dinner? Who is this guy?"

"Wait a moment, Iftach. Are you crazy? What's the matter with you?"

But I was unstoppable.

"This is not the first time we've attacked SAM batteries. We all did it even before you got back with your damn Phantoms and these stupid ideas!"

"Quiet . . . we'll talk about it later."

"And we learned something from experience! So what are you doing now, throwing away everything we've learned? Who is this spy you're meeting at night? Why do you go out against missile arrays with no defense?"

"Will you please calm down? Don't shout, for heaven's sake. This man is on our side, Iftach. He is an expert in fighting against SAMs from the Vietnam War."

"You'll probably tell me EW, now, right? What is EW, huh, Khetz?" I was really steamed.

"Come on, take it easy." Khetz grinned, as if calming down a small child. "Come sit with us; relax. He won't eat you, and you'll have something good to eat. We're going to discuss something." The steam went out of me. I was hungry and thirsty, and I dragged in after him.

Our man rose to meet us again. He was of medium height, tending to heaviness, his skin tanned, and the hair on his balding head black and curly. Two black, agile eyes scanned me swiftly. I observed that he had just now made his dress less formal. He didn't wear a tie, and the upper button of his shirt was opened, as is usual in Israel, but his black shoes shone like mirrors, and his shirtsleeves were fastened with fancy gold cuff links, something never seen here. On one of his fingers he sported a coarse gold ring with a big green stone. I had never met an American before, and he seemed to me disguised, as if hidden behind some kind of camouflage, or perhaps trying to look like an Israeli. A suspicion rose in me. I thought, "This guy probably knows Hebrew. He might have listened to our conversation in the entrance." I vowed that I would not say a single word, no matter what.

Khetz and the stranger shook hands very warmly, and it was clear that they knew each other before, perhaps from America. Khetz introduced me as a friend. We shook hands.

The guest looked at us, asked for pardon, and went to the rest room. I realized that he was extremely sensitive. We sat and waited. Again I whispered, "I think I get what you're going to rely on. It is an electronic barrage, isn't it?"

Khetz waved his hand at me as if waving a fly away.

"That's what you dubbed EW, eh?"

He didn't answer. Perhaps the code name was too secret to mention. But I continued in the same line. "It's black magic you're relying on," I said contemptuously. "They've sold you a bill of goods."

Suddenly two red flares appeared on the thin, pale cheeks before me.

"Listen, Major Spector, stop talking nonsense. What do you know about it? There were tests, there's proof—"

"Proof, eh? What proof, Khetz?"

"Vietnam."

This didn't silence me. In 1970 there were many articles about that war around, and I could read English.

"Vietnam, eh? SAM missile suppression, eh?" I was adamant. "Do you, Lt. Col. Sam Khetz, know these proofs personally, or just somebody told you about them? Did you see in your own eyes something about electronic warfare that convinced you to rely on them? Something I don't know about? Did you?"

I waited for an answer for some seconds. There was none. I knew I hit the nail on the head. "From Vietnam," I told him, "I haven't heard of great success against SAMs."

And when he didn't say anything, I added in a rage, "If I were you, Sam, I wouldn't keep quiet. I would get up and oppose going out on this operation Saturday. But no one can do it instead of you. They all depend on this American knowledge that only you, and perhaps Avihu, can estimate the worth of."

Khetz sat silently.

Only then did I grasp what was so weird in that briefing. It was this: the briefing for the attack on the most massive Soviet missiles array, the strongest antiaircraft system in the world, was not a briefing at all. The commanders didn't command. In fact, they didn't know what to say. In fact, it was an apology.

"I pray you, Sam, don't go out on this mission. Tell them!" Khetz shrugged, and I blew my top again. "You keep it in because your mouth was shut in the briefing? Huh? This is a really bad reason. But never mind, Khetz," I said, "we still have time till Saturday." He was looking away from me.

"Well?" Again, no answer came.

"What are you ashamed of? So what the hell if you're ashamed! Be a man, call Agassi. Call your friend Moti. What are friends for? Demand to cancel the operation. At least postpone it."

Khetz answered quietly, "Now I think it was better to leave you to wait for me in the car . . . but it's over. Here, he's coming back."

Our guest was making his way to our table. We rose to receive him. Khetz added quietly,

"Sit with us, listen, and don't interrupt." His voice was low, but clear and hard.

As soon as possible I went to the rest room, and took as much time there as I could. When I got back candles were already lit on all the tables, and the room was half dark and full of diners. My strange couple was bent head to head, immersed in a quiet conversation that seemed like the continuation of other conversations in the past. I sat down and tried to concentrate on my dinner and not pay attention to them. This was easy, since it was noisy, and my basic English didn't allow me to grasp much of the foreign terms that rolled between these two, in American acronyms. Were these parts of equipment? Or perhaps electronic warfare technology? Maybe methods of flying? I didn't know. The words sounded to me like Chinese. I would learn them in time. Only the face of the stranger was cut deep into my memory, a strong, dark, heavy face that reminded me of the actor Telly Savalas. And I still can hear his voice whispering over that table with Khetz, who suddenly seemed to me thin and weak and very, very tired.

Thirty years after this evening I would meet this man again. It would be in the year 2000, and we would meet almost accidentally, in an Irish bar in the suburb of Rosslyn, in northern Virginia. By then David Brogg's head would be as bald as an egg, but his face was as strong as ever. Over a pitcher of dark beer we would both recall that bizarre dinner in Jaffa, on

July 16, 1970, when Brogg sat and preached the faith to us, his eyes moving from Khetz to me—a somber stranger keeping a gloomy silence, poking at his fish and not tasting it.

THE CITROËN WAS RATTLING on again. We were on the Yavneh road, going from Jaffa to Hatzor, and I was rattling again, too, in agony. "Tell me just one thing, Khetz. Is this what we have learned, to rely on magic?" And when he didn't answer me, I said, "Khetz, missile batteries are dangerous! You can't march in there—into the heart of the killing zone—like it was a parade!"

"I know, Iftach."

"Into the killing zone you slide in like commandos, in small groups, and from several directions, so that if one is hit, the others may still hit the target."

"I know. Enough."

" And to fly as fast as you can! And stick close to the ground—there are always hills to hide behind!"

Khetz said in a calm voice, "Listen, Iftach. There is a good reason why we're going in this way, flying formation and at high altitude. You are just not acquainted with the planning."

I couldn't shut up. "What is it I don't know, Khetz? What is there to know? Okay, so you believe in your electronics—switch it on, who cares? But keep low to the ground! The ground defends you, hides you from their radars and missiles! Khetz, the ground is physics, not electronics. The ground is real!"

"I know."

"Then do me a favor and don't fly in there in formation! Why this parade, Khetz, why all this operazia? It is impossible to fight this way. Where is the personal leeway? How will your pilots see the missiles, break—"

"Enough!"

Finally I shut up.

THE SMALL CAR HOPPED and yawed on the old road to Yavneh. The evening was beautiful, and the air was full of the smell of wild blossoms. A large orange moon, almost full, rose in the east and lit the world. The road shone before us like a line of silver, and all around was white like milk. Khetz switched off the car's lights, and so we drove.

"Yo, like daytime!" But there was no joy in his voice. I was silent. Something bad, bigger than I, was happening right in front of me, and there was nothing I could do. I felt tied up and mute, like in a nightmare.

But when we left the main road and turned into the side road leading to our base, Khetz stopped the car on the shoulder and switched the engine off. Suddenly a thought—a hope—rose in me. Was he going to say I had convinced him? And when we got to the base, would he call Moti and postpone this operation to think a little more?

But Khetz only lit a cigarette and asked me what was going on with the Dagger, that air-to-air missile he lent me. After a pause, I was glad to tell him that the test flights were going very well. It seemed that adaptation of the Dagger with the Mirage was possible. All that was left was to launch the missile on an aerial training target, to see if it launched without problems and scored a hit.

The change of subject was relaxing.

Khetz smiled at me warmly and said that the combination of Mirage plus Dagger might be "almost too good." The cigarette illuminated the wrinkles in his lean face and lit sparks in his small, dark eyes. We both were thinking the same thing: the missile the Fighting First was using for tests came from the Falcons, Khetz's Phantoms. They also had too few missiles. Suppose the tests come out well. Then what? Is all this going to be just a theoretical experiment? Nobody at headquarters had any intention of giving us such good stuff.

Then Khetz said, "If your experimental launch is a success, you'll get six Daggers from the Falcons to take with you down to Refidim."

"Wow, Khetz!"

"But with one condition." We eyed each other. "That you undertake personally to bring me a MiG shot down by a Dagger."

"What do you want, his scalp?" We both laughed.

He lit a cigarette for me, too. We sat a little more, perhaps for a longer time than expected of two busy men whose squadrons await them, but long enough for the moon to set. It became dark, and then something strange happened. Khetz was not the sentimental type, and it was not his habit to open his heart, at least not with me. But then, sitting behind the wheel, he opened up and told me of a strange dream that kept repeating the past few nights: Aki was visiting him. This was the first and only occasion when Aki's name was brought up.

Khetz asked me, and I told him about that awful afternoon, two years before, when the phone rang in Refidim and I was scrambled with Zorik to search the Red Sea south of the town of Suez. Once and once again, and for the third time, we scanned the opaque surface of the water while the sun was setting and the air darkened. I told Khetz in detail how we returned time and again to the oil and jet fuel slick, and how we circled each of the few ships in the vicinity, and of the hopes that rose when sailors waved to us with unclear pieces from one cargo ship—its name was *Iola*. But the two men we were looking for were not there. We harried the *Iola* until she entered the Egyptian harbor at Adabiya, where we were driven out by Egyptian antiaircraft artillery. And when we came back the oil slick in the sea widened and the sun sank behind the Egyptian coast, and the colorful oil rainbows died in the dark water and were gone. And when we returned there at first light the next morning, the thread—if there ever was a thread—had vanished, and Aki was gone.

Khetz hadn't heard this story about Aki's death from me. We smoked and talked. His voice, when he talked with me of Aki, was soft and warm. The dream was pleasant, he told me. Not at all frightening.

And when we arrived home and separated, the hour was already late. The moon set and the darkness was total, and the lawns among the eucalyptus trees began to collect dew. We said good night, and each of us climbed his own set of stairs and entered silently into the opposing door. I saw his outside light going off.

Sleep covered me like a waterfall. But at midnight I woke with a start. A sudden fear nailed my flesh, and I didn't know who or what woke me. Sleep did not return, and I lay gazing at the dark ceiling till I understood, slowly and silently, what my friend Sam Khetz had told me.

‡

The cord between us unraveled on Saturday, July 18, 1970.

When I came out of the house in the morning I stopped at the door, went back, and told Ali that Khetz was going to die today. "Aki came to call him," I told her.

Her eyes grew big, and she waved me away like a fly, saying I was tired and stressed, and talking nonsense. "Go to work, and when you get back we'll take a couple of days off. I have to take you in hand."

"But Ali, Khetz agreed—"

"Go."

I went. I didn't fly that day. We were just a minor side show to that day's performance. Menachem led our four-ship division on patrol. A heavy haze hung over the canal when the Phantoms charged into Egypt, and my Mirages didn't see much of what happened on the other side.

That evening the debriefing of Operation Challenge took place. Again we met in the same barracks building in Tel Aviv, and the same audience was present. Sam Khetz was already gone, and his navigator, Einy, was a prisoner in Egypt, joining his predecessors there. The story of the failure of the Phantoms was told by Avihu, the commander of the second Phantom squadron. He himself got back by sheer luck, with his aircraft badly damaged, and survived a very ugly crash landing in Refidim.

The debriefing was fragmented and disjointed. The audience didn't listen. The officers in the front rows conferred secretly all the time with Moshe Dayan, who looked with one eye at the ground near Moti Hod. An EW man stood and began defending the electronic warfare gear that had failed us, giving out details and data; suddenly the whole thing ceased to be a secret. At last Moti took the podium and said, "Gentlemen, we failed in this operation, but the war goes on." Then Dayan and the senior officers left.

In the door out I spoke to my new base commander, Col. Rafi Harlev, who had just replaced Yak, and sheepishly asked if the Falcons squadron was available. Harlev looked at me for a long time.

"No," he finally replied. "We've named a replacement."

Right away I knew who the man was. Even before the name was announced, before I saw Ran Pecker shaking hands with Moti, it was as clear as day that Ran was the right man, the one in the whole air force on whom this terrible mission was built. Frank Savage, the veteran fighting general, brave as the devil, came once again ready to do battle. Ran unpacked his suitcases—already cleared to go for a year of studies in London—returned the plane tickets, silenced his wife, Kheruta, and the kids, who longed for a happy, calm, green year, and reported to Hatzor to take the broken and ailing Falcons under his wing.

Pecker took upon himself a difficult mission, to restore that squadron and lead it while continuing to fight the war, without one day's rest. And he took on one more thing that even Frank Savage—the original—hadn't done: he did all this with a complicated aircraft he didn't know and had never flown before. Ran took off into battle almost immediately, without any grace period.

Truly, when he first harnessed himself in the Phantom, the War of Attrition was close to its end, and he had only three weeks of fighting before the end came. But neither he nor any of us, who watched him admiringly, could have known that. Battles raged daily, and the end was not in sight. The fact is that the moment Ran took over the battered Falcons, this squadron was energized and continued fighting. They didn't win over the missiles, and they suffered additional losses. But they returned to being a squadron, a fighting unit.

THE FUTURE HAD MORE TROUBLE in store for this interesting and problematic squadron, and in 1973 she would need one more Frank Savage. But at the end of the war of attrition, in July 1970, it was Ran Pecker who grabbed her by the hair and pulled her out of the deep mud she was stuck in.

Chapter

15

Comradeship

Sidewinder: a second-generation air-to-air missile. The principle of heat sensing was revealed in the 1940s, when it was found that lead sulfide was sensitive to heat radiation. This feature was used to build nose cones that can find the exhaust pipe of jet engines.

The development of a heat-seeking missile began in 1946 at the U.S. Naval Laboratories. It was called Sidewinder, after the venomous snake that detects its prey via body heat.

A FIRST OPERATIONAL EXPERIENCE with this missile was attained in 1958 over the Strait of Formosa, when Taiwanese fighters launched Sidewinders against Chinese MiGs. One of the American missiles fell into the hands of the Chinese and was transported to the USSR, where a Soviet imitation received the name Atoll. The basic design was used all over the world for the development of many similar missiles, including the Israeli Shafrir. The Sidewinder and its derivatives are the most common air-to-air missiles in the world and are used in most air forces.

The advantages of the heat-seeking missile are its simplicity, low cost ("electronically sophisticated like an ordinary radio set, and mechanically complex like a washing machine"), and independence. Once the seeker is locked on a target, the missile goes for it without any need to enslave the shooting aircraft or its radar to direct it to the target. The limit of the missile is the necessity to have visual contact; thus it is useful mainly at shorter range.

ONCE MORE I HAVE TO PRESENT a fair picture. The world is not perfect, and so when the air force's pilots were fighting, getting killed, or falling into enemy prisons, not everybody in the air force behaved exemplarily. One day, when I was still in the flight school in Hatzerim, we drove up to the base for lunch. Near the dining hall there is a large field, and some air cadets were playing soccer on it. Among the players was one black-haired, handsome officer, tall and well built. He took balls on the fly and converted them into goals. I remember his happy face and his big laugh. He and his way of playing were very impressive. I shall call him Eddy.

We stood near the field and watched. Suddenly somebody slapped me on the back. I turned and saw Asher Snir. I jumped for joy: where did he come from? Snir was not stationed at Hatzerim, and lately we saw each other rather rarely. As a substitute, we wrote letters. He used to call me Baller and I called him Brainer and we both were happy, since we thought we both had this and that. So we stood there gabbing.

Suddenly, when he saw me watching the game, Snir said in contempt and anger, "Come on, let's go away from here. I can't look at him."

"At whom, Eddy?" I asked. "What the problem with him?"

"Don't you know?"

I admitted I didn't. I had no notion of what he was talking about.

Snir told me that this Eddy, a navigator and instructor in the flight school, had refused transfer to Phantoms.

The new aircraft, already involved in a very tough war, were critically short of navigators. The navigator in a Phantom is the operator of many instruments and weapons systems from the rear seat. It is a special and vital job, and at that time and for years later, too, the shortage was so serious that sometimes the squadrons had to put pilots in the backseat as "weights." The Phantom squadrons were screaming for navigators, and the air force scraped them from the bottom of the barrel and from every hole and corner. Navigators were created from the aging, stiff-jointed transport crews yanked from their seats in Dakotas. Navigators were produced by shortened courses in flight school, kids not yet ready to shave. They were put in the backseat and sent, a day after they got their wings, straight into the maelstrom over enemy territory, to find their way and sometimes death or imprisonment.

"Eddy," Snir told me, "decided he was not ready to go to Phantoms."

"So what is he doing here?" I asked.

Snir didn't understand my question: "He instructs, he gives classes. On the evenings he goes to class at the university."

"That's not what I asked," I corrected myself. "How come he is still here?"

"Fact."

Indeed a fact. Eddy would go on as an educator, sending his friends and students to battle, until he finished his full hitch and retired honorably, handsome with his unused wings, and with all the academic titles. To this day he continues publishing his Zionist articles in magazines.

Back to July 1970. Again, we are in the War of Attrition, and I am just a major, the new commander of the Fighting First Mirage squadron.

The one Dagger missile I got from Khetz was still being test-flown on our Mirages, and it was doing well in spite of the hard time we gave it—jettisoning tanks and so forth. On Tuesday we launched it against a decoy. It launched well, hit the target, and that was it. We typed a one-page report and got it to Joe Aretz's pals at headquarters, asking for approval to use the new weapon in flight operations—and for some supply, just a few of the missiles. No answer.

On the other hand, Khetz's promise was kept in spite of his death. On Thursday, five days after his death, carts arrived from the Falcons carrying six long, grayish tubes. The First flew down to the Sinai, to take over the ready line at Refidim. Three of our seven Mirages carried Daggers, two on each. My direct superior, Colonel Harlev, and all the headquarters staff knew about it without knowing. My squadron was armed with the new unauthorized weapons, and my commanders sat in their offices, keeping silent and waiting to see what would happen.

‡

On July 27, before dusk, we were scrambled to the northern section of the Suez Canal. The controller directed us to search the area thoroughly: "There are MiGs!" The haze was heavy, and the setting sun in the west added to the difficult conditions and created a brown, blinding halo. We kept a safe distance, and the water of the canal looked like a shining strip.

My wingman, Yaari, saw them first and called them out, "Bogies at eleven o'clock!"

Immediately I saw them, too—two small, black silhouettes with swept-back wings. The planes rose from the ground and climbed. It was hard to discern in which direction they were flying, toward us or away. They rolled over in front of me and dived, dropping black dots, and straightened over the Egyptian sands to flee home. In a minute I passed over the blast of the bombs they left behind.

At low level, my Mirage was wild and wanted to go. My speed indicator ran up fast and reached 750 knots—more than 1,300 kilometers per hour, high over the speed of sound. We raced deeper and deeper into Egypt, like tornadoes over the surface of the delta marshes, skimming the water plains that in the setting sun were painted with different textures by slow currents of water and wind. We buzzed dozens of boats with their white sails. The low sun blinded us with reflections in the water, broken here and there by wide, muddy expanses. The closest MiG looked like a small, round dot, black on the burning background of red and yellow. My face heated up under the visor.

"One, you're clean—I am clean." That was Yaari, a good man to have on your wing.

I overtook the last one. Air brakes out just for a second—a hard buffet and my Mirage stood on her head like a horse about to take a hurdle, but soon calmed down again. I had equalized my speed with the target. For a second I sat behind the MiG in close formation, just three hundred meters away. We both were almost touching the water flying at extremely high speed, more than six hundred knots; from the corners of my eyes I felt the water streaming past me like mad, as though I were on the deck of a very, very fast speedboat, sitting high in my seat, my ass above the streaming surface below. To aim right I had to get down an extra two to three meters below my target. So I did it very slowly and gently—I held myself down, led my gun-sight pip into the center of the jet pipe in front of me, and fixed it on the yellow eye of his afterburner's flame. Carefully, I aimed.

A caress of the trigger. My cannons roared. A hit! Something broke off the MiG and flew toward me, rolling, passed near, and was lost behind. The MiG descended just a bit and touched the water. A big jet of spray, and he took off again with rocking wings, came down and touched again, and continued bouncing like a stone. As I pulled up he disintegrated beneath me. Some fire. No ejection. I looked up. There was the other MiG farther ahead, continuing his flight west.

"Number two, the other one is yours." I pulled up and passed over Yaari's plane to the other side and set myself in a defensive formation. My eyes scanned the surrounding area, and right away I saw another section of MiG-17s. They approached from the north, at an acute angle to our heading. They were still far away, and we were much too fast for them, but suddenly one of them fired in our general direction. Flickers and flashes came out of his nose.

"Come on, Hassan," I muttered, "don't waste your time."

We continued at extremely high speed westward, still shaving the marshes.

"Two, you're clean," I informed Yaari. No use bothering him with those new MiGs; let him concentrate on the kill. We would deal with these two later, on the way back.

A LARGE FLARE BROKE OUT on Yaari's wing. For a moment I was stunned. I even thought I had made a mistake—could it be that Hassan had hit him? But then I understood. Yaari had decided to launch a Dagger at the MiG in front of him. What? Was it possible that the Dagger's sensor could pick up the target engine against this hot background at such a long distance?

"Wow," I thought, "the older missiles could never do it." I didn't even think of trying it myself.

I waited to see how the first launch of a Dagger from a Mirage would play out. I waited and waited, but no missile launched from Yaari's plane. What was going on here? Fire continued to flare beneath Yaari's wing; something nasty was developing.

"Number two," I ordered, "you are on fire. Turn back immediately!"

Yaari obeyed and turned hard to the east. I followed to escort him. But as I began my turn, my windshield passed over that distant MiG. My gunsight traversed it, and instantly my Dagger announced a lock-on, humming loud and clear in my earphones. My finger acted on its own, and the missile launched and flew ahead on a large plume of flame. I stopped my turn and watched, spellbound. The MiG and my Dagger raced ahead, the white trail of the missile curling and then going down and uniting with the MiG. A short crack and a large bonfire flared out and smeared the wet, green surface of the Nile delta. Oh, yeah.

Instantly I returned to my sharp turn east, but now I didn't see Yaari. We were flying so fast in opposite directions that we must be many kilometers away from each other. I slapped my brow with an open palm. How could I let myself lose Yaari in this smoggy air! And him with a fire on his wing. To add to my worry, he didn't answer my radio calls. I slapped myself again, even harder: a separation. And my fault!

And so I raced east, looking for some sign of Yaari, my heart thumping heavily. On our super-fast chase west we had gone deep into Egypt, some thirty kilometers or more, and the minutes on the way back seemed long.

And as in a child's game, all the signs left behind appeared again. First the two MiG-17s reappeared, with my friend Hassan the shooter in the lead. For a moment I was almost lured into a little action with them, with my second Dagger. But I passed through their formation like the wind and let them fade into oblivion.

Then came the fire on the marsh: smoke and a large ellipse of wreckage, here and there some small tongues of scattered fires. I lowered a wing to make sure, and no, this was not Mirage wreckage. I passed over the junkyard and continued east to Sinai. Next came the water mirrors, and now with the sun at my back, their light was dimmed, and the wide, muddy expanses with the many white sails. The marshes ended and the sand dunes came, and then, at full speed, I finally pulled up and crossed the canal. Passing under me I saw the outpost of Fortress Alon. A thin thread of smoke still rose from it, a reminder of the bombs the MiGs dropped. Amazing how fast it had been. Such a short time!

Only when I approached Refidim and communication was renewed did I find Yaari. He was on his final landing approach, his wing black with soot, but he and his Mirage were safe and sound.

Back on the ground, we found out what had caused the fire. The rocket engine of the Dagger had burned fine, but the missile couldn't launch. Simply, the mounting of the American missile on its French pylon had been done wrong. The training of my mechanics had been quick and dirty, and this was the price we paid. Before I court-martialed someone, I recalled that Khetz had been right. There was good reason for orderly procedures. True, the Dagger had given us an exceptional MiG kill , but we definitely might have lost a Mirage, too.

I issued a report and waited tensely for the reaction. Somebody surely would wake up now, after we had used Daggers in battle. What would happen now? To my amazement, absolutely nothing. So we trained our mechanics some more, put our four remaining Daggers back on our wings, and waited.

Two days passed, and on July 30 it was again our turn to be one of the first sections to scramble. The red bell rang. When I crossed the canal over the city of Suez I saw, far away to the west, short white trails in the air. I directed my Mirage there and went to maximum speed. When I came closer I saw a bunch of black dots dancing in the air like a cloud of insects in summertime. I climbed up over the mess, lowered a wing, and found a big dogfight under me. Everywhere there were MiG-21s, Mirages, and Phantoms turning and shooting at each other. Missiles' smoke trails streaked through the air. In the middle a lone parachute stood out like a dislocated mushroom.

I selected a good MiG and joined another Mirage who was scuffling with him. I saw immediately red, five-pointed stars on the MiG's wings. The MiG itself was painted beautifully and shone like a new car fresh from the factory. It was clear, these MiG jockeys were not Egyptians, they were Russians! I almost saluted my childhood hero, the defender of the motherland, Alexei Merseyev.

My MiG began fleeing west. I began to chase him. He had a two-thousand-meter head start, a little too far for a good shot. Before I managed to get closer, an order came over the radio: "Abort battle!" and all our aircraft complied and turned east. The area emptied within seconds, and here I was alone again, chasing west. I sent both my Daggers after him and saw them closing on him. The long range gave him time to see them, and he broke hard left and then right. Both my missiles burst right near him, and something sprayed out from his fuselage. Now I had to hustle back before somebody else showed up. I crossed the canal behind all my pals, and when I was again over the Sinai I remembered something.

"Two scalps," I whispered in a low voice, either to myself or to somebody else who couldn't hear me anymore.

We all landed in Refidim, and my Fighting First hosted the happy gang of Mirage and Phantom jockeys from all over the country. It seemed they were all together for that Russian feast. We figured out that there had been twelve Mirages and Phantoms on our side, and some sixteen Soviet MiG-21s on the enemy's side. Four MiGs were shot down. I didn't announce my MiG as a kill, since I hadn't seen him go down. Some years later it came out that this MiG didn't make it back to base—he was seriously damaged and the pilot ejected on his way home. The kill was then divided between the two Mirage pilots who had fired at him.

This battle—the mother of all multiparticipant battles—gave me reason for joy: all the hits were from missiles alone; cannons had played no part. Suddenly we were modern. And all the Soviet aircraft that went down had suffered Dagger hits.

True, we didn't come out completely clean. A Soviet missile also hit my friend Snir, but he managed to land his damaged Mirage in Refidim.

But then there was something else. I was amazed to learn that mine was not the only Mirage carrying Daggers. The other Mirages came to this battle carrying Daggers, too. I asked how they got them, and they told me that in the past two days they had received Daggers. Just like that. And this happened while I was sitting on pins and needles in Refidim preparing to defend myself. This was great news, but I was left wondering when and in which way permission had been given. Did somebody sit down after my kill, and the near accident afterward, and make that decision? Who, when, and on what basis—my short report from Refidim?

I never found the answers to these questions, and I didn't waste much time on it. The war was still on, and this was it.

No one in authority has ever mentioned the series of technical, operational, and safety risks two squadron commanders from Hatzor took on themselves when they passed elements from one weapons system to another, proved it, and sent it to battle. They did it relying on their own understanding of the situation, and taking authority and responsibility when everybody else sat at arm's length. My own chutzpah and Khetz's comradeship under fire had doubled the firepower of our interception force—and just been forgotten.

THE BIG BATTLE AGAINST THE Russians was the last aerial combat of the War of Attrition. This thrilling victory rectified somewhat the heavy, tragic mood that enveloped us all following the Phantoms' wars against the SAM batteries, but in essence it didn't change the situation; Israel lost that war.

Fact: a week after this dogfight, on August 7, 1970, Israel accepted a cease-fire agreement with Egypt, brokered by the United States. This agreement, known as "Roger's Plan," called for both sides to remain in place. From our point of view, the important thing was to keep the Suez Canal out of the killing zone of the Egyptian Soviet missile array, which at that time still lay farther away, some several dozens of kilometers west of the canal. After all, this had been the objective of the Phantoms all along. But on the day after the agreement was signed—and in an obvious provocation—the Egyptians moved all their missile batteries right to the banks of the Suez Canal. Now the threat of the missiles penetrated our area in the Sinai. From a defensive system to protect Cairo, the missiles had suddenly turned into offensive weapons.

This was one of the moments of decision taught in military history books, the moment when both sides stand facing each other for the decisive battle. Both opponents are worn down and tired, and only willpower decides who wins. This is what Itzhak Sade meant when he told the Palmach soldiers that when you are cold and wet, this is the time to keep going, for the same rain is falling on the enemy, and a decision is near. Major General Gorodish portrayed such a moment in his famous, pompous words after the Six-Day War: "We looked Death straight in the eyes, and he lowered his."

On August 8, 1970, the Egyptians looked straight at us, and Israel lowered its eyes.

Strategically, we lost the War of Attrition not just because of our failure against the SAMs. That specific struggle was just one campaign among many, and not a big one—altogether, just fifty Phantom sorties. Besides this failure, the War of Attrition was full of thousands of combat sorties and other campaigns that had worked very well—against MiGs, in the attacking of ground targets, and raiding deep into enemy territory. And at the end of those three hard years our government choked. The failure of the Phantoms against the SAMs was the last straw.

The real reason for our loss had not been tactical. It had been strategic, and bigger even than military power per se.

Our spectacular military victory in the Six-Day War had confused our estimation of power. After it, we were deluded into believing that nothing was impossible. We saw everything through the muzzle of the gun, and forgot how to make realistic evaluations of the power and forbearance of nations. We disregarded the deep pockets of our opponents, who were much richer than we were. Egypt's population was a dozen times more than Israel's, and Syria's threefold. Both were autocratic states with no democratic checks and balances. That, and a low standard of living in their populations, gave them power to mobilize and sacrifice people at will, and supplied them with a multitude of soldiers.

Additional depth was added by other Arab states, and the material and political assistance of the Soviet Union and its satellites. All this was supported by international agreement that Israel was an aggressor, since it held conquered territories against UN resolutions.

Spellbound under the mysticism of our limitless power, we refused to see the true direction the war of attrition was taking. We narrowed our view, as if looking through a straw, at battles, especially at the more successful ones, and whitewashed our failures. With such self-deceit, no wonder that the loss in the important battle against the SAM missile array, which couldn't be covered up, was perceived as a national disaster.

The enemy, on the other hand, was wholly different in essence and goals. The governments of Egypt and Syria had no true conflict of interests with Israel. What bothered them was the dishonor they suffered because of their failure in Israel's War of Independence in 1948. Our conquest of the West Bank and Gaza in the war of 1967 worsened that failure seven times over—the conquered areas gave material and comprehensive meaning to the failure. They also gave a direction for solution of the conflict; the Arab states said it clearly, "the return of every inch of the motherland" (no matter that most of it was useless desert, and was declared "theirs" just yesterday—it all was a matter of pride). The three noes of the Khartoum enunciate, first and foremost a deep insult.

Of course, insult was not everything. There were deep social, religious, and national currents fermenting and waiting their turn. Still, it was hurt Arab national pride—symbolized by the conquered areas—that prevented any political process between the parties. Probably in those first years after 1967 the key to a solution had been in our hands, but old habits and ideas held us captive, too. Soon we attached ourselves to those new land areas. Sharm El Sheikh, the southernmost and most remote point in the Sinai and a magnificent scuba diving site, suddenly became more important than peace.

Within a short time, we had declared we were "waiting for a call from the Arab states," but we didn't want—and soon couldn't use—the captured areas as a deposit and open a political process with Egypt, Syria, and Jordan. Time for such openings was limited, since the Palestinians in Gaza and the West Bank—the only faction that had a real conflict with us, and the real danger to the Jewish state—were awakening.

When we chose to fight over the spoils of war—those conquered territories—we forgot our true goal, the establishment of the Jewish state. Our loss of political focus led to disruption of our military strategy, and since then that reality has been perpetuating itself: war and enmity became the dominant constants in our region, and they awakened deep, sleeping currents and strengthened them. Within a decade those currents had reshaped the warring parties, and the substrate on which they were functioning.

Egypt and Syria didn't have this problem, and they had no military illusions. After the loss in 1967 they pinned their hopes not on victory in any given battle, but on time and depth of resources. The Egyptians and the Syrians looked at war as a process of wearing us down. Their rulers saw losses in battles against the IDF as a reasonable possibility (though some events angered them). On the other side, their (pretty few) wins gave them encouragement and reason to continue the struggle.

A war between sides so different is called, in strategic language, "asymmetrical." Achieving victory in asymmetrical war is not a simple concept, since the meaning of victory is different for each of the warring parties. Whoever gets into a war like that must begin by setting policy and strategy that define "victory," and how to achieve it. If you think this explanation fits only the case of the war of attrition in 1970, you are wrong.

Policy and strategy are much more crucial than any battle, but it is easy to avoid defining them. Thinking about deep concepts requires soul-searching, including examination of conventions that have rooted themselves in us for years. And even harder, it points the finger right at the higher echelons of power. All in all, it is so much easier to deal with tactical questions—how to do this, how to do that. Tactical questions are evident, clear, and tangible. Everyone can relate to them. They are emotional. This is exactly the reason why that tactical failure, in the battle against the Egyptian SAMs, became shrouded in such symbolic importance.

In fact, all that happened there was relatively unimportant: the IDF—and specifically the Israeli Air Force—hadn't found a good answer to one tactical question: how to destroy SAM arrays. But the government of Israel, which didn't bother with policy and strategy and never thought to find solutions to problems within itself, was shocked to find out that the only service provider they ever contracted—the IDF—suddenly couldn't answer a question. Ezer Weizman, a political figure of influence and a military authority, interpreted this failure of ours in universal, almost apocalyptical terms—"the missile has bent the aircraft's wing"—and we were all moved. The national discussion turned into tactical babble about which was stronger—the airplane (ours) or the SAM missile (supposedly theirs). And what was not said, but implied, was even more horrible: the victory of the SAM batteries created a psychological image of an unstoppable steamroller coming toward us.

In this way the government of Israel, on August 8, 1970, faced the Egyptian challenge with empty hands and chose to lower its eyes.

We, the soldiers, suffered feelings of personal failure, even guilt. We had failed militarily, disappointed our nation. And since the elimination of the SAM batteries was given exclusively to the Phantom squadrons, the Phantoms' failure brought about the collapse of a whole tower of expectations. The air force's then deputy commander, Benny Peled, known for his sharp tongue, summed it all up this way, "The knight in the shining armor has been knocked off his horse." Those feelings of failure and guilt were stamped deep into the fabric of the air force, and affected its thinking and actions in the coming decade.

Let us go to the problems that caused our knight in shining armor to fall on his arse. It is important, since this experience defined the Israeli Air Force and all the characters in our story for years.

First, the War of Attrition had been more or less static on the ground. Soon, the emphasis passed to a vigorous air struggle, dogfights, air-to-ground attacks on the front and in the enemy's rear, as well as airborne intelligence missions. This brought about a showdown between our aircraft and the SAMs. Destruction of the SAMs was necessary to give us freedom of flight—air superiority—over our operational areas, and to enable us to provide close ground support. In the first two years of the war, the burden was borne by the remaining aircraft from the Six-Day War, supplemented by light attack A-4 Skyhawk fighters purchased from the United States.

Then, in September 1969, the first four Phantoms landed in Israel. The F-4 Phantom was the masterpiece of American military aviation, and its arrival brought with it very high expectations. Almost immediately the

Phantoms were integrated into the fighting, and soon they took part in all fighter missions. Then elimination of Egyptian SAM batteries was allotted only to Phantoms. Then the SAMs were being deployed in greater numbers and began to be integrated into denser and wider arrays. New missiles and radar were supplied by the Soviets, and soon some batteries were operated by blond, blue-eyed soldiers.

All in all, this mission took about fifty Phantom sorties. Five Phantoms were shot down in those fifty flights, and two more were badly damaged and returned by sheer luck. This is a rate of loss of one aircraft per every 8.3 sorties, or in military jargon, a 12 percent dropout rate. Such a dropout rate—three times higher than in Operation Focus in 1967—is unacceptable in a prolonged war. Simple arithmetic shows that our newly acquired Phantom force lost 15 percent of its machines against the SAMs in a month.

Indeed, the Phantom failed in its war against the SAMs: it didn't find a way to hit without getting hit.

Why were the Phantoms getting so badly torn up?

As a generalization, an aircraft that flies in a SAM-defended area must choose one of two optional flight profiles, each with its own advantages and defects. The first is low-level flight. This profile is relatively immune to detection by the missiles' radars but vulnerable to the manually operated antiaircraft guns. And the second profile is high flight, which is diametrically opposed. Of course, the choice had to be based on estimation of which threat was more serious at any given moment.

Until 1969, the Israeli Air Force believed in coming in low to surprise the enemy, and this profile worked well for us in Operation Focus. From experience we learned what cost (dropout rate) we could expect. It all changed when the Phantom crews returned from their training in the United States. Khetz, Avihu Ben Nun, and their comrades came back with the opposite preference after learning that high flight was used successfully by the Americans in Vietnam. This flight profile was chosen by our Phantom squadrons over Egypt, and indeed, not one Phantom was damaged by ack-ack. But the toll of six Phantoms lost to missiles put this decision in question. Perhaps the conditions in Egypt were different from Vietnam, or perhaps not everything they understood about Vietnam was totally correct. In any case, replicating this method in our own war was going badly.

There was still a last hope for the high flight solution: electronic warfare gear. These top-secret containers were supposed to nullify the SAMs' radar efficiency altogether. They were rushed from America, taken out of their boxes, and hung on the Phantoms in haste by incompetent technicians (no one had time to train and test them) on the eve of Operation Challenge. The theoretical performance of these instruments—as presented by the American experts—led to the flight tactic that caused my friends' and my own dismay. No one in our air force really knew how this equipment would perform or had tested it before. It was a matter of blind faith. But at the end of the day it turned out that this equipment was not appropriate for a new kind of Soviet SAM radar (SAM-3) that had just been introduced into Egypt and was unknown in Vietnam. Low-level flight might reduce the toll, but Khetz, Avihu, and their crews flew in like ducks over a hunters's blind. Operation Challenge failed totally, and the fact that only Khetz's plane was shot down there was sheer luck.

What would have happened had our Phantoms flown to attack the SAMs at low level using an evasive approach, as in the Six-Day War, instead of arriving head high, like Sir Lancelot?

Any answer to "what if?" must be speculative. But still there is a rational, methodical analysis, called operational research. If it did not exist, how could we plan anything for the future? This method begins with laying down hypotheses, then running scenarios using all the data we have at our disposal, getting quantitative results, and finally deriving conclusions. The good thing about this method is that everyone can check the results. In fact, this is the way science works.

So when we assume that our Phantoms attacked the SAM batteries at low level and using evasive approaches—a profile we have good data about—we find that along those fifty sorties we suffered just two losses instead of six. Had we flown this way, clearly the weight of attrition would have been different.

But that's only tactics. Let us look one step beyond the field of view of the Phantom commanders. What about the handling of the air force? What would have happened, for example, had Gen. Moti Hod decided to deploy all the weapons in his arsenal, and not just the Phantoms, against the SAMs?

Aside from its 30 Phantoms, the IAF had 163 other operational fighters (45 Mirages, 82 Skyhawks, and 36 Super Mysteres and Vautours). All these 163 planes were fast jets capable of carrying bombs and attacking ground targets. In fact, they were attacking all the time, and were attacking SAM sites until early 1970. They all had weapons and methods that worked. Nobody is arguing that the Phantoms were more modern and much better in attack than the other aircraft, but their value was well above zero. These other aircraft were less effective than the Phantom, but they had worth, too. If their chances to destroy a target were lower, more sorties could be ordered. There were always a number of sorties that would equalize the chance to achieve the mission with the Phantoms. You only have to consider what price you pay for these additional sorties. This was an easy calculation. We have reliable data about their vulnerability.

So the same results achieved by 50 Phantom sorties would have been achieved by 95 sorties of the whole lot. This is 45 more sorties, and we still would lose 6 aircraft (according to simulations: 2 Phantoms and 4 others). The same? Not at all! The burden now is shared among 10 squadrons and 190 aircrews, rather than by 2 squadrons with 30 crews. The loss of half an aircraft per squadron is far easier to accept.

Had this been the case, the Phantom wouldn't have been toppled and certainly not the air force. Had we met the Egyptian challenge of August 8 in this way, I don't think the Israeli government would have lost its nerve afterwards.

When I was processing the alternative above—this was done long after—I asked myself, "How could it happen that the IAF gave that super-critical mission to just 30 Phantoms, and 163 good fighter aircraft pilots were left on the sidelines, watching their friends get cut to pieces?" I have some assumptions of my own. Here is the first: the air force command didn't see the War of Attrition as a decisive war, but as a linear series of operations, one following another (this fits in with the general perception in Israel of this forgotten war). Accordingly, our command took every mission singly, and gave it to their best problem solver, which in the case of the SAMs was certainly the Phantoms. A supporting factor in this error was the eagerness of the Phantoms' squadron commanders to go. They wanted to prove themselves by having the Phantoms do everything.

This eagerness was very praiseworthy, but in this case it was checked neither by the high command, who were supposed to control the situation, nor by the squadron commanders, who were the guardians of their tools. In simple language, we had a command problem.

And another assumption: the process itself led to rapid loss of the psychological capability to attack SAMs by other squadrons. Immediately after January 1970, when the Phantoms took that mission away, the IAF's groupthink didn't allow employment of other aircraft against the SAMs. It was just Phantoms, a mission too dangerous for ordinary aircraft. In an odd perversion of logic, dogfights were treated differently. In them we were sent to fly freely everywhere. In this way 85 percent of our air force's fighters became irrelevant for the most critical missions we had at the time. The protest of Lt. Col. Uri Even Nir, a Mirage squadron commander who stood up and asked, "What makes those fucking SAM sites so different from any other fucking target?" wasn't even noticed.

And if we allow ourselves an open mind, why shouldn't we get out of the aircraft box and ask what the IDF at large could have done with all its equipment—artillery and so forth—to help in this critical mission except by sitting on its ass and shaking its head gloomily while the Phantoms were crushed, alone.

The carpenter didn't use his tools correctly. He had a shop full of machinery, but he put all the hard work on the new, shiny saw he just bought from America. The saw overheated and broke, and the whole shop stopped production. This, in my humble opinion, is the crux of the story of the Phantoms in the War of Attrition.

‡

Sometimes I think, "Who knows? Had we not been so timid, we might have won that war after all. The rain definitely was falling on both sides; just read the Egyptian reports. And I imagine that after the Egyptian arrogance of August 8, our government stands its ground; the IDF and the air force go out to battle with blood in their eyes, and we hit—all of us, Mirages, Skyhawks, Phantoms, artillery, commando units, and everything else—the SAMs. By then they were close to the Suez Canal and in easy reach, and we chop them up with all the tools at our disposal. We definitely could have done it; all we had to do was exert ourselves just a little more.

Egypt's president Nasser died on September 28, 1970, just five weeks after we threw in our hand, and Egypt was immersed for some time in other things. Had we done as I indicated above, the War of Attrition would have ended in victory—not a strategic one, but at least a military victory. We would have been spared all the complications dumped on us by that failure.

But then, I remind myself that strategic wars are not won by tactical victories. And the deeper problem—the definition of our national priorities, policy, and strategy—could in no way have been solved by the poor carpenter and all his saws. The deeper problem was the business of the landlord, but unfortunately, the landlord was no better than his carpenter, and didn't ask himself what was being produced in that shop, and to what end. Even after the cease-fire agreement, and during the three years that led up to the Yom Kippur War in 1973, the strategic question was never raised. We continued playing by ourselves in cloud cuckoo land, and the political and strategic reasons for our failure in the War of Attrition were repressed.

Only the carpenter, the air force, blamed himself. He explained everything in terms of his tactical failure against the SAM missiles, so he bought himself new saws, trained hard with them, and hoped for the best.

Chapter

16

Clarity

F-4 Phantom (Israeli nickname: "Hammer"): a U.S.-made, two-engine, two-seat jet fighter. The two crewmen sit in tandem, the pilot in front, and the navigator, officially called the WSO, weapons systems officer, behind. The aircraft was developed by McDonnell Douglas for a wide variety of missions. Its maximum speed is more than Mach 2, twice the speed of sound, attack radius 280 miles, and altitude ceiling more than 50,000 feet. It can carry bombs and air-to-ground missiles up to 7,257 kilograms. It can handle diverse attack profiles. For air-to-air, it has up to eight missiles, an onboard radar, and a six-barreled Vulcan cannon with 640 20mm shells.

The first four Phantoms landed in Israel on November 5, 1969. The Falcons squadron was established in Hatzor, followed by the Hammers squadron in Ramat David a few weeks laer. Other Phantom squadrons were established after the War of Attrition.

A YEAR PASSED AFTER THE END of the War of Attrition, and in August 1971, I was ordered to leave the Fighting First to establish a new Phantom squadron at Hatzerim Air Base. My departure from the First was not a happy one.

I left feeling that I hadn't succeeded in my previous assignment the way I had hoped. Although I could take credit for the successful operational performance of the squadron during the last months of the War of Attrition, and few other noteworthy things in the following year, the fact was that I had been pushed out. This was never said openly, but I knew that Col. Rafi Harlev, Hatzor's base commander after Yak, didn't believe in me. This was not a pleasant feeling, but I suffered more from how relations developed between the squadron's pilots and me.

In every squadron there is an "opposition," but the one that faced me in the First consisted of most of the pilots. I knew they respected the operational leadership I gave the squadron. I had never had any difficulties with discipline. But my pilots showed no initiative; they just followed like zombies. My life became unpleasant, especially since this was the opposite of my expectations when I took command of the squadron a year before, at the height of the war. But a year later, after we had gone through a difficult war together and done our jobs well, my squadron became alienated from me. People were distant, dragging their feet. It was difficult to work in such an atmosphere.

Not that I intended to give up on this squadron. I thought long and concluded that it all emanated from the cuts in personnel I had made during the war.

"It's clear," I said to myself assuredly, "that my pilots have a grudge against me, since I've abused their buddies." Then it was just a social problem, and the solution to such a problem should be found also at the social level, shouldn't it? I started an active social program, and we had some good parties and great squadron trips. We took some time off, and the entire squadron went traveling around the Sinai. We spent nights among the dunes, around bonfires, singing with guitars. On camels' backs we climbed the highest granite mountains, and dived on coral reefs in crystal waters. We held lectures, dancing parties; everybody had a great time, all to no avail. The gray atmosphere appeared again the next day. All this activity did wonders for the squadron's mechanics and me, but it didn't help with my main problem: the pilots. Except for Menachem Sharon, loyal to a fault, gloomy faces still filled the briefing room, and no spark of initiative flared in the vacant faces before me.

I recalled a lesson Ran Pecker gave us in the BBN leadership course. "Esprit de corps derives from operational success," he had told us, but somehow this didn't help either. After the war, when we introduced the Dagger missile and had outstanding results in aerial combat, we continued to maintain the highest operational activity: we took over the reconnaissance mission and equipment from the Bats—who replaced her Mirages and became the third Phantom squadron—and began crisscrossing the Middle East, taking photographs. Wearing pressure suits like astronauts, we soared the heights and watched Egypt from altitudes of more than seventy thousand feet. Then we flew at low level to take pictures in all the countries surrounding Israel. We flew operations almost every day. And if this was not enough, when headquarters decided to disconnect the Mirage's airborne radar and take us out of night readiness, our Fighting First didn't give up the right to be operational twenty-four hours a day. After a serious recalibration of radars and pilots, we demanded a nighttime showdown against the new king of the mountain: the Phantoms. In a night of competition using our outdated French Cyrano radar, our Mirages managed to "hit" the same number of "enemy targets" as the American monsters. This was truly operational black magic, and while the other Mirages went to sleep at dusk, we proudly remained night fighters.

All along we did a lot of training. We initiated and organized "war days" and "activity nights," where we attacked simulated enemy opponents in the air and on the ground. We trained new Mirage pilots, and our level of flying was high, with no accidents whatsoever. The squadron was in excellent condition. Still, I got no enthusiastic feedback from my pilots. What else could a squadron commander do? I began doubting myself.

I concluded that in everything involving flying I knew what I was doing, but on the command side something was missing. I felt stuck. I didn't know how to command. I understood I had to go.

It was clear to me that I was to part with my beloved Mirage and the green lawns of Hatzor. This change was taking me down a new path in life. I knew that from now on I would not be dancing in the air anymore, but would be attacking ground targets with heavy bombs and struggling with SAM missile batteries. I knew Ali didn't like it at all, though she said only a few words about it.

And I was leaving someone else.

"Goodbye, Hassan," I thought. "Now we are done forever. I shall leave you in the capable hands of Gonen, Epstein, and their friends."

Well, what did I know?

I did one important thing in the last weeks at the Fighting First: some serious soul-searching.

I opened a new notebook and wrote on the cover: "Establishment of the Orange Tails." The first pages were devoted to a severe self-criticism of my first tenure as squadron commander, where I had succeeded and where I had failed. For some deficiencies I could devise possible remedies, but on a few I just threw up my hands—they seemed to be faults rooted in my nature. It was my capacity for leadership that remained a mystery. So I decided to stop agonizing and moved on. This will take care of itself; time will tell.

Then came the list of decisions: against each line item I wrote what I was going to do differently in the Orange Tails. This process reminded me of my youth, when I had devised my "decisions for life"—always positive, all inside, etc.—but now these weren't decisions of a young dreamer anymore. I was thirty. I had made mistakes in the past; I analyzed them and drew appropriate conclusions, and I was going to do something about them.

When I left the podium after I had passed the squadron's flag to Maj. Avi Lanir, there were cheers and affectionate cries from the mechanics. As anticipated, the pilots stood silently. On my way out I stopped my car near a Mirage hangar. I climbed the ladder onto one of them, and the gentle fighter nodded its beak to me, as always. The Phantom that I was now learning to fly was cumbersome and heavy, and when I climbed aboard, it didn't notice my coming at all. I patted the Mirage, and drove down to Hatzerim.

The establishment of the Orange Tails fighter squadron was difficult and full of problems.

First, there was a delay in the arrival of the aircraft we were supposed to get from America. The Americans were annoyed with us for some reason by then, and at one time they even announced that the contract for the Phantoms was canceled. The whole concept for establishing the Orange Tails was shaken, and my small team, which assembled every Thursday in a small office in Hatzerim, wondered whether our transfers from our units, and all the work we were doing, was going to be for nothing.

And the work was endless. We had to build a fighter squadron from scratch. There were the five of us, each coming from a different part of the air force—three pilots, one technical officer, and one nineteen-year-old female adjutant. No one had Phantom experience, so we started by deciding that each had to go out to see what people were doing in the other Phantom squadrons.

The stationing of the new squadron at Hatzerim was another problem. The Negev base lacked resources for our incoming personnel and their families. In the early 1970s Hatzerim was just five years old, a small, dusty place, limited in just about everything. The roads to the Negev desert were few and patched. There was nothing green or shady there, and the nearby town, Beer-Sheva, was just a border town, with a few narrow streets in which our women could find no shopping. The best restaurant was Romanian Maurice's Chorba Soup Corner. As a substitute for theater and dancing you could wait in line at Sarussi's slaughterhouse till the chicken you had selected for Friday's dinner flew out of the door headless to dance its last in the yard among the rubble and the putrid puddles. No wonder almost nobody in the Phantom community wanted to join us.

Our main lack was in professional air and ground crews. Air force headquarters supplied us mainly with rookies who had just finished flight and technical school. Instantly, even without seeing them in Hatzerim, we directed them to the older Phantom squadrons for training on their jobs. We, of course, had no Phantoms or professional technicians at our disposal. Everybody was aware of our questionable future. Would we be a squadron or not? When I came to our sister Phantom squadrons to learn to fly the aircraft, I was met by standoffish looks. They thought, Who knows? He might use his time with us to steal our experienced crews. Similar suspicions followed the other members of my team. These were false suspicions. I didn't try to lure anybody, and I strongly forbade any of my men even to allude to anything like that. I had no interest in anyone who didn't ask to come on his own initiative. They should come and beg.

We had no idea when—or if—we would get our promised Phantoms so that we could create a new squadron. And so, in some perverse exercise of logic, we worked even harder. We wanted to create facts. Our efforts bore the stamp of a challenge, as if everything would be created from inside us. We strove to be seen and heard, and turned our lives exemplary. We wrote everything and published lessons and conclusions immediately after every stage. People laughed at our openness, but the materials that accumulated began to create a clear agenda of the process of creating a squadron, and every decision we took we could base on preceding actions.

Our base had several subterranean hangars for the new aircraft. Those hangars had been standing empty for a long time, and the systems of infrastructure—fuel, electricity, communication—were out of order. Some were just big holes in the ground, their concrete floors covered by sand dunes brought in by the wind. Then we brought back to Hatzerim all our people who had found no place to study the Phantom, and established a company of renovators. They put on utilities and began cleaning, whitewashing, and pulling electric cables. When parts and supplies began to arrive, we opened a warehouse in one of the hangars and then a shop for treating Phantom components.

We got base housing for our squadron offices. It stood at the far rim of the base, past the runways. It was a lone, empty building, vacant perhaps from the time of its construction, and the rooms were deserted and shabby. There was no telephone or electricity, so for the time being the virtual Orange Tails squadron continued to be run from a small office at base headquarters, near the offices of the rabbi and the welfare officer. In the whole air force there was no written material that could teach us how to build a squadron from scratch. No guru knew what was needed and from whom to get it, what should be done, and in which order to do it. The base commander, Col. Shaike Bareket, was very smart and didn't try to interfere in the process. He would smoke a cigarette with us, listen for a while, and leave with a few words of encouragement. We had been thrown into the water to sink or swim, and it was no wonder that at times we felt alone.

Then air force headquarters saw there was no end in sight and decided to give us two Phantoms from each squadron, to start us off with six aircraft. Then the opposition to the Orange Tails peaked. Everybody was short of aircraft, professional teams, equipment, munitions—and money. At staff meetings in Tel Aviv we were openly characterized as a "toy squadron" that was screwing things up for the other Phantom squadrons. Each time we were called to discuss another facet of the Orange Tails' establishment, the participants would produce lists of their own needs, and somehow they always matched what we were to get. Staff officers began to vaccilate, and soon I felt a lack of assurance spreading. Orders to pass men or equipment to us were delayed.

Once, I entered the office of my former base commander in Hatzor, Colonel Harlev, and told him that in spite of a clear order from headquarters, we hadn't gotten a shipment of Dagger missiles from his base. These missiles were needed to enable us to enter operational readiness.

"You're not getting them," he told me.

"Excuse me, sir?"

"Major Spector, I suggest you take care of your squadron and I'll take care of my base," he lectured me. "Everyone should mind his own business—this is the way to have the air force be successful."

On the way out I met Nathan, the longtime head of Hatzor's construction team. He was a civilian, a gentle giant, a very sensitive guy who always knew how to help and advise the young, confused couples who arrived at family housing.

"What's up, Spector?" he asked me in his Polish accent. Before his warm smile, and the concenetration camp number tattooed on his arm, I opened up. Nathan listened to my tale of woe, shaking his head. A month later, unexpectedly, a truck arrived from Hatzor. It unloaded needed pieces of furniture we had been unable to get. A huge photograph was added, a picture of a Phantom taking off, to be hung in the office I didn't have yet. I understood that Nathan had put his construction unit to work for us without asking his superiors.

When I told my men what had happened to our Daggers, they rebelled. I cooled them off. I understood. Harlev also knew the secret—he was the officer in charge, and so threw his weight around as much as he dared, and whoever wanted to sue him was welcome to try. This was the world I knew, and I didn't take it personally. The order to transfer those Daggers got old in Harlev's files, and the missiles stayed with the Falcons in Hatzor. All that happened was that my Orange Tails flew their initial operational missions without Dagger missiles.

Even so, I didn't feel we were weak.

MAYBE IT WAS JUST THESE difficulties that conjured up the fighting spirit in us. Yes, we definitely were envious of our sister squadrons, the senior Phantom squadrons who sat safely in their padded nests. But we decided that we were in a good position to do well. In the Orange Tails we learned what we could from the other squadrons in order to copy, imitate, and then outshine them. We decided to learn it all and then select the best and filter out the worst. We were in a perfect position, free from any past encumbrances.

THE TIME OF ARRIVAL of our first six Phantoms was set for December 10, 1971. Now we had a timetable, ninety days to define how we were going to do it all a better way. We doubled our efforts. And—well, we were all veterans of the War of Attrition. We knew we had to prepare fast, because the next war was on the way.

AND THEN THERE WAS THE Phantom itself.

After a short conversion course I began to fly with the Falcons and the other squadrons as a guest. From the very first moment, I hated this aircraft. It was very large, very clumsy, very complicated, and always there was somebody in the rear cockpit making noise, and bothering me with advice and instructions. I felt as if I were back in the Harvard trainer, in an unending struggle against a noisy, unresponsive aircraft, together with an annoying instructor on my ass.

It was particularly hard for me to come to terms with the performance of this aircraft in aerial combat. Whenever I reversed turn, or just rocked it a little in the air, the Phantom would react with a long delay, as if the stick were on springs. And when it finally condescended to obey, it would start with a symphony of rattling and drumming, like forks in a dishwasher. At times I stole a sideways look to make sure that all the junk was still attached to the airplane.

During my second flight in the Phantom I sat in the backseat of Eitan Ben Eliyahu, to watch and learn. Eitan wanted to show me acceleration to twice the speed of sound. Halfway, one of the engines began braying. I told him,

"Eitan, this is the Phantom?"

"When you have two engines and one of them goes south," he told me, "you still have the second one to take you home."

"Aha." I was not impressed. The Mirage didn't need two engines to get to Mach 2 or to get me home.

MY PARTNERS WERE ALL HARD, tough men.

Major Uri Shachar, my designated second-in-command, came from the same job in a Skyhawk squadron. Gordon had already been flying Phantoms for few months. All three of us had grown up in the Fighting First, had fought together, and understood each other well. The designated technical officer was Maj. Jacob Baram, also a Mirage graduate, who came from Ramat-David. Everybody called him "Briar," and he was hardwood indeed, much tougher than any of us. The fifth in the team was Lieutenant Shemer, a very sharp young officer, a go-getter, who had replaced the girl adjutant. Now we were a men-only team.

During the week we scattered over all the country, flying and learning what we could from the three active Phantom squadrons, and on weekends we gathered in Hatzerim and sat down to go over what we had learned and our new ideas. Sometimes, when our needs were not met, we were not ready to compromise. We had to squeeze a Phantom squadron into the headquarters of a Mirage squadron two sizes too small for it. We redesigned the space to use every corner, which required big changes in the internal structure—moving walls, power lines, etc. Then we were notified that the air force wouldn't approve the budget for the changes, and we found ourselves facing an insoluble problem. When we realized that no money would be allocated for the necessary infrastructure in the squadron building, Shachar and I rose early one Saturday morning, drove down to the building with heavy hammers, and smashed down all the unneeded internal walls. The base commander appeared, and his face got very pale. He threatened us with dire consequences. But the next morning the construction workers came over with the drawings we had prepared for them before our budget was turned down. Over time I suspected Colonel Bareket, my commander, of sympathizing with his radical new Phantom pilots.

In the same way we fought outside, we fought with ourselves. Our meetings lasted for days and spilled over into the nights, and usually were hot and noisy. None of us was pretty. Each brought with him loads of ideas of how to shape the material in our hands, and each was ready to die or kill for his ideas. We would struggle till late at night with everything: training programs, aircraft readiness, caring for the soldiers, furnishing the operations and technical control centers, and education of future pilots and mechanics. We spread maps and drawings on the floor till there was no place to step, and then shouted at each other from opposite sides of the room. Once I was called to decide on the way information should be transmitted between the squadron's operations room and the technical control center. This is a crucial connection, especially in wartime, and here also we had an opportunity to set up a better system than any other in the air force. I came in and found a heated dispute under way between Gordon and Briar. They both came from opposing schools, and each had his arguments. There was no intermediate solution that could integrate all the advantages, and I had to decide either or. At last I decided, and chose Gordon's way. Briar was entrusted with the preparation of the required tools—boards, magnets, communication terminals, etc. On the next week we met, and the tools were ready, all right, but they were not made exactly according to our specs. There were alterations. I threw a furious Gordon out of my office and shut the door.

"Briar, what's going on here?"

Briar waved a large, bent finger in my face. "Spector, you made a mistake here. Let me explain to you again." He was a warm man, radiating energy and power.

I pulled out a piece of paper, wrote something on it, and folded it in two.

"Give me the Scotch tape, please." I sealed the page all around and put it into my notebook.

Briar stopped and watched me, not understanding.

"Briar," I told him, "we had an agreement and you tried to get around it. The next time it happens I'll use this page."

The conversation that followed ended with a signed agreement that consisted of two words: "Everything clean." Then we shook hands, and Briar went out to do his job over again from the beginning.

I did not really enjoy the bitter struggle of "all against all" I was leading, but I convinced myself that I didn't care. I was already far beyond the Fighting First and my failed tries to find grace in the eyes of my people.

In fact, I went to the other extreme. I had a mission to accomplish, and without realizing it I was hurled back to the forgotten rule of my youth: keep it all inside. I stopped taking interest in the outside. I accepted the reality that I'd lost the popularity contest, and I didn't pay attention to it anymore. Instead, I invested a lot of effort in figuring out what I really wanted to accomplish. I listened to everybody, all the while writing and sketching in my notebook. When I came to conclusions, I worked hard to articulate clear decisions. Everything became technical—organization charts, timetables, construction processes—and every detail after processing came out bright and clear. Manpower was an important part of my equations, but human beings were not.

Home was all but forgotten. Ali and my two sons receded into the background. I learned that Ali had found a place for Etay in the first grade of a primary school in Beer-Sheva, and in passing learned that she had found work and was taking classes. This was all good news. I nodded and fell asleep while my kids fought to climb on my lap Friday nights.

‡

On December 5, 1971, we called in all our men from around the country and opened the new squadron. It was a cold, blue, winter day. A hundred people—pilots, technicians, and clerks—met on the truck parking lot. I sat all of them on the asphalt and told them for the first time why we all were here in Hatzerim, and what I expected from them. They came to a drab and distant place, but the things they heard were clear and resolute.

We took them on a tour of our assets, which were unlike anything they had known in the places they came from: a lone, battered building at the end of the remotest runway. Inside it, in the briefing room, instead of the briefing center with boards and charts, they saw a blackboard standing in front of a line of plastic chairs with metal pipe legs. The temporary operations office was near the rest rooms until the end of renovations of the underground floor and consisted of nothing more than a hand-cranked field telephone on a chair. But the rooms were washed and clean—the setup team had cleaned up the night before.

Our base had no housing for our people, and the Oranges' mechanics were issued large army tents. But before the arrival of our people we all got together, officers and pilots, and fixed up their quarters. We assembled bunk beds for them, brought mattresses and blankets from the quartermaster stores, and on every bed were put two clean blue utility uniforms.

Five days later, on December 10, our six borrowed Phantoms landed in Hatzerim—tail numbers 43, 44, 49, 59, 65, and 67. All six, with their twelve noisy jet engines, rolled down the slope, entering what was definitely the cleanest, most efficient, and best-looking subterranean hangar in the whole Israeli Air Force. The domes were all whitewashed, with plenty of mercury lights. All the required installations—refueling, air pressure, tool storage, office space—were new and perfect. Everything gleamed.

A short ceremony took place, and the flag of the new Orange Tails was raised for the first time by the air force commander, Maj. Gen. Moti Hod, and handed to me. This was Friday noon, and when the sodas and peanuts were consumed and the few guests had gotten into their cars and headed back north, we all changed clothes and washed our new Phantoms with water and soap until even the sooty metal of the jet pipes shone. When Saturday dawned, everyone scattered to his quarters or tents, but not before the hangar floors were washed again. From now on, we all knew how things should look in the Orange Tails.

When that Saturday's morning I couldn't restrain myself and dragged my two small boys down to the squadron to look at my new aircraft, I found a crowd assembled at the hangar, and the guards struggling to keep them off from touching "the dirty half dozen," lest they spoil their virgin beauty.

On Sunday we began to fly, and from then on we squeezed those six Phantoms to the utmost. All we had were those six, and right away we stripped one of them for disassembly in the service hangar—the technicians had to learn the guts of this large and complicated monster—so we were left with five, and no reserves. On these five ships we intended to build the infrastructure for a standard Phantom squadron, equal in size to its three elder sisters. A month after the opening of the midget squadron we became operational. With a bit of chutzpah, we viewed ourselves as "The squadron of the South," the first line of defense against the Egyptian enemy. Though operations were managed via a field telephone on a chair, in early January 1972 we mounted our first operational flight. I led a four-ship flight patrolling the Egyptian border, covering the First, which was going farther in. The Mirages were doing a real reconnaissance mission, and we just flew along as insurance. We didn't delude ourselves that something was going to happen this time, but we briefed the flight as if we were going to fight the whole Egyptian Army and Navy. As we returned proudly from the long, eventless patrol, we knew that on the control map in the air force's command center, the symbol "1/Orange" had crawled down the Strait of Suez, and we had been visible on radarscopes in all the radar units. We were on the map.

And then there were the days when we had only two or three aircraft available for training. The mechanics stayed up nights and worked selflessly to fix every problem and have every aircraft ready to fly every morning. Most of our technicians were young and inexperienced, airmen eighteen or nineteen years old, and when I passed the hangar at night to see what was going on, I found the few veteran technicians with their heads in the fuel tanks or lying soaked with black oil under the bellies of the aircraft, while a circle of the new techs stood around and repeated for them in loud voices, in broken English, procedures from the technical manual for the Phantom. When I first saw it, I was worried.

"Is this the way to get it done?" I asked Briar. But later I was amazed to discover the dialectical beauty of our situation: since our squadron was new and inexperienced vis-à-vis the other squadrons, we gradually developed a strong technical culture built on a fresh and stable foundation.

THE PILOTS HAD NO TIME for self-pity, either. We all were new on the aircraft, and it was necessary to get flight time. We were flying all day, every day of the week. In January we went farther, adding six flight nights, but after we realized that everybody was falling off their feet, we went back to one night a week. To get in even more time, we began flying double shifts. This was a way of getting in two sorties for the price of one: after landing, instead of returning the aircraft to the mechanics for maintenance, we parked for refueling without leaving our cockpits or shutting the engines off, and in essence stayed aloft. When the aircraft was refueled, we took off again for another round. In this way—it was at the edge of the margin of safety—we could get five or six sorties from each aircraft daily instead of two or three. When we didn't have enough aircraft to get a flight of four airborne, we asked other squadrons to join us, either to fly with us or to compete against us in the air.

OUR ORDER OF PREFERENCE was clear—first of all, operations and training, while living conditions were not a topic of discussion yet. The room slated to become the squadron's ready room remained bare. In its center stood a Formica table, and breakfast was jam from a jar and sliced bread. In the hot summer hours at about noon, pilots would nap sitting on chairs in every room, facing the wall, or lying on the cool floor of the corridor. At night, the readiness crews slept on beds near the door that led to the hangar, covering their heads with military blankets against the mosquitoes.

‡

We thought up new ways to improve our flight performance. We divided ourselves into fixed crews of pilot and navigator—not common in the IAF, which prefers standardization. My own partner was Roy Manoff, a thin, dark junior officer who had joined us after his initial training at the Falcons. Manoff knew the Phantom better than I, and I knew more about flying. And so we got together, a twenty-year-old second lieutenant and a thirty-year-old major, planned the flight, and for the next hour shared the work as equal partners. After landing we split up—me to command the squadron, and Manoff to the navigation room to draw maps. He was a serious young man, very reticent; perhaps after five years in Israel—he had come from Argentina—he didn't trust his command of Hebrew. Instead he would smile with a mouth full of gleaming white teeth. While he rarely spoke, his short comments were always on the mark. Soon we all realized that he understood things in a different, deeper sense. At that time I didn't yet know about EQ, emotional quotient, but I began rethinking my former opposition to the two-seat fighter.

We wanted to improve our teamwork and thought that introducing our navigators to the pilot's functions might help. There was a rare asset next door—the flying school with all its two-seat Fouga trainers. The base commander, Colonel Bareket, agreed to approve some flight hours for us. He only asked me, "What happens if all the Phantom squadrons want this, too?" I answered him with the same language I learned from his friend and colleague at Hatzor, Colonel Harlev. He laughed, and then for a while our navigators flew as pilots in Fougas, and trained simulating attacks on each other, operating the gunsight and struggling with pilot emergencies.

In March 1972, four months after our inception as a squadron, we checked and decided we had finished the initial stage. Then we wrote and published a thin booklet announcing the completion of a new Phantom squadron. At the end of the booklet we added a plan for new staffing procedures that was designed to direct everyone—from headquarters down to the floor sweepers—regarding how to establish a new fighter squadron. We gave lists of equipment, timetables, goals, and targets—including those we hadn't reached yet. Our booklets came back with a contemptuous dismissal: who are those nobodies so pretentious as to dictate procedures for IAF staffing? Well, perhaps the process was flawed, but for us the writing itself was a binding public declaration: "We said it, we did it, and we will do more."

After four months of very hard work, the training period ended and the air force took a week off. We decided that instead of taking a week of leave, we would brush up a little more. We asked one of the senior squadrons to host us and prepare a course for advanced students. After a week of training at Ramat-David at the Hammers, we all went back south for another bout of hard work.

The Orange Tails began to take shape. The American embargo was lifted, and the inferiority complex of the "midget squadron" began to go away. We waited anxiously for our new aircraft, and indeed at the end of March 1972 they began arriving from St. Louis, flown by test pilots from the factory. They landed at Hatzor, and we went there to bring them home. I took the first one, tail no. 51, and flew it to Hatzerim. My commander, Colonel Bareket, was a full partner in the greatness of the moment and sat behind me as weapons officer. No. 51 was clean and lovely and smelled like a brand-new car. Bareket proposed that we buzz the base, but I preferred to land the new aircraft carefully and taxi it slowly, holding it like a newborn baby, into my squadron's no. 2 hangar, just prepared for it. Following this flight I noticed with a slight surprise that I also began calling the aircraft not by its foreign name, Phantom, but by its Hebrew name, Hammer.

Still, I didn't love the Hammer. I was repelled by its dinosaur profile, but I caught myself casting sideways looks at it. Something began to drop inside me, like a coin making its way down in a machine. I was almost offended when Briar and his mechanics climbed the 51 on the same day with their dirty shoes and began taking parts from it and peeping into its guts. Briar and his second-in-command, Lt. Mike Lott, noticed my expression, and the next day every ladder in the squadron had rugs for wiping our shoes.

New aircraft arrived monthly, and soon we could hand the original six back to their original owners. We became an independent fighter squadron, proud of our new, shiny aircraft, and of our squadron's emblem displayed on their wide, low tails. We painted those tails orange, like the color of the setting sun I saw at dusk from the windows of my office, sparkling at me on the barren Negev hills. We adopted the name Knights of the South.

WE CONTINUED TO WORK very hard. We already had ten aircraft, so we invited First's Mirages for a week of dogfight training. We were beginning to fly the Phantom the right way. We practiced with the variety of weapons and munitions the big aircraft could carry. We started competing in fast turnaround competitions—how fast could we arm the whole fleet with bombs and missiles and get the squadron on a war footing—and the aircrew team headed by the muscular Shachar competed against the munitions officer, Lieutenant Jimmy with his Indians. The Friday ritual was set, and everybody—pilots and mechanics together—got together to wash down the hangars and shine up the aircraft. This was the prelude to our Saturday off.

More and more aircraft arrived, we opened more hangars, and new air and ground crews joined us. Everyone who came of his own free will made me happy. A real fighting unit settled down around me, one that required no more marketing. The senior commanders of the air force didn't know it yet, but the young pilots already had a sense of what was happening here, and suddenly there were people knocking on our squadron's door. The two-seat, two-engine Phantom doubled everything, and at the beginning of 1973 my Orange ceased to be a small, intimate unit and became big and noisy like her three older sisters. But the hard beginnings had left us all our own culture of noncompromising insistence on clarity, perfection, and cleanliness. This culture became part of us, and remained even as men came and left.

I spent most of my waking hours in the squadron or in the air. Ali carried the burden of our home by herself, and in addition she worked in Beer-Sheva and was studying to be a librarian. We had no private car, and every morning she would stand at the base gate to hitchhike to town, and at noon on the way back at the military hitchhiking point at the southern gate of Beer-Sheva. I suspected that the operations clerks were hiding from me that on rainy days they sent the squadron car secretly to pick her up. I preferred not to know. When we met at night I would tell her about my Phantom shop that was so loud that I was hearing buzzing in my ears all the time, and when I escaped to my cockpit, a navigator was making even more noise. My stories amused her, and the laughing brought little Noah to us, a baby girl after two boys. Back then there was still no way to find out the sex of the fetus, and when a girl appeared we both thought we would faint from joy.

It was a hard time but we were very happy.

And I still couldn't love the Phantom.

I already knew how to control it and manage its clumsy performance, and each time I took the controls in the cockpit I repressed my revulsion and reveled in the efficiency of teaming with the navigator. The Phantom was a very interesting aircraft, and great for ground attacks and bombing missions, and it had all those wonderful computers, but at nights I would sometimes wake up from a dream and ask Ali how we got here, and how could I have traded my noble steed for a hippopotamus?

The Phantom clicked with me only in mid-1972, after I had collected some two hundred flight hours in it. We were on maneuvers against the Fighting First. In one of five repeated sorties practicing advanced aerial combat against Mirages at low level, suddenly something happened inside my cockpit. This was a very intimate thing, as if somebody had strummed the bass string, and I froze and listened very carefully, lest I lose it, while the fight went on all around us. Then I tried very gently to open more, and the Phantom heard and responded, smooth as butter.

I stopped idolizing Mirages, and they became just good models of the MiG-21. In that flight's debriefing I heard Epstein from the First, who had keen senses and a sharp eye, say, "The Orange Tails have become dangerous."

Though I was never as sure of the Phantom as of the Mirage before him, he had shown me that he also knew the game.

I don't want to dwell on the next year, so let's skip the training and the deployments to Refidim and Ophir in the southern part of the Sinai. Let's skip the stories from family housing, the parties, the picnics, the kids, the women, the friendships, and even various operational sorties.

Let's only mention the failed attempt to intercept the futuristic MiG-25, which crossed the Sinai Peninsula at untouchable altitude and speed, like a space satellite, to take our pictures for the Egyptians. This MiG was a secret Soviet aircraft with hypercruise performance, and it flew much faster and higher than anything our Phantom could dream of, but we climbed toward it intending to make an approach at sixty thousand feet and launch radar-guided missiles at it from there. We saw its vapor trail coming toward us on our climb to position, but then we had an oxygen malfunction, and Manoff and I had to stop our climb halfway, choking, and the MiG passed high over our heads, painting a white trail in the sky. We landed at Ophir disgusted and disappointed, the unlaunched missiles still hanging under our aircraft.

Just a line about my old friends from the thirty-first flight school class. Goldie was completing a stint commanding a Skyhawk squadron and designated to take over the Bats Phantoms at Tel Nof; Or Yoeli, who flew my wing that stormy night, and now was commanding the neighboring Skyhawk squadron in Hatzerim; and Uri and Shula Sheani, who lived next door, with four kids. From all Sheani's capabilities, the air force decided to use his talents in orienteering . He became the commander of the preparation stage for flight school. And let's not forget Asher Snir, who had begun to get me into interesting discussions over "space-time" and "the psychophysical problem." Snir was using these discussions as an excuse to come and convince me to vacate the Orange Tails for him, since his time was running out. For me, well, it was just an honor to have someone like him wanting to come down here, in spite of the desert dust.

And for the same reason, to cut to the chase, let us cut short the arguments against "Baban"—the best of all the instructors—who vehemently opposed my habit of washing out of my squadron whomever I didn't approve of.

"Teach them, you bastard!" he would yell at me. Baban had been my flight instructor on Meteors in 1960, the first jet I ever flew, and his beautiful, long-fingered hands manipulated the stick with such adroitness that very few could match him in a dogfight. I thought he was great, but I remembered the lesson Gen. Moti Hod taught me. I was expecting a war, and not about to let my squadron become dysfunctional, as I had seen at the Fighting First. I didn't intend to compromise on the quality of men when I was building a squadron from scratch. I agreed to accept only the good ones, and kept washing out anybody I didn't feel right about. War was coming.

MY SECOND-IN-COMMAND was promoted and Gordon replaced him, and after Gordon came Maj. Shlomo Egozi from the Bats, probably in some clandestine plot with Snir the expectant. They all were strong men and good managers, and they gave me a platform from which I could get the squadron on the right path. Briar also was promoted to a job in base technical management. Mike Lott, his deputy, replaced him as the squadron's technical officer.

Suddenly this was a different Orange Tails, a new group of people, less stressed, brighter of spirit, perhaps happier, but I knew that deep within, the currents of purposefulness and resoluteness were still flowing, left behind from the initial establishing team. We were moving on, to October 1973, and the Yom Kippur War.

THE FIRST SPARKS OF THAT conflagration began to smolder at the end of 1972, in the North. Again, we began attacking in Syria and Lebanon. We bombed and destroyed a Syrian SAM battery in a place south of Damascus called Sheikh Maskin. This operation was deceptively easy. A few days later we attacked a terrorist training camp near Damascus, again with success. These attacks were in the SAM killing zone, but their silence encouraged those who believed that the SAM was a toothless tiger. Later there was a nighttime dogfight.

I was flying in Syria, with Oren as backseat weapons systems officer (WSO). We cruised around, lights off in total darkness, deep in the Syrian Desert, with Israel in the distance as a colorful line of blinking lights. There were MiGs in the void around us, and from time to time afterburners lit up and went out like distant fireflies. Oren managed to catch echoes on his radar screen and we maneuvered to attack, but this time the new American missiles malfunctioned. A fuse connection kept shorting out, and the missiles refused to launch once, and then again. Suddenly a fireball lit up right over our left shoulder, and turning back, we saw a long tongue of fire, striped blue and purple. We pulled up toward a slim shadow that passed over our cockpits, rolled out, shut his afterburner off, and vanished into the night.

Then there was September 13, 1973, a big day just a bit before the big war, in which the Orange Tails shared, with the rest of the air force, thirteen downed Syrian MiGs. The two kills Oren and I brought back, and another one brought by Egozi, were the first for the Orange Tails, and our joy was great even though Oren was busy pulling his long, blond hair in the backseat for having failed to lock his radar on our third MiG of the day. That MiG escaped into a cumulus cloudbank, and we couldn't continue searching because we were alone, and our fuel—as usual—was low. We left that MiG and returned to Ramat-David, into a hornets' nest of the local Hammers' pilots and their mechanics, who claimed we had come from the South to poach. Only among them, in the Hammers' ready room, did Oren calm down and finally agree that opening his backseat career with two kills was not so bad, although—he continued complaining—had we knocked down that third one, too, things would be so much better.

When we landed that afternoon back in Hatzerim, after champagne and kisses from Ali, and the cheers of the mechanics, who carried us on their shoulders all the way to my office, I found a note on my desk. "Spector, it was really something! The squadron deserved it, I deserved it—difficult to express my feelings, embarrassed at how happy I am! Simply unforgettable!" It was signed "Yankele Briar." My tough and aggressive technical officer, a man of the original team, allowed himself only this once such an expression of feeling. His note made me happy indeed.

Whoever connected these events could see how the drum taps were quickening toward October 1973.

‡

Just a word about the men.

After my disappointment in myself over the First, I no longer sought the affection of my subordinates. I believed in command cut and dried, not in comradeship or leadership. Accordingly, I required only two things at the Orange Tails: clarity and efficiency.

Of course, the men were the principal material I had to work with and the principal risk factor, too. For that reason I was checking on them all the time. Whoever didn't fit was promptly washed out, fast, before he put roots down and before he could do any damage. I tried to treat my subordinates hard and fair. This was the new rule of life. And to be hard I built walls to keep myself from becoming too personally involved with the men. I didn't want to become a slave to my emotions or soften my stance. I didn't hide this attitude from them.

From myself I demanded foresight, and the future was all in my men. The men were not just conglomerates of fortuitous occurrences. The behavior of each hid connecting lines, concealed from the untrained eye, that were the causes of all the phenomena that swirled around them. Gradually I became convinced that the men were directing subtle signals my way, calling my attention by their actions, asking me to watch them.

The men, pilots, navigators, and mechanics were many and complicated and interesting, and my memory alone was not enough. I learned to write down a plethora of details so I wouldn't forget. I had a separate page for each aircrew and senior mechanic. There were days when I covered dozens of points in that book, and each point colored—good in green, bad in red, neutral in blue. Soon I found myself connecting dots with green, red, and blue pencils. On every Friday afternoon, when work finished and everybody went home for the weekend, I would shut myself in the empty squadron building and add new points and draw my colored lines in my notebook. Very soon I began extrapolating the graphs into the future.

I had ethical doubts. I began to realize that by just selecting the points to be written down, I was insinuating my own personality into the mix. The graphs I produced were not objective, and the forecasts of the future even less so. Was it fair to judge people, reward and punish, and even wash them out on such a basis? This was indeed a good philosophical question of the kind that interested my friend Snir. Still, I had no other database, so I continued cross-checking. And then one evening I took a big step. Looking at a page full of conflicting data I had collected on one of my more complicated officers, I shut my eyes and let my unconscious speak. My hand played with the pencil, and on the white page the curve of my emotions—what I felt about this man—drew itself. I lowered my gaze and saw a circle, but the circle was broken and I saw where the break was. This way the data porridge on the page formed a pattern, and for one brief moment I was enlightened. I believed I understood what drove this guy, and trapped that understanding in words.

The next morning I invited him to my office, and I almost shouted for joy when he raised offended eyebrows and asked, "How did you know? Who told you?" I hid my Sherlock Holmes excitement, and the next move was simple. We went on to solve a latent problem that could have led to serious trouble in the future, and perhaps even have endangered his life.

From that point on I understood that though the details were important, and I had to continue collecting them diligently, the details themselves did not make a picture. The details came from the outside, but the full picture came from within, and the picture was the important thing. Getting to a valid conclusion was not easy; it required a lot of work from me, and it was hazardous, too. I knew that in spite of all the graphs and dots and my unconscious processes, my conclusions were not infallible. Sometimes, when a conclusion surfaced concerning a person or a situation, it surprised me, too. In the beginning I used to delay it, fearing to consolidate my results, even to utter them verbally. Even formulating a conclusion in words created a new situation. But Dvorah, my second mother, had taught me that to cope with reality one has to bring things into the light. Once, when I feared to utter the word "cancer" in her presence, she said to me, smiling, "Don't be afraid of words, Iftach. Words don't bite."

And so I learned to define people and situations, to confront my conclusions even if they seemed weird in the beginning, to declare them loudly, first to myself and then check them with my officers. The more I practiced the method, the better my capability to hit the mark became.

And in this way I learned gradually to "see."

‡

Sometimes a person who generally was "green" showed "red" deviations, and then it was necessary to take him aside and to find out—directly or indirectly—what was going on with him, and to watch him closely. But "deep blue" also was not good enough, not combat-fit. Blues had to be shaken up. And so I was prying and digging inside myself, and the men talked to me in their secret language from the pages, and more ideas rose in my mind and I brainstormed with myself, and without realizing it I learned to command men. And only when I had finished going over the whole fifty or so pages and the darkness of Friday night was creeping from the windows into the room, would I get up and stretch, yawn, lock the notebook in the drawer, free the secretary standing by, and say good night to the readiness crew who remained to spend the night in the ready room. On the way home I would circle the aircraft hangars to wish all the mechanics a good Sabbath. Later, in the dark of night, I would see those circles again.

I was searching for the path, which is more significant than any single fact.

"The first warning of things going out of kilter in the unit comes in a casual conversation among men on the squadron balcony," I wrote for a lecture to the air force. "Then it is time to get involved. If you miss out on that, you will have to confront more serious trouble later." In Dubi's case, for example, warning lights kept flashing in my head. For long periods he seemed "all green," just a good, happy kid with no stress, but behind this misleadingly bright exterior hid a wild devil who would pop out at times. I numbered those pop-ups meticulously, and I warned him once or twice. Then, one day, one dot too many intersected his red line. I invited him in and on the spot locked him up for thirty-five days.

"For what?" he cried, flabbergasted and humiliated. "For one low pass? How bad is one buzz?"

"It's not just about this one buzz," I told him. "It is your punishment for the accident waiting for you in the future. When you get yourself killed, at least it won't go without punishment."

And off he went to the guardhouse.

I have no doubt that my decisions, which came from inside, seemed at times weird to my men, perhaps on the verge of absurd. The graphs in my booklet crept forward weekly, every man changing. Suddenly, when I felt a premonition of the future, I would call one of them out and talk to him, warning, praising, compensating, and punishing. My decisions regarding different people were not equal, and I admitted it openly. I didn't keep any punishment charts, nor "bonus charts" for good work. I didn't compare people. I was very subjective, all was personal, and they found a way to live with it.

One pilot, we shall call him Bee, kept shooting at aerial targets from too long a range, missing every time. He began to wallow in self-pity. I flew with him, encouraging him to approach to the minimum distance and even beyond it. On the same day I came down hard on some of his friends who were doing the same thing. Eventually some barrier fell inside Bee and he began to hit his targets. Commanding in this way may certainly seem capricious, unstable, even an unfair way of management. But in our case, in the Orange Tails, my men didn't take it that way. I presume they understood there was method in my madness. Some among my men believed, and later said openly, that this treatment did actually foresee things, and for some it even saved their lives. And what's more, some of this nervous alertness stuck to them. This was to bring good results in the approaching Yom Kippur War.

My handling of the formal flight procedures wasn't free of problems. Throughout the term of my command people asked me, and I asked myself, who gave me authority to change air force flight limits. This was a tough moral issue for me. I want to make it clear that when I led Bee beyond the limits, my goal was not to disobey orders. I believed that most standing orders "in the book" were the core of past wisdom and experience, and that as a rule we should abide by them. But the real world seemed to me more complex than the one in the book, and the regulations didn't apply in many cases. And I also believed that responsibility was personal and devolved upon humans, not the book.

For me, the responsibility to free Bee from a problem and make him an efficient fighter pilot was mine. Otherwise I would have to wash him out of my squadron, together with the millions of dollars already invested in his training. I knew how to turn Bee into a good pilot—I myself had learned to get to the right shooting distance after violating the limits—but I didn't think Bee had to go through all that process, to hide and lie and be caught and punished, and endanger his life till he learned. The responsibility was mine, and I thought that if the Orange Tails weren't well prepared, it could only be my fault.

There is a story about an officer who, during a battle, turned to his commanding general and asked permission to change some detail of their plan. The general answered, "I gave you officer's rank to exceed my orders." This is exactly the way I understood it: we don't need officers who turf responsibility up or down. The essence of being a man—and not a tin soldier—lies in making decisions and taking responsibility for them.

My real difficulty was with the question of personal example. This is complicated. Orders must be obeyed, and a good officer—who was given his rank just to exceed those orders—has to explain any deviation from a lawful order. But still you can sort it out.

When it is about ordinary things, I—like everybody else—believe in strict discipline. Such conflicts become important only if it is about crucial things, human life, or the law of the land. It is not by accident that serious concepts such as our notion of black flag, not relieving anyone from the responsibility for war crimes. These terms remind you that the ranking officer is not the supreme commander.

I believe, just like Mota Gur, who taught us in the BBN course, that when you are in conflict on a very meaningful issue, it would be incorrect and disloyal to be silent. You must push the issue up the chain of command, and not give up even though it can cost you in many ways.

But there are situations when even this process is not possible. Sometimes you are alone and there is no time for lengthy processes and discussions, or you are out of touch with your commanders. This is the usual situation for pilots in wartime. Then you must take responsibility and be a man, and decide according to your understanding and beliefs.

In this moment you have to clarify to yourself to whom, or to what, you owe loyalty.

I ADMIT IT—MY WAY OF commanding Orange Tails—prognosticating through graphs and circles—was only a partly logical thought process, and a strange way to command men. Still, there was no mystery here. My inner world joined the dry, logical evaluation of men and situations, with all the data, and together they created a unique personal tool to develop sensitivity I had invented. And this tool evolved later into a most important new concept, that of "kettles." This was a notion that soon turned out to be an exceptionally good weapon in war.

What are kettles? The idea of a kettle was born in the Orange Tails during the Yom Kippur War. The name originated from a children's story in which a Bedouin came to town for the first time from the desert, and his host poured him a cup of coffee from the hot, whistling kettle. Excited with the world's innovations, the Bedouin went out to see the town and admire its wonders. While walking on a railway track, he heard another whistle. Another kettle, thought the Bedouin, more coffee! But then a locomotive passed the corner, and almost ran over him. Shocked, the Bedouin interpreted the situation: "A grown-up kettle."

IN OUR WORLD, THAT OF THE fighting Orange Tails, this joke became a mantra: "A kettle is a small thing that whistles, but if you don't put out the fire under it, it grows, becomes a locomotive, and runs you over." We used it to symbolize the presence of some vague, not clearly defined danger. When anyone felt it, he would say, "We have a kettle here," and everybody understood that we needed to search out the improbable. Gut feelings or hunches sometimes anticipate the brain, which is trapped in rational boxes.

A gut feeling of uneasiness points at a small, invisible sign of trouble—just a kettle, but some of them grow. You might be just a second lieutenant, a backseat weapons officer/navigator, but did you hear a whistle in your inner ear? Then don't be shy! Speak up. This is war and our time of truth, and we'd better check your hunch right now and find out. Tell us everything and don't postpone that investigation till tomorrow, or you might find yourself alone on the track with a locomotive coming at you, and the cost will be high.

I always thought that all the important, difficult things give initial, small signs before they burst on the scene. Not that the interception of signs was easy and simple; there was always a lot of background noise, and the more sensitive the receiver, the more false alarms. But whoever was listening, heard more, and whoever thought about it knew more. I listened to my pilots and heard the malefactors among them sending me signals, as if asking me to deal with them: "Hey, Spector, I'm dangerous. Stop me!" I listened, and we had no accidents.

It was just like that with the enemy: he also kept talking to us during the war—willy-nilly—and sent us signals. All you had to do was work hard and listen closely. And if you prepared for something that didn't happen, so what? This was war, and you just slept a little less.

In general, I don't know of any surprises like lightning from a clear sky. If indeed such surprises exist—and I doubt it—they are extremely rare, and in my opinion they occur because you didn't notice the signs, because you didn't look and listen, because you didn't care to do your graphs.

I suspect that most stories of surprises are excuses from commanders who failed to do their jobs.

And so a new group of young, independent men grew in the Orange Tails. I gave fewer and fewer instructions and orders. I was witnessing the birth of a new sort of opposition group wholly different from the one I had been part of as a young pilot in the Scorpions. Indeed, the Orange Tails' opposition was as sarcastic as any other and could scoff and criticize, but this opposition invested less energy in young pilots' friendly manner, often mistaken for esprit de corps, and instead learned to think clearly and speak truth to power. This informal group, which during the Yom Kippur War would call itself "high society," buoyed up our squadron in the hard days fast approaching.

I saw knowledge and capacity increasing around me, and in myself a new way of knowing, much more refined and delicate than how to fly the Phantom or lead a formation in a dogfight. Command of men began to work itself out through my fingers, and sometimes I needed to suppress a surge of joy when I saw there was no need to pressure them anymore. They knew by themselves. Young leaders stuck out in the squadron, took on leadership roles, and showed me they did things correctly on their own. A group of leaders was growing under me, and they pulled the whole bunch forward. I was there, watching.

Chapter

17

Baboons

THERE WAS ANOTHE IMPORTANT THING without which it is difficult to understand how the Orange Tails fought the Yom Kippur War. This was the course for advanced aerial leadership, the BBN course. No, not that other course, at Ran Pecker's Bats. This time I am talking about the new course, the one I ran at the Orange Tails.

WELL, NOT JUST MY FRIENDS and I remembered that outstanding course we had with Ran on the eve of the Six-Day War. Somebody at air force headquarters remembered it, too, and sent out a feeler to find a squadron that might be ready to prepare and run something like that.

I looked around. No one volunteered. This was the beginning of 1973. We still were in a tense cease-fire with the Egyptians and the Syrians, with frequent violations, and we all sensed war and were preparing for it. We trained day and night. New equipment kept coming and we had to integrate it. All the squadrons were tense and loaded with work. We in the Orange Tails were tense, too, perhaps even more so than all of them.

I hesitated. My Orange Tails, a green squadron from the remote base at Hatzerim, was hardly the obvious choice to host and run such a high-level course. Our squadron was built on very young aircrews and ground crews—kids, really. It lacked a spine of veterans and the deep culture that typified all the other squadrons. Although the senior pilots of the Orange Tails had good operational experience, none of us had spent the War of Attrition flying the Phantom, and we couldn't point to any reserve of exclusive knowledge. The Orange Tails was closed within itself in the Far South, learning feverishly to fly and fight, learning to become a true squadron, ripening from the inside. Senior commanders seldom visited us and hardly ever flew our planes. We were virtually unknown to the air force at large. No senior commander in the air force—except for our base commander, perhaps—suspected the quality that was growing here.

Even I didn't see myself as the best choice among my peers. Certainly I was nothing like Ran Pecker, a natural-born leader who radiated charisma wherever he went. True, I had good battle and command experience, but mine was definitely not outstanding in my age group. Those who commanded two of the other three Phantom squadrons actually had taught me to fly at flight school. Other squadron commanders were sent by the IDF to study, mature, and get academic degrees in economy, social sciences, and engineering. All I could present on my side was a nice record of MiG kills.

I don't know what made me raise my hand. I knew that when I returned home to the Orange Tails my second-in-command, Gordon, would be furious. I raised my hand, perhaps, just because nobody else did. And this was likely the reason why I was entrusted with the job.

The chief of training at headquarters set the time frame for the course, and handed me the list of trainees who were to report to the Orange Tails in April for a three-month stay. I knew most of them. They were ten interesting men, assembled from all the fighter squadrons. They all were good and experienced fighters, but three of the pilots had never flown the Phantom before. Thus another subproject was added, to transition to the Phantom and prepare them before the beginning of the course. All throughout March 1973 we got forty sorties into each of them, doing some of it in Refidim, while the Orange Tails was stationed there in readiness. Some clown from the opposition invented a name for the three old rookies preparing for the

BBN: Baboons. This nickname stuck to all the other trainees of the course who showed up in April.

As I mentioned, there were no clear instructions as to curriculum. I began wandering around the air force and drawing ideas from here and there. Everywhere I found the stardust trail of my predecessor, but almost no practical suggestions. At last I had an idea, and I sent a short letter to the operations department at headquarters, with a suggestion: "What about using the course for analyzing some practical problems for you, and then testing the solutions in the air?"

This, finally, was an interesting suggestion. Soon I was invited to Tel Aviv, and ops loaded me up. Lieutenant Colonel Yossi from the training department came ready with an allocation of the gear for such experiments, flight hours, munitions, dummy targets, flares. When we had reached some conclusions and the meeting was about to end, we all stood up to go, and a thing that had been bothering me for some time came up.

"Perhaps it might be a good idea to test new concepts against SAM batteries?"

The operations department's officers shook their heads. This was deemed unnecessary. During the three years since Sam Khetz had been shot down, the air force had developed a new method for attacking SAMs with fighter aircraft. The elimination of the SAMs had become the most important mission of the IAF. Air force headquarters and all of us had put in a lot of effort to figure out how to destroy Soviet SAM batteries. The method of attack changed, and the air force returned to low altitude—exactly as I had demanded from Khetz before his death—with reliance on basics and not just the electronic warfare devices he kept developing and purchasing.

But the air force didn't adopt the small unit approach I proposed, which centered on penetrating to the targets from various directions and in small groups, independent and free-moving. The approach was still frontal, based on large numbers of aircraft coming in waves from one direction, right into the teeth of the enemy. The weight was supposed to crush the enemy, overwhelm his firepower. The idea was to ensure that at least part of the attacking force would reach the target and destroy it. It was a complicated method, and the whole air force trained and tested it in huge flying drills, employing hundreds of aircraft. The process was very similar to the run-up to Yak's Operation Focus, but with many more aircraft.

In the end, all the battle plans were prepared according to this method and became operational orders sitting in all the squadron safes: Operation Defy to eliminate the Egyptian missile arrays, and Operation Model to do the same in Syria. They both were huge, very sophisticated, and complicated plans, too sophisticated and complicated in my opinion (I called them mockingly operazias). And they were based on the supposition that the enemy's SAM batteries would be in their last known sites, the way enemy planes had obligingly waited for us on the runways in 1967, during Operation Focus.

I said to the officers at ops, "I hear there is a new weapon to deal with mobile SAM batteries. They are called SAM-6s, if I am not mistaken."

They glanced at each other and back to me. This was secret intelligence, but available at my command level.

"True," they finally replied, "there were new releases about this in the Soviet Union. So what?" The SAM-6 was still viewed as something exotic. There were many other exotic weapons in the Soviet arsenal.

"There were indications that a few of them might have turned up in Syria as well."

"Possibly. They get a lot of material from the Soviet Union."

"Well," I asked, "suppose some of them turn up in our area?"

I SHOULD EXPLAIN. The SAM arrays we were familiar with until then, types SAM-2 and SAM-3, were stationary batteries. That is, the enemy could move them from one place to another, but very slowly; it took days. In this situation we had no difficulty finding out where they were at any given time. Enough time to photograph the area—the Fighting First did it regularly—and the new SAM deployment was there on film. The locations of the batteries were fixed for the rest of the day. Under such conditions you could plan attacks on them. Although stationary arrays could kill you, too, attacking them was still a reasonable option. You flew to the target and bombed the hell out of it. Braving enemy fire and taking the hill is part of a soldier's job, isn't it?

But the situation is very different when the threats are mobile, and you enter the enemy killing zone without any notion of where that hill is. You can photograph, but even while you look at the pictures the deployment has changed. The SAM-6 mobile missile batteries were mounted on vehicles, and could move from one location to another in a short time. With such batteries, the area becomes an unknown array of threats. In short, if there really were SAM-6 batteries, all our current doctrine—which was based on the lessons of the War of Attrition—had become obsolete. Defy and Model would be thrown to the winds with all the investment in time and energy. All our plans had to be rewritten, training changed, and more. Everyone in the room knew that.

THE CENTRAL FIGURE who had prepared the air force for the onrushing war was Lt. Col. Avihu Ben Nun. Avihu was entrusted with the planning of fighter operations in the operations department at IAF headquarters. He was a serious guy, and he mandated a series of drills of SAM attacks for the whole air force.

Avihu, one year my senior, had been Sam Khetz's second-in-command during the Phantom project in the United States. When they came back from their training, Avihu established the second Phantom squadron, the Hammers, and commanded it in Ramat-David. Avihu was an outstanding pilot and a brilliant officer. In some ways I happened to follow in his footsteps, first as second-in-command at the Fighting First, later as chief of IAF operations, and finally as commander of Tel Nof Air Base. Each time I found I was following a serious person, a charismatic commander, and a fighter pilot with a clear and well-reasoned approach to air combat. Son of a middle-class family, Avihu was unique in our group of mostly kibbutz boys. He had good manners and took pains with his personal grooming. His good looks added to his special glamour, under which hid uncompromising ambition. Avihu is an upright, slender man. His face is always well suntanned, and his eyes behind his pilot's sunglasses are the color of steel. Even today, nearing seventy, he still has all his hair. He is one of the very few on whom everything looks perfect. Only rarely something peeps out of him and disappears quickly. On such occasions I recall my mother's definition of what a perfect gentleman is.

During nine hard months of 1970, Avihu was squeezed by the same steamroller that had crushed Sam Khetz. The day Khetz was killed, Avihu had a brush with death, too, when he and his navigator, Saul Levy, crash-landed their badly damaged Phantom at Refidim. Avihu got out of the wreck of his aircraft, dusted off his flight suit, got into another aircraft, and rejoined his unit. He was an outstanding soldier and combat commander.

After the end of the War of Attrition he became "Mr. Phantom" and the representative of the wave of the future. At that time, the United States had replaced France as our source of military equipment. France had embargoed Israel in an ugly, nasty way. Then America stepped up and sold us Skyhawks, Phantoms, and then all the technology and equipment we were using. The American technology was much more advanced and very impressive. And more importantly, the United States was fighting at that time in Vietnam against the same Soviet training and equipment the Egyptians and Syrians were getting.

A whole reservoir of applicable knowledge opened for us in the United States. Most of us couldn't get at that knowledge, or even read the language. Avihu could. He returned from America with the Phantoms loaded with knowledge and connections. Soon he taught the Hammers squadron's men to read English, and they raided other English-speakers throughout the whole air force. The ever-growing Phantom community, with Avihu as its uncrowned prince, directed the military thinking of everyone from squadron level up to air force high command.

The method of missile attack developed under Avihu was a complicated and sophisticated accomplishment indeed. Hundreds of aircraft were required to arrive—formation after formation—from the same direction and at very small intervals, and spray the enemy array as if from one hose. It had to be synchronized like a Swiss watch. And truly, the Defy and Model operations were glorious designs, activating hundreds of fast-flying fighters in complex maneuvers, interweaving like decorative Persian epigraphs. Each aircraft had to be accurate to a split second and not deviate from its course in the slightest.

These drills were very difficult and complex, and hazardous, too. I am proud of our wonderful air force, which succeeded in accomplishing these elegant maneuvers again and again in training and in war games, and which got out without casualties. Preparation for a SAM attack drill required bookkeeping any accountant would admire, and the actual performance was more courageous and spectacular than any aerial show by the Blue Angels over Oshkosh or anyplace else. Avihu demonstrated to us and to our commanders what a magnificent air force we were. It's just a shame we were the only spectators—such performances would surely have brought us medals had they been done at the Paris Air Show.

Those drills created in us feelings of enormous satisfaction and great power, but I, and a few of my buddies, felt uneasy about all that. Our argument was that the operational worth of a fighter pilot lay in his being free to maneuver, not locked inside a cohort marching in lockstep to run the enemy over with the weight of their bodies. I saw the air force as wielding quality, not quantity power.

"Why are you putting us in a box?" I kept asking. "Can you imagine sending us to a dogfight in such close formation?"

"Of course not," they would answer. "What are you talking about?"

"Well, in that case," I would shout and pound the table, "fighting against SAMs is just another dogfight, against another kind of aircraft. Let us out of the box and let us fight. Enough of this parade ground bullshit!"

But once again, like that night with Sam Khetz, I found myself struggling against conventional wisdom. Everybody else thought the same way, and I lost the argument.

The real clients—the missile batteries—watched balefully from the balcony. They didn't play our games.

The officers in the ops department looked at me strangely.

"SAM-6s? Where did you get your information?" If headquarters didn't know much about the SAM-6, a squadron commander from Hatzerim who had just read routine intelligence reports definitely had to know less. "We'll know where they are in good time," they said, somewhat hesitatingly. "We'll nail them before they move." They didn't get paid for chasing wild fantasies.

"Well," I persisted, "suppose we don't know. Isn't it worthwhile just to check?" From today's vantage point I know that I was sensing a kettle back then.

The operations officers said, "You are chasing your tail, Spector. The existing batteries were also thought to be mobile, and proved to be clumsy things that move slowly and with great difficulty. The problem is not finding the batteries. Our problem is how to enter the killing zone of the missiles and get out with minimum losses. And our current doctrine furnishes us with this." Of course, they were talking about penetration at low level. But the question I just raised put the whole system in jeopardy once again.

Was it still right to fly at low level?

Low-level penetration is good only when approaching a target whose location is known in advance. But the problem with mobile batteries is, by definition, their unknown position. The pilot has to search and find them on his own. But lo and behold, there is no practical way to search for targets and locate them when flying at low level; the pilot's field of view is too limited.

The idea that the positions of the missile batteries will not be known, and our pilots would have to fly around in the killing zone to look for them, was unbearable to everybody in the room. If this indeed was the situation, then all the work we had invested in planning, equipping, and training had been in vain. This was really an awful idea.

Even so, we had to check it out. We dialed air intelligence. The answer was prompt: "When the air force goes out to hit the SAMs, we will know the location of 90 percent of the batteries." The faces of the operations planners lit up. Yossi from the training section breathed a sigh of relief and went out back to his desk. There was no need to run around and work to get more money and resources for new tests that were not already planned.

The ten Baboons sat before me. This was a company of captains, all excellent fighter pilots and navigators, and I looked into their eyes and saw my friends and myself six short years ago. I also was reading their thoughts. Like me six years earlier, they, too, hadn't come willingly to the course.

What were they going to get out of this? And who were Lieutenant Colonel Spector and his Orange Tails to teach them anything here in the wilderness of Hatzerim?

I understood, and I was determined to give them a course as good as the one we got at the Bats.

And indeed during those three months, until the course ended in July 1973, I gave them my all, and everything available to us at the Orange Tails. Gordon, my second-in-command, had to use the squadron in the service of the Baboons. He ran the Orange Tails' routine in my place, and we both met only evenings to report what happened, to coordinate the work, and to set limits. I couldn't watch the Orange Tails closely enough, so I limited it.

In the mornings, the Baboons flew first, and the Orange Tails received the remainder of aircraft, firing ranges, munitions, and the leftovers of eggs and white cheese from breakfast. When the Baboons initiated extensive flight exercises, the squadron would support them with "slaves" who drew their maps and flew under their command and according to their instructions. And when the course invited lecturers, the Orange Tails would sweep the floors, mow the grass, and serve the refreshments. I met my squadron over those three months only beyond the limits of my other life. A slap on the shoulder of a mechanic here, praise to a clerk there, an interview with a pilot at a critical moment were key elements.

But time kept heating things up, and when I delve into my logbook I find operational alerts and scrambles, and even one real dogfight, against a few Syrian MiGs in the north of Lebanon.

From my patrol area at sea, I watched the vapor trails and saw the MiGs closing on Eitan Ben Eliahu, who was on a photo intel mission over Syria, trying to cut him off. I called in a warning, but the aerial controller—far away in Israel—didn't understand the situation developing on his screen. I made another radio call, but still getting no reply, I announced loud and clear, "There's going to be an engagement out here!"

Still no response. So I took my four-ship section in at full speed and cut off the MiGs from their prey. Eitan sneaked out of there unscathed, and a MiG went down. But my call was heard, and Benny Peled, second-in-command and air force commander designate, thought I had decided to rebel against the air force's central control or mount my own war against Syria. After landing I was summoned promptly (Don't change, come right away!) to Tel Aviv.

Dark cumulonimbus clouds covered the boardroom's ceiling, and high electric tension filled the air. Lightning was primed to strike and thunder to roar. Benny climbed the podium with his mustache bristling and called on me, and everybody waited to see what would happen. I got to my feet and explained what had actually taken place, then drew on the blackboard a sketch of the situation as I had seen it from my cockpit. Of course, I was not alone there; an additional twenty eyes had seen it all. Benny's whiskers gradually went to half mast, and when I asked him what I was up there for, if not to get Eitan out if he got into trouble, he even said he was sorry. To Benny's credit, he always was ready to think anew. He canceled his preliminary decision to court-martial me, and the whole thing ended as usual: no medals, no jail time.

To me, this was nothing new. Authority is what you make of it, and the responsibility ends up on your shoulders no matter what happens.

I can't find the summary of the advanced leadership course I published among the few papers I still have, and this is indeed a pity. Perhaps there is a copy of this document in the air force's archives. It was a slim, blue booklet. All I can find is a letter from Benny Peled in my logbook. There, in his own handwriting, are the following words: "I trembled reading your work. In a word, 'beautiful.' Surely we shall attain our goal. Benny." This letter was stuck on the page from August 1973, two months before the war. But the fact is that when the war broke out, we were not even close to the target set by the Baboons in their experiments.

And this is the crux of the story. In spite of the negative opinion of the operations department, the ten trainees of my course went out to do research, trying out ways to attack mobile SAM batteries on the move. The name we invented for such creatures was Wild in the Savanna. Later this name became the official designation.

To be sure, we didn't disobey orders this time. In a long conversation with Colonel Agassi, chief of operations and Avihu's superior, he listened and confirmed that I had analyzed the problem correctly. Agassi even proposed some ideas of his own. But permission alone wasn't enough. I needed vast resources for this job, mainly dummy mobile batteries that could run around the Sinai so my pilots could face the practical difficulty in finding them and devise new ways to do it. In short, I needed several dozen four-wheel-drive vehicles, drivers, mechanics, a doctor, a nurse, a ground officer to run the show, rifles for the guards, gas and oil, communication sets, blankets, food and water, and a bunch of administrative stuff. Agassi shrugged. He was the chief of operations, not administration.

My base also didn't have this kind of ground resources. Again at air force headquarters, the training department would not accept Agassi's oral promises.

"You are talking nonsense!" Yossi raged at me. "I have no place to get all this stuff from!" I found myself going from door to door, descending the chain of command from captain down to lieutenant and then to the quartermaster sergeant. There was no one to talk to in the air force about land vehicles, so I was sent back to Hatzerim.

I stopped the car in Beer-Sheva, at the door of Ariel Sharon's office. Major General Ariel Sharon was at that time the commander of the Southern Command of the Israeli Army, the general responsible for the ground front with Egypt. I didn't know Sharon personally, and he didn't know who I was. He was ending his military service, but he was not dismissive of the story I told him. I saw before me a very-good-looking man, still not fat, his full hair white. He was wearing a green uniform with a red beret. I stood in his office door in my flight suit and no hat, and perhaps the only reason I was allowed in was my unruly appearance. General Sharon had a broad view and could make decisions. After fifteen minutes I got a division of command cars and access to all the target ranges in the Southern Command. All I had to do was instruct the commander of my "division"—an officer who came running and stood at attention in front of me—when to go, where, and what to do in the area.

I left General Sharon and returned to Hatzerim. I never met him again in person, but following that short discussion I received an interesting note from him. This was in the midst of the Yom Kippur War. Sharon was fighting with his corps against the Egyptians on the Suez Canal front. Whenever he saw the orange tails of the Orange Tails streaking over him into Egypt and out again—so was the message he sent me—he knew I was there for him.

My command cars, in small companies, began raising dust in the wide expanse of the Sinai Desert. They roved around and stopped in places according to instructions by our exercise management team. Then they arranged themselves in deployments similar to our estimations of how those new mobile SAM batteries would. From their hidden positions they would watch us and launch signal rockets and smoke grenades, to simulate missiles launches.

The Baboons had prepared themselves well to do battle. They patrolled outside the danger zone, and they devised methods to locate the small, scattered groups of vehicles over the vast distances (we called it independent intelligence-gathering). Sometimes we employed our Phantoms as simulated missiles. They came at us from the "enemy area" at top speed, emerging and pulling up to us. Each "damaged" Baboon left the game, made a circle to cool off and think it over, and then returned for a second try and then a third. Slowly we found ways of locating the mobile batteries from a distance. We tempted and threatened them, and the batteries reacted: they launched and exposed themselves. Only then did we go in and attack the targets. Whenever we succeeded in scoring a hit on our target, it would set off colored smoke as a sign that they were *hors de combat* for the current drill. The radar controllers followed our approaches, and our gun camera films were analyzed. Our successes and failures were analyzed qualitatively and quantitatively. Our methods kept changing, and our scores improved daily. We were getting better at killing without being killed.

At the end of the BBN advanced leadership course, every participant on the course and some leaders of the Orange Tails had preliminary knowledge of how mobile SAM batteries on the loose could be located and hunted down. We nicknamed our product, the method we invented, "SAM hunting." It was an extremely difficult and challenging way of flying, and the maneuvers required of the pilots and navigators were extreme and on the edge of safety limits. But it worked.

Indeed, our SAM hunting was just an initial step on a new path, a far from perfect method, and couldn't be used all the time. But there was promise in it—that there was a way to fight SAM batteries even without preliminary location intelligence. And it had another, surprising benefit: it was not an operazia. In this method you could start attacking the SAM arrays with any force you had at your disposal, with no need to involve the whole air force and concentrate all its power, the way Operations Defy and Model required. At that time I didn't understand the constraints such operazias put on the commander of the air force in wartime, sucking him dry and conditioning his decisions. Who knows? Had I understood that aspect of the story better and said it loud and clear at the time, would someone have heard me?

It seems not soon enough. Benny Peled didn't think any differently from his operations planners, and after the war he argued that his superiors promised him that the air force would get the first couple of days free of any other requirement, just to execute its SAM plans. Until his dying day Benny blamed himself for his believing this alleged promise, but this is how the air force got ready for the coming war.

Like all the attack squadrons, the Orange Tails also were slated to be part of the operazia of the SAM attacks using the method for static batteries with known locations. But the Orange Tails—out of the whole air force—had a possible alternative. Only we had taken part in the experiments and maneuvers with the Baboons, devised a new method, and continued to work on it.

For me, this experiment was an escape from a conceptual box. I felt just the way I had four years before, when the method of "specification of one target" in massive dogfights showed how a section of two could compete in multiparticipant battle against any number of MiGs.

In July 1973 our BBN course ended. The command cars division returned to Southern Command, and the Baboons went back to their units. Major General Sharon was replaced by General Gorodish, and the new commander of the South began a campaign of chasing cars and throwing speeders into jail. Benny Peled replaced Moti Hod as the IAF commander. Everything returned to normal. The Orange Tails began a course for new Phantom pilots and navigators. The war was closing in.

I was the trainee who had learned the most in the BBN course for advanced leadership. The lectures and the visits, Ran Pecker–style, and especially the intellectual leadership I had to supply for those smart, rebellious Baboons, started new thought processes inside me.

I took a new, clean notebook and wrote on its cover, "Thoughts about the air force." On the first page I drew a simple table, like a chessboard, and I labeled the X and Y axes respectively "missions" and "tools." The squares soon filled themselves in, and I saw it was out of balance. I was surprised to find some of the squares empty. The significance was that some missions had no tools, and some tools had no missions. I began thinking about it, asking myself new questions.

I was changing fast. Without asking, I got out of the circle of "shouters" and "being shouted at" of my friend Goldie and found myself in no-man's-land. From just a squadron commander, a lieutenant colonel heading a battalion, I turned into an amphibian, a fighter pilot slouching about with the thoughts and worries of a general officer.

I told Ali all this and she, laughing, cited Miguel de Cervantes. I wasn't surprised. Dvorah, my mother from the Galilee, used to call me "Don Quixote."

Chapter

18

Model

The Yom Kippur War was initiated by Egypt and Syria on Yom Kippur, October 6, 1973, at 2:00 P.M. Almost all Arab states were in this war, including Syria, Jordan, Iraq, Algeria, Morocco, Libya, and Kuwait, and for the first time the Arab world used oil as a financial weapon. At the end of the war there was danger of a confrontation between the two superpowers, the United States and the Soviet Union.

The war took Israel totally by surprise. A total of 2,569 Israeli soldiers were killed, 7,500 wounded, and 301 taken prisoner. The war shocked Israel's citizens, caught the IDF off balance, and left a deep scar on many souls.

THE OFFICIAL HISTORY says that this war caught us by surprise. Some say that if we hadn't been surprised, the air force would have attacked first, as in the Six-Day War, and all would have been different.

I don't think so.

Because when the sirens wailed on Saturday morning, October 6, 1973, at 6:30 a.m., I was seated with the other unit commanders in the office of our new base commander, Colonel Shumi. We had just gone over our preparations for war and only lacked accurate knowledge of when it was going to start. This was the same as in the Fighting First six years before. The base was ready, we had enough people standing by and ready for action, and we had plenty of time: the war began at two o'clock in the afternoon, so we still had a full seven and a half hours.

Thus when the wailing of the sirens began, Shumi nodded to us and said, "That's it—to your squadrons." I started my car and drove very slowly to the Orange Tails. There was no need to race. In my Phantom squadron, all the aircraft were armed and ready for war, according to orders, my readiness crews standing by. The squadron was ready and briefed for the first action. So I drove slowly. And I had another reason: I wanted to show the base personnel, who were peering out their doors in their pajamas, rubbing their eyes on a holiday morning, that the sky had not fallen, that everything was okay. I knew I was their barometer, and I wanted everybody to know that as far as I was concerned, we could start anytime.

I understand that with Israel's reserve forces as a whole the situation was totally different. For the hundreds of thousands of citizen soldiers who slept at home, or were praying in the synagogues on this holiest day of the year, during which no one goes anywhere and the streets are literally empty, the sound of sirens came as a shock. But as far as I was concerned—and from what I learned since, for the air force and the IDF high command, this war came as no surprise. Only the soldiers who were not prepared by their officers were surprised.

No surprise, but what I found on arrival at my squadron was a big mess. All the telephones were ringing, and every call brought contradicting orders, do this and then . . . no, never mind, do that. All our people were trying to figure out the orders and carry them out on the double. At noon the war still hadn't started. We made an all-out effort to complete the last munitions changes on all the aircraft, and hurriedly prepared maps and plans for different targets. At the same time, a flood of reservists was pouring in. They filled the aircraft hangars and the corridors of the squadron building, needing rations, mattresses, blankets, and a place to store their gear. They needed to be given jobs. They needed officers to tell them what to do. I felt

I was going to lose my focus.

I called my deputies, Egozi and Krieger, my technical officers, Mike and Jimmy, and the adjutant, Shemer, and told them, "Don't bother me with administrative stuff anymore. I have to try and see the main thing."

And Jimmy asked, "What about the the mechanics?" He knew the mechanics were the apple of my eye. I answered,

"Their problems don't interest me anymore. As far as I am concerned they can burn to ash, just let them get the aircraft ready on time." Now it was clear. There were no more questions.

And then, in early afternoon, the balloon went up.

Shumi, our base commander, received a telephone call. We were in his office. He turned to us, his voice shrill, "Enemy aircraft approaching the base! Get the Orange Tails—everybody—airborne!"

I drove back rapidly to my squadron and shouted down the empty corridor, "All pilots scramble, fast!"

I grabbed my flight gear, found a navigator, and we raced to the next hangar. All the other pilots were running ahead of us, so I jumped into the first empty aircraft I found—it was sitting there with a full load of bombs—and started its engines. In all the other hangars other aircraft roared to life, all carrying tons of bombs. Somebody was already taxiing out and passed in front of me, blasting the whole hangar with his heavy jet exhaust on his way to the runway. Objects flew all around us.

I began opening my throttles to go after him, intending to take off fast and once in the air to take command and organize whomever I might find into a defense of the base against the incoming MiGs. We still had to figure out where to jettison those dozens of tons of bombs hanging from our bellies.

Then I got a call on the radio.

"Spector, where are you?"

In the IAF we do not use our real names on the radio, just call signs. But in all the confusion, nobody had gotten a call sign. The thundering of the first takeoffs was deafening even through the helmet, and I might not have heard this call hadn't that voice called my name again and again. "Spector!"

and one more time: "Iftach Spector!"

"Spector here," I finally answered. "I am in hangar five, on my way out."

"Iftach, listen to me," continued the voice, and now I recognized it was my second-in-command, Shlomo Egozi. "Hold it for a moment. As you were! There is no attack right now."

"What?"

"Let me get some order here!" He was talking fast, but his voice was firm and clear. "Gilutz has already taken off leading a section; they'll circle the base. That's enough defenses for now. Stand by with your engines running; be ready to scramble at any moment. Your call sign is Ascot. I'll get you a four-ship section in a minute."

I said, "Okay, take it." And immediately a series of calls began, identifying the pilots in the aircraft one after another.

"Krieger here, started up, with Oren."

"Gordon here."

"Goren."

"Kamay here." the navigator talked for the pilot in his front cockpit, who hadn't put his helmet on yet.

And even a voice of one of the "chicks," the students in the transition course to the Phantom, broke into the radio, "Gino here, standing by."

I almost laughed aloud.

Egozi continued to manage things, fast and serious and very accurately, selecting formation leaders, assembling formations.

"Gino, exit your aircraft and return to the building. Panay is on the way to replace you in the cockpit."

"Roger." I felt his disappointment.

I knew we were in good hands, but I was standing in my stirrups. The MiGs were out there on the way, hanging above our base like clouds full of hail, and I worried that too much management might delay our defense and fuck us up.

"Ascot, how do you read?"

"Five," I answered for my whole four-ship formation he had collected for me.

"Ascot, stand by with your engines running. Every one of you, tell the mechanics around him to unload the bombs off his aircraft, fast." Every aircraft was loaded with some four tons of bombs.

"Take note: fuses are in," I protested. When a bomb is fused it is dangerous; you don't touch it.

"Copy that. Do as I said." I realized that Egozi knew something about authority and responsibility, too.

"Roger, will comply."

The mechanics around me reacted in disbelief to the signals I gave them, then were convinced and came with their yellow carts and got under the big aircraft's belly. Hard knocks were heard, and the Phantom hopped when four tons of bombs, with fuses, slipped off.

"Ascot, when you are clean, taxi out to the runway. You will replace the airborne flight."

The attack on the base never happened. After some time on the runway we were sent back to the hangars, and gave the aircraft back to the mechanics to arm them again with the same bombs. Egozi had prevented us from throwing away huge loads of fused bombs in the expanse of the Negev or into the sea, together with the rare and expensive weapons pylons. Within a short time the Orange Tails was ready and armed again, and I knew I had a young battle commander under me.

But even though Hatzerim hadn't been attacked, the war had really started.

The Egyptians and the Syrians attacked in force, large, armored columns moving toward the Suez Canal in the South and into the Golan Heights in the North. I took command in the operations room, and the squadron began scrambling on various missions. By sunset we began to get some startling reports. Egozi and Duby caught an aerial convoy of Egyptian helicopters full of commandos crossing into the Sinai and shot down six of them. I was happy to learn that my young partner Roy Manoff had been Egozi's navigator, and with five aircraft shot down, was now officially an ace. An even more fantastic item came from the Far South. A section from our squadron, led by Captain Nahumi, defending the Ophir airfield in the southern tip of Sinai against aerial attack, had shot down seven Egyptian MiGs.

‡

Darkness fell at Hatzerim, and all our aircraft returned safely. After the noon madness, that good news instilled a feeling that we had gotten off on the right foot in the war. But it was too early to celebrate.

After the daily debriefing, Egozi sent the pilots to get some sleep and conserve their strength for the next day. We decided to keep all of them in the squadron building, to have them close by. The administration of Egozi and Shemer was excellent: mattresses and blankets were spread in every office, and the squadron's operations clerks wrote down who slept where and when. That enabled us to dispense with the loudspeaker, and if somebody was needed they would wake him quietly without disturbing all the others. We all stayed in the squadron building; in fact, for the next three weeks, until the end of the war, that's where we lived. Similarly, the mechanics lived, ate, and slept in the subterranean hangars, by their aircraft. This arrangement prevented any physical or mental distraction. Everybody in the squadron had only one thing on his mind: the war.

After everybody hit the mattresses, the managing crew remained in the operations room. We looked at each other. We had only a very partial picture of what was happening, but we knew well that our squadron's successes were just local affairs, just defensive reactions. We got the news that the Egyptians and the Syrians were attacking from the south and the north, and because the defending Israeli units had only skeleton personnel on the line because of the Yom Kippur holiday, they probably had already crushed them. It was clear that defense alone was not going to get us to victory. The big game had just started, and things were going to change. We waited for orders for the morning attack so we could arm our aircraft accordingly, draw the required maps, and prepare our briefings.

But that night was different from what we expected. Beginning at midnight, orders began to arrive, and the craziness of the previous day was repeated: as we were figuring out the first order, and had awakened all our men to get ready, the telephone rang again.

"Stop! The mission has changed." We stopped the mechanics and ordered them to strip and then rearm all the aircraft with new ordnance, and the navigators had gone to prepare their maps, when the teleprinter clattered and out came a new roll of crap. Do it all over again—truck new weapons from the stores, undress and rearm the aircraft—the navigators threw their maps away and spread new, clean ones on the tables. The intelligence officer repacked his target files and tore open new envelopes from the safe. The duty officer erased the boards and began to draw new briefing instructions on them—and the telephone rang again.

At three o'clock in the morning, with all the squadron red-eyed and frazzled, I decided this had to end. I instructed Jimmy to load all the aircraft with simple iron bombs, eleven half-ton pieces on each, and that was that. No matter what target we were going to attack on the morning's first sortie, this was what we were going to use. I sent my pilots and navigators to get some sleep. They were left with only one hour of sleep, and one more hour to plan and draw maps for whatever mission we got before dawn. I had no intention of updating the chain of command about my decision.

And so we learned how this nocturnal war had to be fought. On subsequent nights we let our people sleep. The duty officers in the ops room went through the stream of orders flowing in, from which they gleaned some idea of what was on their minds at high command. Then they took notes and filed them. We took seriously only orders that came in after three o'clock in the morning. This method required our technical and operational staffs to be very efficient; they had to prepare anything—everything—within two hours, come what may.

I was not worried; the Orange Tails knew their business.

WHEN DAWN NEARED ON October 7, the second day of the war, air force command finally knew what it wanted to do today. They decided to start with Operation Defy and eliminate the Egyptian array of SAM batteries along the Suez Canal. This was the right thing to do to attain air superiority there and attack the Egyptian army, which was crossing the canal and encircling our positions on the east bank.

Operation Defy required the full involvement of the whole air force for a day or two. We rolled up our sleeves and went out to do our part in the first sortie. At first light I took off, leading twelve Phantoms, and we crossed into Egypt and attacked Beni-Suweif, a fighter airfield south of Cairo. This was part of the necessary preparations before attacking the missiles. The MiGs had to be grounded so they wouldn't interfere with Defy. We hit the airfield's runways hard, and the first job of the day was done as planned. Then we went home, ready for a fast turnaround for the real thing, to begin knocking out the SAMs waiting for us at the canal.

As we landed, more madness: Defy was canceled.

"Everybody take off on Operation Model!"

Model was a different operation in the opposite direction—attacking SAMs in Syria. This time there was no preparation, just hysteria.

"Hurry up, hurry up, we have to knock out the Syrian missiles as soon as possible!"

I admit that words such as "madness" and "hysteria," which I use above to describe the first days of the Yom Kippur War, offend my ears. A lot of time has passed since then, and as it happens after every disaster, we all have internalized some formulation of what happened. The past has rearranged itself by itself; the uncertainty is gone. Today there is a view of the whole situation, and there is an explanation for everything that took place then. True, one still remembers even after thirty years that it was hard, but one is not supposed to exaggerate in words and tone; it's not proper, not respectable.

Well, believe me that I am not writing hysterically now, just as the sailors from Pearl Harbor and the firemen from the Twin Towers were not hysterical when they were writing their memoirs. But in the war itself, in our squadron's operations room in Hatzerim, we had no view of the whole. We saw the world through a straw, and it broke on us in a series of surprises. When I landed back from Beni-Suweif on the morning of October 7, no one told me that Gen. Moshe Dayan was saying to the air force commander, "Benny, the Third Temple is falling." (A reference to the First Temple, destroyed by Nebuchadnezzar, and the Second Temple, by the Romans). I didn't hear the tone, nor understand the reason for Benny's spontaneous reaction to throw whole the air force at the Golan Heights.

But when I saw how a well-organized operation to attack missiles in Egypt turned into everyone running amock to attack missiles in Syria, I had doubts about the stability of my world.

‡

Nothing in that flight resembled anything I had seen before.

The missile attack operazia that I had been so pressed to agree to in its totality was thrown to the winds once it was really needed. What was taking place now was a catch-as-catch-can kind of flight. The clock was ticking, so there was no time for briefing. Everybody grabbed an envelope from the safe and ran to his plane while the mechanics were still arming it, and tore his envelope open to study the procedures and his target while being strapped in the cockpit. And once in the air, the pilots spread the maps on their knees, trying to find their way while maneuvering to avoid other aircraft racing north.

In this way the main battle doctrine of the Israeli Air Force collapsed the moment it started. The IAF broke into the Golan Heights in many formations, helter-skelter, and found itself skimming over Syrian armored columns that had advanced into the heights the night before. Their antiaircraft artillery shot the hell out of us.

We, the Orange Tails, had a unique advantage, and not by luck this time. A few months before, when the planning of Operation Model was reaching its completion, we had stubbornly insisted on penetrating our allotted targets in the missiles array from the rear, not by frontal attack, as planned. I preferred a circuitous, indirect approach. My battle experience—even from my Mirage period—taught me to avoid crossing "hot" front lines at low level. Just like my Uncle Aronchik at El-Hamma in 1946, I believed that it was much easier and safer to cross into enemy territory somewhere else.

We argued about that approach, and I was ready to give up the advantages of a direct approach from the front with all the others. And indeed the Orange Tails' attack routes, unlike everybody else's, went around the missile arrays and penetrated from the rear.

The squadron took off formation after formation, and I, after some management duty, happened to be the last leader from our squadron to take off, leading a three-ship section; we lacked a fourth ship. We entered the missile array from behind, as planned. As I had anticipated, nobody expected us to come in that way, and everything was quiet. No one shot at us, but we found nothing where our SAM-6 battery was supposed to be. The place was empty. The battery, like most of its kind, had deployed forward with the attacking Syrian Army, in the direction of the Hula Valley in Israel.

All I saw around were columns of armored infantry. I found myself in the heart of the Syrian ground forces. Groups of vehicles were driving west, and antiaircraft farted smoke balls shooting west. I flew over there, and the Syrian soldiers looked up at me; my target was nowhere to be seen, and I felt like an uninvited guest at a party. So I pulled up and made another, higher circle, searching, hoping to find that battery somehow.

This was the moment when the Baboons began paying off on that investment—I was not at a loss. In their trials they had analyzed techniques of tempting missile batteries and threatening them to make them launch a missile and expose themselves. It was totally clear to me that circling around in easy radar range and in the heart of the fire zone, my navigator and I were juicy bait, and I hoped the idea would work. And at last somebody nearby woke up and launched a missile at us. The missile's fire and trail of smoke exposed his location. But I was not just bait but also a threat, carrying eleven half-ton high-explosive bombs. As soon as the missile took off—Erel saw it first and pointed it out—I rolled down and dived right on its source. My wingmen, who had seen the SAM the same time we did, pulled up from ground level and came in after me. And indeed when I put my gunsight there, I could see a group of vehicles comprising an SAM-6 battery there. They shot another, smaller missile at us. We needed no extra assurance that this was indeed our target. All three aircraft unloaded all our ordnance on the site, blowing it to kingdom come. Then we turned back and went home very satisfied with ourselves.

And only when we landed, overjoyed to see that all our pilots were back safely from the Golan, were we stunned to hear that all was not well. Not only had the air force missed most of the SAM batteries and bombed vacant land, it also had lost seven Phantoms in this operation. The Syrian SAM-6 array—except for the minute part that we probably took out—was essentially untouched. Operation Model, which was planned to deal with the fixed SAM batteries, failed miserably when it met the mobile array.

‡

WELL, I THOUGHT WHEN I understood what had happened, we'll just refuel and rearm and go back to the Golan Heights and finish the job." I had seen the Syrian army on their way to the Hula Valley, and I knew firsthand that the Galilee in northern Israel was in real danger. It was already afternoon, very little daylight was left, and we hadn't accomplished anything yet. But then came the next incredible order: "Fly at top speed—TOP SPEED—to Egypt."

"Egypt? What about the Golan Heights?"

"Forget the Golan Heights."

"Do we go back to Operation Defy from the morning?"

No. This time this was not the continuation of Defy. Now it was to attack the bridges that the Egyptians were laying over the Suez Canal to bring armor into the Sinai.

"Bridges? What bridges?"

AND AGAIN, LADIES AND gentlemen, pardon me for the politically incorrect utterances you hear here. I was not in the high command at the time, and I know only second-hand about the pressures they were under. And I heard our leaders arguing later that they had been much firmer than it appeared from down below, and that perhaps we were so whipped only because we were just the knot at the end of the lash.

Well, maybe.

When I last visited Benny Peled, a year before his death in 2002, he tried to convince me that this indeed was the case. He even gave me a good show, reading from some document or other (it turned to be a high command protocol from that time) and playing various roles in bass and soprano voices, stopping at times to fix me with his angry lion's eyes and draw some oxygen into his poor, emphysema-clogged lungs. Indeed, according to Benny's show, some of the top brass had stepped up to the plate. But I still don't think this was the whole truth. I don't believe that the high command assessed the situation coolly, setting priorities for its limited aerial force. I find it hard to believe that only we, down at the squadron level, were confused. No. Mass hysteria had reigned on our side, from the top down.

The military problem was, of course, how to get out of it and make the enemy hysterical, the enemy that was continuing to penetrate the Golan Heights in the North and the Suez Canal in the South. This was not a simple thing, even if you had Phantoms. The enemy had foreseen our reactions, and we were paying a high price in casualties and matériel from all our running around trying to clean up spilled milk. This price was the result of our intellectual laziness during the years since the end of the War of Attrition, and no "but we were surprised" excuses can cover it up.

So there were bridges on the canal.

I didn't know what a "military bridge" was and how it should be attacked. This was something that if somebody had thought about it before the war, we pilots never heard about it. Bridges were at Waterloo, over the Yarkon Brook in Tel Aviv, and over the River Kwai in the movies. If you read about the war in Vietnam, you would know that the Americans were continually bombing the Paul Doumer Bridge in Hanoi and had been unable to knock it down or even stop traffic over it. Rumors had it that the IDF was developing secret bridges to cross into Egypt, but this, of course, was not for pilots to know. My men and I knew nothing about bridges. And headquarters also had nothing clever to add.

But we did have Phantoms and iron bombs. So we loaded our aircraft with as many bombs as we could carry. It was reasonable to expect that bombs, if they hit a bridge, would do some damage. Now, since we didn't accomplish anything with Operation Defy—that is, we hadn't taken out the Egyptian SAMs—the Suez Canal was a hot spot for us. We had to enter the heart of the missiles' killing zones to attack those bridges. Still, this was not the problem. Entering the SAM killing zone in Operations Defy and Model required exactly that. And if this time the target was going to be bridges instead of missile batteries, so what? After all, there always comes a moment in battle when the soldiers have to stand and take fire. My men showed no signs of being upset by this idea.

But the truly serious problem was again location: nobody knew where those bridges were. They could be anywhere along the 150 kilometers of the canal. How many bridges were there? Ten? A hundred? Nobody knew. We were left with the problem of how to enter the zone, search, find, and destroy however many bridges there were. And even their looks and size were not clear. Were they large or small? Yellow or green? Nobody knew anything. There was only one way: go there and find out for yourself.

And even though the problem we faced was similar to that of finding a mobile SAM battery, the Baboons' hunting solution for SAM-6 arrays was not relevant here. You can't tempt a bridge to get it to show itself. And anyway, this was in the afternoon. No hunter would hunt birds with the sun in his eyes. But we had to attack those bridges now. There was nobody else to do it but the IAF's Phantoms.

So we put together as many formations as we could and improvised some attack doctrine. And so, with Roy Manoff in my backseat, off we went to the Suez Canal. We left the rest of our formation to wait outside and came in alone at low level, avoiding radar detection, then pulled up above the band of water with the setting sun in our eyes. We circled over a section of the canal. You had to go over to the other side to see anything. We ignored the black flowers of ack-ack that bloomed around us and the smell of burning cordite that filled the cockpit. And so we scanned kilometer after kilometer but found nothing. We cleared out of the fire zone and flew back over the safe dunes of the Sinai, took a breath, and returned for a second look.

At last Hawkeye Manoff saw a bridge. Believe me, it was hard to see. I was stunned to discover that these bridges were nothing like the Golden Gate Bridge. These were just two steel ramps for vehicles set on submerged pontoons. They were very thin threads, like sewing lines on the black water, almost invisible, especially in the dim light and the hazy air just before dusk. But we found one.

And then we called the rest of our formation waiting outside—ready to replace us if we were shot down, and continue the mission. All three of us went in and bombed that bridge.

And more formations from our squadron acted as we had improvised just an hour before, and attacked nearby. Perhaps we disrupted something or scared the Egyptians down there. There were other formations from our sister squadrons operating in other sections of the canal, but I don't know how they found their targets and made their attacks.

And this time it was dumb luck that the Orange Tails ended this mission without losses. October 7, the second day of the war, ended with a few night sorties, and some bombs dropped in the dark in the general area of the canal. Perhaps they interfered with the Egyptians resting on their laurels.

After this day ended we gathered in the briefing room to find out what happened to us during this long day. Many eyes were fixed on me, so I tried to move slowly and speak little and in a low, manly voice, so they could all see that everything was okay—just another one of those wars.

I was hiding from them what I knew, that the command structure above us had collapsed.

The terrifying and worrying thing in those first days of the war from my point of view as the commander of a fighting field unit was neither the enemy nor the missiles. For these I was prepared. Also, the madness didn't terrify me. I could handle the toilet paper that came rolling out of the teleprinter, and deal with the craziness of "load/unload ordnance" that harassed my mechanics during the long night. And even racing from one front to the other didn't scare the interceptor pilot in me. Ours was a superb fighter squadron (that day I began to realize how good it was) and was built to handle such things. We knew how to improvise, and when all the rules were thrown in the trashcan and procedures torn up, the Orange Tails found ways to survive in the heart of danger and do our jobs.

The terrible thing was the loss of trust in my superior officers. I couldn't grasp what had happened to them—they seemed to know nothing, their voices were hysterical, their instructions incoherent. They didn't listen to feedback from below and made the same mistakes over and over. The ground I stood on was crumbling under my feet, and I didn't know what tomorrow would bring.

This was like an earthquake for me. I hadn't the slightest idea of what was going on in Tel Aviv in those days, no notion of the tumult and loss of collegiality that reigned in the high command of the Israeli Air Force. I didn't know about the hysterical running around in the poisonous atmosphere of cigarette smoke inside an underground bunker, of the pale faces of senior staff when every hour brought news of the collapse of another part of the front—the gains of Syrian armor in the Golan Heights and Egyptian infantry crossing the Suez Canal into the Sinai Desert, about the fall of encircled positions and the collapse of their own plans and expectations. I knew nothing about the shouting and the arguments.

That day had shaken something in me. From that moment until the middle of the war I suffered from a chill up my spine; I felt alone and the entire world around me full of simmering kettles, not all of them enemy-made. I felt alone in battle.

All I had was the Orange Tails.

Chapter 19

Room for Decision

THE MISSION OF THE ORANGE TAILS in the Yom Kippur War was long and complicated and lasted nineteen days and nights. There were 760 battle sorties. This work was done by a rather small group of pilots (one in five were cadets training on the Phantom) and even fewer navigators, and maintained thanks to a couple of hundred mechanics, most of them reservists.

Of the two dozen Phantoms we had when the war broke out, four were lost, and three others were seriously damaged and grounded. Many others were damaged, some several times, but were fixed and returned to fly and fight. Three used Phantoms arrived during the war from America, were absorbed into our fleet, and replaced lost aircraft. The squadron attacked enemy airfields and SAM batteries in Egypt and Syria, and gave our ground forces close air support. We shot down twenty-two enemy fighters and seven helicopters.

We all got to the end, some a bit battered, with two of us in the hospital.

It seems I was not alone.

As soon as war broke out, like an animal sensing danger, the Orange Tails woke up and began thinking and functioning. As if by themselves, original fighting techniques grew in the Orange Tails. Some new ideas were extremely important, and got funny names such as High Society, or Kettles, or Living Map.

High Society rose on its own out of the midlevel of the squadron. These were the more prominent leaders—pilots and navigators. They were involved in everything. Their voice was heard in the briefing room, in the ops room, in my office. These seven or eight guys—formerly our squadron's loyal opposition—gathered around me, and took the weight with me and my officers. They backed us and added to our collective brainpower.

This might sound like a trivial thing, but what else do you expect soldiers to do in war, if not give their commanders their hearts, brains, and loyalty? Maybe, maybe not. I know of other cases. But in our case, my High Society led and the squadron followed. It showed faith in me and in itself, and suddenly I could do anything, make any decision, initiate and demand any kind of effort, and take any risk, and found all my pilots and mechanics behind me. As a result the squadron functioned beautifully. We only got better.

But there was something else, something almost spiritual: the Orange Tails gave me something I never asked for and wasn't expecting. Since its inception all I wanted from the Orange Tails were clarity and efficiency. And suddenly, in the hardest moments of that war, I found the men themselves. I was like Saul, who looked for jackasses and found a crown.

Everything was the opposite of what I had experienced in the Fighting First; back then I wooed the men, tried to pull them with me, and the squadron was lost. But in the Orange Tails, where I had given up on PR and was interested only in the core mission—the operations—it all came to me on its own, and the squadron pushed ahead, with me in the front.

In the beginning I didn't expect this boost, this strong approval I received from my men. I was suspicious, fearing to enjoy it. I asked myself, "How did I get so popular suddenly?" I looked to be proven wrong, to find out that this was just a passing fad. But nothing went wrong.

One event from that war still cries out for closure. The story is not new, but for the first time ever, I'll tell what really happened.

It happened on October 9, the fourth day of the war. We came back to land at dawn after attacking the Egyptian airfield Kutmiya, halfway between

Cairo and the Gulf of Suez. On the way back Gilutz and Yaari's Phantom was hit, caught fire, and went down in the Red Sea. After some time the two injured pilots were rescued, taken to the hospital, and the Red Sea gave up two points to me. When we landed after Kutmiya, a new mission was waiting for us: to attack Syrian headquarters in the center of Damascus.

Our eight-ship formation was supposed to hit the target after another eight ships from the Bats. The time for preparation was short, as usual, but it was necessary to prepare well—the air defense array around Damascus was formidable. Ten missile batteries surrounded the city, and flying in there at high altitude was totally out of question. But we were lucky to get an excellent flight plan to the target. Our route passed over Lebanon, over mountainous and forested areas, and the final approach was between mountains. In this way we could fly down the last slope into Damascus very low, under the missile radars. Then we would burst out of the wadi and appear over them all of a sudden, taking the antiaircraft batteries by surprise. A quick dive on the target, and then out over the mountains again.

I was well acquainted with the Damascus area. In the last year before the war I had led several sorties into the region. We attacked terrorist camps there, successfully eliminated the missile battery at Sheikh Maskin, and more. And in this war, too, I had already managed to roam around the city once or twice. I had a feel for the area. And my navigator for this mission, Kamay, could be trusted completely. So I gave my crews a short briefing, emphasizing the importance of flying low, right until the last moment.

"Use the land for protection," I told them seriously, as I had told Khetz long ago. And then I had another order. "Aim carefully this time. This is a city, not a military base. Don't scatter your hits!"

We crossed over the beach at Ashkelon and went out to sea. The morning was blue and beautiful, and our eight-ship formation coasted north at medium speed in total radio silence. Going deeper into the Mediterranean, the Israeli coast vanished behind us and we cruised calmly, alone over the high seas. Once in a while we passed a lonely ship. And when the clock and the navigation computer came to agree in some nowhere between sea and sky, Kamay turned me southeast, in the direction of Lebanon. The second element of our formation, four ships led by Gordon, slid back into line astern, and the heavy Phantoms were moving to the target in two elements, one after another, Ascot and Dubek.

Approaching Lebanon's coastal radar, we descended to very low altitude and picked up speed, plowing the still face of the sea, and leaving furrows of foam in the water behind us. The tops of Lebanon's mountains rose over the rim of the huge azure basin we were hovering in and peered out at us. Now it was time to get our maps out and prepare for battle.

The closer we got to the coast, the higher the Lebanon Mountains rose before us. I could already see their sides, mottled with black patches of forestry and scarred with whitish channels. Now I could see that clouds were heaped up over the mountain crests. The clouds were large, their tops white and shining in the sun, while their bottoms were dark, covering the mountaintops. The view was stunning, snowy mountains overlaying a white, sandy beach. What a vista, a Levantine late summer dream.

The mountain reflections played before us on the surface of the water, and finally, between the mountains and their reflections, a thin white line appeared. It was surf on a sandy beach. I rocked my wings twice as a signal, and we opened our throttles and accelerated to combat speed. We thundered over the beach and began climbing the mountain slope, to cross the first barrier on our way into Syria. Shadows of the great mountains covered us, and the sky above us became cloudy. The atmosphere around us changed instantly into the dark of winter.

"This is October?" Kamay chuckled from the backseat, but there was no humor in his voice. Our two pairs of eyes looked forward up the slope, searching for clearance between its tops and the clouds, to cross over to the other side. Finally there was something.

"Here, over there," and I pointed my nose between two high peaks that stood like pillars under the cloud ceiling, creating a gate. The air was brighter in there. My Phantom squeezed heavily into it, turning, and the other seven slid in behind me. Mountaintops passed over our heads on both sides, disappearing in the gray cloud cover above. Streams of tiny water drops slid down our canopies. And then we passed the summit, and the ground dropped away abruptly below us. A sigh of relief in each aircraft, and we lowered our noses and dove into the valley, away from the ominous atmosphere above us.

Everybody took time now to prepare for battle and to arm his switches. The Lebanon Valley under the thick clouds was dim in the wintry light. I turned back in my seat and counted my buddies: Ascot was here, three Phantoms cruising in my wake, dark gray like sharks in the foggy aquarium around us. Dubek was just a blurry movement in the background. Good; everybody was in place. The target picture was almost black, and Kamay switched his cockpit's red night lighting on.

The Lebanon Mountains receded in the distance behind us, and in front of us—on the other side of the valley—towered the next chain, the Anti-Lebanon Mountains, heavy and high. It also had its tops in the clouds. The light around us was soft and smooth, as though we were underwater, and the greens of the Lebanon Valley passed under us rich and lush, checked and variegated with lines of light. No sound on the radio, total communication silence, as usual. Five minutes to target. Fine.

The mountain slope. Again full power, nose up, and the Phantoms began climbing the slope of the Anti-Lebanon chain. Our altimeters rolled up, and the clouds in front of us came closer, growing in the windshield Again, Kamay and I searched for a break between the mountaintops and the cloud ceiling. This time it was seven times more important, since beyond this chain was the enemy. There, on the eastern slope down to Damascus, we would start our last approach to the city, and there the radars and the SAMs waited. We had to keep close to the bosom of the earth, descending on them, shaving the ground, and using every groove in the ground to hide from the missiles. Our eyes searched. Where was the break? We became more and more tense. Here it was, the unknown, the X factor in this sortie.

The aircraft gained altitude and the clouds were already close, but no break to be seen. The steep climb bled our airspeed, and the Phantom felt tired and heavy, its steering clumsy. The slope came nearer and nearer as I pressed my aircraft to the ground to gain some seconds before I hit the clouds. Trees passed by my wings; my belly skimmed the rocks. A few hundred meters ahead of me, right in the windshield, the clouds merged with the mountain into one foggy, amorphous mess. There was no brightening whatsoever that might signal a break. Seven heavy Phantoms, loaded with fuel and bombs, dragged behind me. What I saw before me was a barrier of clouds filled with rocks. If I didn't decide soon, the mountain would decide for me.

I decided. Lighting both afterburners, I broke radio silence. "Ascot, Dubek, everybody climb full power, above the clouds!" Immediately I pulled up with what speed I had left.

Immediately my aircraft cockpit was shrouded in humid, opaque cotton wool. My hand groped blindly for the cockpit lighting switch, my eyes wandered among the flight instruments. There was no voice but the aircraft's sounds around us. I could hear Kamay's and my own heavy breathing on the intercom in the gray silence. The climb went on and on. Did I make the decision to pull up in time? Did all of them hear and pull up immediately?

The Phantom climbed, its altimeter turning slowly. A sigh of relief as the instrument's hand passed the height of the mountaintops, hidden somewhere in the fog around us. But we were almost out of speed. When will we finally get out of this mess? At last the light around us began to flicker. The murky fluid that enveloped our canopy changed from gray to white, and all of a sudden our Phantom broke out of the clouds, and before us we saw vast blue skies and yellow sunshine. Gasping, we found ourselves hanging at twelve thousand feet over a white, brilliant cloud carpet that went all the way east, where Damascus waited.

Our heads turned in search of the rest of the formation. One by one and two by two, black Phantoms popped out of the white, wavy rug. I lowered a wing and began drawing a wide circle, to collect them all and organize them again into combat formation.

A FULL CIRCLE AND THEY were all here. Once again we were in formation, the bombs were still with us, and we were ready for battle. But the situation had changed. From where we are now, how do we get through the clouds and then reacquire the ground for our final approach? There were no holes in the clouds. I was disconnected from the ground, just as I was ten years ago in my Super Mystere, but this time I was not on my own. Seven other Phantoms depended on me and my decisions.

Meanwhile, a warning light began flashing and I heard a chirp in my earphones. The advantage of surprise had been lost while we were circling up here at altitude, like geese on the horizon. Our warning gear told us that Damascus missile radars had already acquired us.

I did not know what to do. It made no sense to continue at altitude, to push eight aircraft above the clouds right over a locked-on missile array. The missiles would burst out at full speed from the clouds, leaving us no time to react. How many Phantoms would survive the first salvo? Two? Three? No; a low approach was the only option. But the ground was nowhere in sight, hidden under this white cotton wool. Then, maybe bite the bullet, give the order, and plunge head down into the clouds? No; this would be insanity. I could bang eight Phantoms on the rocks, eliminating a whole fighting unit from our order of battle. No.

I didn't know what to do. I finished the circle in formation, and when we were headed east I straightened hesitantly toward Damascus and began inching there, groping. I lowered one wing, then the other, looked down, searching for holes, for a piece of land so I could squeeze us through and reconnect to the ground and the original plan. I was hanging in blue space, over white carpet, and my whole formation trailed behind me. No one said a word to me, not even my navigator, but I felt their nervous eyes on my back. They awaited instructions, any instructions, from their leader and squadron commander, but I didn't know what to do. We flew east, already encroaching on the danger zone. The red light came on and the horn chirped. The batteries' radars were tracking us through the clouds. There had to be a way! A hole, just a small hole in the clouds! I looked around fervently.

Nothing.

Now, for the second time in this flight, I had to make a decision.

I heard my own voice talking on the radio, cool and businesslike: "Ascot, Dubek, turn one-eighty; head west."

Perhaps this is a good time to remember the IDF tradition of no turning back before the mission is accomplished.

This tradition was stamped into the IDF after a period of weakness that followed the War of Independence in 1948. The combat performance of the Israeli Defense Force dwindled, and then was saved thanks to the bravery and personal example of some daring operations led by Ariel Sharon during the 1950s. Moshe Dayan, the chief of staff, ordered that only 50 percent casualties justify aborting a mission. In the Six-Day War I had my own example of this: our base commander, Benny Peled, ordered us to fly to the Egyptian airfields without stopping for any reason, and if someone fell out along the way it would be "his own problem." I was brought up on all this, and it lay heavy on me when a mix of stupid mountains and stupid clouds turned me back from Damascus. I had aborted before I suffered 50 percent casualties, and my hands were clutching my aircraft's controls, my knuckles white. The formation trailed behind, every one of them aware of what had just happened. The whole trip home lay before us, and we were still carrying sixty-four expensive and desperately needed bombs, and we had to ditch them before landing.

Suddenly voices broke out on the radio, on the combat channel. I heard voices coordinating a pull-up, a dive, and for a second I didn't get it. Flinching in my seat, I looked to both sides onto my buddies around to see what was happening. But they were all around me, cruising in formation above the pastoral vista of clouds.

And then I heard that somebody was hit. Cries of "Break, break!" and "Fire," and a navigator fired off a geographical position—the location told me it was right near Damascus—and then another voice in a ridiculous but clear New York accent, like the narrator of a documentary, croaked, "Oh, it's just a small fire." And then it came to me that these were from Bats, a sister Phantom squadron. Actually, they had an American navigator, Grossman. Or was it Joel Aharonoff, another immigrant from the United States?

And—yes, I suddenly recalled, the Bats were supposed to attack the same target right before us. How could I forget about them? And now they were there, hitting our target in Damascus. I recognized the voice of their leader, Arnon Lavushin.

"Clear target area, heading south," which meant they had completed the mission.

I had turned back, but Lavushin hadn't. He reached the target. And oh, boy, he was paying a price for it.

"How did the bastards get in there?" Kamay mumbled behind me in awe.

What the hell, I thought. Didn't they encounter mountains, clouds? Lavushin, that cool bastard! God damn him! How did he get through that mess?

I learned after the war from Lavushin how he found a way to Damascus. The route the Bats took was a little different, just a few kilometers away from mine, but there—thanks to luck—they found a nice hole and cleared the ridge easily. "I had no problem at all," Arnon told me.

Luck is important, too.

This story of two squadrons that went to Damascus, and their very different adventures, has been told many times since then. It was a subject of discussion for the whole air force, as an example of decision problems and dilemmas flight leaders might face in battle. In one of those discussions the air force commander, Maj. Gen. Benny Peled, established a position toward aborting missions.

"As a rule," he said, "I permit every leader to abort and return to base, but I reserve the right to check why he did so, and decide if he should continue to fly and lead my men into battle. I have no rule book regarding this," Peled said, "but remember that as you are volunteers, this obligates you as much as it acquits you. I shall not force anyone to fly."

In actuality, Benny devised those principal directives only after the war—when I raised publicly the story of my aborted mission to Damascus. During the war nobody cared to talk about it. I brought this issue up after the war, when I was entrusted with the operational training of the air force. To better learn the lessons from the war I thought that dilemmas like this one might help the education of our pilots. Although I remained content with my decision to abort in this particular instance, the discussions of the event were hard for me emotionally.

‡

But back to the Orange Tails, before we landed after the aborted flight to Damascus. There was an interesting sidebar to that flight, which the squadron never bothered to advertise. On our way home I called the northern controller and reminded him that we still had sixty-four five-hundred-kilo bombs, and asked for an alternate target.

"Find out where we might be needed," I told him. "We'll stand by for orders." And for added impact I told him, "We have time—plenty of fuel." We had very little fuel by then, but no one in my formation demurred. So we circled over Galilee, conserving fuel and waiting for a target. At last the controller came back on and passed us over to ground army control in the Golan Heights. A familiar voice answered my call on that channel. It was Sivron, a veteran from ops. His voice was excited when he came on and said, "You're a gift from heaven!"

I had no fuel for friendly banter, and I cut him short: "I have thirty tons of ordnance for you. You have a target for us?"

"I sure do! I have a fat target for you, Ascot!" Sivron's voice was different from his usual slow talk; he spoke fast.

"Then let's have it, and fast." Sixteen pairs of eyes were watching fuel gages. Sivron directed us to use this and that map.

"Look," I told him, "we have no maps and no time to waste. Get us there somehow, and quick!"

"I'll find a way," Sivron answered. "Stand by."

We kept circling over the northern part of the Sea of Galilee, with engines on minimum. I refrained from asking my pilots about their fuel levels, so as not to require them to answer. I was waiting for the first of my pilots to announce "Short on fuel, returning to base." We were all below the required minimum to continue, and I imagined how the dropping out would go. But my sixteen men were still with me, mouths shut. I kept my mouth shut, too, using all my willpower to avoid bugging Sivron down there. He was doing his job, and it was better not to interrupt him.

As far as I was concerned, we were going to attack in any case. If Sivron took any more time we would have to penetrate and attack in a more economical way, at lower speeds. This would be more dangerous. But I didn't care about danger anymore. By this time I almost wanted to pay. I guess all my pilots were aware of what was going on, and I was becoming prouder—in a dark and bitter way—of my men, with their hearts in their mouths, still silent.

Sivron came back on, gasping for breath. He was a great navigator, and had found a way to direct us to the target without maps. He gave us a starting point—the estuary of the Jordan River into the Kinneret—and calculated for us headings and time to target. When we finished writing down the numbers, he described the target itself. This was the main axis of attack of the Syrian Army going from the east toward the Jordan River.

"When you pull up," he explained, "you should see before you two black hills, between them a road, and on that road and around it there should be massive Syrian forces moving west— tanks, artillery, trucks of all kinds, everything. Those forces are the target," he said. "Divide your fire, hit as much as you can."

"And where are our own forces?"

"Far to the west. No sweat; you won't hit them."

I replied with a laconic "Thanks" and went to work. I had no time to waste. I ordered the formation in line behind me. I gave brief instructions and hurried in first. They followed me one after another, each aircraft taking a slightly different heading—two degrees right from its predecessor—and so we penetrated into the Golan spreading like a fan, each Phantom racing toward another section of that axis to engage another Syrian target. We all flew very low because the whole area was covered by SAM-6 missiles. It was more than an hour and twenty-five minutes since takeoff, and we were really short on fuel, and avoided lighting our afterburners, because it was fuel that was going to dictate how this improvisation turned out.

On the way, Sivron suddenly broke in on the radio and doubled our flight time—he had made his first calculation with the wrong scale and discovered his mistake at the last moment—but the change came in time. We just changed the clock, and when my second hand reached zero I pulled up from among the basalt rocks and thorn bushes, looked down, and there it was.

Here was the road, and there were groups of vehicles and tanks scattered on and around it like black flies on a cord. Field artillery flashed, leaving black clouds. I rolled over, put my sight on the largest group of the lot, and eight half-ton bombs made a line of bursts on the ground, blooming with clouds of dust and smoke. With the last kick I turned immediately west, reduced power to the most economical setting, and circled a little to see my men coming out one after another. Finally we all were out, and the touchy question could be asked. Those with less than 1,500 pounds of fuel—that is, several minutes left to keep airborne—were sent to land immediately at nearby Ramat-David to fill up and return to our home base. The war was still on, and we had to get ready for the next mission orders.

When I got back from Ramat-David and entered the squadron building, there was already a call for me. Sivron was on the phone. His pleasant voice had resumed its regular slow, drowsy rhythm, and I tried to cut him short again, thanking him for the extraordinary efficiency in the planning of that attack, and to please go away, I had work to do. But Sivron had a lot to say, and before he got to the point Maj. Gen. Moti Hod got on the line, too. I gathered that our former air force commander was now working in the northern command post. I had difficulty in understanding their voices; they both spoke as if they were a little drunk.

They enthused, blessed me, blessed the Orange Tails, described again and again how tough the situation was on the Golan, our ground forces almost breaking under the ferocious Syrian attack, and how they kept calling for air support and there was no support to be had. The air force didn't have anything to spare—and then, when hope was almost gone, the Orange Tails had appeared. Suddenly, as if from nowhere.

"You came to us right from heaven! Eight Phantoms!" cried Moti, and said, "Do you understand what that means?"

Yes, I knew what eight Phantoms were worth.

"And what an attack it was," he said, "right on the money! You completely broke the Syrian attack. Don't you understand what you did?" Sivron asked me. Embarrassed, I admitted that no, not really. The Damascus fiasco was still filling my head.

New, deeper voices joined the telephone conversation. It happened that our unexpected hits had halted the Syrian ground thrust to the Jordan River along that axis. Some of the senior officers in the North wanted to add personal praises and blessings for saving the day. Someone remembered the

Ad Halom Bridge, where Israeli Air Force Messerschmitts had stopped the Egyptian Army on its way to Tel Aviv in the War of Independence in 1948. Baffled, I asked permission to hang up the receiver. I had a war to fight, a squadron to run, and already a new mission order was coming down for the Orange Tails.

Even years after that, people kept appearing to visit me, men who were there, from simple soldiers to major generals, to tell me what happened there, to say thanks, how lucky we were to have you in time. I answered them all, blushing, that I got there only by chance.

Yes, luck is important, too.

The Aborted Attack on Damascus
and Defense of the Golan
October 9, 1973
and the Dog Fight on Mt. Druze
October 10, 1973
Hims
Al Qusayr
Tripoli
LEBANON
Ba'labakk
SYRIA
Beirut
Zahlah
Bekaa Valley
Az Zabadani
Mediterranean Sea
Sidon
Damascus
Mt. Hermon
Tyre
Golan
Zefat
Sea of Galilee
Haifa
Teverya
Nazerat
Mt. Druze
Megiddo
Yarmuk
Jordan
Netanya
Nablus
Zarqu
West Bank
Az Zarqa
Tel Aviv
Amman
Ramla
Ashdod
Jerusalem
JORDAN
Gaza
Gaza
Hebron
Dead Sea
Khan Yunis
Hatzerim
Beer Sheva
ISRAEL
El Arish
Nizzana
Wadi al Arabah
El Quseima
Negev
Sinai
El Thamad
Elat
Etzion AFB
Al Aqbah
Route to Damascus October 9, 1973
Route after attack on Damascus is aborted October 9, 1973
Syrian tank assault on the Golan Heights
Route of failed attack on Blay, and ensuing dog fight on Mt. Druze October 10, 1973
Airbases
0 25 50 75 miles

Chapter

20

Hassan Again

IN THE NINETEEN DAYS of the Yom Kippur War I flew forty-two combat sorties. Some of those were simple flights, but quite a few were complicated and dangerous. The summit of my personal efforts was on October 10, when after two attacks on airfields in Egypt and Syria, and two more on ground forces at the Suez Canal, I made a fifth sortie, late at night. We patrolled over the Red Sea, south of the Sinai Peninsula. It was pitch dark and we were both dead tired. Ofer, in the backseat, was alternately snoring and waking up. I was so wasted that so as not to sleep at the stick I scratched my thighs with my commando knife.

Near the end of the war the drum beat faster. I find today in my logbook four sorties on October 22, two on SAM batteries in Egypt. This was the Orange Tails' first opportunity to test the hunting tactics we inherited from the Baboons. The new tactic worked. We located and destroyed two SAM batteries unscathed.

In one of these sorties, I met Hassan again.

LOOKING BACK ON ALL THE COMBAT flights in my life, most were not difficult, especially when compared to our training flights. No MiG pilot I ever met was a rival equal to Epstein, Salant, or Slapak, and no enemy as scary as

Ran Pecker. But real-life dogfights had unique elements: breaking at the right second and having a missile—or a MiG firing its cannons—overshoot and miss. Or arriving just in time to clear a MiG off a friendly tail (this especially is an emotional experience). Or to get into a hot fight and find that one external fuel tank refuses to drop from your right wing, and your Mirage—like a race car with a flat tire at top speed—rolls right on its own, and only right, spiraling almost out of control toward a MiG growing fast in the windshield—whoa! And then you hear yourself yelling like crazy, "Break right, Hassan! Yil'an Dinac, RIGHT!"

I don't know which was my toughest aerial action, but one of them was no doubt the worst. And this one was in the Orange Tails, in the Yom Kippur War, on October 10, 1973. MiGs were active throughout that war, and huge, multiparticipant dogfights were taking place between them and our Mirages over the front lines. There were "harvest days" when Mirage pilots felled dozens of MiGs. My squadron, on the other hand, was busy attacking ground targets, and we saw much less of those MiGs, but when it happened, it was always under tough conditions, deep in enemy territory. I met MiGs five times during the war, three times in Syria and twice in Egypt, and on four of these occasions I hit them only out of necessity.

Except for that one fucked-up sortie.

That time it was a duel, a single Phantom versus a single MiG-21, nothing complicated. But by the end this dogfight was the most difficult and dangerous of them all, and overall it was bad, bad. And it occurred just due to my own personal guilt, and I got out of it miraculously. Just like our mentor from the old Scorpions Rami Harpaz used to say, "Smart enough to get out of a situation smarter people avoid in the first place."

But first let us discuss the order of preferences.

The moment I became a Phantom pilot, I understood and accepted that from then on I was not a hotshot pilot anymore and that my squadron and I were taking on a hard and necessary job, less romantic than air-to-air combat. We were entrusted to put ordnance on ground targets. As attack pilots we Phantoms do not chase MiGs but fly to our target, attack it, and return by the shortest possible way to reload and get ready for the next sortie. Our contribution to victory depended on us not deviating from our routes on the way to the targets.

This may sound obvious, even trivial, but it is not. Fighter pilots brought up on the tales of the Red Baron, Manfred von Richthofen, want to shoot down enemy fighters, and they find it extremely hard to see them and still go on their way. They have to fight the desire to "clean the aircraft" (that is, jettison the bombs) and go get a fine kill. And the Phantom is certainly a good MiG-killer. Avoidance, then, is a matter of principle.

True, it is not always possible to live up to principles. There are the times when a MiG dives and threatens you or your buddies directly—then there is no choice and no argument. You give up your ground attack and take him on; otherwise you die or end up a POW. But life is not black and white, and most situations are marginal. You fly and see a MiG in the distance. He is not a threat—yet—but he could be one very soon. Then the question is whether you continue to your target, keeping the bombs on your belly, or get rid of them and go for that MiG. And there is always the dilemma of what comes first, you reaching the target or him sitting on your tail.

In such dubious moments, when one can decide this way or the other, everything depends on the formation leader, on his integrity and morality. He has his own emotional conflict. Leading your buddies on to an attack when MiGs are tailing you and not dealing with them is as hard as keeping both hands on the steering wheel when angry wasps zoom around in the car. Hard indeed!

We in the Orange Tails—and by this I mean not only myself as the commander, but also the high society of the squadron—were aware of those centrifugal forces, and thus we issued several rules of engagement to assure first of all the completion of the primary mission—if at all possible. "A pilot who shoots a MiG down during an attack mission," said the first rule, which was written large on the blackboard, "has by definition committed an offense. His action shall be liable to immediate inquiry, and if it comes out that the situation did not warrant it absolutely, he will be washed out of the squadron." Later, after we got into trouble, we made this rule even stricter: "Downing MiGs is legitimate only after the attack, on the way back. And even then, on condition that you are cleaning the MiG off a buddy's six." And for more impact, we even got to specific names: certain pilots were forbidden even to look at a MiG, under any circumstances. These were some of the hot doggers whose judgment I didn't trust.

"MiGs are not on the menu for you," I told them. "Your aerial kills will come during the next war."

Those rules, which the squadron took seriously, protected operational discipline, and the Orange Tails' formations as a rule remained tight and got to their targets. Behind all this lay a moral obligation.

So, late in the afternoon, we took off in an eight-ship formation to attack the Syrian airfield Blay, on the other side of the Golan Heights, south of Damascus. We crossed the Jordan River and in a fast, low sweep went deep into Jordan to come in the back door. When we were deep in the Trans-Jordanian Desert, we turned north and passed east of Jebel Druze, a high ridge. After that we turned and headed west, racing at full speed toward Blay from the interior of Syria, with the setting sun in our eyes. But when we finally pulled up over the target airfield, we ran into something we didn't expect.

I never saw weather like that before or after. The moment we climbed, the air, which was normally clear at low levels, became so hazy that Blay totally disappeared. We could see absolutely nothing. A thick layer of dust engulfed us, and the sun melted into a radiant ball of red mud. The dirty air became a screen, and the ground far below first darkened, then simply disappeared.

We began searching for the airfield. We organized into pairs in a line astern and began going over the estimated position of Blay, looking down and seeing only yellow. The haze was like porridge, glittering streams of minuscule particles flowing beneath us in waves. Billions of tiny lights. Our eyes were tearing behind our dark glasses. And though we repeatedly wiped away the tears, we couldn't see the ground. We couldn't see anything, and began to wonder—

Suddenly somebody called out on the radio, "MiGs! MiGs! Break!"

I looked up and saw an air-to-air missile, like a blackish, thin toothpick, diving from above and dragging a fiery tail, pass inside the formation and explode near one of my Phantoms. We broke hard left, and during the break my navigator, Erel, followed the trail of the missile back up to its launch point. He located and pointed out to me sparks on the yellow background of the sky. And soon several small silhouettes materialized—black triangles: MiGs. In that situation there was no sense anymore in pursuing our former mission, just defense and get the hell out of there.

I ordered, "Emergency jettison!" Instantly bomb clusters and fuel tanks flew around like a rain of black drops, rolling in the yellow, shining air. "Everybody out! Head east!"

It was clear that our attack had failed. Now I had to get everybody home. I wanted us to fly back in the same roundabout way we had arrived, since the direct line from there to Israel was blocked by Syrian SAM arrays on the Golan Heights. We all turned east. The formation's order was now reversed: the rear aircraft became the first, and now everybody was flying ahead of me and I was the tail-end charlie. The formation flew east, afterburners glowing on the dark background of the eastern sky like pairs of fireflies.

"MiG on our six, Iftach." This from my navigator, Erel.

Again we broke, and the distance between our Phantom and all the others opened more, but the MiG wasn't after us. Perhaps he hadn't even seen us. He passed over us very fast, heading toward the rest of my Phantoms. We slipped in far behind him and saw him launch another missile in their direction.

I warned them in time; they broke, and the missile missed.

This was the second strike mission we had screwed up. No doubt some personal frustration had gathered in my gut. Additional stress was that on sound off, after we first broke away from the MiGs, one of us hadn't answered. I had seen someone hit by the MiG's missile, and he didn't answer my calls. In the end it turned out to be Duby Yoffe, a tall, blond kid. He lost communication because of the missile hit but made it home with a badly damaged aircraft. But at the time I had no way of knowing that, and I was upset that we had lost a ship and two men. And so the dormant Mirage pilot in me apparently woke up and overrode the squadron rules of engagement.

According to those rules—which I had set down and enforced with an iron hand in our squadron—there was no excuse for a dogfight now. I should have let that MiG alone and led my men home. But he was right in my sights. But I was not thinking clearly at that moment.

Instead of sneaking away and racing south, I put my Phantom's nose on that MiG, and when he—who had much more speed and momentum than I—left the other Phantoms and turned back to me, I didn't run away. He pulled up, and I lifted my nose to him, too, and we began the invitation to the dance. Probably deep in my heart I thought I would finish him off quickly and catch up to the formation on the way home.

Big mistake.

Major Goren, who was a senior reserve pilot and a cool customer, saw it all and wanted to help me out. But I had very little wisdom in me at that moment. I instructed him harshly to take command of the formation and take them home. Goren complied, and they vanished quickly into the darkness that was beginning to fill the hills and brooks below.

Erel and I remained behind, riding our Phantom No. 10, against a MiG deep in Syria. So began the duel in which I met for the first time a rival who was my equal.

All conditions were in his favor. We were far away from safety and limited on fuel, while our opponent was just a few kilometers from his home base. Already at the start, the Syrian had considerable advantage in speed over me. And finally, he was flying a MiG-21, a lightweight, agile fighter—the Mirage kind—while we were flying a Phantom, which by nature is a heavy, sluggish, and unforgiving machine. And worst of all, no one could guarantee that that MiG would remain alone in this fight. Fortunately for me this last threat never materialized.

The moment he turned ferociously on me I realized this wasn't going to be easy. A second later we were stuck there with the MiG, and all that was left for Erel and me was to call on all our strength and fight for our lives.

The hour was late, and the sun had just touched the horizon on its way down. The dominant landmark in the area was Jebel Druze, the Mountain of the Druze. This is a large, black mountain. Our struggle began over the eastern slope of that mountain. The sun went down behind it and disappeared over its crest, and we were soon in the shade. It was that beautiful hour of twilight when all is peaceful and the light of the world is soft and gentle.

The MiG used his extra momentum for a tight turn, and began closing on us from behind. I let him come in, and when he came close enough I used Yak's old trick of stopping my Phantom in the air abruptly, hoping to throw the MiG in front of me. The Syrian was surprised, but he was an excellent pilot. He lifted his nose almost vertically and reared his stallion, too, right along with us. Now we both were flying together almost in close formation, both very slow, "standing in the air" on our engine downwash. Both our noses were raised high up, and we both were at the limit of our ability to hold the air, slowly sinking down on our tails. Luckily we were over the mountain slope—sinking together with the descending slope.

We hovered side by side, crossing each other's path and the distance between us shrinking and opening alternately. In pilot lingo this is called a scissors. It's a maneuver in which the slower of the two should eventually win, after his opponent gets in front, into killing range. It's a tough struggle. Whoever lets his aircraft loose even for a second loses his life. You slow your aircraft to its minimum speed—just above a stall—and hold it there, turning and twisting, on the verge of losing stability before a tailspin. You have to maintain this attitude in order not to go forward. At very slow speeds the lift on the wings decreases and aerodynamic drag overcomes the engine thrust, causing the aircraft to sink.

All in all, the scissors is a very difficult and dangerous maneuver, at the edge of flight limits, where both fight stubbornly against each other and the laws of aerodynamics. It can be compared to wrestling on a tightrope: besides your rival, the abyss also waits for you. But the problem is that once you are in this situation, it's very hard to get out. Whoever tries to escape shows his tail to his enemy. As a rule, getting into a scissors with an enemy fighter is a mistake. One-on-one duels between hot contenders tend to develop that way, but smart pilots do their best to avoid it. Once in a scissors, you are out of alternatives. The fight becomes about superior aircraft handling, and you are tested not on brains but on who flies his aircraft better and on the willpower of the pilots.

So we struggled on, fighting and sinking down the slope, toward the foot of the mountain, both of us skimming those black rocks very, very closely.

The Phantom has an advantage however; it knows well how to "stand in the air," supported by the power of its two great engines. On the other hand, it is a very heavy aircraft, and it has terrible difficulty maneuvering at low speeds. But lightweight fighters such as the MiG and the Mirage maintain a certain maneuverability even in such conditions. As result, we were standing in the air, and the MiG maneuvered around us. Our situation was not good.

Just then, Erel called my attention to the most amazing sight I ever saw: both aircraft were digging up the ground with the streams of fire from our tailpipes. The afterburners blasted down, licking the black rocks and raising huge pillars of dust. For some time we struggled among those pillars, and the MiG's afterburner exhaust—which in the dark around us shone like a long, sharp tongue mottled with blue and orange lines—was dimming beyond a pillar and reappearing, illuminating the whole temple around us. So we hovered and ducked among those dust columns like two fireflies playing hide-and-seek on a lawn, twisting around stalks of grass.

This was a singular moment, one of the few in which there is no story, when "before" and "after" vanish. Only the moment remains.

The MiG and we were totally exhausted, hovering side by side on the verge of stalling, sinking down along that slope. The slope kept us airborne, but was a limited playground—we were getting near the foot of the mountain, and there, on the plain, there was going to be a decision. Any mistake would be fatal. I was very tense. My hands clutched the stick and the throttle; my movements were stiff.

Erel totally understood the pressure I was under, and worried that I might lose my nerve and do something rash. He said to me on the intercom, "Take it easy, Iftach, be cool." And this was the turning point. I relaxed. Erel helped me overcome the nervous impulse to tighten my turn toward the MiG, who was trying to turn his nose toward my tail. Had I done that, I would have been competing with him on his terms. I would have lost the last of the lift on my wings, and we would have spun out and crashed there in Syria.

I took a deep breath and reminded myself of the training fights against the Mirages. I forced myself to relax, forget the MiG, and concentrate only on my own actions. I stopped fighting against the MiG, focused on my Phantom No. 10, and flew him the best he'd ever been flown. Since we had no way to copy the MiG's agile maneuvers, we did the opposite and "gave some air"—not too much—to those wide wings of our Phantom. I softened my hold on the stick and rudder pedals, and when No. 10 breathed air again—just a little—it was out of the question to let him go forward very much, but this little bit was enough; I could once again lift his nose up, then higher, and then, standing even more erect on our engine plumes, I turned very gently, very carefully aside, using only the foot pedals, the way Tsutsik used to stall-turn the Harvard. And when the big aircraft realized that I was giving him the best flying of my life, he also relaxed, stopped trembling and vibrating, and was suddenly sailing along with sleek, gentle movements. We merged into one, and our Phantom breathed air and showed us he could do better than I ever expected. Gradually, turn by turn, he began overpowering the MiG, cutting it off with delicate, cruel resoluteness and attaining degrees in the curve. My Phantom flew as well and as comfortably as any Mirage.

Suddenly Hassan realized what was happening and was terrified. His movements became erratic, and he began to be thrown meter after meter forward. And then, when we began gaining that advantage, I knew we were going to beat him.

Once or twice, when the MiG crossed in front of me, I fired my cannon in its general direction. I was unable to aim with my nose pointed high in the sky above it. Had I lowered the nose even one degree we would have gone all the way to the ground. But I fired over his head so that he could see the flashes and would know we meant business. And it worked. The Syrian pilot, who until that moment was flying well indeed, got even more frightened and pulled in his reins for a hard stop. The air on the MiG's wingtips whirled like heated glass. He, who flew a single-seater and had no one like my Yoni Erel, had lost his nerve.

‡

Suddenly Yoni cried, "Look! Look!"

A line of dim light shone out of the dark figure that hovered a little before us. The MiG's vertical stabilizer glinted. It was turned sharply to its maximum. We both knew that that was that, the last move. The knight in front of us spurred his mount one last time, trying to get one more jump out of him, the decisive one. The MiG lifted its nose. Clearly Hassan was giving me the show of his life.

My legs trembled, and once again I had to restrain myself from pulling up against the MiG—just fly and watch. I couldn't lose our wings' frail hold on the air. We simply hovered there, waiting.

And then, really close to us, Hassan's horse rebelled against its rider. The MiG's nose reared up in an abnormally fast, light movement, almost reaching the vertical. The MiG stood on its tail like a tower in the air. We were very close and I saw Hassan's canopy glistening like a soap bubble above us. Then he lost it—the MiG suddenly rolled in the air and spun down toward us, almost falling on our heads. The canopy blew off, and the pilot flew out of the cockpit like a small parcel and hit the ground with his parachute still closed. Instantly the MiG fell right on him, and they both blazed among the black rocks like a napalm bonfire.

Yoni and I breathed a sigh of relief and released our wonderful Phantom No. 10 down to the horizontal, freeing him, too, and breathing the air. We slowly accelerated and turned west among the black Syrian hills, on half power. When we climbed the big mountain going home, we took a last look back: a dirty red fire was burning on its feet, sending up a black pillar of smoke.

We were so short on fuel that on the way home we shut one engine off and flew home directly across all the missiles. They somehow gave us a break and let us pass, and we reached Ramat-David on a wing and a prayer.

This story ended early the next morning at a debriefing. I called in all the pilots and told them what had happened—not that they didn't already know everything from the grapevine—and then I told them seriously, "This was an egregious offense of squadron rules. The pilot who did it is here and now washed out of our squadron. He is to pack his bags and go. We don't need pilots like him in the Orange Tails. Let him go home and watch from there how those who know to fight continue to defend Israel." I saw their surprised faces. We were in the middle of a terrible war. I saw in their eyes the question "What the . . . ?"

Then I explained, "I will make a technical distinction between two men. The pilot Iftach, who committed a serious offense endangering a crew and an aircraft, is washed out right now. But Squadron Commander Spector is needed in this squadron right now, and he stays. Your squadron commander shall continue to command and lead you as usual."

They looked at each other.

"And this MiG is scratched and goes into oblivion. No kill will be claimed in this case."

They kept silent.

"And let me make it clear, the rules have not changed a bit, and their enforcement shall be, if anything, more strict. Any wiseass who commits an operational offense shall be punished without mercy."

Again they looked at each other, and back at me.

"Is all this clear to everyone?"

They all understood. There were no discipline problems in that squadron after that.

Chapter

21

Wholeheartedly

I AM NOT GOING TO RELATE EVERYTHING about the Orange Tails in the Yom Kippur War, nor tell stories about other battles I was in during that war. I have already tried to do part of it in another book, and I shall likely never finish the whole story. I only want to say now that the combat effectiveness of this squadron has nothing to do with the happy fact that it didn't lose a single pilot in the war. This fact was evident, of course, only after the war ended.

As a rule, the index for the combat effectiveness of a military unit must in no way begin with counting its casualties.

I DON'T LIKE THE NEVER-ENDING praise for the Orange Tails—coming even from generals and air force officers who should know better—for "bringing all the boys home safe." This is an unlooked-for compliment. In my eyes, these kinds of commendations represent a fundamental misunderstanding of war and set the wrong standard for officers and men. A good combat unit does two things: accomplishing the mission well is primary, and then—and only then—a good unit looks to minimize casualties. Whoever turns this order on its head better not fight at all.

The Orange Tails fought and behaved well because we had been prepared well for war and understood the situation from the beginning, and because we had the right mixture of toughness in combat and flexibility in thinking. The Orange Tails managed not to sink into laziness or stupidity even in its toughest moments. This was no small feat. And we never had slogans such as "The hard things we do fast." It was all business.

The Orange Tails was a dynamic battle unit, alert and always thinking. We all watched for kettles, and prepared to douse the fire under them in time. We kept correcting and re-correcting our combat methodology. Thanks to all the above, the Orange Tails met every challenge in the Yom Kippur War.

So nobody was killed in the Orange Tails? Great. But this is just the dessert, the cherry on the whipped cream. The Orange Tails fought well because we put the bullets in the targets and because we had some of the art of war drummed into us.

Squadron commanders were ordered to write fitness reports when the war was over. The last sentence in my very brief report to air force headquarters summed it up this way: "The Orange Tails are fit and ready for another war." I knew that all my men stood behind these proud words.

This was such a wonderful feeling that it's hard to convey in words. I knew I had done my job right. I felt like a carpenter who cut the wood without breaking the saw.

And my happiness welled out of a hidden personal satisfaction, too. Now, after four years of commanding squadrons in two wars, I finally knew how to command men.

In December 1973, two months after the end of the Yom Kippur War, I handed the Orange Tails' flag to their second commander. The event was modest, with only a small audience. Again, just like two years before, it was a cold winter day and we had the ceremony inside the squadron's first aircraft hangar, still shining and clean. Our families watched from the sidelines. They had just returned to base housing after they were dispersed to a boarding school for the duration to bite their nails and await the outcome. The women returned, cleaned up their homes, threw out the putrid remnants that were still in the refrigerators after three weeks, reactivated the kindergarten, and tried to smile through their personal troubles.

Every family had someone dead; names kept coming in from everywhere. We ran around nights, driving all over Israel to visit, to console, to hear stories, to try to understand. Ali's brother, Maj. (Res.) Yair Dgani, returned from the dunes of the western Sinai to Givat-Brenner still picking the thin steering wires of the antitank Russian missiles out of his hair. Yair was physically unhurt but as shaken as I, and for similar reasons. I heard about how some of his senior commanders had performed only after the war, and later read about it in the report of the Agranat Commission, which investigated the conduct of the war. Sheani was dead. And Goldie. They joined the eternally young faces in the photo of flight school class 31—just six of us left now to get older. Only after the war did I tell Ali about the death in battle of Col. Arlozor Lev, Zorik, the commander of Ramat-David, that beloved man who had welcomed us to the Scorpions and into his home when we were a young couple.

THE NEW COMMANDER AND I saluted each other. I left the podium full of conflicting emotions. Like all of Israel, I was shocked by the failures of leadership in the war and by the removal of Chief of Staff David Elazar—definitely not the guilty party, and perhaps the one man who'd showed any balls in the high command—and with Moshe Dayan's ugly evasion of responsibility. But on the other hand, I myself was full of pride and felt very lucky. I was delighted to have been one of the field commanders who took the war in hand when those above us dropped the ball, and of my standing as a man in those ten days until the high command realized that the Third Temple wasn't falling after all. And over all, I knew I reached my peak of professional capability as fighter pilot and combat commander exactly when my country needed it. That was a hell of a good feeling.

But it was hard to show pride and happiness after this war. There were too many hard feelings all around. Thus I kept silent and never shared with anybody either the pain or the personal exaltation I felt—to this day.

Ali was in the audience. She was painfully thin. Our sons stood beside her, and she held baby Noah in her arms. When I looked at her, she unconsciously squared her shoulders, like a soldier, and I recalled the old photograph of Grandma Bracha Tatar "at attention" behind her cart-driver husband. A shaft of pain ran through me. Had the wheel come around again? Doesn't it ever end?

The short ceremony ended and the squadron's women pushed in to hug Ali and shake her hand. I could see by Ali's face that she also was filled with emotion. My nine-year-old son Etay embraced me, coughing deep in his throat. That nervous cough, something like a bark, was to linger until he grew up.

I reported to air force headquarters in Tel Aviv. Everybody was digesting the outcome of the war and working on postmortems. I soon realized that not everything was open for discussion. When I asked the air force commander why he had ordered all copies of the Orange Tails' war debriefing collected and destroyed, he answered me facetiously.

"An alien from space who decides to study human society on Earth"—Benny was renowned for his colorful images—"should better not use Walt Disney films for that research."

"What?"

"In the Yom Kippur War," Benny interpreted for me, "we arrived as a 'Mickey Mouse' air force, a grotesque imitation of the real air force we should have been. It's no use wasting our time studying Mickey and Minnie's love life. It's a similar waste of time to study the lessons of this past war. We'd be better off preparing for the next one."

He didn't fool me. I knew he knew that was not a good excuse and that he didn't sleep nights after the war. I also knew that some of his senior subordinates were discussing secretly how to get him out of the top spot. And I was certain the Orange Tails' war debriefing booklet had been suppressed because it had criticized the workings of air force high command during the war. Many years later somebody sent me that suppressed booklet. I reread what I had written at the end of October 1973, and I agreed that it contained some harsh criticism:

"This war suffered from a lack of designated targets."

"Feedback was met with negative reaction from the high command."

"We failed in blindly believing our intelligence."

"Headquarters lagged behind the field in tactical analysis."

"Field units feel they can plan operations better than headquarters."

And finally the sentence that was deleted with a black pen: "In this war, the real enemy was air force headquarters."

Rereading this after many years, when I was much more mature and distant from the hard feelings of that time, made me able to understand a letter a former commander of mine, Gen. Rafi Harlev, had sent me: "The lessons you wrote about in the Orange Tails' war debriefing booklet are doomed to be discarded, not because they are mistaken, but because they are written in this unique fashion of yours." But at the end of 1973 I was on fire, and said bluntly that my commanders had failed in their duty.

I was not alone in my opinion. The whole of Israel was furious when the results of the war were known, along with the number of dead, wounded, and prisoners of war. No family came out untouched; every community buried sons. The whole nation—I included—wanted an accounting. The Agranat Commission ran its meetings behind closed doors, but the media spread allusions to leaders and senior officers. I had my own memories of the collapse above me, beginning with confused telephone calls, contradicting and ever-changing orders, and ending with letters I got from people who were inside that cauldron at air force headquarters during the war.

"As to command performance," one wrote to me, "it was extremely bad. Your evaluation that 'the command post was under stress' is nothing in comparison to what really went on up there."

And another one wrote, "One day we shall have to talk at length about the war . . . for reasons I am not free to detail, the air force didn't do what it should have done. My white hairs are the result of it. But never mind," he added with dry humor, "better white hair than a bald head."

A third man, who spent the entire war in the air force command post, conveyed the following: "The command post was crowded, fussy, and noisy all the time. Officers and enlisted personnel ran around in the corridors, shouting. People worked around the clock with no place to eat or sleep, and became exhausted. There was no calm place to sit and read, and so information that came in from the field was set aside. Commanders didn't look at feedback from the squadrons after execution of their missions." When he saw my astonished face, this officer went into further detail: "Radios blared from all sides. Crazy rumors flew around. Everything was interpreted in an extreme manner, everything was black or white, and everything caused immediate reactions. When they became overwhelmed with fatigue, officers simply disappeared from their posts and couldn't be found. The air force commander would suddenly show up and issue orders, and nobody understood what and why. There were times when arguments verged on mutiny." He concluded his indictment with the following words: "When an operation began, decisions to continue or stop it halfway were made on the basis of casualties but without regard to accumulating results. Simply, information about losses came right away, but real results were known only much later."

For a soldier like me, who was expecting efficiency from his commanders, such descriptions were a damning finger pointed right at Benny Peled.

Today I can imagine how Benny felt when I sat in front of him demanding to know what happened to the Orange Tails' debriefing document. I wanted to use it in my new job. Besides blaming my superiors' performance, that booklet contained concrete lessons I, as a new staff officer, intended to use. And when I realized that I touched a nerve in a touchy person, I expected that Benny—who was known as an aggressive guy—would hit back at me. But he didn't in that conversation.

Instead, he grabbed my shirt and didn't let me get up. He sat me back down and began explaining and explaining. The tense atmosphere lessened with the seventh cigarette he lit, and then I reminded him of our previous conversation in the middle of the war. I had called the command post in Tel Aviv from the Orange Tails, found Benny and told him on the phone, excited and happy, "Benny, a helicopter found Yoram and got him out!"

Yoram Peled was a pilot in my squadron, a hot dogger, and his aircraft had been shot down. For a full hour there was no information on what had happened to him.

Benny roared back at me, "Stop filling my mind with crap!"

"But Benny, it's about Yoram—"

"To you I am the air force commander, not Yoram's father!"

I hung up silently and said to myself, "Benny is a damn fool." Then I cooled down and understood what was going on in his head and said to myself, "All right, then, for now I am Yoram's father."

I reminded Benny of that conversation and we both laughed a little.

In the end, he entrusted me with changing operational training in the air force. I hesitated.

"According to the lessons of the war?"

"Yes," he finally conceded, halfheartedly. "According to the lessons I shall confirm." I understood that instead of fighting we had to turn a new leaf together. I shut up and went to work.

AFTER TWO YEARS OF CHANGING our operational training, which involved hard work from a military organization recovering from war and dealing with a host of problems, I was sent for an advanced degree in the United States. There I found out that war had more dimensions than a clean shot or getting the bombs on the target. For instance, I discovered the economic side of war.

The understanding began with a deeper look into the issue of the missiles. Missiles—all types—could be thought of as unmanned aircraft drones, weapons that could be launched from a distance and could fly independently, navigate to targets, and hit them. The common denominator for all those weapons was that they enabled hitting without being hit. The chief cost factor for aircraft and pilots was rate of loss, and aircraft and pilot costs were rising fast. Drones were cheap. They could perform missions too costly for manned aircraft and lowered the cost of decision-making and the economic impact of war. When I came to that conclusion, I found it had far-reaching, strategic results.

BEFORE I WENT FOR ADVANCED study, I had no interest in model planes of any kind. Only a very few men in the Israeli Air Force at that time had minds open enough to discuss such things. Lieutenant Colonel Dotan, for example, was doing experiments with radio-controlled model aircraft with cameras, to get intelligence from enemy areas. I admit I didn't understand what made one of our best fighter pilots get involved in such a perverse and arcane subject. Drones, like computers, seemed to me as irrelevant for attacking missile arrays and other difficult ground targets as helicopters carrying little green men. In short, I remained a simple fighter pilot, a knight among knights. A pilot is a pilot is a pilot, with all the panache and limitations that come with this profession

In 1976, when I was sent to study for a master's degree at UCLA, in the United States, and especially after I began visiting the RAND Corporation, I got out of the fighter pilot box. Suddenly I saw new ways to look at war, not just as a medieval knight might have disdained the new technology of gunpowder.

I saw two clear technical developments relating to missiles and other unmanned aerial devices that changed my worldview: One, the accuracy of those devices was consistently getting better; and two, the cost of these systems was coming down. Then I recalled that the same process had taken place with our air-to-air missiles, and with the Soviet antiaircraft missiles that had killed us.

This was interesting. I gathered data, connected colored dots, and produced lines—of performance, of cost, of accuracy. I divided the X axis into years and found that the ratio of improvement in all aspects was accelerating. Suddenly a trend emerged: drones were capable of doing certain jobs very well, and were getting better. I understood that these devices were headed for some point in the future when they would be more cost-effective than manned aircraft in other jobs, too—for example, in attacking ground targets. And since they were so cheap—no human life was involved—their use was less conditioned: you could employ them even in tough situations with high loss rates; this was almost just an economic consideration.

I stretched my graphs into the future on a military setup I knew well. My calculations pointed to a nexus in the future in which a state using this kind of technology could inflict a fast, lethal, and above all unconditional blow on enemy forces. This was stunning. You could go for it all at once, with very few limiting military conditions.

The more I thought about manned aircraft and their missions and remembered Yak's dictum, the more I thought it would be inefficient to fight antiaircraft systems with aircraft. And my new opinions went even further than that: I thought that antiaircraft systems, including missile batteries, were not targets in themselves. They were just nuisances, impediments on our way to our real targets: the enemy's military assets. Elimination of the missiles, which employed most of our attention, was in principle a "parasitic" activity, a detour. I began to see things I had thought heroic before in a new, critical way. I began to think that we would be better off building weapons systems against the real targets. The new weapons opened a way to develop a first-strike capability to hit the enemy's war machine directly without dealing with those antiaircraft and missile batteries. This required that we arm ourselves with systems other than fighter aircraft. The fighters were expensive, and since the Yom Kippur War seemed to me not efficient enough—even with aerial superiority—against the multitude of targets presented by the enemy's military. The fighters were good to destroy specific, expensive targets, but you couldn't get them to produce high-elimination capacity on the battlefield. And the enemy's ack-ack and mini-SAMs, which could never be completely eliminated, kept promising a fall rate of more than 1 percent, which would keep manned fighters too far away from their targets. On the other hand, unmanned vehicles, which could suffer a much higher rate of loss due to their low cost, seemed to me a workable solution.

I began imagining thousands of small, cheap, unmanned missiles ignoring the enemy's antiaircraft systems, passing through them and hitting his tanks and armored personnel carriers. I envisioned a first strike, not a nuclear bomb on cities in the style of Giulio Douhet or psychological devastation like Operation Focus in 1967, but a new strategic shock that would paralyze the enemy's military power at the start of a war.

AND SO, WHEN I REPORTED to air force headquarters after a year of leave to take command of the operations department from Col. Avihu Ben Nun, I brought with me a notebook full of ideas, but my mind was mostly busy with that first-strike idea.

After a year in America I found that the Israeli Air Force of 1977 continued to invest its best resources and brightest brains in finding solutions for the problem of the SAM batteries. My department of operations was busy gathering alternative techniques and supporting systems for the elimination of the Egyptian and Syrian missile arrays. Even Benny Peled mocked their collecting of "thirteen backups for backups" to assure victory over those missiles, but still he signed the chit approving Avihu's request to develop an additional backup—number fourteen. Every investment was considered legitimate to beat the missiles next time.

The main difference from 1973 was in the argument for attacking the SAMs. Before, the necessity to attack the missiles had grown out of the tactical need to achieve air superiority. But in 1977 the missiles were somehow promoted to a strategic target. Officers in my department claimed with deep conviction that the destruction of the missile arrays would have similar results to Operation Focus, the destruction of the airfields in the Six-Day War in 1967. They thought that the Arab regimes had invested so much in those missile arrays that a fast, elegant elimination of them would be such a defeat that the earth would quake under their feet. For my officers, the missiles were a be-all and end-all, both tactical and strategic assets, and the most worthy targets. It was put in logical terms, but in fact the determining factor was emotional. It was a matter of honor. The air force was conditioned to attack the missiles, and it couldn't rest until it did just that. It had to avenge Sam Khetz's death on the same battlefield.

Personally, I also hated the missile batteries as much as any of my friends and commanders, but I asked myself if they were really that important. And were we really capable of inflicting a massive aerial blow to enemy ground forces with our fighter force once we finished the SAMs? With an air force consisting of just fighter aircraft, I was far from sure of that.

Five years later this debate came to a head. On the evening of June 9, 1982, I was a brigadier general, commander of the air base at Tel Nof, and was summoned to Tel Aviv for debriefing of that day's brilliant operation, the complete elimination of a Syrian array of missile batteries in Lebanon.

We finished them off in half a day without a scratch on our planes. The hall was full, and everyone who was anyone was at that briefing.

Like all of us, I felt enormously happy and proud of this achievement. I was even proud personally to show pictures from my Skyhawk bombing sight: a SAM-6 mobile SAM battery, my archenemy since Operation Model in 1973, could be seen under my bombs. And so much did I rejoice in that victory that I ordered preparation of a special emblem of honor, and submitted it in the name of Tel Nof's pilots to the officer in charge of the operation, Col. Aviem Sela. Since 1974 this man had designed and developed this mission, and his part in releasing the air force from the nightmare was great. When I was invited to the podium, I began by calling Aviem up and awarding him the prize. This was certainly an unusual action, almost pompous. The commander of the air force, David Ivry—who certainly deserved that prize no less than Aviem—gave me a look.

If there ever was a point in which strategic, not just tactical conclusions could be drawn from the elimination of SAMs, this was it. Feeling this way when my turn came to present Tel Nof's part in the victory, I just skipped the common habit of counting the scalps my base had collected and instead proposed to use our proven capability and eliminate the missile batteries around Damascus.

"The elimination of twenty missile batteries may bring that army to collapse," I said. "Syria is isolated and loaded with problems. It is like a fragile glass vase; one ping on the right spot can cause it to disintegrate, just as happened to Nasser in 1967."

I began to suggest that once the bonfires burned around Damascus, the Syrian regime would realize how exposed it was, and this would be a good time to propose a settlement and even begin moving toward a political solution between our states, but I didn't manage to say much of it. David Ivry stopped me, remarking sourly that this is not what I had been invited to the stage for. He said angrily, "Military officers should stay out of politics!"

ALTHOUGH HE HAD CONFUSED the concepts of strategy with politics, Ivry was certainly right. Had I not been in a state of euphoria, I would have recalled what I kept arguing years before when I was chief of ops, against conventional wisdom: that those were just SAM batteries, not strategic assets. The Syrian rulers probably just blinked in embarrassment when they heard of the destruction of their SAM-6 brigade and the hundred MiGs we shot down that day. It was far-fetched to believe that they would fall from power just because of the destruction of another twenty batteries around Damascus. The missiles and the MiGs were just pawns to them, not treasure. So much for strategy. But the missile elimination proved not to be a tactical achievement, either. The ground war against the Syrians in Lebanon in 1982, however successful it had been, was executed by our ground forces and not the air force. The air force fighters may have helped, but they definitely did not play a decisive part.

Thus, the marvelous elimination of SAMs in 1982, the product of years of investment and the resources of a whole country, was neither strategically nor militarily meaningful. Its meaning was mainly emotional, for us Israeli pilots. The destruction of that missile array was first and foremost an act of pride and revenge. The Israeli aircraft had paid back the Soviet missile for "bending" its wing. Only two good things can be said in favor of this vaunted elimination of the SAMs in 1982: the operation was well planned and well executed. Today we know that these, too, are not obvious.

But there was another reason why Ivry was right to stop my strategic proposals. He probably was already suspecting what we didn't, that this war was a "war of deception," a political game that had no long-range, government-approved national plan. None of the military men in that hall could imagine Prime Minister Begin and his government being led by the nose step after step to places they never imagined going. Perhaps Ivry already suspected that we were sinking into activities the government never intended and never approved—deeds that would bring us down in many ways. Perhaps he was thinking of his next moves to keep the air force sane. It made no sense to waste time on strategic proposals in a war that was mainly politics.

So much for 1982; now back to 1977, to those eighteen months in which I served as chief of operations, until I submitted my resignation and left the military. In that job I didn't spend my time only on debates for and against missile attacks.

This was an interesting and exciting time, full of crazy fun. The department under me, which was responsible for the planning of all aspects of war, was involved in everything. We dealt with every operation, either day-to-day or long-range. All intelligence data and all the IDF's programs and secret weapons were open to us. We entertained new ideas, issued new operational demands, developed new battle doctrines, and arranged exercises and war games to test them. Every six months we submitted a situation report that affected budgets, training, and new weapons. We did surprise readiness checks on all air force units. I enjoyed very much scrambling a squadron or a base for simulated battle, day or night, and watching them deal with it. It brought back mountains of lessons. And most interesting of all, we worked in close cooperation with the land and sea arms of the IDF.

I used to devote one day every week to flying. I visited all the fighter squadrons and flew Phantoms, Kfirs, Mirages, and Skyhawks. I got aboard flights in helicopters and transport aircraft, visited our control and radar units, and met with these branches of military aviation totally different from fighters. On such visits I met with officers and pilots and gave them ideas for the future, discussed operational plans and doctrine with them, listened to their reactions, and gathered impressions. I took part in many exercises and learned new ideas that welled from below. I discovered outstanding men and women. Sometimes I was amazed how the air force had come so far from those pioneer days of flight school sixteen years ago, and even since the establishment of the Orange Tails. Notwithstanding my criticism, this was a different air force, clever and purposeful. It was a dynamic world of sophistication, always interesting. I had to stay on my toes all the time.

For example, there were the long-range targets. During the late 1970s the Iraqis were building an atomic reactor, and this threat worried us a lot. We began testing our capability to operate a thousand kilometers from Israel. The independent range of our fighters was much shorter than that. The air force began to develop aerial refueling capability. I started using this new, still limited capability and mandated operational test flights to very distant points, day and night. On one of these tests, formations of Israeli

Phantoms and Skyhawks got out to two thousand kilometers, the Italian coast, and returned. I used this opportunity to learn to refuel my Skyhawk in the air somewhere among the Greek Islands. One night we sent Kfir aircraft to the east, to circle targets at their maximum operating range. I spent other long nights flying odd missions to faraway, unnamed places.

And there were the day-to-day, ongoing operations. The air force didn't rest for a minute. Preparation for those operations, and the meetings and presentations for their approval, always ended in the minister of defense's office and sometimes in the prime minister's. Those presentations were challenges in themselves, and one always heard interesting ideas and was exposed to perspectives from new, surprising angles. At times I had the opportunity to take part in such operations as a "front-line manager," always in a forward command post, either in a jeep, a plane, or on the deck of a ship, following the process closely, ready to intervene and send in air support at any moment. This was a mighty great feeling.

One of those operations—the Litani operation in Lebanon—continued for several days and nights. The air force worked at high capacity, and in that instance I experienced the operation of the air force command post in wartime. Of course, this operation was nothing like the Yom Kippur War, but I was glad to see that this time the atmosphere was different from the stories of confusion that had reigned there during that war. I exploited that Lebanon miniwar to instill and examine correct working procedures—for instance, processing of feedback from the line squadrons and integration of our conclusions into the next orders being planned. The means we used for it were still primitive—paper maps and intelligent clerks with logbooks and colored pencils—but in essence we created "living maps."

Helicopters were another distraction that the new head of operations wasted his precious time on instead of going over the minute details of fighter plans for war that were brought daily to his desk.

I discovered late in life this curious vehicle that could land and take off almost anywhere. But when I joined the operations department I noticed that it could fill some of the more problematic empty squares in my notebook charts. And in this I found a good base left by my predecessor, Avihu Ben

Nun, and Benny Peled also had seen the revolutionary military possibilities hidden in helicopters long before I did. Still, the man who most influenced me was Maj. Ido Ambar, the officer who planned helicopters operations under me.

Ido believed that commando units could be flown to an enemy's rear by helicopters, and attack his weak spots. Such an aggressive approach fit my own thinking. Conditions that disturbed activating fighter aircraft—for example, bad weather or missile batteries—didn't affect helicopters in the same way. Helicoptered commandos could attack important targets at night and in adverse weather conditions, and enable us to continue the war even when our fighter force was grounded. And perhaps the most important: the helicoptered force would be able to continue the fight even if our airfields were paralyzed.

And there was another good thing: Unlike futuristic unmanned aircraft, helicopters were ripe and ready. Here there was no need for risky technological development. The helicopter squadrons were there to be used and were organized and ready for action. We had large American CH-53 Sea Stallions—we renamed them Petrels—that could transport commando forces with their weapons and gear and put them right on their objectives. Such possibilities were so dazzling that we began imagining a new type of battle unit, mobile, quick, and aggressive, that could be deployed alongside the cumbersome IDF and know how to use the various capabilities of the air force and direct them to a plethora of new targets. This theoretical unit fit into my first-strike concept. We called it in our discussions the Israeli Attack Force.

But the main component was missing: the air force didn't have commando units. Indeed, the Israeli military had several elite infantry units—all of them full of top-quality soldiers, but they all belonged to other service branches. And whenever in the past the IDF had put infantry with helicopters for joint operations, it had been improvised, since there was no responsible body with unified doctrine and efficient management. During all our wars, commando operations in the enemy's rear were extremely rare, and the little that was done was usually improvised and amateurish. Only in peacetime, and after long preparation, did such operations succeed. One such case was the hostage rescue at Entebbe Airport in Uganda. But in wartime you don't have time for such delicate preparations.

The existing elite infantry units were the apple of the eye of the army, and there was no way to get a ready infantry unit from anybody. So we mounted an effort to build a new commando unit of our own from scratch. We wanted an infantry unit that would belong to the air force and be integral with our helicopters.

Simple? No. We found out that we were stepping on the toes of the commanders of the ground army.

"It's unthinkable," said the regular army, the "greens." (The air force was called the "blues.") "To give the air force permission to build an airborne commando unit. They'll be drawing water from the same well of first-class recruits. What about us?"

Those greens were ignoring history. Infantry units had operated in other wars under air force command and had had a fair amount of military success (and failure as well). And the navy had a superior commando unit, Flotilla 13, which did dangerous jobs successfully, although it was commanded by officers wearing not green but white uniforms. The reason for this unit was historical. As early as 1941 the Hagana had sent infantry units deep behind enemy lines in boats (remember the mission of the Twenty-three?), and in the War of Independence in 1948 the Palmach was already using PT boats for special operations. In a natural way, maritime commando operations were seen as legitimate from the beginning of the IDF. But the blues were different, since in 1948 they didn't have helicopters. Nobody had helicopters in 1948, and only visionaries such as British general Orde Wingate had imagined using helicopters in the 1940s. From its inception the Israeli Air Force focused on fighters. This is why no airborne commando force was ever developed.

"So what?" I responded when I grasped the context. "We just missed the first train. Well, 1977 is as good a year as any other to buy a ticket and start this journey."

I began pushing this idea, too, and to my joy in this matter I didn't find myself alone. Ido, of course, worked shoulder to shoulder with me, but even the fighter planners picked up on the idea. In the beginning, they certainly saw in it "backup, no; fifteen for missile elimination," but in time some of them developed a more general outlook. Our voice began to be heard in the corridors of the General Staff. Right then we stepped on real land mines.

Most of the land generals saw in our idea an invasion of their territory, and naturally they reacted vigorously. The paratroopers were insulted more than everybody else. "Why can't the air force just fly us to the targets and get us back, as we did in the good old days?" they asked. "Why does the air force need an infantry unit under its own command?"

Those operations from those "good old days" had plenty of bad operational examples, and good reasons not to do it that way. When we reanalyzed those improvised operations, we found in them many failures and mistakes, and always there was no integrated command structure to take responsibility and make corrections.

"Why do we need infantry?" we answered the paratroopers. "Because waging war behind enemy lines requires tight coordination of infantry with helicopters and fighter aircraft. This is expertise that must be learned, practiced, and commanded in place. And for this, an organic command structure is needed, to prepare in peacetime and control it in war." "Opportunistic copulating," I once told the paratroopers' commander, "bears only orphans."

The greens were hopping mad, but the alternative they proposed, taking the helicopters from the air force and putting them under the army, was just a provocation and unrealistic, and they knew it. They got even madder. The new vice chief of staff, Maj. Gen. Raphael Eitan (Raful), vehemently opposed the idea of letting the air force develop a special commando unit for itself. Raful was suspicious by nature, and I believe he had figured out our hidden plans for a future Israeli Attack Force. In one of many staff discussions he labeled me "General Popsky." This was a ridiculous name taken from a book called *Popsky's Private Army*. In spite of his rough exterior, Raful was an avid reader.

The chief of staff, Lt. Gen. Mota Gur, didn't want to take a position on the matter. He also was a paratrooper, and in his last days in command. For some time it seemed we were at an impasse.

‡

I first met Col. Raphael Eitan when he commanded Paratroop Brigade 35. This was in the middle of the 1960s. Young Lieutenant Spector, a Super Mystere pilot, was sent south to the Negev, to join a training exercise with the paratroopers. The brigade was training to take some barren hill. I was given a radio, and my job was to direct close air support, what soon became known as a forward air controller.

The brigade commander was short, stout, and tough, his red nose peeling and his face pockmarked under his battered Australian field hat. He took me under his wing and sat me in his jeep. Before us was a rather large hill, its rocky sides mottled with bushes, and on the top were some whitish dugouts. We watched the soldiers advancing in line, running and falling face down. When the sun went down, a break was ordered. The battalion commanders assembled at the brigadier's tent. I sat among them eating jam from cans with them; they were all legendary figures from my childhood.

In the morning there was another dry fire drill (with no live ammunition), and in the afternoon came time for the live fire attack. We stood, the forward command staff, on another hill. All was spread before us like a chessboard. The soldiers hopped among the rocks up the slope, firing in short bursts and raising squirts of white dust. From our position the shooting sounded like explosions of chains of caps. I saw another group of soldiers climbing the other side of the hill. Suddenly a great fart came from our side—a jeep had launched a round from a black pipe. The smell of burned powder spread, and a second explosion roared in the distance. A pillar of smoke sprouted on the hilltop.

"Loretta," the commander's female clerk said to me with a lovely smile.

"Call me Spike." I clutched her hand warmly. She was only a little chubby, and the upper button of her collar was open. She had magnificent dimples.

"Not *Loretta*!" She recoiled and pulled her hand away. "*Lo reta!*" *Lo reta* in Hebrew means "recoilless." I still didn't get it.

"Some cannon," she snapped. The way she turned away made me see that my chance of her seeing me as a real cannon was over.

The aircraft called me on the radio. They were already circling above us, waiting their turn. They were loaded with napalm. Raful turned to me: "Hit the target, now!"

With my hand on the mike, I scanned the battlefield again. The soldiers were already too close to the top in my opinion, perhaps 150 meters.

"Sir—" I began. Raful turned his back on me.

"Call him 'Raful,' not 'sir,' " advised "Loretta." I tugged at his sleeve.

"Yes, Spector?"

"The troops must pull back from the target . . . they're already inside the safety perimeter."

Raful threw me a contemptuous look. "The air force is not willing to fight?"

Embarrassed, I shrugged. I brought the aircraft in on a "dry pass."

"Do not drop any ordnance!" I warned them. I felt the stare of the brigadier burning in my back.

The two Vautour fighters, large and noisy, passed one after the other low over the hill. I saw the soldiers getting up, waving, and applauding. Raful sent me a shadow of a smile. And again the soldiers began to run, firing their rifles.

A messenger came running. The drill was immediately stopped and the soldiers were called back.

"What happened?" I asked my confidante.

"Two soldiers were killed," she whispered. Apparently someone was caught in crossfire between the two units that attacked the hill. A commotion began. The company commanders came running, got together, and conversed quietly. A command car started its engine in a din of noise and smoke, and drove down to the wadi below us, bouncing in the dust. I saw that it carried stretchers. The forward command group began to fold itself. Blankets, maps, binoculars, and water tanks were thrown in the jeep. The soldiers turned back down the slope. The aircraft still buzzed overhead.

"Sir . . . excuse me, Raful."

"What now?"

"Permission to napalm the target hill?"

"Do as you like."

The Vautours thundered in and loosed their bombs. A boom, and the hill was covered with flames and black smoke. The soldiers froze, then turned around and jumped excitedly and shouted "Bravo!" Chubby sent me a dimpled smile, and Raful shook my hand strongly. His hand was thick and hard, a hand of a farmer.

This struggle to establish my "private army," which went on for a long time and became nasty at times, found the beginning of its solution from an unexpected direction: the soldiers themselves. One day Ido brought two men in green uniforms to my office. Both of them were big names. Dodik Rothenberg was the hero of the legendary Battle of Ammunition Hill in Jerusalem, a bloody battle during the Six-Day War. And Muki Betzer, tall and balding, was one of the most decorated soldiers from Commando Force, the top elite infantry unit. He had taken part in many operations beyond Israel's borders, including the rescue at Entebbe. Both were heroes and thoughtful men.

Muki said, "Instead of fighting the army over their beloved assets, let's establish a new reserve unit. It should consist of ex-commando reservists. Let's train them specifically for air force missions."

"Are there such things, released commando guys who can fight?" I saw in my mind's eye flabby, grizzled veterans.

"There are. And they are okay." Muki seemed to read my mind.

"Who will establish this new unit?"

"Me," Muki said.

"And who'll command it?"

"Me."

Still, I had reservations about this kind of ex-commando fighter. I knew their mode of action. They prepared their operations years in advance, looking for absolute certainty. In fact, they were peacetime soldiers. I told Muki, "In aerial warfare there is no time and no certainty. I need guys who can get an order in the morning, prep till noon, mount helicopters in the evening, and fight at night."

"They'll do it."

I made it certain he understood me: "I want to be able to scramble them to targets like fighter aircraft."

"Can do."

"And the same next day?"

"Same next day."

I was impressed. Only one question remained: "How can I trust you to be at my disposal in time of need? At the first opportunity the greens will steal you for their trenches." I wanted soldiers wearing blue berets, so it would be clear to whom they reported.

"Blue berets? Not yet," said Muki. "Let's go slowly. Let's begin green, quietly. Later, the greens will get used to it, and finally they'll give in. Let's do everything gradually." Clever Dodik nodded, but I, paranoid as I was, couldn't rest until we succeeded in squeezing permission from Raful to establish the new unit—"not an air force unit, you hear me, Spector?"—in an air force base. If not under the air force command, at least they would be nearby, under our supervision.

And indeed the "battalion for air force missions"—a vague name was given to it intentionally—began to become a reality. Muki's reserve soldiers were smart and agile, worked hard, and reported for long months of service. They developed tools and methods that inspired even me, and I was glad to see helicopter and fighter pilots mixing with those commandos routinely. These soldiers and officers were still wearing green berets—it took a long time before they changed to our blue ones—but the language they used began to sound like ours, and I could read their maps. I found myself dragged at night with Muki into all kinds of infantry maneuvers, inserted by helicopter in dark places, driving odd vehicles, and using unfamiliar weapons. On one of my visits in our battalion I saw a familiar back bent over his work. I slapped it, and Brutus the night fighter turned to me, a welding torch in hand. We hugged each other warmly. It came out that he, an engineer by profession, had volunteered to design and build some equipment for the air force's new commando unit. If Brutus was there, then the whole thing was becoming a seriously scary weapon.

But while I began celebrating the birth of the helicopter commando, an unexpected weakness was revealed. Painfully, that weakness was in the helicopters themselves—the air force end of the deal. The flight profiles were too demanding, and the helicopters didn't have sufficient instrumentation to ensure safe flight and landing on target. Their instrumentation was antiquated—on a level with the Harvard trainers I had flown in 1958. With such instruments, navigation and spatial orientation at night in enemy territory were difficult at best. The helicopters were capable of doing single, very special operations, like plucking with tweezers, but not the extensive deployments I needed from the commando unit.

In one of the exercises I took part in, a helicopter crashed due to loss of spatial orientation, and the dozens of soldiers aboard survived only by luck. This was really bad; Muki's warriors knew how to attack the targets we selected for them, but we couldn't guarantee getting them there in one piece and extracting them safely after the operation. This problem remained unsolved.

Of all the issues I wanted to address as chief of operations, the most important was a lesson I had learned in the Yom Kippur War: the integration of fighting units into the war as "heads," not just as "hands."

Air force headquarters, and my department of operations with it, saw themselves as the brains, which processed plans and doctrines and sent them down as detailed orders to the limbs—the squadrons and the air bases. This was exactly the system I was familiar with from my time as manager of one such limb. When I commanded the Orange Tails I became distrustful of this system, and my dissatisfaction grew later, when I headed the aerial training department. It wasn't about the authority of headquarters to decide what should be done and who should do it. What bothered me was them dictating the method of execution in minute detail, as was the rule in their orders. In short, I was after central control of the what and the when, and for local control of the how.

I could cite many examples of blunders by a headquarters remote from the field that had produced plans such as Challenge—a bizarre doctrine that had sent Khetz and Avihu out to be sacrificed. Headquarters had rejected—without even checking—the idea of arming Mirages with Dagger missiles, and then it didn't care to attend the debriefing when this force multiplier was successful. Headquarters was too lazy to reevaluate the attack methods against mobile SAM batteries. It didn't think about the possibility of the Egyptians building bridges over the Suez Canal, nor did it have an answer to that problem. Immersed in its plans for various operazia, headquarters had made serious tactical errors, was not aware of actual weather and lighting conditions, of the performance of the bombs' fuses. It rejected feedback from the battlefield. The reality the pilots had to deal with in the Yom Kippur War was different from anything the brains expected, but still, imprisoned in its old doctrines and its underground bunkers, headquarters continued to send down to the limbs orders full of errors that one could either fight against or just ignore.

The main problem was that neither the staff officers nor the field commanders were prepared for this. We hadn't built any systems that would enable our limbs to function when the brain was confused or paralyzed.

And now, when I was part of the brain, I couldn't avoid the possibility that the same problem could recrudesce.

"Uncertainty is basic to war," I explained to my officers. "And even the newest doctrines and plans that we geniuses are developing now may fail." This had no organizational solution. Even getting the best people to headquarters won't help—who do we have more capable and knowable than Avihu, Sela, and the like? It was clear to me that I was no better than they, and in spite of all the improvements we had made, we could end up repeating the same mistakes if war came on our watch. I felt as if I were walking on eggs.

Against this background I changed my view about the orders we were issuing to the fighting units, and saw them just as "thought drills" and not plans to be executed word for word. Any dictation of tactical details was undesirable—it petrified pilots' brains and impeded independent thinking.

The problem was that at the same time, peacetime operations—with which we were dealing, too—did require going down to minute details. In those peacetime operations there were sensitivities, involvement of commanders and civilians, and there was plenty of time for the planners to invent complicated methods that could be employed and controlled only in peacetime. Those intricate performances succeeded, and the complicated planning, with emphasis on detail, overflowed into the war orders and the operational culture of the force. I was afraid that the war plans my department kept sending down to the units were cooking up for the air force the same surprise that my predecessors had cooked for me.

‡

From the moment I was named chief of operations, I began working to restructure orders into tables of who does what and when. The how was a wholly different story, an issue of doctrine and not of plans and orders, and the source of the doctrine in my opinion was not in the operations department but in the air force at large. My department should be only the engine fueling the creation of doctrine. I returned to the way Operation Focus had been prepared. Our orders had served only as guidelines for the field units in order for them to know what to prepare for.

"If we give the fighting units some responsibility for fighting methods," I told my officers, "they'll begin to think and prepare, and new ideas will surface." Of course, I remembered the Baboons.

My men were furious.

"The field units have no general understanding," some of them said. "Pilots deal with flying, and their knowledge of everything else goes in the slot under our office door."

"Why not supply them with information?" I asked. "Most of it is not confidential." But my planners opposed the idea. They were clever and able, and like most people of our kind they preferred to play their cards close to their chests. Also, my directives hurt their aesthetic sensibilities. I had relegated the "art of planning" to a simpler level, replacing colorful and sophisticated crochet with simple cotton checkered blankets.

"We are better off having mediocre fighting methods as long as the pilots understand and believe in them," I told my planners. "Give the field commanders freedom to manage the details."

My men didn't like it.

I turned to the field commanders. If the problem lay in the disconnection between the brain and the limbs, then the time had come to activate the neurons in those limbs. The method I used for it was "planning exercises." The operations department mandated to the bases and the squadrons war games, in which we dictated to them a general situation and ordered them to use the tools at their disposal to achieve certain results. No indication was given to them of how to do the job. "Use what you have" was the rule.

The units, sometimes competing against each other, had to call in all the expertise they could lay their hands on, open books and maps, and issue plans for their battle. Sometimes those war games included elements of actual execution—arming the aircraft, briefing, taxiing, and even attacking target ranges. This gave their planning a dimension of reality in timing.

At the end of the war games, there was a general debriefing in which the plans were evaluated, and the units' solutions were compared against each other and against the "teacher's solution," which my department prepared clandestinely. There were hot arguments. The bases and the squadrons went deeper into the doctrines, initiated tests of their own, and the staff began to get fresh ideas and solutions to operational problems and had to compete against a smarter opposition.

But the deeper meaning was that the actual fighters—even though they executed the orders—took part in the thought processes and operational responsibility of the air force. There were even some exercises in which I paralyzed headquarters totally in the middle of a war game, and the bases had to continue the war by themselves, coordinating their actions.

In the first war games I met a phenomenon that surprised and repulsed me: some field commanders were not happy with any added work or responsibility. They preferred to receive detailed orders.

"Give us complete orders!" they demanded. "What else is headquarters for?"

I turned a deaf ear, and these voices weakened in time but never ceased entirely. There was another reaction: Benny Peled, who was at the end of his tenure as commander of the air force, was uneasy about this change.

"Are you taking the command away from me?" he kept asking.

David Ivry, who replaced Benny, understood the idea much better.

I still ask myself when the exact moment was that I decided to close my notebook and leave my desk job, since I had concluded that I was becoming a nuisance and should do something else. No doubt this happened when I felt my ideas conflicted with the air force's ethos and got everyone's back up.

As long as I wanted to add new, sophisticated weapons to the air force's arsenal, all was well. But it was much less nice when I began thinking about the future of fighter aircraft. I also agreed that we still needed fighters and that they still were very efficient on some missions. But I could show the empty squares in my chart and argue that fighters were unable to fill them successfully, and thus fewer aircraft were needed.

I raised an idea called "a quality air force": an air force one-third the size of our existing force but consisting of only super-modern aircraft, such as the F-15. At my request, research compared this model against the existing air force in several war scenarios. The researcher—Dr. Yitzhak Ben Israel, who later became a major general in the IDF—showed that within a framework of identical current costs, such a small and agile force could achieve better results in almost all scenarios. Only one assignment was left open: who would attack enemy ground forces and destroy thousands of tanks? Quality aircraft alone were too few for that. I had designated my imaginary remotely directed drones for that. I wanted us to develop and acquire such weapons using budget from "surplus" manned aircraft. I stepped on a lot of toes.

The prevailing wisdom pointed in the opposite direction, to adding fighter aircraft. Since the Yom Kippur War, the IDF's command, headed by the chief of staff, Mota Gur, believed that the rehabilitation of the IDF and its preparation for war required massive force enlargement. The IDF and the Ministry of Defense got unprecedented finance and political power after that disastrous war, and used it. Our confidential defense budget—for Israelis, anyway—was discussed freely abroad. I found the numbers at UCLA and in the American press. I found that Israel was spending 30 percent of its national annual budget on defense—twice the expenditure of before the war, and five times other "normal" militarily active nations.

The IDF and the Ministry of Defense wanted to achieve military independence, and with excited assistance from the defense industry they pushed for development and production locally of combat ships, main battle tanks, fighter aircraft, and other projects needing a lot of infrastructure and full of economic risk. Even superpowers could barely afford these risks. Such ventures were hot topics and were protected by special interests. In this atmosphere, to talk about reducing the number of aircraft and developing drones was like swimming up Niagara Falls. The real issue was power—as fast and as much as possible. And power went to those who knew how to direct large streams of government finance into waiting hands. Getting and spending big money was vision, strategy, and leadership.

The need to buy many more fighter aircraft was supported by ground forces, too. They wanted to receive close air support in their war, and for this they needed lots of aircraft.

Professor Amnon Yogev, a colonel and respected physicist, came to me and said, "Spector, here's the answer: if we give every fighting unit a laser-designating projector, the air force can give close support with accurate bombing." Amnon was entrusted with laser-directed weapons. Technically, he was absolutely correct: a soldier could illuminate the target with his laser projector. The aircraft could drop a bomb that would home on the laser beam and hit the target. QED.

I told him, "Look, Amnon, you are promising every soldier that a fighter plane can support him in time of need. We don't have that many aircraft."

Amnon said, "One of the missions of the air force is to support the ground forces. Buy more aircraft."

I reminded him that aircraft can't work under threat of SAM batteries. If this is the way we take, we will have to achieve air superiority. I reminded him that this is exactly what we had promised before the Yom Kippur War, and exactly in this we failed.

"The air force," I told him, "must concentrate its firepower on quality targets, not chase thousands of calls for support from companies and battalions."

"Then what do we do, Spector?"

I didn't have drones to solve his problem. I told him, "Buy a lot of machine guns and ammunition for your troops, because if they rely on air support they'll end up facing the enemy with just a laser projector in their hands."

IDF command was furious with me, and so was the air force.

OF COURSE, I KNEW AT THE TIME that my idea about changing fighter aircraft for drones was ahead of its time. Even I could understand this, and knew that the first smart bombs we developed had not been so smart.

But I remembered the leap in quality that air-to-air missiles had made right before my eyes. And one more thing was clear to me: those weapons would improve and their cost of production decline only when we started to mass-produce them. This could be done only by placing orders to industry.

The first chit I signed my first day in office as chief of operations was an order for a thousand glide bombs. A thousand bombs was an unbelievable number, ten times over the original budget that was allocated to this in the annual program. Each bomb was a hundred times more expensive than a normal iron bomb, and this requirement came at the expense of several other important needs. My commanders raised their eyebrows—clearly there was no need of a thousand such bombs to destroy SAM batteries. But since it was against missiles, they approved the requisition. Still, the number I ordered was only one-tenth of the quantity I really wanted because they were intended for more things than just attacking SAMs. I wanted to get those bombs to action to accelerate the tempo of learning and improving them and their use. I wanted to equip all the squadrons with those bombs and begin employing then routinely in training to accelerate the process of getting to the next generation of weapons. I was ready to use those glide bombs in operations at the first opportunity and I almost succeeded, but had to cancel: Yassir Arafat failed to show up at the meeting.

No doubt I was too pushy and impatient as a staff officer. I didn't consider political correctness, and my commanders were reaching the limit of their patience. In one discussion Benny got out of his seat and yelled at me to stop grinding him down with these ideas, or—as he put it in English—"I'll shoot you down in flames!" Benny was scary even in English, but he also had warmth and grace. Very early the next morning I was invited to his office. Over the first coffee of the day and the eternal cigarette, clean-shaven and his eyes still drowsy, he conversed with me at length. In the end he sent me to continue with "my craziness."

David Ivry replaced Benny as air force commander in October 1977. Ivry was extremely intelligent and understood my worldview pretty well, and I believe he even agreed with most of it in principle. But Ivry was a pragmatic person who knew that a heavy ship such as the air force could not make sharp turns. I lost patience. Even though I saw progress in some of my requirements, my main ideas seemed to me as far from fulfillment as ever. I could continue blabbering about "filling empty squares," "quality air force," "first strike," the need to replace fighter aircraft in some missions by helicopter commandos and drones, and the need to decentralize war planning—still, the main product of my department was plans and orders to eliminate SAM arrays with Phantoms and Skyhawks. And the imagination of the air force and most of its energy were invested in its next fighter aircraft. This was a worthy subject for fighter pilots, and many plans and many interests protected it. It was clear to everybody, even me, that the real attention and the real finance would go there, not to any other idea.

The Americans proposed their fighter aircraft, put political pressure on us, and lent us money so we could buy them, and in Israel, heavyweight sectors—our aerial defense industry most of all—pushed for the development and production of an Israeli-made jet fighter. The air force was the client and its word was important, but very few pilots or commanders cared to discuss the deeper question of what was needed, and for what ends. The air force knew what it really wanted—it was an American modern jet—but at the end, the air force reconciled all the competing parties. It convinced the government to buy American F-16s and at the same time voted for the development of the locally produced Lavi, which was going to be practically identical to the American fighter, and even undertook to order both of them. In this way, by the right hand doing the opposite of what the left was doing, the State of Israel was led into a huge double investment, and part of it went down the drain in the end.

During my studies in the United States I learned the interesting notion of the "military-industrial complex"—this integration of partial interests that affects national decisions. Now I had the opportunity to see this phenomenon firsthand—and in my eyes, this whole process was improper, or at least illogical.

‡

Inside the general ooze that my ideas were floundering in, my personal break point arrived. I remember clearly where this happened. It was at a convention of reserve pilots at Tel Nof. The reserve pilots, a big part of the power of the air force, were then a focal point of distrust of the high command. Although ready and willing to contribute, serving a day every week, they harbored deep resentment regarding command failure in the Yom Kippur War. The goal of the convention was to strengthen their trust in our plans for the next war. My departmental officers climbed the podium one after the other and presented them with our new, improved plans. When we got to the crux—attacking SAMs, of course—Tsutsik got up in the audience. The big, swarthy man, my instructor in flight school, was now a captain at El Al Israel Airlines. All those years he continued to fly Skyhawks in the reserves—a feat that not all pilots could match. I looked at him with great affection. His temples and his chest hair, sticking above his shirtfront, were already white.

Tsutsik said, "I don't understand."

Nahumi began to explain the new methods of attack on the missiles from the beginning.

"Not that," said Tsutsik. "Don't you have anything new to show us?"

The audience of reservists supported him with a growing murmur of catcalls. The room became noisy, and all eyes turned to me. I was the senior staff officer, so I got up to the podium to defend our plans and fighting doctrines.

I knew with whom I was dealing here. The people I faced were not cowards. They were ready to risk their lives and enter the missile killing zones once again, and I presumed they saw our plans as practical, but they needed to be convinced of the reason to do it. So I supplied it. I described to our reserve pilots how the elimination of the missiles would change the situation, shake the enemy strategically, and enable us to break his army tactically. I reminded them how after air superiority was attained on June 5, 1967, the sky opened and the enemy lay open to us. I spoke, but I did not believe what I was saying. The convention ended on an up note, but since then, whenever I approved operational plans, I saw before me Tsutsik's skeptical eyes.

‡

For a while longer I kept signing operational orders and sitting in on staff discussions, but more and more I understood that the man entrusted with operations cannot be in opposition. For some additional time I kept coming to work with red eyes, and at last I went to David Ivry's office and asked to be relieved and leave the service. Ivry, a moderate man, tried to calm me down—perhaps a short leave would do—but my feelings were too strong. I had my strategic thinking, but I failed to convince the air force to follow. I knew how to fly, lead, and command, and also to think and write, but I didn't know politics nor how to say one thing and mean another, and I didn't care to learn.

"I don't fit here, and I can't stay in the air force," I told Ivry painfully. The conversation ended. When I exited Ivry's office I thought, "Here's where we part, my beloved air force. I am leaving you in the good hands of Ivry, Avihu, and others like them."

It was August 1978. I took off my uniform and left.

I didn't have much time to mourn this second break in my life. We were poor, and we had to pay the mortgage on our home. We both had to find work, and quickly.

Within a week I found myself picking apples in the orchards of Kibbutz Tsuba, near Jerusalem, the same kibbutz my Uncle Shaike hoped to establish before his death. Ali stood like a rock behind my decision and my torment, and worked in the kibbutz kitchen. We came down from the heights of the air force and folded ourselves into the narrow, warm niche of the kibbutz.

Tzuba's members accepted us very gracefully into their society. We received a small, nice apartment with a bit of lawn in front. The end of summer in the mountains of Jerusalem was sweet and cool. I worked in the fruit orchards, picking, pruning, spraying, and shoveling powdered bird shit on the roots of the trees. Our fourteen-year-old, Etay, learned to drive a tractor, too. Our kids went to live and study in the children's houses, and while I was in the fields my nine-year-old, Omri, carried six-year-old Noah on his shoulders to the opening of the first day of her first-grade class. Soon we all found new friends, and the children got a dog. Every weekend, friends from the past, from Givat-Brenner or the air force, came to visit us, and we sat on the lawn and peeled cactus fruit, or walked around collecting berries and figs in the deserted Arab gardens on the hilly terraces. I continued flying in the reserves, and every week I drove Ali's red VW beetle to Hatzor, to fly Phantoms in Aviem Sela's Falcons as an ordinary section leader. It was nice and calm in Tzuba, the people of the kibbutz were wonderful, and the socialist way of life was still romantic, but we both knew well that this was an intermission. The kibbutz was not the solution to our lives. We recalled Shoshana's life at Givat-Brenner and my own run-in at the general meeting there, and decided we were not ready to give up our personal freedom. But the days were beautiful, and we lived from one to the next. Shosh came to visit us a few times, to see the grandchildren. I noticed that she was cool to me, and could see in her eyes criticism for my "dereliction of duty," but I was already in another place and not involved in national security anymore.

In autumn, the fruit harvest season in the mountains, my thoughts flew far with the clouds and the migrating birds. I entertained new career possibilities. I thought about going back to get a Ph.D. in the United States. I sent a letter to UCLA, and to refresh my English I translated a book about American fighter pilots in Vietnam from English to Hebrew. Then I reconsidered. I rejected the idea that I would go back to the issues I had left behind, justifying and formulating reasons for the failure of my main intellectual achievement. Then winter came, and the pruning of the apple and plum trees. The mornings were misty, and the chill air between the rows of bare trees cleaned my lungs gradually of the residue choking them.

The family gathered in the chill evenings around the tiny kerosene stove. This was our time for closeness. I got to know my three kids. Ali and I talked, grew close again. She became pregnant. Spring arrived, and optimism sprang anew. I hummed songs to myself to the rhythm of the tractor hopping over the terraces, mowing and spraying the orchards. I connected with friends, discussing, writing, and weighing many ideas.

The world was full of exciting choices. I waxed passionate; there were so many new prospects.

And then one day the chief of staff of the IDF, Raful, showed up in the orchard.

It was the spring of 1979, and the days were bright and blue. I led a group of young volunteers from America in thinning out the flowers on the peach trees to assure that the remaining fruit grew out to commercial size. This is great work, the peach trees in full pink bloom, and it almost hurt to extend the hydraulic shears into the tree and cut entire branches with one trigger pull. The boys and girls carried ladders and climbed into the trees after me to complete the final pruning, using manual shears.

The tractor behind me roared, and due to the noise I didn't hear anything, but suddenly I saw blue working shirts crowded around a stranger in a green uniform. I went to see, and the commander of the Israeli Defense Force was standing on top of a ladder, pruning branches. Lieutenant General Raful refused to get down, and he didn't stop working with the shears he took from one of the girls until we broke for breakfast. We went some distance from the volunteers and sat together on the green, warm grass, eating sandwiches and sipping tea from styrofoam cups.

"You're coming back in the service." I grinned. I told him that rumors had reached me already, that command of Hatzor Air Base would be offered to me, and I had turned it down.

"I am not going back," I told him, "I have other ideas. And," I added angrily, "it's time you told them to release my retirement pension account. I need the money to start my new life."

"You're not getting a penny. First, go talk to Ivry."

"Ivry has nothing to say to me."

"Ivry is waiting for you. Go talk to him." The chief of staff rose, brushed the back of his pants, put on his red beret, and walked to his car, which waited near the orchard.

"We decided to buy F-16 fighters from the United States. The aircraft will arrive within the year," Ivry said. "I want you to come back and take command of their integration and assimilation into the air force."

My jaw dropped.

"And you're to command Ramat-David Air Base, too."

When I could breathe again, I said, "David, how can you do this, after what happened? Didn't I let you down?"

"This is for the Orange Tails," he answered, "for the Yom Kippur War."

I don't remember if my eyes filled, or if I managed to control my emotions. I was moved indeed, but not because I was hungry for compliments. I was moved because during all those years I learned not to expect any honors from my superiors. No commander of mine had ever bothered to mention, one way or another, the principal occurrences, decisions, and risks that had shaped my life. Not one of them said a word about the establishment of the Orange Tails, or its performance in 1973. Ivry's saying that was completely unexpected, and the more so from such a closed, critical guy, stingy with his feelings. It was like getting a love song from anybody else. To this day I am grateful to Ivry for that single sentence.

And still I knew that what was proposed was conditional. The air force hadn't called me back so I could preach heresy about its future organization and equipment. Intellectually, I received a proposal to turn the clock back ten years. For a moment I sat and weighed it. I was aware that it was absurd. I—who declared from every podium that the air force should change direction from fighters and invest in other alternatives—had received a proposal to take command of the newest fighter force.

At last I decided. In one stroke I buried my strategic ideas and all my other plans for life, and chose to take command of Ramat-David and the new Israeli F-16 force. The cost was removal from the circle of those who influence the agenda and future of the air force, but a romance with the hottest plane in the world, and living a few more years among the best people Israel could assemble, was going to be a great joy, a dream of any combat commander. And more battles were in the future, for sure. How could I turn this down?

We shook hands and I rose to go. At the door I stopped, turned back to Ivry, and said, "Ivry, you know well that I'm coming back for one more hitch, that's all. In two years, three at most, I will leave the service for good. We both know that I came on a mission, and I am not out for command of the air force." He looked at me with his blue, hard eyes and waved his hand. Ivry didn't like pompous declarations.

AGAIN THE MOVING VAN. We left our friends in Kibbutz Tzuba, who had given us a home in time of need, and on a blazing noon in the autumn of 1979 loaded our tattered furniture for the umpteenth time, and after a four-hour drive arrived in family housing at Ramat-David Air Base in the Izreel Valley, into clouds of stinging gnats. It was harvest time, and almost without a breath I was hurried back to military command and into the cockpit of a fighter. Here we go again.

Chapter

22

Halo

AFTER TWO YEARS AT RAMAT-DAVID came three years more in command of Tel-Nof Air Base, and my military service finally ended for good five years later, in October 1984, when I turned forty-four. My picture was added to a long line of yellowing faces on the office wall in Tel Nof. I said good-bye to Abraham Yoffe, David Ivry, Ran Pecker, Avihu Ben Nun, and the clerks, entered Ali's car, and we drove together home to Ramat-HaSharon, a suburb near Tel Aviv.

On the next morning I went to my mother. I found her sitting outside in the autumn sunshine, wrapped in a blanket.

"Shosh," I asked her, "how much money do you have?"

The bright eyes looked at me uneasily. Cancer had already destroyed their hard, self-assured clarity.

"What do you need money for? What do you intend to do?"

"I want to go away for several months. I need time for myself, to think. There's no silence here."

"Listen well, Iftach. I am not so healthy anymore . . . "

I understood. "I'll pay you back to the last penny when I get back."

"Where are you getting money?" I saw before me a very sick, scared woman.

"I will have money. From my discharge bonus."

"Ach, why did you have to leave? What will come of it?" She dug deep in her closet and produced ten thousand U.S. dollars in bills, folded with rubber bands. I knew it was all she had.

I was going abroad for an undefined period of time, for as long as it would take, as far as my mother's money would get me. I had no other cash resources. I had a list of addresses, and an introductory letter from air force commander Amos Lapidot.

Ali took me to the airport. When we kissed good-bye, I told her, "I'll come back with something good. I'll get it from inside." And Ali said, holding our little Ella's hand, "Go in peace, don't worry. Don't think about us here, we'll be all right." And she added what I didn't ask from her. "I'll take care of your mother."

I spent the ten hours on the plane browsing in my small notebook, erasing, correcting, and adding lines to the fifty-odd I had already put there in the past few days. Each of those lines was a possibility for new work, for our next life. Some of the ideas were interesting, others curious, and others totally crazy. I was going to check out some of them and come back with one.

I stayed in America for two months, traveling from place to place on buses and in trains, sleeping in cheap motels, washing my own underwear and socks. In the morning I went for the meetings I had arranged, wearing the one suit I had pressed the night before, sporting my only tie. I met people and visited companies. I collected and read the materials they gave me, and made synopses. I tried to reject forty-nine thoughts and select the right one for me. Gradually I began to see some light.

The Israeli Air Force and the defense of Israel still flowed in my veins. At that time I didn't know yet how to build houses, run farms, develop and market computer programs, write novels, initiate ecological research, or join political struggles for national sanity. In 1984 I was focused on the future of aerial warfare.

AMONG OTHER THINGS, helicopters interested me most. The military uses of the vertical-takeoff-and-landing vehicle had captured my imagination for a long time, since I took part in the establishment of the air force commando battalion, which since then became an established fighting unit in blue berets. I knew that the old problem of the helicopters' flight instrumentation hadn't changed. When I returned to military service, and after my two-year F-16 venture, I became commander of Tel Nof Air Base. There I met the helicopters again. In the next three years I fell in love with the large CH-53 Petrels, their pilots and mechanics, and the intoxicating operational possibilities they hid.

I liked to spend long hours with them (a helicopter operation is a process that takes days and nights). After years of flying solo on the limits—the way fighter pilots fly—I found the teamwork of the helicopter crews interesting and fun. Their crews were less arrogant, perhaps because in the first place they were seen as second-class pilots. Their society was not so structured, and they had a better sense of humor. There was always humor in their cockpits, sometimes a little stupid, but I enjoyed it, anyway. Most of all I liked their special vocabulary: where fighter pilots confirm with "roger," the helicopter pilots used the word "straight," a wonderful idiom that has special meaning in Hebrew.

In those three years commanding Tel Nof I learned to fly those complicated machines and joined in their operations, and I still have several stones I collected in dark, remote fields, in places with foreign and strange names. I flew helicopters in training, in war games, and on the battlefield, and I experienced the great variety of helicopters' activities: the winding, clandestine penetration into enemy areas, to insert men and supplies in various places, on mountains, in deserts, and onto various vehicles; hovering to rescue wounded and dead people, pulling them up out of canyons, floods, and every other place. I caught a parachute that carried valuable equipment while still in the air; transported heavy loads by a hook under the craft's belly and deposited them gently on the summit of a high mountain, with the rotor blades clawing at the thin air at the limit of their power. And more.

Helicopter work was amazingly diversified. They penetrated and emerged, sometimes under fire, carrying soldiers, vehicles, and weapons. They attacked, collected intelligence, and chased terrorists in small wars. Gradually I perceived that helicopters went to the limit no less than fighter aircraft, although in different ways. There was enormous combat potential in helicopters, but their flight was complicated and problematic, very different from the beautiful, geometric clarity of a fighter's movements. Helicopters moved in their secret ways as in a thicket of uncertainties, as in the depths of a jungle. They had to orientate in difficult situations and react quickly to survive.

I was surprised again by the kind of instruments helicopter pilots had. A powerful helicopter such as the CH-53 took dozens of soldiers with their weapons and vehicles great distances by night and at low altitude, crossing hot battlefields, and winding in complex topographical areas. These were difficult and dangerous flights, and the pilots had to navigate flying low and fast and safely in the darkness among many threats without triggering any of them. The crew had to navigate with perfect accuracy, and to keep spatially oriented all the time. As a fighter pilot myself, I was expecting a serious instrumentation system for what this task required, but the instruments at the disposal of the helicopters' pilots were years behind the times.

In the three years I flew with helicopters I waited for somebody to propose new instrumentation, but in vain. Salesmen and marketers showed up, but they proposed just gadgets, pieces of instrumentation that dealt with parts of the general problem but not the whole. The modern fighters were sporting integrated flight systems for their less-complicated missions, but helicopters had nothing. And the helicopter pilots themselves didn't take any interest in avionic instrumentation. They didn't understand the concept of integration at all. This is why there was no market for real systems for helicopters—no one had thought much about it.

I believed that the time of the helicopter had arrived. Somebody with imagination was needed to create new associations. The helicopter's problem was very different from the fighters', and the idea was stimulating intellectually. I thought, Perhaps it could be me? Perhaps just because of my strangeness to their world I might come out with a fresh look at the problem and devise an avionic solution that might answer their questions and resolve those difficulties.

GENERAL PARKER, THE vice commander of U.S. Army aviation, received me at Fort Rucker as if I were a king. Right after a first meeting in his office he drove me to the officers' quarters. I was housed in a villa with white rugs. For breakfast I sat alone at a table for ten, and a servant, looking like a captain of an ocean liner, wearing a white uniform with shiny gold buttons, served me, passing plates over my shoulders.

For two long days I got an educational tour. I saw helicopters—lots of different kinds of helicopters. There were long rows with hundreds of them. I conversed with the commanders of various units. Then I had meetings with pilots, flight instructors, simulator instructors, chiefs, technicians, and instrumentation people. I looked into their flight profiles and the instruments they were using. At night General Parker and I flew together in a helicopter, simulating combat flight. I observed the way Americans did things and the different tools they used. At the end of those two days at Rucker, which came after visiting the main industries that produced instrumentation and weapons systems for helicopters, I summed it up this way: "All over the world people cook with the same water." That meant that their problems were identical to ours. I proposed to Parker that I present my impressions to him and his staff.

Some ten officers sat before me in Parker's briefing room. On the wall hung a white board. I got up and wrote on it a group of sentences in red marker, and at the end of each I put a question mark.

"Well, gentlemen?"

A colonel raised his hand. "General Spector, all these are well-known things. You've written a list of our troubles."

Parker nodded to me to go on.

I added a few more sentences, this time in black. In fact, what I wrote there was an initial characterization, first lines for a full avionic system for military helicopters, but nobody knew it yet. The officers looked at each other and began grinning. These were just empty words, hollow promises. Nothing existed yet in the real world.

"Gentlemen" I asked, "suppose there could be something that does all this. What then?"

I didn't know how those problems could be solved, but at least now I knew for sure and formulated what was needed.

"If you have such a thing, bring it to me," said General Parker, "and I'll buy it. There's nobody in the world who would pass it up."

There was nothing more to do in the United States. My time abroad was over, and I flew home. On the airliner to Israel the general definitions of the first integrated avionic system for helicopters took shape. I required the system to combine night vision, spatial awareness, navigation, communication, battlefield orientation, and direction of weapons systems. The year was 1985, and combined systems were operational only in the most modern fighter aircraft, such as the F-16, and those systems didn't even come near to supplying the services I intended. Had General Parker been a less open-minded person, he certainly would have suggested I join George Lucas in producing science fiction films.

I called the avionic system I designed Hila, a woman's name. In English it translated to Halo. Besides the outstanding operational requirements, my Halo had some serious material difficulties that designers of fighter systems didn't face. The first was price: air forces that were ready to invest five million dollars in avionic systems for an F-15 fighter wouldn't invest anything over a hundred thousand to buy avionic systems for a helicopter. Why? I could tell them how wrong they were—a helicopter mishap involves human life, more lives than the crew of a fighter. But what difference would that have that made? Thus I decided that for my final presentation the price tag of the complete system would be a quarter million dollars, but the system would be built of independent subunits that could be sold as modules for a much lower price, and deliver partial services.

A second major hindrance was the system's weight: all existing aerial instrumentation—computers, scopes, gauges, etc.—were heavy. A fighter aircraft that carries four tons of bombs can easily carry a few hundred added kilograms of radar, computers, wiring, screens, terminals, and even electronic external tanks. Helicopters, on the other hand, are sensitive to every extra kilogram. So I decided that the complete system could not exceed twenty-five kilograms. The modules, some of which had to be on the pilot's body and helmet, were limited to grams. In this way I defined more parameters and Halo began to take shape. I finished when I knew exactly what I wanted.

When functional requirements were completed, the general system designed, and the parameters set, I couldn't do any more by myself. I needed an engineer. My discharge bonus arrived, and finally I had some money. I contacted engineering companies and bought data and technical help.

After I got back to Israel, my mother died.

As if she waited for me to return, she collapsed the same night I arrived. Ali and I spent the next ten days taking turns at the hostel, and at home with the kids. During the long nights, when my mother was unconscious, I sat by her bed, and there I completed the functional engineering description of Halo.

One night I dozed off in the chair. When I woke I saw Shosh looking at me. At first I thought she didn't recognize me, but her eyes were again bright and steady. I rose and approached her.

"Go home. Get some sleep, Iftach."

"Do you need anything, Mom? Shall I bring something, or call somebody?"

For a long time she didn't answer. I thought she had fallen asleep, but then I heard her say in a weak, almost inaudible voice, "Those last years . . . were unnecessary." She sighed and then whispered, "I am so worried." I could imagine what was worrying her. It was not her future, not even mine.

A nurse came and took over. I went home. In the morning they called us from the hostel. She had died.

Shosh left Givat-Brenner in 1962, after she realized that the Zionist-socialist community had ceased to be her home, if it ever had been. She was named administrative manager of the Naval Officers' School in Acre, in the north of Israel. That ancient city, a mix of Jews and Arabs, was very similar to the Jaffa of her youth. At the school she worked with the school head, Maj. Gen. (Res.) Shmuel Tankus, a former Palmach soldier and former commander of the Israeli Navy. In her ten years at the Naval Officers' School Shosh was an excellent manager, and to this day I receive greetings from students who respected her tremendously. During her service there, she changed the name of the school, and now it is named after the lost Palmach Twenty-three. In the mid-1970s she retired and settled in Ramot-HaShavim, a village in the Sharon Valley. She was still active, and began to work as a volunteer in the plant development nursery of agronomist Dr. Yosef Shuv. She was a clever and industrious worker, and under Shuv's direction she worked in developing new varieties of the flower gerbera.

Shosh was a feminist before feminism was popular, and a committed Zionist. She named the twenty-two new varieties she developed after Palmach women soldiers who fell in battle. Among them were 'Haviva' and 'Hanna', after the two parachutists who jumped behind Nazi lines in World War II and were caught and executed. And there was another gerbera flower named 'Zohara', after the Palmach pilot Zohara Levitov, who was shot down in her plane during the War of Independence in 1948. And there was 'Bracha', after Bracha Fuld, who was shot by the British when she stood, hands raised, between them and the illegal immigrant ship *Orde Wingate*. And there was also 'Yardena', in memory of Yardena Grinstein, who fell during the battle for the northern city of Zefat during the War of Independence.

And more new kinds of flowers bore more names, and each had a story behind it: 'Shulamit', 'Miriam', 'Naomi', 'Laila', 'Leah', 'Bilhah', 'Esther', 'Tamar', 'Hava'. In her way, Shosh immortalized the role of women in the establishment of the State of Israel. After her death on February 19, 1984, Dr. Shuv completed the development of the last flower she had been working on. It is a red flower with a black heart, and Yosef called it 'Shosh'.

We buried Shosh in the cemetery at Ramot-HaShavim, the village where she lived out her last years. Some hundreds of her friends and our own friends assembled to pay their last respects. On her gravestone we engraved a line from the Palmach anthem: "Our heads shall not be bowed." When we finished shivah—the ritual seven days of mourning—I went through her things. The clothes, furniture, and electrical appliances were donated to charity, and we kept only the beautiful mosaic table she made with her own hands. It is in our kitchen to this day.

I don't think I ever really knew Shosh. She, like the maze in her eyes, was a mystery to me. In the picture before me I see a young woman about thirty, very straight and serious. On her face I see keen attention, and that tense, alert, and clever expression that characterized her throughout her life. Her mouth is closed, but her lips are relaxed. It is closed because this is how she felt at ease. Only the corners rise slightly, gracefully—not quite a smile. She wears no jewelry, no makeup, and no earrings, only a large ivory brooch in her collar, with the head of Pallas Athena, which she always liked. Her eyes look straight into the camera lens. The picture fails to show the sharpness of her bright eyes.

When I opened one of the drawers in the empty house, a wave of letters poured out. I opened one of them and instantly closed it. Outside, in her garden that already had begun to go back to nature, a light rain was falling. It didn't dampen the bonfire I lit, burning all her papers to the last one. I believe that's what she would have wanted. All remained inside.

THE PROBLEMS I FACED in the technical characterization of Halo were far from trivial, and every iteration sent me back to basic definitions. Every problem was intertwined with other problems, and sometimes the whole thing seemed a bag of snakes. None of my helicopter pilot friends could help me figure out where the main flight difficulty was, to enable me to build my system along an order of preference. The most complicated of all was the decision about the flight profile according to which the system would be built.

Was the main problem the loss of spatial orientation? That loss—and the resulting vertigo—were closely associated with looking at the outside world through artificial screens and night vision goggles. In the Jordan Valley stands a memorial for fifty-three soldiers and pilots who died in a crash due to loss of spatial orientation of the crew of a CH-53 Petrel helicopter. I thought I had found a solution for that—a new optical lens that would put all the instrumentation data right on the pupil of the pilot's eye. Then I found that describing the lens was easier than making it. There was no lens in the world that could spread the required data on twenty-eight degrees of the area of the pilot's goggles. I had to invent a new kind of lens.

But then, maybe the main problem was in geographical orientation? At low altitude, especially at night, it's very easy to get lost. And the area would be full of hidden dangers, enemy forces, and power lines that lurk in the wadis in the dark to snare helicopters. If you got lost, you had to gain altitude, and then you were exposed to the enemy's antiaircraft and missile batteries. A navigation system was definitely a priority, but no existing system fit helicopters. They all were not accurate enough—they talked in miles, whereas helicopters needed meters—and they all were very expensive and very heavy, way beyond the budget for my complete system. So for navigation I had to break new ground, too.

Another problem looked even more important to me. I called it the living map. I thought that this was the main problem with military helicopters, if not with any military system. I am talking about the distribution of enemy threats in the area, including mobile ones. This was the same problem that made things difficult for us, the fighter pilots, in our wars against the SAMs. And when you talk helicopters, the problem is twice as difficult. Threats were not limited to few dozen mobile SAM batteries, but included every ground unit. When crossing enemy territory a helicopter must avoid any contact with enemy forces of any kind. They all can do harm. In short, the pilot needs an updated and current battle picture. And my problem was that there existed no precedent nor any idea of how to create such a detailed living map. This problem was really tough.

The solution to the living map occurred to me suddenly at night, like an epiphany. I was awestruck—how clear it was! I was thrilled.

During those months of definition it was easy to lose hope. Almost nobody understood what I was after, and whoever did understand, didn't believe it could be done. There were nights when I felt I was wandering in a maze with no exit. But I believed that the spring did exist somewhere inside me, and at the end it would break out. I would get up from bed and go back to my desk, pushing, pulling more and more out of myself. When my release bonus money ran out, Ali sent me to the bank, and I borrowed against my retirement pension.

At last, after four months of work, I could hire a typist to type three copies of a fifty-page booklet that described Halo in enough detail for a reasonable presentation. But the turning of my drawings and definitions into a flightworthy system, to be acquired by air forces and armies, was way beyond the capability of a single person like me. I contacted two companies, Elbit in Israel and Hughes in Mesa, Arizona, and asked them to develop Halo under their auspices. In the synopsis I sent them, I put forward clearly the two question marks that hovered over my solution. The first was the required optical lens. Halo depended on successful development of a novel lens for the pilot's goggles. But I had a solid theoretical base—I attached a theoretical analysis I had bought from a specialist; it that ended with a sentence I was to learn was typical: "It seems the said lens is not out of the limits of physics." And the second bet was on the then-futuristic global positioning system, GPS, a network of communication satellites that in 1984 was just beginning to be built in space. At that time the performance and even the existence of the GPS were questionable. This was certainly a long shot, but no other solution would be in spec for Halo. And I had a third thing to show them: letters from General Parker and the Israeli Air Force commander, Amos Lapidot, both of them informing me that if such a system became available, it would fit their requirements. Amos was even willing to give me a CH-53 helicopter for flight testing of Halo. With all this, both companies said yes and wanted me to develop the system with them.

I chose Elbit and went to work in Haifa, Israel. In parallel with the development of Halo I was entrusted with the company's aerial systems marketing. I had only three requests for Elbit's president, Emmanuel Gil, before we signed our contract: loan of one great systems engineer; a one-year time frame, and $2.2 million for development. The estimates of time and money were based on the thin blue booklet I gave him. As to the men, I knew that when I had one really good person, others would follow.

Gil was as good as his word. Haim Kellerman, a young, redheaded engineer, reported to my new office. His former experience was in developing of artificial kidney, and when he first met me he couldn't tell one end of an aircraft from another. After a week he understood Halo and began to use words I didn't understand. In a short time other good men joined us—engineers, test pilots, and program managers. Soon Halo became a sea of complicated technical papers that I couldn't grasp anymore. Meanwhile, GPS had become a reality. The new lens with requisite optical properties was developed also, and a global patent was acquired. This lens became a business unto itself, and serves in various other machines besides Halo.

When I saw that my men knew better than I how helicopters should fly, I backed off to where I was just working with the main concept. I dealt with management and mainly in marketing. Within a year the CH-53 flew a test flight at Tel Nof Air Base. Even before that, I made the first sale to a foreign country, for our first fifty million dollars.

When I left Elbit after four years, components of Halo were already installed in all Israeli military helicopters, and the system was being exported. Soon all U.S. Army, Navy, and Marine helicopters were equipped with spatial orientation components of Elbit's Halo. Although parts of Halo—mainly the "live map"—still needed to complete development, the system and its various components and derivatives brought in hundreds of millions of dollars to Elbit. I was very proud of the success of my brainchild Halo. My concept took wing, and suddenly world avionic producers could propose to their clients integrated, computerized systems for helicopters.

Halo strengthened my belief in the formula I found for my life: all possibilities came from inside, all from within.

Chapter

23

Tammuz

TWENTY YEARS AFTER I HAD ENDED my active duty service, and my active participation in the air force (except as a flight instructor in the reserves) ceased, it all came back for one amazing evening. For long time I had been living my life without any connection to aviation, and lo, at the end of May 2001, some fifty of our friends from that time got together in Ali's and my new home.

This was on the twentieth anniversary of Operation Opera, the 1981 attack on the nuclear reactor Osirak—which the Iraqis called Tammuz—near Baghdad, Iraq.

THEY CAME IN THE EARLY evening. Our home has only four rooms, but they are bright and spacious with very large windows, and daylight flooded in, together with the smells of our spring garden.

When the conversation started it went right to the time we were pulling out of the bombing pass, when Zeevik Raz—the flight leader—sent the word "Charlie" on the radio. Aviem Sela, flying relay, got the word and passed it to David Ivry, sitting at the air force control center in Tel Aviv. The meaning of the word was "Mission accomplished; all safe."

All of us, men and women, were meeting as a group after many years. We were delighted to see each other again and to talk openly. We wanted to relive, for just a few hours, that stormy period in Ramat-David in the early 1980s. All of us were twenty years older now, more stooped and wrinkled, and we all wore civilian clothes. No one in uniform or any active politician had been invited to our meeting.

Everybody had prepared himself well for this reunion. Men and women wrote notes and intended to read them. Some brought objects they had hidden for years and never showed to anybody, and many intended to discuss for the first time things they never had revealed. On the large table along the wall, objects piled up: documents, used maps, logbooks, albums, notes, and strange money, as well as other objects. Everything carried with it some personal connection. On the walls hung photographs, paintings, original maps, and drawings that "were there." During the break, when dinner would be served on the veranda and lawn, we all would go through these artifacts and study them.

Everybody had cleared his schedule for the whole evening. But evening passed, night came, and then early morning. We all parted reluctantly at about three o'clock the next morning.

Major General (Ret.) David Ivry, who had been commander of the air force in 1981, spoke. He and his wife, Ofra, had come from Washington, D.C., where he was serving as Israel's ambassador to the United States. In his calm, restrained way, David reminded us of the global and historical importance of the destruction of the Iraqi atomic reactor.

"General Ivry," Dick Cheney, the American secretary of defense at the time, had written to him, "If you hadn't attacked that reactor in 1981, the Gulf War of 1991 would have looked totally different."

As Israelis, we knew the significance for ourselves: in 1991 Israel was hit by some forty Iraqi Scud missiles, all of them aimed at our cities, and most of them fell on Tel Aviv. We all heard the explosions, we all wore gas masks and sat in sealed rooms with doors and windows taped with plastic sheeting. Bad as this was, we could remain relatively sanguine. There was no nuclear threat: our F-16 fighters had taken out the Iraqi nuclear reactor ten years before.

In his natural and humble way, Ivry segued into a personal account of how he had first met this small but magnificent fighter aircraft. It happened in the second half of the seventies, when he was visiting the United States. The F-16 prototype was being tested at that time at Edwards Air Force Base. While there, Ivry was shown this fighter of the future. After flying it, and being impressed with its aerial combat features, the IAF commander had no more doubts. And when he was surprised with a proposal to acquire seventy-five of these, three whole squadrons—this was a batch of F-16s that had been produced for Iran but that had no buyer after the fall of the shah—Ivry said, "I'll take 'em." Smiles all around the room.

But Ivry saw beyond the performance of the F-16 in aerial combat. He told us how he had spoken to the two officers he had earmarked to head the first two squadrons, Lt. Cols. Zeev Raz and Amir Nahumi, and ordered them to research one subject: how to attack a ground target at the longest distance possible, by surprise.

"I saw doubt and bafflement in their faces," he told us. The F-16 was a marvelous air-to-air machine. This was not the directive they expected to receive from him.

"I calmed them down," Ivry said. "There'll be MiGs, too, plenty of them."

He was already thinking about the Iraqi nuclear plant.

THE IRAQI EFFORT TO ACQUIRE nuclear weaponry began in 1959. Following an agreement with the Soviet Union, a first atomic installation was erected at the Tweita site, some ten kilometers southeast of Baghdad. In a few years the French hurried to help, too. France supplied the Iraqi dictator Sadaam Hussein with an advanced research reactor designed for uranium enrichment. The plant name was changed to Tammuz One. At the same time, the Iraqis continued to seek diligently for ready-made fission materials—including military-grade plutonium, the substance of nuclear warheads—from every possible source. This activity contradicted their announcements that their intention was just to produce nuclear energy for civilian applications. On October 25, 1979, Saddam Hussein declared, "The struggle against Israel will be long and hard—the Israelis may try to use atomic bombs—for this reason, Arabs must prepare the tools for victory."

"Prepare the tools for victory." This was hardly anything but a lame excuse. Israel hadn't been threatening anybody. There was no doubt that Iraq was trying to justify its acquisition of the atomic bomb.

There was only one real meaning: a clear and present danger to the people of Israel.

In mid-1979, when the Iranian F-16 deal finally passed to Israel, it became clear that seventy-five new ultramodern aircraft, together with their equipment, would arrive in Israel starting in mid-1980. The air base chosen to absorb all of them was Ramat-David, the northern base in the Izreel Valley.

The Ramat-David of 1979 was an old base, and they had only one year to reorganize it for the new acquisitions. The base commander, Col. Rami Harpaz, began preparations.

Rami was a broad-shouldered, robust guy with a curly white forelock. I first met him twenty years before, when I arrived at the Scorpions. He was one of the central figures in that talented squadron. Later Rami became one of the first Phantom fliers, together with Sam Khetz and Avihu. In the War of Attrition, in one of the battles against the SAM arrays, Rami was shot down and spent the next four years in an Egyptian prison. After the 1973 Yom Kippur War, prisoners were repatriated, and Rami, who was intact physically and mentally (he once told me that being a POW had been a very educational experience), returned to active duty while keeping a kibbutz member, which he remains to this day.

Rami began with the story of the early days of the F-16. When we first heard about it, some felt it was going to be hard. But he had been the project manager.

"I said, 'So they are coming a year or two earlier than expected? Bring it on.' "

For someone like Rami, who personally had experienced the difficult integration of the Phantoms in 1969, saying that might sound reckless. But he knew the quality of his northern base's men.

"There is no such thing as 'impossible' in the lexicon of Ramat-David," he said. From my seat in the corner I smiled to myself. When I inherited the base and the project from Rami on January 1, 1980, the clock already was running toward the landing of the F-16s, and I saw with my own eyes what he meant.

"Ramat-David was an obsolete field," said Lieutenant Colonel Amikam, the construction officer, when his turn came to speak. "All the underground hangars were old, and the worst thing was that the entrances into some of them were too small for the new aircraft." Amikam projected photos on our living room wall. They showed how huge concrete chunks had to be sawed off the revetments to provide larger entryways for the new fighters. This was a difficult and hazardous engineering task. The F-16, though relatively small, was a tall machine with a wingspan wider than that of a Mirage, which had fit into those hangars like a hand into a glove.

"The technical labs also couldn't absorb the multitude of new technical systems coming in. We began a vigorous effort of construction and renovation. We worked around the clock."

Even twenty years later it was hard for us who were there in 1980 to understand what a revolution had occurred at our base. Rami had to arm and service the new, expensive assets he was about to get, and he had neither place nor services for them. It was impossible to rebuild the whole base, or to evict its current inhabitants, so he and his staff had to think outside the box.

Rami and Amikam armored old parking lots and sheds with concrete, precast plates, then routed into them electricity, fuel, and communication lines. Everything they touched needed to change, and every day a new plan had to be approved and budgeted—power generators, fuel lines, ammo stores. They built housing and installed water and sewage pipes. They even invented a theory to convince themselves that those updated shacks were much better than the traditional underground shelters.

"The pressure was so great," said Amikam, "that we were forced to deviate from our own schedules and began working on the most pressing matters. When the first four F-16s landed in July 1980, they found just one hangar ready for them (the night before, workers were still hanging lamps on the ceilings, and painting), and the next hangar was still in pieces and surrounded by scaffolding. It was scheduled to be opened on the very day the second formation of four planes arrived. And so on. The technical servicing equipment was put to work in provisional labs, while building blocks were being set, roofs cast, cables and pipes laid out for it somewhere else."

Lieutenant Colonel Ami Rabin, the maintenance officer of the base and a serious guy, had his own problems. The F-16 was a very sophisticated, innovative machine. It was the first aircraft in the world to be an unstable, "fly by wire" fighter. This meant that the trim was computer-controlled. It could not fly without constant computer monitoring of its flight. To this end, Ami had to develop a whole new culture of computers and computer engineering in the maintenance of the base. The jet engine was very special, too. No one had experience in maintaining this aircraft or operational know-how. The Americans themselves hadn't put the F-16 on an operational basis yet. There was a shortage of good men, so Ami drew whole technical teams out of the existing fighter squadrons of the base—the Skyhawks, Phantoms, and Israeli-produced Kfirs—and almost stripped them of their technical staffs. This, of course, caused hardship and risk—the squadrons based at Ramat-David, like the rest of the air force, continued to fly and fight—but people were needed, and he took them from every other mission, and told them to concentrate on the F-16 alone. A local technical school was opened, and hundreds of technicians were retrained there, using books sent from the United States. The demands were enormous, and the pressure built up accordingly on all levels. Sometimes it was difficult to cope. One day Ami returned with the base commander from a discussion in the air force's headquarters in Tel Aviv. Rami said to him, "Take note, Ami, you were wrong."

"Why?" asked Ami Rabin, who was still recovering from an argument over something.

"You were right about everything you said," said Rami, "but why did you have to shout?"

"How can one keep calm—"

"One can. You just decide that you won't get angry, and you don't."

After four years of outstanding leadership among his ten comrades in a Cairo prison, Rami definitely knew how to control himself.

And truly, Ramat-David of 1979 didn't seem the right place to base a large number of modern fighters. It was an antiquated RAF base that had had repeated face-lifts for decades, and was all patched and speckled with tar barrels, among which the aircraft taxied. The base's installations were inferior even to Hatzerim's in the time my Orange Tails were established there, a decade earlier. As in all the other installations we inherited from the Brits, you could find in Ramat-David ultra-modern machines and super technologies functioning inside shacks with patched ceilings.

We all recalled that stormy and rainy night at the end of December 1979 when the brook outside of the northern fence overflowed its banks and flooded the base. This was the surprise from hell. Aircraft revetments were filled with streams of murky water. Fuel tanks floated down slopes like kayaks, jet fighter aircraft were covered with water up to their air intakes, bombs and missiles sank and were lost under layers of mud. Soon the electricity also went out, leaving black winter darkness. Water kept falling from the skies and gushing out of the new river, the pumps died, and the water level rose.

I was then just a visitor in Ramat-David. We had moved there few days before, since I had to assume command the next week. I saw this and understood the meaning of having only seven months to turn this junkyard into a decent place for seventy-five new F-16s. But it was still that night, and I left home and hurried to the operational sector of the base to try to help not as a commander, but as an ordinary pair of hands. With the lights of my car, I found my way to hangar sixteen, where there was only a lone figure, the technical officer, Lt. Dov Bar Or, working in the water with a small tractor trying to drag a Phantom from the underground hangar up to the runway. The hangar was pitch dark like a huge cave, and full of chest-high, muddy water. Closing my eyes, I dived in and felt my way around in the freezing, dirty water. With fumbling fingers I connected the tractor fork to the Phantom's front wheels, and watched how it began moving through the mud and up to the still-open taxiway.

We did this six times in a row, and the tiny diesel tractor, skidding in the mud, pulled six Phantoms one after another out of the shelter, cruising submerged in the rising water like a submarine, sucking air from the pipe on top, and farting bubbles from its exhaust pipe under water. Even a year later I was still dealing with inquiries and lawsuits over who had been responsible for the loss of expensive equipment and weaponry that night.

In those muddy moments I understood that nothing was free, and it all depended on hard work and covering every aspect of operations and maintenance, from digging to deepen the wadi to feeding the last mechanic trainee; from good absorption of the new F-16s to correct employment of the older squadrons on base, Skyhawks, Phantoms, and Kfirs. Still, creating the conditions for the establishment of three F-16 battle-ready squadrons was the main mission and demanded every bit of experience and good sense I had accumulated in the establishment of the Orange Tails. And indeed I hurried to put my stamp on all the programs Rami left me, and implemented the lessons I had learned from those earlier days.

During those two stormy years 1980 to 1981 I sent nobody to fend for himself and find the materials he needed. My entire base, and through it the whole of the air force, stood behind the three new "children" I was raising. If what they needed was somewhere, my people ran and got it for them. If somebody wasn't diligent enough, he was gone. Those who thought to use the situation to gain personal power—gone, too. And when things needed were not in existence anywhere, I didn't forget the contract I had signed with Briar in the Orange Tails—"all clean"— and kept tough and fair. Then at least my subordinates received clear explanations and the commander's instructions on how to get it done another way, and not just empty promises.

After my experience from the Phantom era I demanded and got mutual cooperation from my new three squadrons. Their commanders were trained to help each other. When after a year one of the three was relocated to a new base in the Negev, her two sister squadrons equipped it with their best men—pilots and technicians—and the base's best equipment, greased, clean and newly painted. Not a word of envy or complaint was heard.

‡

In July 1980 the first four aircraft landed, and in less than one year, on June 7, 1981, we attacked Tammuz.

Duby screened on my white wall the gunsight video of the eight F-16s that attacked the nuclear reactor. Square, irrigated fields passed rapidly through the windshield, then roads and high-tension towers. This was the delta of the Euphrates, its looks reminiscent of the Nile delta on the other side. A bend of a river, then Relik's voice mumbling either to himself or for the pages of history: "It's all the way we hoped—the SAM batteries are silent, no MiGs." And then the flight leader, Zeev Raz: "Light ack-ack."

The sound of rapid breathing filled the speakers, and the windshield revealed an empty sky: the attacking aircraft had just executed a high-G pull-up and was climbing over the Tammuz, readying himself for his dive to the target. An electronic system chirped. Ilan Ramon's voice muttered: "Yes, some ack-ack," and then went on, reminding himself in a calm and measured voice, like a student doing his exercises, "afterburner on, deploy chaff." Lieutenant Ilan Ramon was the kid of the operation, the youngest of us all. The gunsight rolled and a large, square yard appeared, growing fast as the aircraft dove on it. Details became visible, the dirt walls around it, the inside crammed with square structures and narrow alleys. At one side there was a very large building. This was the French nuclear reactor, Osirak—Tammuz itself. It was as large as Madison Square Garden, with a white dome over its center.

The bombsight aligned and began to advance slowly toward the dome. In the distance, the water of the Euphrates River gleamed. A muddy island could be seen in the middle.

And now the bombsight clicked in place, touching the base of the building. A small black dot appeared on the side of the picture, and a short beep indicated that the trigger had been pressed. The small F-16 trembled as two tons of iron and explosives—a fifth of its own weight—leaped free to speed to the target. And again the measured voice went through proper procedure, "Afterburner off."

"Cluster," demanded Nahumi of his three following aircraft, "sound off."

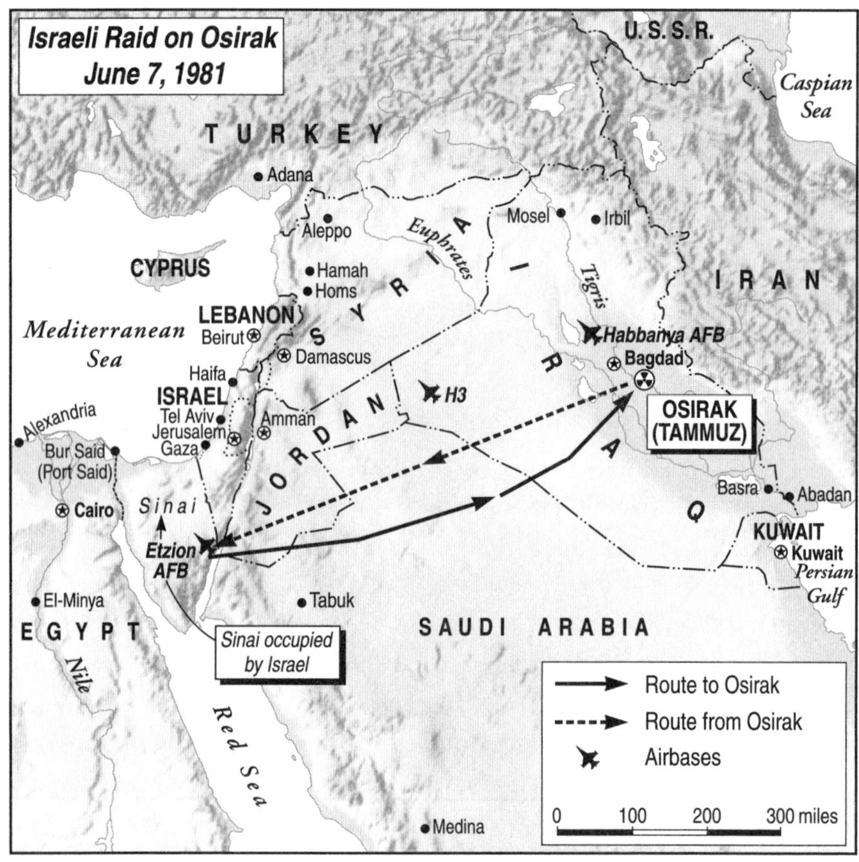

"Two," I answered him. I was out, following him east.

"Three." That was Relik.

Silence.

"Cluster four?" and again, now in a harsher voice: "Cluster four, come in!"

We all breathed a sigh of relief when at last young Ilan Ramon, Cluster Four, finished his postattack checks and got around to answering, "Four here."

Now the operation commander, Zeevik Raz, could confirm to the relay man, Sela, and through him to the chief commander: "Charlie all."

We came out fast, leaving the cultivated delta behind, and again we were over the desert. It was time to go for some altitude—we still had a thousand kilometers to go. Lighter now, but low on fuel, we climbed to thirty-three thousand feet. Six F-15 air-to-air fighters were waiting for us, to escort us on the long way home. We had carried two tons each all the way to Baghdad, and now we had no fuel left to take on any enemy fighters on the ninety-minute flight back to Israel. We finally landed with minimum fuel, but safe. Ramon's complicated calculations proved out; he had brains, the kid.

"You, the pilots of Ramat-David," Ivry resumed with a reality check, "know only what you saw from your cockpits. But reality is multifaceted."

Ivry, the air force commander at that time, described to us the big picture in which our mission had played its part. He laid out for us an array of situations, pressures, considerations, and even emotions that ordinary people rarely know about and that we, on the front lines, could only imagine. If we thought that Opera, our attack on the Iraqi nuclear reactor, was the main item on the agenda of the leaders, we were wrong. It was not the highest in importance. There were other issues, no less critical.

"At the same time Opera was being mounted, the peace process with Egypt was under way," Ivry told us, "and there was a danger that this crucial development might be brought to a standstill because of the operation. At the same time, there was something else: the IDF was evacuating the Sinai Peninsula. And at the same time, the fighting in Lebanon kept heating up. After you F-16s shot down the two Syrian helicopters in Lebanon"—this was the first aerial victory achieved by our new F-16s, and Duby Yoffe permitted himself a slight smile—"the Syrians introduced SAMs into Lebanon." The entire world was occupied with Lebanon. We all were sure that the next clash would take place there.

And truly there were many aspects in my command of Ramat-David in that fateful time that reminded me of the establishment of the Orange Tails. Ramat-David was farther away from Tel Aviv and isolated in the North, and the air force at large was occupied in other, more important things than the building of its new combat spine. And so it happened that the absorption of the F-16 into the force was given to us in the North almost exclusively, as in the days of the Orange Tails in the South. David Ivry, the all-knowing, was informed of every detail, but still I felt that sometimes this worked like a private business. The whole project was handed to me as an add-on to the command of Ramat-David. I even received the formal title of "project manager," which confirmed that I had two hats to wear on my one head. This was an unusual management quirk that gave me considerable freedom.

I admit that I liked this exceptional arrangement; the assignment was totally mine, with all responsibility and authority. Rami left me good plans, which I could alter if necessary. All the budgets allocated to the project were at my disposal, and as an added gift I received a civilian comptroller to watch my documents and check my decisions and expenditures, lest I was stealing anything. Throughout these two years, my staff officers and I squeezed out of Ramat-David everything that fine base could give us, and stood the new backbone of the air force on two firm legs. My men and I streamlined and saved, stretched every dollar, and at the end—after the project goals were fully achieved—we were so proud to return the few millions that were left over.

Of course, the comptroller looked at this with a jaundiced eye, and dragged me to Tel Aviv explain that improbability to the Ministry of Defense chiefs. I didn't mind; it was really fun to answer that yes, I sent my F-16s into battle before the designated date and even though we hadn't spent all the allocated money, and they brought back good results. The chief laughed, and the comptroller collected his papers and vanished.

It's not wholly disadvantageous to be an orphan.

"The decision to attack the Iraqi reactor," continued Ivry, "was taken only when it became clear that a quantity of nuclear fuel had left France on its way to Iraq. These seventy-five kilograms of nuclear material, once inside the reactor, would make it 'hot.' After that, the implications of an attack would be far more serious. The attack would spread nuclear contamination over a wide area. This compelled the government to decide quickly, before the material reached the reactor."

Ivry was very well prepared. Every now and then he pulled out of his file a handwritten note and showed it to us silently, as proof. This is how secret objects began to be shown.

"Menachem Begin, the prime minister and minister of defense, required full consensus in his cabinet regarding this attack, so there were delays. Meanwhile the Iran-Iraq War went on, so every time the Iranians attacked near Baghdad, more SAM batteries were added around the Tammuz plant. More antiaircraft was deployed there, defensive walls were built around the site, and barrage balloons were anchored in the air above it. Finally, a division of mobile SAM-6s was deployed there, too. The degree of difficulty of the attack went up and up, and together with it the difficulty of deciding whether to do it or not. On January 1981, the last minister who until then had opposed the operation—Deputy Prime Minister Yigael Yadin—consented."

When he finally agreed, the attack on the reactor was approved, and Opera was ready to go.

"After the attack, some people criticized Prime Minister Begin for arranging the attack with the elections in mind," Ivey reminded us. "I don't agree. Had the attack failed, it wouldn't have helped him get reelected. In my opinion, Begin felt a genuine responsibility to the nation. He feared the next government might be too late to catch the window, before the reactor became hot. And the decision was hard. The intelligence organs opposed the attack; they argued that the Iraqis would only build another reactor within three to five years. Some thought the American reaction would be harsh. We had to prepare for a possible Iraqi military reaction as well.

"Menachem Begin," said Ivry, "took full responsibility on himself."

If Begin took on national responsibility, it was David Ivry who had to take on operational responsibility. Our F-16 aircraft were new in the air, with no combat record. They hadn't even concluded their ordnance testing. The flight profiles of F-16s with two one-ton bombs—the only bombs we had that could penetrate the structure of the reactor—were not verified yet. Anyway, we began training with these bombs hanging on our wings.

One day Ami Rabin, the base's maintenance officer, entered my office, closed the door behind him, and said: "Iftach, I don't know what you plan to do with these Mark 84 bombs you keep training with, but if you ever intend to jettison external fuel tanks while those bombs are hanging near them, you better think twice; this configuration has not been tested yet. This can lead to serious trouble."

We definitely intended to jettison our external tanks on the way to the target after emptying them—this was mandatory to get to Baghdad—and the bombs would be still on the wings. So what? I didn't understand what was bothering Ami. In Phantoms and Mirages this was standard operating procedure. But Ami was an experienced aeronautical engineer, with a background in munitions, and he taught me that jettisoning empty tanks in unfit conditions might end with the tank hitting the fuselage of the aircraft and even lead to its breakup in the air. Such things had happened before. A warning light flashed in my mind and I shuddered—just imagine our eight-ship formation in a snafu like that on its way to Baghdad.

The air force didn't have an instrumented F-16 for this kind of testing, so we had to do it "by the seat of our pants." Within a few days the squadrons themselves conducted an experiment in a rather amateurish way. They found a set of flight conditions in which it was safe to jettison the tanks. This was one example of the uncertainties that came with the new aircraft, and luckily it was exposed in time. It was just luck that we had Ami Rabin with us—he definitely wasn't the usual maintenance officer. Still, we didn't know what else we don't know. We were vulnerable to error.

And there was the issue of the aircraft's vulnerability to hostile ground fire. The antiaircraft defense around Tammuz was considerable. The reactor and nearby Baghdad were circled with rings of SAM batteries and antiaircraft—not to speak of MiGs from nearby airfields. The radar coverage was perhaps only equaled around Moscow. The chances of some of us getting hit were well above zero, and the F-16 carried with it many unknown factors. It was a new aircraft with a single engine, and nobody knew how durable it was under fire and for how long it would stay airborne and get its pilot out once it took a hit.

Some protested against the use of F-16s on this dangerous and uncertain mission, and suggested sending the double-engine F-15s instead. The large F-15 seemed so much more massive and robust. A heated debate broke out in the air force commander's office; everybody wanted the mission for himself. But Ivry knew he had bought jet fighters, not toys, and to become the backbone of our attack force they must prove themselves under fire. Ivry knew it and I knew it, and in the last discussion in his office—the two chiefs of the opposing tribes, and a few technical people participated—we both were on the same side. Ivry concluded,"This is what we bought the F-16s for. They can do it, and they will," and I came out holding the bag.

To the delicate question the government asked him, how many of the attackers were likely not to make it back, Ivry came up with a percent "casualty estimate." He calculated the number from past missions with limited similarities, according to the methodology of operational research. Then the term "casualty estimate" began to make the rounds, and the thinking regarding this nasty subject got to Ramat-David and the few pilots who were preparing the operation, drawing maps, calculating fuel quantities and experimenting with long-distance flight and attack profiles. These pilots began to wonder how many of them would end up staying in Iraq. Somebody estimated that we would lose just one; others put it at two. Later, the ugly question of who among the chosen eight had the best chance to be hit came up, too. Everybody thought he might be the one. There were even secret betting pools.

And all this time, above us, decisions were being made, then canceled. A few times the government decided to go for it. On one occasion we had even started our engines, and the mission was aborted.

"You don't have the slightest idea," Ivry told us, "of how many times we kept all that shit from falling on your heads. You had F-16 squadrons to build, and had we driven you crazy the way they drove us . . . "

As an example, he presented a handwritten note sent to him by the IDF's chief of staff, Raful, from one of the cabinet meetings.

"I told them," wrote Lieutenant General Raful to Ivry, "it's either-or. Either you decide to do it, or stop driving us crazy." Raful, who sat next to me with his sturdy arms folded on his considerable belly, grunted, "Had I known you kept all my notes, Ivry, I would have written twice as much."

Laughter filled the room.

And there was also a personal secret. Ofra, Ivry's wife, told us that on the day before the attack she and Ivry had visited Tel Nof.

"On the way back home, right near Mughar Hill, David stopped the car."

Mughar Hill is a high, barren, red clay hill, and everybody who grew up in the area knows it. David Ivry was a native of the nearby township of Gedera, and so was Ofra. Surely as kids they picked anemones on the hill in the winter, just the way Ali and I did. Kibbutz Givat-Brenner is on the other side.

"And standing there, David told me," Ofra continued, "that tomorrow the atomic reactor at Baghdad would be hit."

Ofra is a delicate woman, and excitement showed on her face. Silence fell over the big room. This operation had been absolutely top secret. Nobody was supposed to say a word about it. David brought his head closer to Ofra's in an affectionate way and she continued, as if apologizing, "I didn't believe it. This was the one and only time during our whole life together that David had told me about a mission. And how had it suddenly come to be the reactor? All Israel was talking about Lebanon then."

When they went to bed, David fell sound asleep, but Ofra didn't shut her eyes the whole night.

Nobody told Anat Shafir, Relik's wife, about the forthcoming operation, "and just for this reason our marriage stayed intact."

Anat is a sculptor who works in iron. The story of the attack on Tammuz, when she finally learned about it, she imagined as "a very precise and sturdy structure of iron pieces, welded into one by a superb artist." For a moment she caused all of us to see this operation through different eyes, those of an artist. She read her comments from her notes.

"The full story got to me years later, and suddenly I realized what a risk we took there. Only then did I grasp that we all were living on borrowed time," and here she paused, struggling with feelings brought on by her memories.

Relik, her husband, Nahumi's deputy, took over and told his own story: "At the end of the last briefing, Major General Raful got up and said to us, 'The fate of the Jewish nation is in your hands.' Then I remembered my grandfather."

"My name is Israel," explained Relik. "My parents named me after my grandfather. My first daughter's name is Rachel, after my father's sister. Both Israel and Rachel died in Stutthof, a Nazi concentration camp in northern Germany. They were taken there from the Vilna Ghetto, in Lithuania."

I thought, Good God, where are they going with this?

True, I was expecting some odd stuff to come out here, but nothing like this. I had never imagined that a tall, bright guy such as Relik might think when hearing Raful loading on him the fate of the whole Jewish nation such grandiose things as I might not return from this mission, but at least I won't die the way my relatives did.

But he went on. "This was the first time in my life," Relik revealed, "that my dead relatives came to me before a mission." And then, a split second before the atmosphere turned morbid, he added mockingly, "After that, I didn't worry anymore about fuel consumption. All I needed was to get there; no need for fuel to return."

Laughter broke out and filled the room, breaking the tense silence that had reigned until then. Fighter pilots usually don't talk like that. But although I didn't have any such thoughts, I still keep to this very day a handwritten note another high-ranking officer sent me: "You won't need fuel to get back."

EVENING CAME, AND THE LIGHT coming through the large windows faded. Ali got up and switched on our many lamps, and the atmosphere in the room brightened considerably. Now it was my turn to tell my story. And first I had to explain for the thousandth time why I, the base commander, went on the mission to Tammuz. In most military organizations, colonels and general officers do not go on such missions. Colonels and generals are supposed to manage things from the rear, to sit in front of screens and give orders, not to pick up rifles and go with the enlisted men to the battlefield.

Why, indeed, had I gone?

I admit there was my fighter pilot nemesis—that "black demon" that Ali always accused me of having. It was there as always, urging me to go, see, and do. But this time that demon was not the whole story. There was an angel of my better nature. I was moved by a feeling of responsibility.

David Ivry thought otherwise. He ordered me not to fly the mission, but then the chief of staff, Raful, gave me a hearing. We were sitting in his car. It was very early in the morning, and we were waiting for the pouring rain to slacken so I could allow the amateur pilot general to take off in his plane to Tel Aviv. Those 1981 winter days made it a regular ceremony between us. I would get up very early and go out to see if the weather would be a problem for his level of experience, and at times I halted his takeoff right on the runway. He complained but always complied, and I believed he relished the drama. This time the rain was really heavy, so I got in his car and we had few minutes of privacy till a hole opened in the overcast.

We talked about the forthcoming operation. When I told Raful that Ivry wouldn't let me go to Baghdad and requested his help, he cut me off rudely.

"Spector, you're trying to become General Popsky again? Forget it. This is not your own private mission."

I pointed to his left hand, where he was missing two fingers. I said, "Everything is personal, Raful."

He was stunned, then got it.

"Hah!"

I have to explain that. In this conversation I relied on something that had happened a few years before, when I was chief of operations of the air force. The deputy chief of staff, Rafael Eitan, Raful, asked me to his office.

When I entered he was sitting there alone, writing. When he noticed me at the door he looked up and demanded without any preamble, "Give me a proposal on what to do about the plague of accidents in the IDF."

This is how Raful was, right at you straight and simple.

"Right now?"

"Right now." Raful didn't like to wait for reports.

Well, prevention of training accidents was an issue I was interested in. I was very proud of the fact that after four years of commanding fighter squadrons, in two wars, I had lost not a single man. I began elaborating on this, but Raful waved me off. He was a peasant, an artisan. He did carpentry at home, and on weekends he sawed planks and made furniture. He needed something physical.

On his desk among the papers lay a fancy dagger. I bent forward, took the dagger, and stuck it forcefully into the top of the desk. Raful looked at me and then at his wounded desk, and then at me again, his black carpenter's brows rising in amazement.

"If you really want to stop accidents right away," I told him, "whenever you are told about an accident, stab your hand or thigh with this dagger. You'll see that this will get the desired effect very quickly." I got up to leave.

I stopped in the doorway. He was looking at me. I added, "Accidents continue to happen because the commanders see them as fender benders. Nothing will change until they hurt you personally."

He grinned at me and waved his hand in dismissal.

Not long after, I heard that Raful had injured himself in his carpentry shop. I came to his office to see. Again the deputy chief of the IDF sat alone in his room, writing, his bandaged left hand resting on the paper as a weight. He gave me a look that said, "Well?"

I pointed at the bandage and he said, "I got careless with the big saw and cut off two fingers. An accident. It happens."

"And what happened afterward?" I asked.

"Ah, nothing." He grinned. "I threw the fingers to the dog." Raful was not very softhearted, even with himself.

I couldn't keep from laughing. He already wanted to get back to his papers.

"Does it hurt?" I asked.

"Quite a bit," he admitted. "From now on I'll be more careful."

"As I said, it is all personal."

As I had expected, Raful approved my request to fly the Tammuz mission.

To nail it down, so he wouldn't backtrack when Ivry complained, I equipped him with a parable. "When you are the division commander and two of your regiments go to fight," I asked him, "where should you be?" Raful was a real fighter and excellent field commander.

"What a question!" he barked at me. There was no way he could answer differently. The rain was letting up, and he was getting restless. Getting out of his car, he summed up. "Well," he said, "so you'll be flight leader."

"No."

"What?" he almost roared at me. "Now, Spector, I really don't know what you want!"

I had no intention of taking command of the operation, although Raful was amazed at and perhaps disappointed by my decision. I explained that I wanted to fly the tail of the formation. I chose to fly as number six or seven of the eight.

"But why?"

I told him. I knew that my strength was not in flying the F-16, for as a base commander I couldn't train enough in it. For sure my two squadron commanders, Raz and Nahumi, were better in the F-16 than I was. The meaning of my flying had nothing to do with leading the mission. Deep in my heart I was expecting the unforeseen, and believed that maturity and plenty of experience were called for. I could imagine so many uncertainties, bad weather on the way in or over the target. MiGs might suddenly show up. One of us might fall by the wayside for technical or other reasons. I was sure hard decisions were in the offing. There were many possible things that could happen to eight fighters a thousand kilometers away from home, crossing three enemy countries.

I was sure something unexpected would happen, and there and then, Raz would need someone like me at his side. Just a word, even a nod might suffice. Oh, how I had needed such a person once above the clouds over Damascus.

Ironically, the attack on Tammuz went like silk, nothing went wrong, and nothing was needed from me.

And now the time has come for me to reveal my own secret, one I have kept inside for exactly twenty years.

"As everybody here knows," I said, "I missed the target. I was the only one of us whose bombs didn't hit Tammuz. I was very disappointed that I missed, but that's not the important part. The important part is that I avoided telling the truth about the reason for that miss. Now you shall be the first to hear it." I saw them perk up, and everyone was watching me.

"On the pull-up for the attack," I told them, "I was blind—blacked out.

"I was not at the peak of health then. A few months before, I had begun having asthmatic symptoms. I was in denial, didn't believe the doctors, and convinced myself this was just a 'passing something.' I was taking pills to ease my breathing at night, and only later learned they thinned the blood and lowered my resistance to g-force."

"Until this flight to Tammuz, I had done my flight training with no physical difficulty, so I didn't expect what was coming. Then, on the night before the mission, I had breathing difficulties and couldn't fall asleep. After takeoff the next day I felt very tired, and throughout the flight to Iraq I kept nodding off."

I remember this long flight as an unending nightmare. It dragged on for more than ninety minutes, eight aircraft wobbling slowly along at low altitude, saving every liter of fuel. First I felt okay, but after ten minutes, when we crossed the spectacular Edom Mountain ridge close to Eilat, the view turned flat and monotonous and I began to feel tired. Gray, barren expanses crawled along, cut at times by wide, dry wadis, and it went on seemingly forever. My aircraft crept along on its own. Lying on my back, strapped in the comfortable armchair of the F-16, I caught myself time and again dozing off. It was awful. I tried slapping myself the way I did that night in 1973 over the Red Sea, but I couldn't overcome it. Simply, there wasn't any danger in the air, all around was just nothing, and we were gliding through a gray, hazy, totally empty nowhere. I didn't even need to navigate to stay awake; the goddamn F-16 did everything on its own. I knew it was bad. I took off my gloves and pinched my thighs with my fingernails. I tried to move around in the seat, to inhale deeply, and still my head fell, rose, and fell again. From that whole trip I can visually recall only some low, hilly crests that appeared from nowhere and passed slowly beneath me, then were lost forever into another nowhere.

At last, when we had crossed into Iraq, jettisoned our external fuel tanks, and turned onto the last leg approaching the target, I woke up. When we accelerated over the fields of the delta of the Euphrates, I was again alive and alert, but an ugly flaw lay curled inside me. When the time to pull up came, I pulled up, and to my surprise found myself totally blind. I didn't lose consciousness, my brain continued working all right, but I was climbing fast and all I could see before my eyes was darkness.

All pilots know the blackout phenomenon, when the g-load of turning acceleration forces the body's blood down to the legs, leaving the head with diminished blood pressure. The first thing that happens is that vision becomes blurred, then totally lost, and the pilot becomes temporarily blind. Sometimes it can result in fainting. This is a similar phenomenon to what we experience when we get up too quickly after a long period of lying in bed. We sometimes black out. Recovering takes time—long seconds. Blacking out in flight can be real trouble. Fainting can be fatal.

"So when my vision came back," I told them, "I found myself diving in a wholly different direction and not at the reactor's yard. The reactor itself was way outside my line of approach, and I couldn't get my bombsight on it. I thought about circling back and making a second pass, but I couldn't forget we had orders. Ivry had absolutely forbidden us—the trailing section—to make a second approach. 'One pass and out of there' had been his order. Ivry hadn't wanted a lone aircraft straggling ten or twenty kilometers behind the main force, getting everyone into trouble."

Ivry nodded sternly.

"And I understood that. And also I wasn't a wild kid anymore. I was a high-ranking officer and was supposed to set an example. There was no way out. I saw my target was out of reach, so I dropped my bombs on what I could in that Tammuz yard."

I heard Nahumi gasp, and then he said, "Iftach, you have no idea the weight you took off my heart right now."

All those years, as I hid my secret, Lieutenant Colonel Nahumi had been hiding his own secret. Nahumi, the commander of the second F-16 squadron, had led the second section of the attackers. I was his wingman. It came out now that he had blamed himself for my miss—he thought that the way he pulled up had interfered with my approach, and this was why I had missed the reactor. I hadn't told the truth, and for twenty long years he kept his guilt inside.

Zeevik Raz said, "I'll never forget Iftach's face after we landed. I thought, Why is he so sad? The mission is done, and we are all back safely. What is that?"

And truly, I was very sad. And since then, whenever asked about this mission, I would answer, "Let me tell you about some other good misses. I have quite a few." But in my heart I knew that missing the target was not my problem. The real stone that lay on my heart was not the missing, but the silence.

"I was so humiliated and ashamed," I told them. "How could I miss such a big target, as big as Madison Square Garden? And so important?" For some inner reason the fact that my body had failed me was the worst part. I was a forty-one-year-old male. A psychologist might make a big deal about what had bothered me so much, but I just couldn't share the fact that my body had betrayed me with anybody else.

"I buried this story, and you, my friends, are the first to hear it."

Looking at Ali, who sat at the back of the room, I concluded my confession. "To this day, I hadn't even told Ali, the same way I just kept her in the dark about the whole Baghdad mission. She never knew before the flight that we were going on that flight and that I was going there, too." I looked at her. She looked up and sent me a quiet smile.

A good word came from Duby. He, who had fought with me in the Yom Kippur War, on whom I inflicted many punishments when he was a young, wiseass pilot, was sensitive. He saw my face after we landed, approached, and said, "Iftach, your two bombs missed, but we stuck seven bomb loads out of eight in the bull's-eye. As our commander, look at the final result. You should be proud."

And again Raz recalled something: he produced the champagne bottle I had bought for the team after the operation. On it was written, in my handwriting, a mysterious mathematical formula that even Einstein couldn't have grasped: "7/8=100%."

All of us in the room laughed.

I knew some people thought I shouldn't have flown that mission in the first place, and in hindsight they may be right. Some of them told me their opinion straight out. "High-ranking officers," they proclaimed, "should manage, not fly." There is some truth in that, but still I want to add something I didn't say that evening. I had a friend from childhood, Daniel Vardon. He had personality for sure, and he also crawled into the enemy's fire not once, but several times. Danny was decorated for heroism in battle not less than three times, the last of them after he was killed in the Six-Day War, when he tried to break through enemy fire to pull out wounded soldiers. He acted knowing his duty from inside, and doing without asking "What for?" and "How?" and "Why?" He didn't pass the buck to others or bother his commanders with questions such as "Which way?" or "When?" or "Who?" I believe that even if there were radar screens in his time to sit behind and send others forward, he wouldn't have used them. Danny was my example, and a reason for many things I have done in my life.

Karen Yadlin sat with folded legs on the table at the side of the room, among all the artifacts. Karen is also a character, and wanted to say something different, "to burst this heroic, happy macho bubble." Her own secret began with the two-family house at Ramat-David housing. On one side the Yadlins lived, and on the other side the young family Ben Amitay.

Udi Ben Amitay was not there. One of the first F-16 pilots, he no doubt would have flown to Tammuz had he not been killed some six months before, in an aerial collision. Udi was the first loss in the new F-16 force. His widow, Esty, and their daughter, Maya, who was a just a newborn when he was killed, were there in the room.

Anyway, Karen, after asking for pardon from Esty and Maya, continued, "On January 20, 1981, I got home from work. In the parking place near our house I saw Spector's big, black official car."

What a mistake! I forgot Yak's lesson from the War of Attrition that my official car should be kept out of family housing during daytime. I should have taken Ali's red Beetle for that visit, but I didn't. A few years later I made this mistake again: on my way back from Tel Aviv to Tel Nof, my last command post, I decided to visit Tali, Zorik's widow and a very good friend. I drove my big, black official car into her parking lot without thinking about it. Her daughter, Ophir—yes, the same Ophir—happened to be home. She saw "Spector's car" coming. When they opened the door I saw their faces. What an idiot I was! I should have parked two hundred meters away and walked to the house.

Anyway, back to Karen.

"I parked my car," she continued, "but I couldn't, just couldn't, get out. I was in my ninth month. It was clear to me that it was either my husband or Esty's. I won't say what I prayed for." Again she asked Esty's pardon, and Esty nodded to her to go on. "Then suddenly Nahumi appeared from behind the house. He saw me sitting there and winked at me. So it was not Amos.

"There, for the first time," concluded Karen, "I understood the burden of the 'hero's life.' I realized that this way of life had its cost, that the risk was truly there. After three months"—and here her secret came out—"I squeezed out of Amos what all these preparations were about, what was the mission you were training for."

Raz and I looked at each other, and then at Amos Yadlin. He kept quiet.

‡

I was very surprised at the things coming out here. First Ofra Ivry, and now Karen Yadlin. Operation Opera had been top secret. Not just our lives were dependent on its strict confidentiality, but also the one chance to eliminate the nuclear threat to Israel.

The women had begun to talk, and I thought, "Uh-oh, what do these disclosures say about us?"

The wives' rebellion continued. Michal Yoffe was ready with five or six pages. She read her speech from them.

"I met Ali a few months ago," she began, "and Ali, in her wonderful, easy way, said, 'Michalush, why don't you write something nice for the meeting.' I was so glad we, the women, mattered. Suddenly they want to hear us, too."

The Yoffes were part of my own life. Duby is the son of Abraham and Mitka Yoffe, both of them ex-Palmach members. Their blond child grew up and in 1972 arrived at the Orange Tails to fly and fight with me. Duby began as a reckless boy. The circle I drew in an effort to figure out his personality had a grave breach, which I called irresponsibility. So I treated him harshly and punished him when necessary. I thought if I didn't act decisively now I would lose him. I think, and Duby also knows, that I was right. He is alive.

During the Yom Kippur War I kept Duby in the hotshot group, whom I warned not to leave formation no matter what.

"You stick to the leader's wing like glue," I told them, "and do what he does. Don't even think about MiGs. MiGs are for other people, not you," I warned them seriously, and Duby did his job during the war and made no trouble. And I was happy to see that my next prophecy—that he would get his MiGs some other time—also came true.

Duby is a very good-looking guy, light-haired and tall, and with a winning smile. His affair with Michal, who was a cute and verbal operations clerk, was not without difficulties. Michal is the daughter of Ezer Weizman, the former air force commander and later minister of defense and president of Israel. Between the Yoffe and Weizman families there were some past issues, but the young, handsome couple refused to carry the same baggage as their parents and so united the families.

Michal continued her story. "On the morning of Independence Day, early May 1981, I was getting up with my first son, Iftach, then a two-year-old. It was a typical late spring morning in Ramat-David housing. The boy toddled off to kindergarten. The air was clear and I felt no premonition. For weeks Duby had been reassuring me there was no problem, it was going to be a simple operation, just get into Iraq, total surprise, pull the trigger, and out."

Duby had been lecturing her for weeks! Karen's surprise was hardly over, and now here was Michal. I couldn't help thinking, Oh, boy, had I known this in 1981, Duby would have been locked up again, this time not alone and surely not for just thirty-five days. But I kept quiet. Tammuz had been bombed twenty years ago, and my time of imposing discipline also was over.

"I asked Duby," continued Michal, " 'Why did you tell me? Isn't this a violation of orders?' and Duby answered, 'If I am hanged in Baghdad's Central Square, I don't want you to be surprised, since you would never forgive me. It's important to me that you know why I'm risking my life.' For the first time in our life together," said Michal, her eyes on her papers, "Duby revealed his vulnerability."

That was true. Duby was never pathetic. He was the total opposite, light and happy, the classic golden boy, succeeding in everything without perceptible effort, enjoying himself and finding grace in everybody's eyes. Such dark musings really didn't fit him. And I thought, "So this was what my pilots, even lighthearted ones such as Duby, were talking about on Independence Day 1981, a whole month before the mission? Duby, Raz's deputy and supposedly not in the loop, knew of the forthcoming operation. Who else knew? Who among them all didn't?"

"And on the morning of the attack, on the Feast of Weeks, the housing became empty," continued Michal, "and little Iftach and I went to spend the holiday at my parents' home. We sat in the pickup that took us to Caesarea and hugged like two abandoned children."

She couldn't talk freely even with her father, Ezer Weizman. He, who was accustomed to know everything, was out of the loop.

"My father asked, 'Where is Duby? Let's call him,' and I lied to him. 'Duby is on standby, Duby is tired from a hard week, he is asleep in the ready room now, we can't call him.' I disconnected myself from everything, kept busy with Iftach's doll, with his diapers. No, I am not at the Central Square in Baghdad, I am here in Caesarea with my parents and my child. And then, at four o'clock in the afternoon, the telephone rings. Mitka, Duby's mother, who was then a secretary in the government, was on the line: 'Michalush, pour a glass of cognac.' I couldn't hold it anymore and told Father, 'Duby is on his way back from Baghdad.' "

Michal fell silent. I kept my eyes on the floor.

‡

Ilan Ramon got up to speak. Our astronaut was, as usual, very well turned out, and very handsome in his crew cut. He began by declaring that he would speak briefly, and he did. He also said that his talk was going to be out of synch with our conversation, and in this he was totally wrong.

"As number eight, the tail-end charlie, the one destined to be hanged in Baghdad's Central Square . . ." That's how he began.

Again, Central Square.

There was some truth behind this macabre image. There is a common belief among fighter pilots that the tail of the formation is a more risky place to fly than at its head, where the leader flies, and that the chance of the last ones being hit is greater.

There is some logic to it, together with very meager statistics, and a lot of superstition. The problem emanates from the fact that the more senior and experienced pilots fly in the lead: they navigate and command. In the air battle commanders can't lead from behind—find the target and make critical decisions in changing situations. The natural outcome is that the younger, less experienced pilots fly in the back, and there they nurse their fears. Actually, in the Yom Kippur War I was aware of this superstition, and assigned senior leaders—mainly myself—to fly sometimes as tail-end charlie. I believe I occupied that slot for three or four missions while others led the formation. It had some advantages: it provided opportunities to supervise other leaders in action, and it gave everybody a good lesson. In short, I never gave much credence to the myth that the tail end of the formation was more hazardous.

But now, in 2001, when I first heard what kind of thoughts were going through the minds of the two pilots in the last pair—Relik with his Concentration Camp Stutthof and Ilan with his Baghdad's Central Square—I thought maybe I hadn't been tuned in enough to the feelings of my men. Perhaps I had been too remote from them—an "old man," a senior, busy officer. I had lost contact with their secret pilots' culture and didn't understand the vocabulary. Did it come from being burdened with work? Had I really lost contact? Or had my inner child refused to regard that mission as a really serious risk?

I do remember the usual operational tension in me before that mission, more or less the same as in many flights into Egypt and Syria. After all, Baghdad's Central Square didn't frighten me more or less than those of Damascus or Cairo. So when those morbid images were revealed to me for the first time in 2001, I was angry at myself. How dumb was that, experienced combat leader that I was supposed to be? And then I asked myself whether my squadron commanders, Raz and Nahumi, had been any more tuned in than I. Did they sense what was going on with their men? What did they do about it? How come I haven't heard a word from them?

ILAN CONTINUED, "MY MOTHER is a survivor of the Holocaust. She survived Auschwitz. And before I went on the Tammuz operation—and I understood there was a chance of my staying on in Iraq—I thought about my mother, and Auschwitz, and what had happened to the Jews, and decided that such a thing must never be repeated. And if for that reason I must remain in Iraq, well, so be it."

While Ilan spoke, and he was speaking in a way free from any suggestion of pathos, I realized that this was different from any debriefing I had ever been to. Such words, clear and simple, could never march together with analyses of tactics and summing up of battles. They simply had no place to be said, and no commander had ever heard his people describing their mission in terms like these. And I looked at Ilan Ramon the astronaut of 2001, and recalled this fine young man of twenty years before, and thought I probably should have taken my place even farther back in the formation, to strengthen the tail. I was number six in line, and Relik and Ramon were seven and eight, and I probably should have flown as number seven or eight. But no one can fix the past according to deep secrets disclosed twenty years after, and anyway, Relik and Ilan were much more capable on the F-16 than I was, and better shots. I flew there for a wholly different reason.

As Ilan promised us, he didn't indulge in long descriptions of the flight but had something special to say. "These days I am an astronaut, but the interesting thing I bring here tonight is not space, but our Jewish nation. We in Israel are sometimes too closed inside our small pasture and forget that we are but part of the great Jewish people.

"I met some Holocaust survivors in America. I asked them what I should take with me into space, something symbolic that might connect that dark time to what I do now. And one of them, an eighty-year-old man with a simple knowledge of English, came over and handed me a letter. Let me read it to you."

Ilan drew a page out of his pocket and read it to us: "To the glory of the people of Eretz Israel and the diaspora, and to Mr. Ilan Ramon. I would propose that you take into space with you as a symbol, the dirty towel of my seven-year-old daughter, which she made into a doll. I wouldn't give my daughter's doll to just anyone, but she took it with her to Auschwitz, and her ashes are still there. But you, Ilan, when you are close to heaven, open it and let them there apologize for not answering our prayers. I still keep asking, 'Why? Why?' " It was signed "Leo Agen." Ilan folded the page and put it back in his pocket.

"This is the connection that moved me in 1981 and made me ready to sacrifice myself," he said. "We must not forget that the Tammuz operation was done for the whole Jewish nation."

‡

Later, when we all scattered around the colorful tables for the night's dinner, I scolded Ilan again for not bringing his wife, Rona, with him from the United States. Ali and I still hadn't met her.

"She had to stay with the children," Ilan apologized. The names of their four children are identical to the children's names in our own family: Tal, Assaf, Iftach, and the girl, Noah.

Later, Ramon sent us a letter from the United States: "To Ali and Iftach. Thanks, thanks, thanks for the most special and fascinating evening. Perhaps with age we become more open and express our feelings better. Iftach," he added, "I was surprised by your disclosure, and I have only the highest regard for what you said. And in general, I appreciate you, your calm way and even disposition."

And like a directive, my former subordinate added, "You must give more to the education of the younger generation, especially in these hectic times. You have so much to give!"

I never saw Ilan Ramon again. He invited me to come and watch the launch of the space shuttle. I was busy and didn't go, and only sent him a blessing by mail. I didn't come for the landing, either, the landing that never took place. Ilan took off into space on the space shuttle *Columbia* in January 2003. He flew sixteen days in space and was the happiest of men. On February 1 the shuttle disintegrated on reentering the atmosphere on its way to a landing. All of its crew were lost, and Leo Agen's letter was burned to ashes, too.

I don't know to what extent his letter, in which he spoke to me like a father to his son, influenced some of my deeds afterward. Perhaps his last sentence had something to do with my reaction, when I was stunned and dismayed by the attitude of some officers in the IDF toward the illegality of their actions in the conquered areas, and so I signed that famous letter, a refusal to take part in war crimes. And perhaps Ilan Ramon wrote these words to me because he knew me, and saw things that were hidden in me that I didn't even know about.

‡

THE LAST VISITORS WHO left our home, at three o'clock in the morning, were Ofra and Raful Eitan, who stayed and talked a long time. We washed the dishes, carried chairs, and got the house squared away, ready for the next day's attack by our grandchildren. This is how a long, magnificent, and exceptional meeting ended. Its uniqueness was in the willing of all those present, men and women, to open up and speak the truth. And this made the difference between this meeting and other, more regular ones.

Ezer Weizman once said mockingly that the past—unlike the future—could be manipulated. Sometimes I fear that this is what some generals and politicians are busy doing in Israel and the rest of the world.

That evening at our home was not like that.

Chapter

24

A Refusenik Speaks

IN 2003 A YOUNG PILOT put a sheet of paper on my desk. The reason for my signing was emotional: a feeling of disgust to the reaction of the commander of the Israeli Air Force in a magazine interview after a bombing that had killed children in Gaza the year before: "How do I feel? Nothing. Just a light buffet on the wing, that's all. I sleep well at night." And the accompanying chuckle.

I was surprised at the public outrage against us, the signatories of that letter, instead of the other way around. But that storm did something good for me: it forced me to activate my head, not just my heart.

These changes came about under difficult conditions. The insults and dismissals against us "refuseniks"—pilots, commandos, and other soldiers who had heretofore seen themselves as "the salt of the earth"—twisted by the balls and stabbed in the heart. One day a young pilot, my son's age, called me, all choked up. He told me that he had trouble holding up against the pressure.

I asked, "Son, do you have a backbone?"

"Yes, sir."

"Then use it." These hard words came from the 1970s, from the Orange Tails, and I said them not just to him but to myself, too. My situation was similar to his. My long journey in the sky was nearing its natural end at the time, and I intended to fold my wings and settle in my Ithaca, full of respect and honor. Suddenly the pilots' letter forced me to remember the rules of my life again. Always positive, I had to get up and make a second voyage, on another sea.

On this voyage, which has yet to end and has become even more remarkable than its predecessor, I discovered friends who were not friends and enemies who were not enemies, and a multitude of people, some colorful and spectacular, and weird creatures whose existence I never suspected. I was borne on currents from here to there, landed in curious islands, but soon I began to search for clarity. And just as in former days, I found events that were not coincidental. There were connecting lines, buried, concealed from the untrained eye, linking all the things that occurred around me.

THE GOAL OF ZIONISM was simple: the establishment of a Jewish state in the Land of Israel, to save the Jewish nation. In 1948 the occupying British forces left, and we declared a Jewish state under UN auspices. In 1949, after the Arabs had attacked and been defeated, we had an actual country—not very big, less than the full biblical promise, but it was in Zion and had part of Jerusalem, and its space sufficed for the absorption of the remainder of world Jewry after the Holocaust and for any future development. The Arabs opposed us—I will not get into who owns the rights to this land, nor to who began the violence. I don't think these questions have any answers. But they attacked us, so we defended ourselves. In short, the efforts of three generations bore a new Jewish state in the Land of Israel. Then came the fourth generation, my generation, and we screwed it up.

What confused us was the victory in the Six-Day War. First, we forgot the goal—saving the nation—and changed it to saving the land. Second, we ceased to be realistic.

WHEN THE ORIGINAL GOAL—the establishment of a Jewish state—was forgotten, we became passive, reactive. From creators we turned into mere watchdogs guarding a "treasure" (by "treasure" I mean the conquered areas that fell into our hands as a result of the Six-Day War, totally unintentionally and with no plan, with their large population of Palestinian Arabs). To this was added a measure of arrogance: after the "miracle" of 1967 we were caught up in a cycle of superciliousness and mysticism, creating our own reality that ignored existing factors. In this way we became caught up in a vortex of events that led nowhere, and our wars just "happened" with no rhyme or reason.

In "events that led nowhere" I am talking about more than wars per se. Clear goals, realistic orientation, and strategy are necessary also in economy, education, international relations, building of infrastructure, law and order, and all systems of government and state organization. In all of them we began to falter, because everything derives from the goal; he who has no goal, scatters in place. Perhaps other states, older, larger, and richer than we, not surrounded by enemies, can use their inertia and have it all—capitalism and social justice, Western culture and equality to immigrants, etc. (and perhaps even they can't), but this definitely is not within the reach of Israel. With our limited resources we don't have this luxury.

In the past, we had a single, clear national goal. Since 1967 we have been playing with several alternatives, some of which are mutually exclusive. We have no other choice but to decide on one primary goal and reduce the others in importance or even give some of them up entirely. If your supreme goal is a Jewish state, you have to leave the occupied territories to exclude their non-Jewish population. If your topmost goal is the whole biblical land of Israel, you have to give up the dream of an exclusively Jewish state and establish a binational state. And if the goal is just "security" (an unrealistic target, like a war that "brings the boys home")—you must realize that you are opting for military governance. And the same with every other goal you choose. But if you pursue this, this, and that, you may end up with nothing.

We suppress such deliberation, since we fear polarizing the nation (in other words, civil war). Instead of thinking, we prefer to compromise, speak in lofty language, and hope "it all works out somehow." Such behavior was called by Benny Peled, a man of few words, "chicken shit."

And so, with no national goal, we have been muddling through for forty-one years with no coherent policy or strategy, careening from one crisis to the next as things degenerate. First, the system of principles rots, then the hierarchy of command, and after a while soldiering and readiness for national service. I am talking about more than military matters. Without a national goal all the values and capabilities that enable public life wither gradually, from top to bottom. Even clarity of thought and language degenerates; concepts intermingle and become tools in the hands of cheats to deceive the politically immature. Was the aim of our "disengagement from Gaza" to advance us toward a Jewish state and thus an achievement? Or was it intended to improve our security and thus a failure?

Each proclaims his own different understanding, and it all becomes chicken shit.

The pilots' letter didn't deal with all this. It was just a protest against one aspect of degeneration in the Israeli Defense Force in the fields of law and morality. Not one of the signatories, me included, ever believed that the killing of children in Gaza was done intentionally. It certainly was done by mistake. But that's not so with the statements of Maj. Gen. Dan Halutz, who declared publicly that the killing of innocents was not important to him. His words require an answer.

I had a closed-door, face-to-face meeting with him after that failed attack. He took off his insignia and gave me a speech full of high moral tone. I was amazed at the cognitive dissonance, but only after I had seen the pilots' letter did I realize that the speech in his office was directed at men like me, and the "small bang and it's over" speech to his superiors, serving to quiet their doubts about themselves and their responsibility by his impudence. It served also to ingratiate him with some in the Israeli street who simply wanted revenge on the Arabs.

But this interview did one other, even worse thing. It proposed a deal to the soldiers of the IDF: "I'll cover for you if you commit immoral, unlawful acts in the occupied territories."

For officers and soldiers involved in a complicated war, this was much nicer to hear than a loud and clear demand that they fight lawfully.

This was a case when an officer was trying to buy personal popularity, and promotion, in exchange for national assets that had been entrusted to him. I, too, could have been "nice" had I ignored indiscriminate firing of the First's air-to-air missiles. There were similar opportunities in the Orange Tails, in Ramat-David, Tel Nof, and in every position of command. But the education I had received taught me that buying leadership and comradeship cheaply is not just immoral and unlawful, but also has heavy operational costs at the end. Good commanders are busy preparing for war, and not buying and selling. In short, we are not rich enough to afford cheap things as leaders.

In the wake of the storm that battered me after the pilots' letter I began thinking, reading, listening, and talking. I realized that our existence here, and indeed the existence of the Jewish nation all over the world, are still far from secure, and that we can't sit still and avoid decisions, because nondecision is a decision in itself. And I found to my amazement that during all those years and wars, when I thought I was defending my motherland, all I did was buy time. I had been serving the status quo, helping unknowingly a series of governments to postpone the need to set national goals. And time spilled, like milk.

Thus—and here I take the risk of being called naive—I concluded that the future of Israel depends on a renewed decision to build a Jewish state. And please don't ask me what a Jew is. For me, a Jew is everyone who sees himself as a Jew and whose community sees him as one, even if his name is Tatar. A Jew is a Jew is a Jew.

No doubt the renewed commitment to a Jewish state would not be easy. It requires the postponing, or even renouncing, of several less important aspirations. Let it be said clearly, I propose to give up the occupied territories and their non-Jewish population, because not doing so contradicts our national goal. The evacuation of those areas is not to placate the Arabs, nor does it promise security or peace, certainly not now. I propose only one thing: a Jewish state.

People say that Arabs do not agree that we have a right to exist whatever we do, so what's the point in negotiations, unilateral withdrawals, establishment of a Palestinian state—these things only work against us! My answer is that we should do this not because of anyone else, but because these things help us secure a Jewish state for our children and ourselves. Negotiations, unilateral withdrawals, and the establishment of a Palestinian state are tools that get us to our goal, and the question of security and peace should be managed in parallel, but is secondary. No one vows to solve it soon—we may have to manage this conflict for a long time to come—but we can do it only as a Jewish state. And the very existence of the Jewish state will make it clearer where the Palestinians should live and who is really responsible for their situation, for better or for worse. Then the Israeli Defense Force could renew its true mission, to defend our state, as a decent army should do, rather than dulling its edge occupying others.

The Israeli Arab minority's position in our Jewish state would be defined, together with the meaning of citizenship. National economic priorities would change, investing development in the now-neglected Galilee and the Negev, not wasting itself on new Jewish settlements in Palestine. When our borders become clearly defined, many of our internal problems will ease significantly. Israel's standing in the world will be moral and clear. And security and peace can be sought better from a clear position, rather than from inside the tumult of a boiling pot. And Israeli educators, officers, and judges will again be able to look people in the eye.

Once we decide on our national goal, we can begin strategizing how to get there. I know it won't be easy, but the problem is ours and no one else's. Status quo leads down a slippery slope to a binational and finally a Palestinian state. Thus the next logical step is to define a place for the Palestinians, and this place has to be reasonable, so that future reconciliation is possible. This place is present-day Palestine—those still-conquered territories that we should now set free, and let the Palestinians solve their national problem. We should take part in their efforts in an active and positive way, with no patronizing whatsoever. We must mobilize the whole world for this. This is strategy.

In the short term, we must secure our safety. We have to prevent terrorists from attacking us, and outlaw countries from threatening our existence. With good strategy there is hope that such threats will diminish over time, but until then we have to use our weapons, too. So we'd better do it wisely and efficiently, smashing only the guilty and avoiding collateral damage. And if something bad happens by mistake, we should admit it, explain, apologize, and even pay reparations. These are tactics.

Let me say clearly that I also understand that hitting terrorists without any damage to innocents is hard. This does not mean that the problem has no solution. It just means that it is not a trivial problem. We have seen so-called unsolvable problems before—for example the problem of the SAM arrays. The fact that the military problem of hitting a terrorist who hides within the civilian population hasn't been solved yet (and one can solve a problem without achieving 100 percent success) doesn't mean it is not insoluble but only that not enough work has been invested in solving it yet.

The requirement to hit a terrorist hidden in a civilian population is nothing new. This has been an issue for more than a hundred years—it has been discussed philosophically and defined legally—and there is an array of possible solutions—offensive, defensive, and others. It may be a difficult problem perhaps neglected for too long, but the solution lies not in abolishing civilized law and going wild. Perhaps just the opposite is true. Of course, this requires leadership.

These are the real tools: a clear goal and well-balanced and rational navigation in that direction, without whining or aggressive rampages. Rational behavior, tough but ethical and decent, without panic and without giving up our unique qualities and mental stability, is the only strategic option left for every sane government in the world. Sycophantic political leaders with no map or compass are our worst enemies, no matter how sweet their smiles.

In short, all comes from within. This is my answer to the question I was asked by my daughter Noah.

In spite of the old air force maxim, I was never too proud to explain or apologize, and before I end this book I want to do some of that, too.

First, about its length. When I began writing I thought to explain to myself the meaning of three difficult years, and somehow I ended up covering the other twenty-five years, too. Second, I apologize for talking so much about myself, and perhaps misrepresenting the fact that I wasn't there alone. The truth is that behind every word in this book stand many friends who were there—fought, laughed, toiled, lived, and died beside me. They were witnesses to my story, and I remember them all. And one more thing should be said, that I am aware that my truth is subjective. All I know is myself, and this, too, is not a small thing. And if I didn't tell everything, it is because you wouldn't believe it anyway. In fact, some of the most interesting stories I left out of this book. Maybe I'll tell them sometime, perhaps in the third person.

But I am happy with this work. For the first time I looked back and saw my vapor trail across the azure sky, and my white line is beautiful in my eyes, and well closed.

I HAVE MANY MORE WONDERFUL years ahead; there are many things I want to do and many places to wander, from the depths of the sea to the caverns of Earth and up beyond the stars. I raise my eyes and look, and lo, the world is full of new colors, no less beautiful than azure. Green, for example; green appeals to me tremendously. And I know more good days are on the way. And like everything in my life, they come from within.